To Dance Is Human

By the Author

Urban Dynamics in Black Africa (with William John Hanna)
*The Performer-Audience Connection: Emotion to Metaphor in Dance
 and Society*
*Dance, Sex, and Gender: Signs of Identity, Dominance, Defiance,
 and Desire*
Disruptive School Behavior: Class, Race, and Culture
Dance and Stress: Resistance, Reduction, and Euphoria

TO DANCE IS HUMAN
A Theory of Nonverbal Communication

Judith Lynne Hanna

With a new Preface

The University of Chicago Press, Chicago and London

The University of Chicago Press, Chicago 60637
The University of Chicago Press, Ltd., London
© 1979, 1987 by Judith Lynne Hanna
All Rights reserved. Published 1979
University of Chicago Press edition 1987
Printed in the United States of America

96 95 94 93 92 91 90   5 4 3 2

Library of Congress Cataloging in Publication Data

Hanna, Judith Lynne.
 To dance is human.

 Reprint. Originally published: Austin : University
of Texas Press, c1979. With a new preface.
 Bibliography: p.
 Includes index.
 1. Dancing—History.   2. Nonverbal communication.
I. Title.
GV1603.H36   1987   793.3'09   87–13875
ISBN 0–226–31549–5 (pbk.)

To the memory of my mother, Lili Selmont,
whose love for life's beauty and energy
and sense of family duty inspired my studies of dance

Contents

Illustrations

Plates

Figures

Tables

Preface

THE INTRODUCTION IN *To Dance Is Human* describes the growth of the anthropological study of dance. Dance scholarship generally has expanded since the 1960s. Because the understanding of dance in its full complexity must necessarily be multidisciplinary (like the understanding of all human activity—the subject of anthropology), I attempted in this book to synthesize and systematize key dimensions of the accumulated knowledge of many fields.

During the period that has elapsed since the original 1979 publication, reviews of it have continued to appear (the latest of which I am aware only last year), new dance research has been published, and new scholarly periodicals, programs, and centers have been launched. For example, The University of Surrey, England, has founded the National Resource Centre for Dance along with a graduate program in dance; Mexico has established the CID-Danza INBA, Centro de Informacion y Documentacion de la Danza at Instituto Nacional de Bellas Artes; and France has begun a dance program, Cursus d'Etudes supérieures en Danse, Université Paris-Sorbonne).[1] Delighted to participate in the groundswell of long-overdue serious attention to dance as expression and communication, I have continued to explore the topics presented in the book or issues catalyzed by it and others' discussion of dance.

Studies since 1979 have either supported the propositions in *To Dance Is Human* or have not invalidated them, and I believe its theory and supporting data still best explain the multiplicity that is dance, and offer a prologue to current and future investigation. In light of the fact that the first version of *To Dance Is Human* apparently "works" for many readers, and in response to today's burgeoning

1. Next on the agenda should be greater university recognition worldwide of dance as worthy of resources to pursue enlightenment about dance. Most research comes from departments other than dance where performance takes pride of place.

interest in dance, a new printing of the book is in order. This 1987 volume reprints the 1980 paper edition with but minor revision. Identified errors or cloudy phrases have been corrected and a couple of new analytic categories added.

A few comments on matters raised about the book are appropriate. One of my concerns was to counter the mistaken emphasis in much literature that dance is merely emotional by explaining why and how dance is cognitive and language-like. The subtitle, "a theory of nonverbal communication," refers to a set of interrelated propositions about a phenomenon that has empirical manifestations. A theory indicates the types of structural and processual, or ongoing but not necessarily recurring, variables that can be apprehended through the senses or inferred from sensory cues. In this volume, the propositions center on dance, a conceptualization of which forms the work's cornerstone.

The conceptualization of dance, not necessarily any particular dancer's or group's definition, attempts to permit cross-cultural discussion. My phrase "from the dancer's perspective" applies not to the conceptualization but to the *purpose* of dance. This proviso is meant to deal with ethnocentrism—the rejection of other people's dance simply because it differs from one's own—as well as the contrast between human intentional selection of movement and other animals' programmed action sequences.

Describing the physical actions of dance, like transcribing speech, is a beginning step in studying dance; making sense of these movements (comparable to literary analysis), requires further effort. Although when I began my research, there were guides to describe physical movement, such as Rudolf Laban's movement analyses, which I used, there were no guides for probing meaning. To meet this need, I developed the semantic grid as a tool for eliciting, reading, and interpreting the meaning of dance movement and other forms of nonverbal communication. In this revision, I have added an additional category to the grid: the sphere of *presence,* denoting the charisma or magic so often emanating from dance.

Drawing upon semiotic analyses of visual and verbal texts and the variety of dance found in history and different places, I identified what appear to be six devices and eight spheres of encoding meaning in the webs of significance people spin in kinetic images. Similar to verbal languages, images are a reality-defining discourse.[2]

2. Use of the grid is a far more encompassing and in-depth way to probe for dance meaning than merely accepting the four "conventions" or "modes" of representation (resemblance, imitation, replication, and reflection) Susan Foster proffers for *Reading Dancing* (University of California Press, 1986), specifically contemporary Western concert dance. The grid is applicable to dances from all times, places, and cultures.

A reader of *To Dance Is Human* may gain the impression from the chapter on the warrior tradition illustrated with cases from Africa that men danced more frequently than women. However, this chapter should be read in the context of the fact African women commonly dance to celebrate the birth of a child, and there are more births than wars. Moreover, women also usually dance at rituals for the dead and occasionally even perform men's warrior dances.

For interested readers, I note below selected publications where I further develop ideas presented in the various chapters and draw upon others' work, in addition to recent bibliographies of dance scholarship. I am grateful to the many colleagues who have stimulated my thinking with constructive criticism and invitations to address themes in the volume for talks, seminars, journals, and chapters in edited books. These individuals are acknowledged with appreciation in the respective publications.

1   INTRODUCTION

"The Anthropology of Dance." In Lynnette Overby and James H. Humphrey, eds., *Dance: Current Selected Research*. New York: AMS Press, 1989. Updates an earlier assessment of the primary discipline from which this book evolved and suggests the contribution anthropological studies can make to choreographers, dancers, and audiences.

"Semiotics and Dance." In Walter A. Koch, ed., *Semiotics in the Individual Sciences*. Bochum Publications in Evolutionary Cultural Semiotics, Vol. 10. Bochum, Federal Republic of Germany: Brockmeyer, 1990. Reports on the approach to dance that examines its signs, their production, and the problems of meaning in communication.

2   DANCE?

"Is Dance Music? Resemblances and Relationships." *The World of Music* 24, 1 (1982): 57–71. Points out the misperception of a universal dependence of dance upon music.

3   PSYCHE AND SOMA

"The Mentality and Matter of Dance." *Art Education* (Special Issue: Art and the Mind) 36, 20 (1983): 42–46. Summarizes the interpenetration of psyche/soma in choreography and dance performance and education as well as the relevance of dance to learning in nonarts disciplines.

The Performer-Audience Connection: Emotion to Metaphor in Dance and Society. Austin: University of Texas Press, 1983. Discusses attitudes toward the body and emotion and illustrates the communication model in *To Dance Is Human* by focusing on the sending and receiving of messages of emotion in eight concerts of different American and Asian dance genres. What actually transpires between dancers and spectators challenges the fallacious notion of dance as a universal language. The documented use of dance in vernacular and literary language to explain politics, science, and technology attests to the emotional impact of dance that lingers beyond a performance.

Dance and Stress: Resistance, Reduction, and Euphoria. New York: AMS Press, 1988. Explores relationships through historical time and across geographical space (including professional, amateur, and therapeutic dance in contemporary United States) and concludes with guidelines for coping with stress in modern society.

4 DANCE MOVEMENT AND THE COMMUNICATION OF SOCIOCULTURAL PATTERNS

"Dance and the Cultural Heritage" (keynote address). In *Dance and the Child: Children and Youth Dancing.* Report of the Dance and the Child International Conference, August 16–20, 1982, pp. 9-25. Stockholm: Swedish Division of Dance and the Child, 1983. Depicts how dance is created and transmitted.

"Audience Development Through Education." *Design for Arts in Education.* 85, 6 (1984): 21–25. Assesses the communication of individuals' cultural orientation through early childhood experiences.

"Gender 'Language' Onstage: Moves, New Moves and Countermoves." *Journal of the Washington Academy of Sciences,* 77, 1 (1987): 18–26. Shows how dance images in American theatrical dance change over time.

Dance, Sex, and Gender: Signs of Identity, Dominance, Defiance, and Desire. Chicago: University of Chicago Press, forthcoming. Focuses on messages about what it is to be male and female from the images we see in American theatrical dance within a perspective of other cultures' dances. Sexuality, conflict, and the cultural construction of gender options surface in the production and performed imagery. Signs in dance take and give meaning in relation to the offstage social intercourse of men and women.

5 DANCE IN RELIGION

"Dance: Dance and Religion." In Mircea Eliade, ed., *The Encyclopedia of Religion*, 4:203–12. New York: Macmillan, 1987. The result of renowned anthropologist Victor Turner's request for an original article following the outline of chapter 5 in *To Dance Is Human*. The article extends the typology of religious dance practice to include creating and re-creating social roles, merging with the supernatural toward enlightenment or self-detachment, and revelation of divinity through dance creation. Other articles on dance and religion appear in the encyclopedia.

"The Representation and Reality of Divinity in Dance." *Journal of the American Academy of Religion*, 56 (2): 281–306, 1988. Investigates bases for various peoples' perceptions of what is symbolic and what is.

"Feminist Perspectives on Classical Indian Dance." In David Waterhouse, ed., *Dance of India*. Toronto: University of Toronto Graduate Centre for South Asian Studies, forthcoming. Examines some implications of the religious basis of dance for social hierarchy and women's lives.

6   DANCE RITES IN POLITICAL THOUGHT AND ACTION

"Foreign Policy and the Arts." *The Newsletter of International Dance Alliance* (Winter 1985), p. 4. Presents a case for government support of the arts.

"Interethnic Communication in Children's Own Dance, Play, and Protest." In Young Y. Kim, ed., *Interethnic Communication*, International and Intercultural Communication Annual 10:176–98. Newbury Park, Calif.: Sage, 1986. Describes race relations among children and between children and adults in a desegregated magnet school in Dallas, Texas. A full report appears in *Disruptive School Behavior.* New York: Holmes & Meier, 1988.

"Patterns of Dominance: Men, Women, and Homosexuality in Dance," *The Drama Review* 113, 31(1) (1987): 22–47. Raises questions about gender and power in American theatrical dance: Why do women and gays outnumber other groups in Western theater ("high culture") dance? And why are men disproportionately the choreographers and managers and women the dancers (workers)? My aforementioned *Dance, Sex, and Gender* (University of Chicago Press, 1988) amplifies this article. Kinetic visual models of who does what, when, where, how, why, either alone or to whom, reflect and challenge society's expectations for each sex's activity. Demanding to be agent instead of object, females protest male dominance; gays and lesbians call for alternative life-style tolerance; and revolutions spawn backlash.

"Dance and Women's Protest in Nigeria and the United States." In Guida West and Rhoda Lois Blumberg, eds., *Women and Social Protest,* (Oxford University Press), 1990. Illustrates common themes in Africa and America.

8   THE URBAN ECOSYSTEM OF DANCE

"The Artist in the Community." *Dance Research Journal* 13, 1 (1981):
52, 60. Notes the contribution performers make to the American
community and the benefits of such activity that accrue to dancers.

"Tempest in a Toeshoe: Public Policy and the Performing Arts,"
Practicing Anthropologist 4, 1 (1982): 14–15. Reports a conflict between private and public offerings in a suburban area.

"From Folk/Sacred to Popular Culture: Syncretism in Nigeria's Ubakala Dance-Plays." *Critical Arts* (3, 1 (1983): 44–54 (Special Issue on
Popular Culture and Performance in Africa), Rhodes University,
South Africa. Portrays transformations that evolved as dancers
moved between rural and urban areas and traditional and modern
society.

9   DIRECTIONS FOR THE FUTURE

"The Impact of the Critic: Comments from the Critics and the Crit-
icized." In John Robinson, ed., *Social Science and the Arts, 1984,* pp.
141–62. Lanham, Md.: University Press of America, 1985. Con-
fronts issues about the dynamics of communication, influence on
the growth and continuity of an art form and its audience, and
critics' constraints and reservations.

Two recent bibliographies that provide readers with rich resources
that further amplify the understanding of dance deserve mention:
Bob Fleshman, ed., *Theatrical Movement: A Bibliographical Anthology*
(Metuchen N.J.: Scarecrow Press, 1986), is a compedium of dance
research from various parts of the world. Fred R. Forbes, Jr. *Dance: An
Annotated Bibliography, 1965–1982* (New York: Garland Publishing,
1986), presents material within the categories of aesthetics, anthropology, education, history, literature, physiology, psychology, and
sociology.

As scholarship grows, *To Dance Is Human* continues to provide a
basic foundation and a research agenda of propositions about dance
as human thought, feeling and action.

Judith Lynne Hanna
May 1987

Acknowledgments

TO EXPLORE DANCE IN some of its complexity as human thought, feeling, and action is to explore the nature of being human: such is the challenge. With the help of many friends and acquaintances, I have begun to meet it. There are some individuals who have had a long-term impact on my thinking; others were helpful on specific chapters in their earlier transformations. I acknowledge my indebtedness to these people and free them from any responsibility for my heresies and errors.

My musician parents, Lili and David Selmont, first imbued me with a love for dance and other performing genres. Over the years I have experienced the magic of dance and have seen dance thrill and powerfully move others.

I owe most to William John Hanna, my husband-colleague: his encouragement led to and sustained me through my second and third graduate careers. This study is largely the result of that training and our cooperative field work. His insightful suggestions have been consistently and generously given.

To long-time, continually supportive mentors in my work in the anthropology of dance, Alan P. Merriam and Gertrude P. Kurath, and more recent teachers who led me to new ways of thinking about dance, Alexander Alland, Jr., John Blacking, Margaret Mead, and Conrad Arensberg, I am especially thankful. Also, Alvin Magid, Anya Peterson Royce, Ray Birdwhistell, Sol Tax, Genevieve Oswald, Thomas Sebeok, and Barbara Burnham have encouraged my scholarly pursuit of dance.

Some of the material in this book appears in preliminary form in journal publications or edited volumes: *The Anthropology of the Body*, *Current Anthropology*, *Dance Research Journal*, *Journal of Asian and African Studies*, *The Performing Arts*, and *Semiotica*. Permission to use the material is gratefully acknowledged. Portions of Chapter 1 appear in Hanna 1979*a*. References to other publications are specified in the following paragraphs.

Chapter 2 benefited from the comments of William John Hanna, Alexander Alland, Jr., Conrad Arensberg, Judy Hendin, Barbara Burnham, Jane Tyler, Pamela Squires, Joann Kealiinohomoku, Suzanne Youngerman, Gertrude P. Kurath, Adelaida Reyes-Schramm, Manjusri (Chaki) Sircar, Dina Miraglia, Sharon Leigh Clark, Allegra Fuller Synder, Gloria Strauss, Selma Jeanne Cohen, and Gretchen Schneider. Drid Williams commented on earlier versions of this chapter which were originally prepared for the Pre-Congress (IX International Congress of Anthropological and Ethnological Sciences) Research Session on Art and Anthropology: Theory and Method in Comparative Aesthetics, August 28 to 31, 1973, Chicago, organized by Justine Cordwell (Hanna 1979*c*).

I thank James Fernandez for questions about imagery and symbolism in dance, the members of the Fall 1975 York University Dance Seminar in Research and Writing under Selma Odom for their enthusiastic response to my initial presentation of a tool for probing meaning, and Alexander Alland, Jr., John Attinasi, Margaret Mead, Abraham Rosman, William John Hanna, Leanne Hinton, and Barbara Kirshenblatt-Gimblett for their helpful comments on many of the ideas related to semantic analysis. Some of these ideas appear in Hanna 1975*b*, 1976, a paper prepared for the Conference of the Committee on Research in Dance and the Annual Meeting of the American Folklore Society, November 1976, Philadelphia, and 1977*a*, 1977*b*, 1978*b*, 1979*a*, 1979*b*.

Chapter 3 draws upon the comments of Alexander Alland, Jr., Adina Armelagos, Eliot D. Chapple, William John Hanna, Ralph Holloway, Carlos Medina, James M. Murphy, Pamela Squires, Suzanne Youngerman, and especially John Blacking, who provided the provocation to explore the psychobiological bases of dance. I thank him (the convener) for inviting me to share these explorations with the Conference of the Association of Social Anthropologists held at the Queen's University of Belfast, April 2–5, 1975, on "The Anthropology of the Body." A preliminary version of this chapter appears in Hanna 1977*b*.

Materials from Chapters 4 and 6 are derived from my doctoral dissertation in anthropology at Columbia University. Appreciation is due Alexander Alland, Jr., my supervisor, Margaret Mead, Abraham Rosman, Joseph Higgins, Adelaida Reyes-Schramm, George Bond, Conrad Arensberg, and Joan Vincent for their guidance. Preliminary versions of Chapter 4 were presented in papers at the Joint

Meeting of the African Studies Association and Latin American Studies Association, Houston, 1977, and the Society for Ethnomusicology, Austin, 1977. I appreciate Victor Turner's insightful commentary on the ideas in Chapter 6 which were presented to the "Arts, Values, and Social Action" session of the American Anthropology Association Meeting, Houston, 1977. The study of Ubakala dance-plays was possible through the warm friendship and generous cooperation of the people of the Ubakala clan of Nigeria. Robinson Adibe, from the neighboring Ohuhu clan, assisted me in analyzing the data.

I am grateful to James Fernandez, Alexander Alland, Jr., William John Hanna, Suzanne Youngerman, and Judith Gleason for their comments on earlier versions of Chapter 5; Hanna, Youngerman, Marie Adams, and Brantly Womack had useful suggestions for portions of Chapter 6, which is a revision and expansion of a paper presented at the Conference on Social Theory and the Arts held at the State University of Albany, April 2–4, 1976. This chapter has its roots in field work, literature on dance, and pes planus (a pediatrician suggested that dance would make my feet strong). In Africa my dance interest led me to political situations in rural villages as well as urban national capitals where I serendipitously could pursue interests in politics per se. I appreciate Richard Newbold Adams' acknowledgment of the compatibility of the ideas here with his approach to a theory of social power.

The study of Anáhuac dances developed through Shirley Gorenstein's exciting introduction to the theory and method of archaeology and her helpful comments, as well as those of William John Hanna, Suzanne Youngerman, Barbara Price, and Elizabeth Burtner on an earlier version, which appears in Hanna 1975.

Thanks are due Ali Mazrui for asking me to consider the topic of Chapter 7 for a special issue of the *Journal of Asian and African Studies* on the "Warrior Tradition in Modern Africa," which he edited (Hanna 1977). Jane Bennett Ross, Anthony Shay, David Lindner, and Margaret Drewal suggested comparative source material and Alexander Alland, Jr., and William John Hanna suggested editorial changes.

Chapter 8 is a revision of a paper presented at the Committee on Research in Dance-Society for Ethnomusicology Conference in 1974. It grew out of William John Hanna's invitation to make some remarks on dance in urban areas throughout the world for the Comparative Urban Studies Roundtable at the Graduate Center, City University of New York, March 8, 1973. I am grateful for the stimulation of the Roundtable participants, particularly the comments of Eric Lampard, Charles Keil, and Charles Tilly. Thanks are due Natalie Demon Davies, Meyer Schapiro, Conrad Arensberg, and Suzanne Youngerman, who gave me useful leads. I also appreciate the remarks of Joann Kealiinohomoku (and her later written comments), Nahoma Sachs, and Gabriel Moedano at the Indiana University Conference on New Directions on the Anthropology of Dance, March 21–23, 1974, and the comments of Jeanne Beaman, William John Hanna, Judy Hendin, Adelaida Reyes-Schramm, Edwin Segal, and Jane Tyler on earlier drafts.

For institutional support in various phases of the development of this book, I am grateful to Michigan State University, the University of Ibadan, and the American Council of Learned Societies.

Finally, I am indebted to Jane Tyler and Sue Chisholm whose dance insights and editorial skills helped me clarify and present the ideas in this book.

To Dance Is Human

1   Introduction

TO DANCE IS HUMAN, and humanity almost universally expresses itself in dance. Dance interweaves with other aspects of human life, such as communication and learning, belief systems, social relations and political dynamics, loving and fighting, and urbanization and change. It may even have been significant in the biological and evolutionary development of the human species. When dance is suppressed for moral, religious, or political reasons, it rises phoenixlike to assert the essence of humanity. Dance appears primary among aesthetic forms and the instrument of dance, the human body, contributes to other forms which use its spatial, temporal, and kinetic elements. Such dance dynamics persevere in the broad spectrum of nondance aesthetic phenomena.

Dance as Human Behavior

We can view dance from a number of different perspectives. Dance is *physical* behavior: the human body releases energy through muscular responses to stimuli received by the brain. Movement, organized energy, is the essence of dance. The body or its parts contract and release, flex and extend, gesture and move from one place to another. The action, or existential flow, of dancing is inseparable from the dancer: the creator and instrument of dance are one. Dance is *cultural* behavior: a people's values, attitudes, and beliefs partially determine the conceptualization of dance as well as its physical production, style, structure, content, and performance. Dance comments reflexively on systems of thought, sustaining them or undermining them through criticism of institutions, policies, or personages. Thus action and awareness merge.

Dance is *social behavior*. Social life is necessary for human mastery of the environment; dance reflects and influences patterns of social organization (relationships between individuals in groups and among groups). The dancer may, for example, play a specific role with a special status, both of which are determined by society's standards for proper dance behavior. Dance is *psychological*, involving cognitive and emotional experiences affected by and affecting an individual's personal and group life. Thus dance serves as a means of knowing and coping with socially induced tensions and aggressive feelings. As *economic behavior*, dancers may perform for a fee to supplement or to earn their livelihood, or perhaps to enhance occupational skills or values. Some people spend their resources to take dance instruction or to watch others perform. Societies require a system of decision making and enforcement. As *political behavior*, dance is a forum for articulating political attitudes and values; it is an arena for training which carries over to important positions in other spheres of life, and a vehicle of control, adjudication, and change. Dance is *communicative* behavior—a "text in motion" (Hilda Kuper 1968:57)—or "body language." This critical behavior underlies most other dance motivation and actions. Dance is a physical instrument or symbol for feeling and/or thought and is sometimes a more effective medium than verbal language in revealing needs and desires or masking true intent. Because humans are multisensory, they act and watch or feel more often than they verbalize and listen. The dance medium often comes into play where there is a lack of verbal expression. Movements in dance become standardized and patterned symbols, and members of a society may understand that these symbols are intended to represent experiences in the external and psychic world. Ray Birdwhistell explains: "Humans move and belong to movement communities just as they speak and belong to speech communities. . . . there are kinesic [body motion] 'languages' and 'dialects' which are learned by culture members just as speech is learned, and which have a matching distribution with speech, languages, and dialects" (Alan Lomax 1968:229; see also John Blacking 1971:39–40). While I agree that movements supplement verbal communication, dance movements alone have the capability to communicate affectively and cognitively. Through communication, individuals learn a culture—the values, beliefs, attitudes, and behavior a group shares. Through communication they also contribute to the dynamic ever-changing phenomenon of culture. But humans do not communicate by words alone. Nonverbal behavior, including dance, is a part of the calculus of meaning.

Communication is the mechanism providing the interface between the individual and group.

Dance is a conceptual natural language with intrinsic and extrinsic meanings, a system of physical movements, and interrelated rules guiding performance in different social situations. The theme of this book is that dance is human thought and behavior performed by the human body for human purposes. Humans, as do other animals, have needs of the flesh. As social animals, humans work with one another to fulfill these needs and to cope with various kinds of problems. Dance is one of the resources they may draw upon. Just as humans reflect upon themselves through different forms of creativity—oral tales, written documents, sculptured forms, constructed edifices—they also reflect upon themselves through dance.

In this study I treat dance as a phenomenon in itself and also as part of the web of human existence. The potential of dance is of critical importance. At one level of analysis dance has always and everywhere the same distinctive features. These pertain irrespective of the scale and complexity of societies, the type of dance, or the relationship of dance to other performative genres, for example music and ritual. However, at another level of analysis, each dance culture and society has its unique characteristics. Underlying the various chapters, then, is a communicative theory of dance, that is, dance as an expressive form of thinking, sensing, feeling, and moving, which may reflect or influence the individual and the society. Although this theory is derived from various axioms of the social and behavioral sciences, humanities, and arts, it recognizes a basic anthropological principle: significance resides in the whole. The social science of anthropology, the study of humans in all their various dimensions, is especially relevant because of its overlap with other disciplines, its broad historical and geographical scope, its search for explanations of similarities and differences among human groups and other animals, and its emphasis on "holism," the complex interrelation of phenomena.

Several survey chapters (5, 6, 7, 8) which suggest the potential of dance omit the detailed cultural and social contextualization necessary for a valid systematic cross-cultural comparison because of the research "state of the art." Rather, the intent of this book is to generate theory and insights into dance as human thought and action and to stimulate dance research.

The discipline of anthropology is comprised of four fields, but these are not mutually exclusive in theory, method, and substantive concern. Each field has subfields, or schools of thought. The study of dance draws upon their theories and methods and, of course, upon the practices, interrelated concepts, and literature of dance from other disciplines and sources. What follows is a brief sketch of the general concerns of each of the four fields in relation to the study of dance–from village Africa to the bright stage of New York City's Lincoln Center State Theater and from about thirty thousand years ago to contemporary times:

1a. Ethnology–descriptive, analytical, and comparative–generally includes social and cultural anthropology. A major task of social anthropology is to discover the characteristics of social life and social structure (regular categories of social behavior, such as sex roles; residence rules; descent customs; stratification or ranking patterns; rites of passage; allocation, distribution, and regulation of resources; and processes of change). Social anthropologists seeking to understand dance study correspondences between social life and structure, on the one hand, and the concepts, processes, performances, functions, structures, and styles of dance, on the other. They attempt to construct a model of reality to explain the existence of dance patterns in the recurring relationships between people and groups of people.

1b. Cultural anthropology investigates the way of life of a people, its behavior, ideas, and artifacts. From this perspective, scholars may seek to understand dance as a system of communication, a system of symbols and meanings for a particular space-time entity. Analyses of dance patterns aim to identify the models (maps, programs, templates) of and for behavior. The goal is to comprehend those reflecting, refracting, or innovating mechanisms of dance that provide orientations to the realities of a group and to the ways these realities are to be conceived, felt, and acted upon. Human cognitive processes are the focus. Just as plants and animals are used in totemism, economic products in caste behavior, and speech in class dynamics, so the visual, motional configurations of dance in simple and complex societies may serve to categorize social groupings and thereby structure social behavior. The subfield of ecology focuses on how people adapt to their physical environment and in this context the book examines how dance is used as an instrument to harness energy to meet basic needs. Chapters 4 through 8, on dance in communication, religion, politics, war, and urban dynamics, illustrate these concerns of cultural anthropology.

2a. Linguistic anthropology studies language as a closed system.

The researcher attempts to identify and describe the vocabulary and its groupings, syntax, and semantics, and to discover the basic generative forms and their transformations. From this perspective, dance is treated as a language to discover a set of rules which describe how the realm of movement is related to the realm of meaning. Scholars need to distinguish between competence (internalized rules for dancing) and performance (what someone does on the basis of knowing such rules). Furthermore, they should also distinguish between the choreographer (creator of dance) and imitator (recreator of dance choreographed by another).

2b. Sociolinguistics, the "ethnography of speaking," examines a language in relation to social situations and socialization patterns. From this perspective dance is explored as a system of movements, a system of meanings, and a system of rules which include use–the when, where, who, why, and how. Concern is with the dynamics of variation within a single form of dance, dance repertoires, and ways of dancing and choosing among them. In dance events, the focus of analysis is on exchanges between dancers, choreographers, and observers. Chapter 4, "Dance Movement and the Communication of Sociocultural Patterns," draws particularly on the theory of language in society.

3. Physical anthropology concentrates on human psychobiological foundations, mechanisms, and evolutionary perspectives. Its concern is with the organic, animality of humans, whereas the other fields focus on the superorganic, human creation. Physical anthropology considers differences between human dance phenomena and other similar animal patterns, *Homo sapiens* universals (i.e., species-specific phenomena), and biological mechanisms which modify the thoughts, behavior, and social relations of individuals. It takes into account aspects of the body, cognitive functioning included, which have an impact on social interaction (cf. Blacking 1977). Some scholars believe that the processes and products of the arts reveal the evolutionary aspects of symbolization, cognition, and values and attitudes more obviously than in the strictly utilitarian objects of human creation (cf. Erika Bourguignon 1973*a*). Chapter 3, "Psyche and Soma," addresses the concerns of physical anthropology.

4. The archaeological field deals with prehistory. It examines dance through time and is concerned less with what each era was like than the processes of transformation from one to another. Archaeologists share the interests of social and cultural anthropologists but have a different data base and consequently special theoretical and methodological concerns. Chapter 6, Case A, provides an example of how dance may have contributed to social processes and structures in prehistorical times and illuminates our understanding of social development.

Status of the Anthropological Study of Dance

The brief overview of the four fields of anthropology suggests the breadth of human study, and thus of the study of dance and the perspectives in this book. From the earliest studies anthropologists have referred to dance and often describe it. Such topics as drama, ritual, folklore, recreation, magic, religion, culture, music, or mask accompaniment involve dance behavior. Yet, among the approximately ten thousand members of the American Anthropological Association and thousands in other scholarly associations, there are relatively few who have studied dance from the perspectives of the discipline, and less than a handful who have concentrated exclusively on it. Perhaps a hundred have published or written doctoral dissertations on some aspect of dance. However, interest in the study is growing[1] coincident with the groundswell florescence of theater dance performance and the study of the arts, nonverbal communication, play, and biosocial phenomena.

The comparatively lagging state of dance studies has several explanations. Scholars generally have a limited view of dance, although it is a nearly universal and often complex behavior. "Then they danced" is the common remark *ad nauseam*. Ethnocentrism reigns to such an extent that scholars call dances which differ from their ballet or jig a "lewd ambling" or "imitative fornication"–there has been little awareness that some dances involve body parts other than the limbs. Scholars' notions about dance in their own cultures influence their views of dances in other cultures: false dichotomies are drawn between "primitive" and "nonprimitive," and they both often have comparable complexity in their movements and meanings, and in the rules for combining these.

Scholars often fail to distinguish dance from similar motor behavior. Franz Boas set a precedent in anthropology: dance to him was "the rhythmic movements of any part of the body, swinging of the arms, movement of the trunk or head, or movements of the legs and feet" (1955:344). The problem here is that we can apply this description to many work activities. Dance as emotional behavior is overemphasized (R. Marett 1914, Suzanne Langer 1953). Curtis Carter (1976) calls the conceptual plague besetting the understanding of dance a misguided separation of dance from intelligence. The history of the mind/body division can be traced from the writing of the Greeks to current critics. Viewing dance as a primarily conditioned phenomenon (cf. Alan Lomax 1968) perpetuates this problematic conceptualization.

Those who focus on the promotion of social harmony (such as A. Radcliffe-Brown 1964) often neglect dance's disharmonious consequences (E. Evans-Pritchard 1965:74), its performance as duty (Marie Reay 1959) and work, and its impact on sociocultural change (James Peacock 1968). Even when dance is shown to play a critical part in sustaining social institutions, the properties that enable it to do so are rarely discussed.

The social scientists' long-standing avoidance of dance can perhaps be explained by a combination of Puritan ethics, social stratification, concepts of masculinity, and a sense of detachment from nonverbal behavior. Dance has only recently been thought of as a significant element of human behavior and culture and, therefore, as a legitimate concern for study. It has been disparaged as a minor art unworthy of study in the West due to the survival of many obsolete prejudices. Those who saw dance in this way shared the Puritan distrust of body beauty and gaiety and allowed only an inferior status to theatrical performers. Dance, a playlike form, was, in the Puritan ethic, the enemy of work and permitted only to children. Thus people repudiated the body and, therefore, dance, equating it with the devil's handiwork, animal instincts, and lower forms of life. Because they attributed the collapse of the French monarchy in part to moral laxity, the emergent bourgeoisie, anxious to protect its power, transformed the body from an instrument of pleasure into one of production. Furthermore, the body became a victim of social snobbery—a brute linking the bourgeoisie to the lower classes (Stephen Kern 1975). Most scholars of an "art" form have at least some minimal experience in it. Disparagement of dance discouraged participation in it. Besides, scholars tended to be men, and in Anglo-Saxon culture men's dancing had effeminate, homosexual overtones. Observers of dance were not acquainted with the body's use of space-rhythm-dynamics dance elements. Because dance appeared more complex than words and music, and often combined with both, observers felt not only dislike, shame, or curiosity toward the body, but also detachment from it. Thus developed an inability to "read" the dancing body.

Some scholars rationalized their neglect on the grounds that the behavior was not subject to notation and recording. But certainly its social, contextual relations could have been subjected to the same objective, systematic observations, analyses, and reporting as other forms of behavior, for example, kinship and economic patterns. In fact, verbal definitions of movements as well as several systems of notation which permit some levels of analyses, have existed for hundreds of years. More understandable is the lack of detailed analyses of dance. On-the-spot notation requires repeated performances and many dance activities are performed only for special occasions and in unique ways. Until recently, methods for a relatively accurate recording of dance for systematic movement study were limited. Cinema began in 1872 when Edward Muybridge made the first chronophotograph in San Francisco in order to settle an argument over the manner in which horses trot. In 1895 Dr. Felix Regnault used film for a comparative study of human behavior, including modes of walking, squatting, and climbing of a Peul, Wolof, Diola, and Madagascan (Jean Rouch 1974). Even with the advent of motion picture film, researchers could not utilize it in many places. Only recently did humidity-resistant, durable, and portable cameras and tape recorders become available to overcome the problems of portability and tropicalization. However, the costs, including those of transportation and processing, often remain prohibitive.

Social scientists have felt the need to emphasize "science" in their disciplines, and thus they have tended to avoid the more "humanistic" cultural domain. They considered discourse, verbal speech, to be the primary key to human thought and behavior and viewed the sociology of sport and leisure, akin to dance, as demanding little rigor and being the hobby of antiintellectuals. Furthermore, there was not an assembled literature on the theory and method of the social scientific study of dance to provide guidance.[2] Nor were "dance studies" very helpful. Although ancient wise men, such as Plato, Aristotle, and Bharata, discussed dance, limited dance scholarship has emanated from the fields of history, English, music, theater arts, folklore, physical education, and dance. Only as recently as 1926 did the University of Wisconsin establish the first dance major program. In 1934 the esteemed *New York Times* critic John Martin taught what was probably the first dance history course (Selma Cohen 1976).

Actually, the anthropology of dance has had a gestation period nearly half as long as the history of the discipline; precursors go back to the last half of the nineteenth century. Over the years we find some notable contributors to the anthropological study of dance: the literature speculates on the function of dance (e.g., Ernst Grosse

1909); relatively rich descriptions occur (e.g., Ian Hogbin 1914 on the Kaoka speakers of Guadalcanal); Marett (1914) conceived of religion as danced; and in 1922 Radcliffe-Brown pleads for anthropology to realize the central importance of dance (p. 249) and does so himself in his study of the Andaman Islanders. Evans-Pritchard's 1928 article on the Azande beer dance provides one of the fuller case studies in terms of function and description of dance. Franziska Boas's seminars on the function of dance stimulated further interest (Boas 1944). Curt Sachs (1937), a musicologist, offers a theory of dance in culture and society. However, he relies upon poor secondary sources and a high-ly distorted view of the dance of nonwestern peoples (see critiques by Suzanne Youngerman 1974, Joann Kealiinohomoku 1969–1970). In his 1955 study of the structure of art, Boas breaks ground in recog-nizing the significance of dance as having symbolic and expressive aspects. Margaret Mead in her 1928 Samoa study, in Bali (1940), and with Gregory Bateson (1942), approaches dance from the perspective of culture and personality, the arts being a reversal of social norms or a projection of child-rearing sociocultural patterns. Blacking (1962, 1969), Marcel Griaule (1965), Robin Horton (1960, 1963, 1966, 1967), Lorna Marshall (1962, 1969), and Peacock (1968) provide relatively full dance descriptions and discussions of some forms of symbolism.

Gertrude Kurath, a dancer with a master's degree in the history of art and archaeology, has been the most prolific contributor to the dance ethnology literature.[3] Her 1960 *Current Anthropology* article, "Panorama of Dance Ethnology," describes the state of the field at that time. Kurath mentions few studies of dance conducted by social scientists and even fewer explanatory studies.[4] Calls for the anthro-pological study of dance remained essentially unheeded until recent-ly. The development of the anthropology of dance, in light of Ku-rath's overview and subsequent events, has had two phases. Phase I, ending as Kurath wrote, has an upward, soft, sloping curve of prog-ress lasting about sixty years. During this period scholars urged that dance be studied and the functional paradigm reigned. Phase II, dis-playing more rapid growth, began in the middle 1960s; conflicting paradigms have appeared (cf. Judith Hanna 1975*a* on the largest as-sembly of dance anthropologists to date, their notions of the anthro-pological study of dance, and priorities). Most of the participants in this generative, turbulent phase are younger professionals who have recently acquired their doctorates or are now completing disserta-tions (e.g., Judith Blank 1973, Hanna 1976, Kealiinohomoku 1976, Krebs 1975*a*, Nahoma Sachs 1975, Anita Volland 1975, Stephen Wild 1975, Drid Williams 1976, Sue Jennings, and Richard Marcuse). Some senior anthropologists (e.g., John Blacking, Jon Peter Blom, Simon Ottenberg) are also systematically examining dance. For the first time in the literature, different approaches (both old and new) are under critical examination: the 1977 advertisement for the new *Dance Chronicle* calls attention to "a new generation of writers on dance, questioning the accepted accounts of cultural history and looking at the world of dance in new ways."

The structures, in which its practitioners are enmeshed, shape and limit every stage of a field. A course in the anthropology of African dance was taught at Michigan State University in 1965, and since then, several other social science dance courses have been taught, as well as similar courses in the arts, music, and folklore which include sections on dance. "Dance ethnology" courses have been offered in departments of dance, physical education, and music by nonanthropologists. However, the instructors and literature tend to be constrained by unidimensional, theoretical perspectives and the circumscribed training for the study of dance that exists in all academic departments. Although some anthropological training for the study of dance occurs in the aforementioned courses and those on general theory and method, there is no specific program designed to meet the needs of scholars interested in understanding human thought and behavior through the study of dance. Training in different dance forms, performance, observation, and movement analysis is invaluable.[5] Being a dancer, however, differs from being an analyst of dance. A preliminary step in the analysis of an alien dance system is the search for an area of discourse in one's own language or metalanguage which can appropriately serve as a translation instrument (cf. Horton 1964:93 on the analysis of a religious system). Training in filming or videotaping is appropriate for recording dance for later detailed analyses (John Collier 1967, Paul Hockings 1975, Krebs 1975*b*). Reliance on this technique alone is insufficient, for even with several cameras, film cannot capture everything. In situ learning is also necessary.

In spite of these difficulties—neglect, misconceptions, and different theoretical and methodological approaches—the study of dance is viable and productive: it illuminates dance and human existence and uncovers their potential.

Itinerary

This book provides a theoretical framework for ordering present and future dance knowledge. All the chapters are rooted in a dynamic communication model which has interrelated concepts, propositions, and hypotheses. The model accounts for different aspects of dance concept, process, product (performance), and impact from any time and place. It posits an explanation for what dance is and how it works in the interaction between human dancing and other dimensions of human living. The model attempts to recognize a basic anthropological axiom: significance resides in the whole. This collection of theoretically interrelated essays addresses some implicit but underdeveloped issues in the literature. The breadth of anthropological interest, in which I have had training and experience, and the status of the ethnographic and analytic literature dictate the choice of illustrative aspects of dance in human life. I portray some of the basic manifestations of dance in key dimensions of human existence: sociocultural socialization and organization, religion, politics, war, and human use of environmental space. The data come from field work as well as other studies.[6]

The following chapter, "Dance?" specifies the meaning of this critical concept–the keystone of a theory of dance which informs subsequent chapters. I build upon the foundation others have laid[7] and develop a concept of dance for the purpose of future cross-cultural study. The term *dance* has a myriad referents, such as emotional expression, play, work, duty, union with the sacred, theater, ceremonials of authority, and art. On the basis of current knowledge about dance, I suggest a set of features that characterize dance generally. Chapter 2 also addresses the issue of origins and categories of dance. Not only is it necessary to identify our subject, but a broad anthropological approach also requires an examination of psychobiological bases and evolutionary perspectives.

Chapter 3, "Psyche and Soma: Some Bases of the Human Phenomenon of Dance," draws upon physical anthropology in exploring the differences between human dance behavior and other animal motor ritual patterns, questions of nature-culture, and bases of dance similarities and differences among *Homo sapiens*. This chapter shows that dance has its roots, first, in predisposing psychobiological processes, and, second, in social experience. What are the factors which seem to generate or modulate dance, forming perhaps a common substrate, those deep structural elements which manifest themselves in a multiplicity of diverse dance forms? This chapter directs attention to those properties which may help to explain why dance is a common attribute of transcendental behavior in the religious and secular world; why it is a component of sociopolitical manipulations; and why it has potential for individual and group self-assertion, education, and therapy. I present a theoretical framework for interrelating psyche, soma, society, and environment. This model can integrate knowledge from studies using various approaches and foci.

Chapters 4 through 8, addressing some concerns in social, cultural, sociolinguistic, and archaeological fields of anthropology, illustrate dance as reflecting and influencing some other important dimensions of human existence. The themes of these chapters are not mutually exclusive; rather they are parallel and interrelated. For example, social roles are often based on religious precepts and political dictates; conflict resolution may be handled through peaceful political processes or through violence; warlike behavior often reflects sex role differentiation, economic structure, and the confluence of religion and politics; and the physical structuring of space in complex societies reflects the ramifications of sociocultural patterns, religion, and politics. These chapters all have cross-cutting notions of human creativity, the dialectics of continuity and change, and of the repertoire of human possibilities.

The fourth chapter, "Dance Movement and the Communication of Sociocultural Patterns," focuses on information of and for social interaction which exists in a people's dance. For example, the Nigeria Ubakala use particular movement devices and spheres of semantic encoding in their dance-plays to communicate aspects of their world view and to order social relations as well as mediate conflict and introduce change. Dance movement patterns are homologous with sex role differentiation when men and women have the most distinct physical and social roles.

"Dance in Religion: Practicality and Transcendentalism" is the subject of Chapter 5. Within the context of the sacred, the chapter further explores the notion of dance movement providing information of and for social interaction. Why and how do humans use dance as a medium for dealing with the supernatural? Four broad categories of danced religious practice (worship or honor, conducting supernatural beneficence, effecting change, and embodying the supernatural by possession and masquerade) are the focus. Creating a virtual world of time and space, dance appears to be a cultural code or model enabling the human being to order and achieve distinct experience. Chapter 5 examines the expression, in symbolic dance actions, of self-extension or loss of self, transcendence, life as a process of becoming, and the assertions of continuity in defiance of the threat of mortality.

Dance practices also have the potential to organize and mediate social relations in the political realm. In Chapter 6, "Dance Rites as Political Thought and Action," I propose that dance is significant in

its influences over a performer's mind and body and over o̶th̶er individuals or groups. A theoretical argument support͟s ͟t͟h͟e
previous two chapters. The relationship of da͟n͟c͟e ͟t͟o ͟t͟h͟e ͟s͟e͟l͟f
and others centers on the expression and ͟r͟e͟l͟e͟a͟s͟e ͟o͟f ͟p͟o͟t͟e͟n͟c͟y,
social control and conflict containment, co͟m͟m͟u͟n͟i͟c͟a͟tion to subordination or its threat, constraints on the ͟a͟b͟u͟se of power, and
redress and transformation. The communication model, psychobiological patterns and their intermesh with sociocultural variables, and
findings from social psychology on how opinions and attitudes are
changed help to explain dance-power dynamics.

An illustrative case study, "Dances of Anáhuac: For God or Man
in Prehistory?" highlights the intermesh of religion and politics. This
essay discusses dance as a medium of political integration for diverse
ethnic groups. The argument is that dance can be data for theory
and method in archaeology.

"Ubakala Dance-Plays: Mediators of Paradox" is a second case
study in the use of dance in politics. Drawing upon more recent history, attention focuses on Ubakala principles. We also explore dance's
potential to encapsulate issues and phases of social drama–communicating the breach of norms, fomenting the crisis, ameliorating and
avoiding social drama, and proclaiming the schism or celebrating
the reintegration.

Some schisms lead to aggression, symbolic or actual. The violence
in warrior dance play may divert or incite real aggression. This is
one of the topics discussed in Chapter 7, "Warrior Dances: Transformations through Time." The "warrior tradition" in Africa captures
such aspects of human organization and symbolism as the idea of
adulthood related to notions of self-reliance and the concept of manhood linked to violent valor and sexual virility. I explore the relationship of dance to the warrior tradition: its multifarious manifestations, the Eurocolonial impact on warrior dances, and the transformation of "traditional" warrior dances in the postcolonial independence period.

After discussing the changes in one genre of dance vis-à-vis a significant manifestation of human self-presentation, competition, and
conflict resolution, we turn to another arena of change. Dance is part
of highly complex societies as well as ones with a recent history of a
warrior tradition. Chapter 8 examines the impact of the physical environment and social relations on dance and the contribution of
dance to urban life. This chapter, "The Urban Ecosystem of Dance,"
hypothesizes that in the urban area sociocultural factors are the primary determinants of dance concept, process, product, and impact;

but that these are influenced and modulated by the constraints and opportunities (substrate) of relative settlement heterogeneity and density, and by the concomitant physical infrastructure and the elimination of spatial friction. I begin to spell out the conditions under which certain dance patterns appear to be operative in the urban area, viewed as an ecosystem, which relates individual and interacting, interdependent people to the total sociocultural and physical environment. The ecosystem is the complex, reciprocal, cybernetic effect of all factors.

Following a portrayal of some key aspects of dance in society, the concluding chapter, "Directions for the Future," extends the theoretical and methodological considerations that lace the previous essays. Chapter 9 addresses ways of applying the dance theory that this study presents: research pitfalls to avoid; searching for meaning with a semantic grid; eliciting techniques to fill the matrix cells and analyze data; and potential applications of dance research.

The image of a kaleidoscope clarifies the book's approach: the perspectives of various disciplines and their subfields reveal different patterns of similar elements. From such perspectives this study will contribute, it is hoped, to the growing body of dance knowledge, supplement the subject matter of the interrelated fields of social science, humanities, arts, and science, and foster a greater understanding of humans.

Of course, a study of dance cannot begin to capture the multisensory, multimedia performance. Systematic analyses of dance can neither recreate the liveliness of dance nor imitate poetic dance description or popular dance criticism. There are different levels of gaining understanding–the dancer dancing, the choreographer creating dances, the spectator observing, the poet conveying dance imagery, the critic evaluating, and the dancer–humanist–social scientist probing within the constraints of a corpus of theory, method, and knowledge in order to translate the images and energy of dance into another language and a different order of presentation.

In many ways the synthetic theory of dance and its application trace pathways through a largely unmapped world. The ensuing discussion offers the student of human behavior, professional dancer, dance devotee, occasional observer, or newcomer to this genre new insights and understandings into the potential of dance within cross-cultural and historical perspectives. The researcher may modify the theory through testing some of the hypotheses. Posing more questions than it answers, this study attempts to unravel part of the Gordian knot of what dance is and how it works.

2.   Dance?

THERE IS OBVIOUSLY a need to define or, using Abraham Kaplan's phrase, to "specify the meaning of" (1955:527)[1] a behavior before exploring its complexities. For the anthropologist who strives to identify, describe, and explain phenomena within a cross-cultural perspective, it is essential to adopt a definition which both indicates the sets of features which are referents for a concept and, also, remains flexible about empirical issues. Of course, our choice of conceptual apparatus, our working distinctions, need constant refinement, and we must be alert to indications that something may be escaping us because our approach has blind spots. This chapter attempts to define dance using these guidelines and in doing so, considers types of dance and the origin of dance.

Toward a Cross-Cultural Conceptualization of Dance

Some people believe they have an intuitive understanding of dance. Lay people, social scientists, and even dancers often use the term *dance* with the vague and uncritical connotations of ordinary speech. After having danced intermittently for more than two decades, I had an intuitive sense about dance without being able to articulate the necessary and sufficient criteria of its manifestation. Various definitions are offered in dance and social science literature (Kealiinohomoku 1969–1970, Richard Kraus 1969, Kurath 1960, Langer 1953, and Alan Merriam 1974, discuss these definitions). Kealiinohomoku, Kurath, Lomax, and Williams have developed definitions which incorporate anthropological perspectives. However, I think another attempt to clarify the meaning of dance is now appropriate.[2]

A decade ago I began (as observer, participant, and/or field researcher) to examine dance forms ranging from classical theater ballet to popular dance in the West to Latin American, Caribbean, and African social and ritual forms; later I examined a variety of dance forms from other parts of the world. I wondered if there were common characteristics in the kinds of phenomena different people call dance (or what westerners would generally categorize as dance–as a westerner I am obviously influenced by my culture). Examining dance cross-culturally to formulate hypotheses, to establish the range of variation of dance phenomena and their commonalities, and to demonstrate relationships among different aspects of culture or social organization, I was forced to develop an overarching analytic definition. Such a definition should, I thought, transcend the participants' concepts of dance, which undoubtedly include some criteria that other groups exclude and debar some they encompass. Further, the definition should include behavior which has the appearance of what is generally considered dance, even though, for the participants concerned, it is not dance, because they have no such concept. I have observed or read about a number of groups who seemingly have quite different ways of conceptualizing what I think of as dance.

Many societies have multiple words for different dances without having a single generic term. In Japan there are men's dances known as Utamai (song dance), for example, Azuma Asobi, Kumenai, and Yamato. Odori refers to emphasis on the feet, whereas Miko-mar, or women's dances, tend to be quiet dances emphasizing the hands (Carl Wolz 1971). In Hawaii a single word has several referents: "The dance; the dancers; to dance; song or chant used for the hula; to twitch; throb; to palpitate" (Mary Pukui and Samuel Elbert 1957:82). For the Ubakala of Nigeria, drum accompaniment is a necessary part of dance and, thus, the word denoting dance also denotes a drum and a play. Elsewhere in Africa, for example among the Akan, Efik, Azande, and Kamba, dance involves vocal and instrumental music, including the drum. On the other hand, many African groups, such as the Zulu, Matabele, Shi, Ngoni, Turkana, and Wanyaturu, do not use drums, and some even denigrate users of drums. Among the Tiv of Nigeria, the word for dance also encompasses activities we exclude from the performing arts: games and gambling. The Hopi Pueblo Indians of North America call dance their work (Kealiinohomoku, personal communication 1973); and similarly, among the Kuma of New Guinea, men regard dancing as a "duty" and as "work." Marie Reay points out, however, that these terms also denote the business of the moment, the most pressing demand on a person's time (1959:17). And among the Australian aborigines of Northeastern Arnhem Land, the term that "comes closest to a word for 'dance'–the word 'bongol'–has," Richard Waterman reported, "both a larger and a smaller reference than our term 'dance.' *Bongol* includes music as well as dancing, and at the same time it does not include the patterned steps and bodily movements performed in some of the sacred ceremonies or certain activities of the children's age group that we would certainly characterize as dancing" (1962:47). Because black slaves in the United States, members of Nigerian Yoruba Assemblies of God, and a number of white religious groups were forbidden to dance–the Protestant church branded it as sinful–these individuals often performed what appeared to be dance, although they called their movements something else: play, the shout, or feeling the Lord. Some groups continue to forbid dancing. These and other examples of cultural differences constituted my challenge.

For research purposes, abstract terms must eventually have (provisional) empirical indicators. The following conceptualization of dance is a researcher's abstraction (an etic concept) partially generated from analyzing native (emic) definitions. This working definition was reached through empirical observation, a survey of literature relevant to dance, consideration of dance movement elements and the human body (the instrument of dance) in motion, and through adhering to a holistic approach. Holism does not mean an attempt to know everything, but it assumes that dance is essentially meaningful in its sociocultural context. It implies functional relations within a system but does not assume total interrelatedness nor relationships of equal importance. Dance movement elements are those basics generally accepted by movement analysts as intrinsic to motion: space, rhythm (time), and dynamics (force, effort, and quality). It is implicit that dance exists in time and space and is as affected by its physical environment (light, precipitation, heat, topography, etc.) as are other motor phenomena. The instrument of dance is the human body, and its analysis is dependent on kinesiology.

Dance can be most usefully defined as human behavior composed, from the dancer's perspective, of (1) purposeful, (2) intentionally rhythmical, and (3) culturally patterned sequences of (4a) nonverbal body movements (4b) other than ordinary motor activities, (4c) the motion having inherent and aesthetic value. (Aesthetic refers to notions of appropriateness and competency held by the dancer's reference groups which act as a frame of reference for self-evaluation and attitude formation to guide the dancer's actions.) Within this conceptualization, human behavior must meet each of these four criteria in order to be classified as "dance." That is to say, each behavioral characteristic is necessary and the set of four constitutes sufficiency;

1   Choreographers at work: George Balanchine, *left*, and Jerome Robbins, *right*, working with Edward Villella in "Harlequinade." Photograph by Martha Swope.

the combination of *all* these factors must exist. For example, intentional rhythm as an indicator of dance is necessary, but an activity with this property is not necessarily dance; weight is merely added to the assumption. Some of the indicators may have more significance than others in different sociocultural contexts.

Other definitions have been proposed. For example, Kurath writes: "What identifies 'dance,' which uses the same physical equipment and follows the same laws of weight, balance, and dynamics as do walking, working, playing, emotional expression, or communication? The border line has not been precisely drawn. Out of ordinary motor activities dance selects, heightens or subdues, juggles gestures and steps to achieve a pattern, and does this with a purpose transcending utility" (1960:234–235). It is not clear whether Kurath considers dance as human behavior including the animal ritualization that ethologists often refer to as "dance" (Thomas Pitcairn 1976). The distinction is important and is discussed in the following chapter. Dance may not always have a purpose transcending utility: some people believe their deities love dance, and so the devotees perform for the sole purpose of appeasing them. Dances are often a means of training and motivation in work activities. In numerous cultures, dance and aesthetics are instrumentally motivated and used. Intentional rhythm, nonverbal body movement and gesture, and the importance of motion having inherent value are absent in Kurath's definition. Extraordinary as well as ordinary motor activities may be the material of dance. Kurath's most recent definition of dance appears in *Webster's Third International Dictionary* as "rhythmic movement having as its aim the creation of visual designs by a series of poses and tracing of patterns through space in the course of measured units of time, the two components, static and kinetic, receiving varying emphases (as in ballet, *natya*, and modern dance) and being executed by different parts of the body in accordance with temperament, artistic precepts, and purpose" (1961:572).

My definition differs from this by leaving purpose open-ended (not all dance has as its *aim* the creation of visual designs), attributing cultural patterning to dance, focusing on nonverbal body movement rather than a static "series of poses" and "tracing of patterns," and emphasizing that motor activities are not ordinary and that motion has inherent value. The concept of poses may be too limiting: Twyla Tharp's dances rarely use the end-stopped poses that we are accustomed to see in ballet: the dancing just keeps spiralling and shaking through every part of the dancers' bodies. Tharp is a contemporary choreographer in the modern dance tradition which is firmly associated in America with Isadora Duncan, the figure most noted for loosening the restrictions of ballet. She was one of the many, albeit their stories have yet to emerge according to dance historian Gretchen Schneider, who rebelled against the rigid formality and artificiality of the European elitist classical ballet and its superficial themes. The "great figures" arise out of a cultural context: early vaudeville and theater dance created a ripe climate for Duncan's "art, panache, or political bearing."

Kealiinohomoku defines dance as "a transient mode of expression performed in a given form and style by the human body moving in space. Dance occurs through purposefully selected and controlled rhythmic movements; the resulting phenomenon is recognized as dance both by the performer and the observing members of a given group" (1969–1970:28). This definition recognizes dance as human behavior, purposeful, and intentionally rhythmical, body movement. However, the concept of transience requires qualification. Dance may more appropriately be called ephemeral, continually becoming in the phenomenological sense. Moreover, at another level of analysis, it may last in the memory of the performer and observer, and sometimes endures in notation, film, or video recording, as drama lasts in scripts and synopses. Dance may affect behavior of performers and observers beyond the dance situation. Kealiinokomoku only distinguishes dance from nondance by the criterion of a group having the concept of dance. (George Mills and Roy Sieber, 1973, raise a similar problem of cross-cultural aesthetics and whether a group has the concept of aesthetics.) This criterion creates problems for cross-cultural studies and places undue emphasis on verbalized forms of knowing, expressing, and communicating. The definition also ignores two factors which I think are important: culturally patterned sequences of nonverbal body movements which are not ordinary, and motion having inherent and aesthetic value. In refining her definition, Kealiinohomoku (1972:387) states: "It is understood that dance is an affective mode of expression which requires both time and space. It employs motor behavior in redundant patterns which are closely linked to the definitive features of musicality." However, dance is also a cognitive mode; it can convey concepts in much the same way as verbal language, especially poetry. A person can dance without expressing emotion. Redundancy does not characterize all of dance. Indeed, climaxes are often unique patterns. It is not clear how motor patterns are linked to definitive features of musicality: some groups do not dance to music. Perhaps music is linked to the definitive features of dance! Or perhaps the human psychobiological bases of rhythm generate both.

Lomax (1968:xv) compares dance to everyday movement to verify the hypothesis that "danced movement is patterned reinforcement of the habitual movement patterns of each culture or culture area." Furthermore, he hypothesizes, dance "is an adumbration of or derived communication about life, focussed on those favored dynamic patterns which most successfully and frequently animated the everyday activity of most of the people in a culture. . . . Choreometrics tests the proposition that dance is the most repetitious, redundant, and formally organized system of body communication present in a culture" (ibid.:223–224). If this is a working definition, the criterion of motion with inherent, aesthetic value has been ignored. Also, I submit that danced movement may not only reflect the habitual movement patterns of a people, but may also reflect athletic feats and "exotic" or unique movements requiring specific training. The proposition that dance is the most repetitious and redundant system of body communication is questionable (Paul Ekman 1971, Ekman and Wallace Friesen 1969), since dance is not ordinary motor activity and not everyone dances.

Williams provides a relatively comprehensive definition:

> Dancing is essentially the termination, through action,
> of a certain kind of symbolic transformation of experience.
> . . . 'a dance' is a visually apprehended, kinesthetically felt,
> rhythmically ordered, spatially organized phenomenon
> which exists in three dimensions of space and at least one of
> time. It is articulated in terms of dancing on the level of the
> articulation of the dancers' bodies; in the body-instrument
> space which . . . is ninety-dimensional. It is articulated in
> terms of 'a dance' on the level of a pattern of interacting
> forces; the form space of a dance . . . [is] the empirically perceivable structure which modulates in time . . . Whatever
> its surface characteristics, a dance has limitations, "rules"
> within which it exists and which govern any of its idiomatic or stylistic expressions. (1973)

She argues dance's social base and cultural patterning elsewhere. However, it is not necessary to apprehend dance visually: it may occur in the dark. For example, the Iroquois of New York State and Canada have a "Dark Dance," a women's medicine rite, which is always performed at night in complete darkness (Kurath 1964a:13–14,

143–149). A blind person may perceive dance through the auditory, olfactory, or tactile senses. Furthermore, a person may dance in the absence of an observer. Kinesthetic perception also appears to be an unnecessary requirement, particularly in the case of a dancer in a trance or drugged state.

From this review of previous definitions of dance, it is obvious that the proposed conceptualization is partly consensus. It remains close to established usage while attempting to eliminate the difficulties which have been identified. The following discussion identifies more clearly the components of dance: purpose, intentional rhythm, culturally patterned sequences, and extraordinary nonverbal movement with inherent and aesthetic value. To keep the definition in focus, I will not employ extensive ethnographic illustrations.

Purpose

All dance has purpose or intent. The purpose may be primarily movement, the creation of an ephemeral, kinetic design in which concept (ideas about dance), process (what leads to performance), medium (the body instrument), and product (the dance performance) merge. In this case, physical motion is the primary end, what Alan Anderson and Omar Moore (1960) call "autotelic." Yet Merce Cunningham, who claims the purpose of his dances is movement, also demonstrates another intent when he breaks rules of former styles by choreographing solo dance movement which had been dueted or orchestrated with music or thematic material.

When movement is the focus, dance is viewed as a semiautonomous system (Table 1) separable conceptually and practically from its sociocultural context. (Complete autonomy of the dance is precluded by its sociocultural determinants.) Dance can be observed by the human eye, captured on film, or objectified by systems of graphic notation. Meaning in dance is thus found internally, in the stylistic and structural manipulation of the elements of space, rhythm, and dynamics, and the human body's physical control. In the embodied meaning of dance, one aspect of dance points to another rather than to what exists beyond the dance performance. Attention focuses more on the formal qualities and the sensuous surface of dance than on the processes that may lead to performer recruitment and dance training, or on the choice of movement, expression, or concepts that the dance may represent. Robert Armstrong argues that a work of art is a thing in itself, "its own significance incarnated within its own existence and not external to itself" (1971:xvi, 31).

Table 1   The Semiautonomous System of Dance

PROCESS	MEDIUM	PRODUCT	IMPACT — PERMANENCE	
Confluence of environment-al and socio-cultural ele-ment choices and expres-sion	Human body (other accou-trements pos-sible)	Human body in motion	Dancer's and observers' mem-ory, affect, cognition, behav-ior, film, notation	

The purpose of dance can be understood also in terms of the larger social structure, the standardized social form through which concep-tualization and action occurs. The social structure may dictate the criteria for participation and the dancers' relation to, and means of coping with, the broader social structure. Dance is part of those net-works of social stratification that organize the interconnected activi-ties of members of a society. Jacques Maquet, among others, argues that societies strain for cultural consistency and that aesthetic phe-nomena are "parts of a system, involved in an interplay of actions and reactions with other parts of the cultural system" (1971:19).

Within the category of sociopsychological functions, the two per-spectives of dance as a self-sufficient system and as meshed with the sociocultural system can be conceptualized more effectively. Dance has both cognitive and affective dimensions within these functions. It communicates some kind of information; communication is used here to include the performer's intention to communicate and also the performer's transfer of information (D. M. MacKay 1972). "To separate communication from overall information pickup and trans-mission capabilities of the individual would be a tour de force on the part of the human observer," write Emil Menzel and Marcia Johnson (1976:131). Like other cultural codes and patterned interactions, dance is a way of ordering and categorizing experience: it may even be that statements made in the dance form cannot be made in an-other. (The manner of dance communication or style of presentation is discussed in the following sections.) Nonverbal communication is used where there is a lack of verbal coding, for example, in the case of shapes, emotions, and interpersonal attitudes. Dance is an effec-tive communications medium—it functions as a multidimensional phenomenon codifying experience and capturing the sensory modal-ities: the sight of performers moving in time and space, the sounds of physical movement, the smell of physical exertion, the feeling of kinesthetic activity or empathy, the touch of body to body and/or performing area, and the proxemic sense. In this way dance has unique *potential* of going beyond many other audio-visual media of persuasion. Three key actors are possible in dance communication: choreographer, performer, and observer. The choreographer and performer may be one and the same; one actor may play all three roles.

Dance is a whole complex of communication symbols, a vehicle for conceptualization. It may be a paralanguage, a semiotic system, like articulate speech, made up of signifiers that refer to things other than themselves. Substantively, information necessary to maintain a society's or group's cultural patterns, to help it attain its goals, to adapt to its environment, to become integrated, or to change may be communicated. Dance may support or refute through repetition, augmentation, or illustration, linguistic, paralinguistic, or other nonverbal communication; it may anticipate, coincide with, or substitute for other communicative modes. Obviously dance may not communicate in the same way to everyone. Within a culture, differential understanding of symbols may be based on, and sometimes be exclusive to, the dancer's age, sex, association, occupation, political status groups, and so on. Someone just learning the dance may know less than the dance-initiate, who may, in turn, know less than the dance expert. And it may be that what is communicated is not translatable into a culture's other codes or into the concepts of a different culture. Figure 1 illustrates kinds of variation in understanding. Some dance behavior has a generally shared meaning, some is intended by the performer to transmit information, some is interactive in the sense of evoking a deliberate response from the spectator (cf. Conrad Arensberg 1972), some is aimed toward a few, some is unintentional, or has latent meaning. Meaning is thus transcendent, going beyond or outside the dance. (Devices of symbolization are discussed in later sections.)

The affective function of dance is to provide an immediate and sensuous experience. The appeal of the processual, sequentially unfolding dance form, with its arresting, seductive essence, is made through all or some of the sensory modalities mentioned above. The presence of dance may evoke a single emotional response or range of responses, sometimes for pleasure or well-being, sometimes to cope with problematic aspects of social involvement. Dance as a psychological defense mechanism, embodying psychologically or socially unacceptable impulses, falls within this latter category. Such emo-

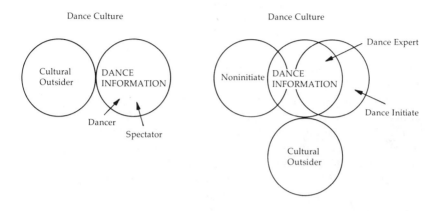

Figure 1.   Realms of dance understanding.

tions as anxiety and fear, made sensorily perceptible, thereby become, according to certain psychological literature on the arts and play, accessible to purposive action by the individual, group, or society. Thus dance may be, like play, rituals of rebellion, or cathartic outlets for deviance, a way of representing a segment of the psyche or world to understand or cope with it. Symbols with established, emotional associations may be employed; emotion-arousing events, people, or supernatural entities depicted; or combinations of dance elements capable of arousing emotions in themselves used, for example, rapid whirling (James Fernandez 1974, Raymond Firth 1973). Aesthetic motion (further discussed under nonordinary behavior), as an end in itself, lies within this function.

Dance may provide affective security as a familiar experience for performer or spectator. Herein, there is an emotional expectation that, within a particular dance style, a dance element (e.g., rhythm, dynamic, or spatial pattern) will be recognized, repeated, and/or followed by another such element at some specified point. Alternatively, dance may arouse interest, what Victor Turner describes as liminality, the suspension of usual rules (1969); what D. E. Berlyne calls the collative variables—novelty, counter expectations (surprise and incongruity, uncertainty, absence of clear expectations), complexity, conflict, ambiguity and multiple meaning, and instability (1971:141–161); what Hans and Shulamith Kreitler refer to as remoteness from the habitual (1972:163); or what Arnold Ludwig refers to as altered states of consciousness (1969:13).

States of consciousness are always altering: they range along a continuum from reduced arousal (tranquil states) to increased arousal. These states are conceptualized as the individual's symbolic interpretations of the state of his or her own central nervous system. The dancer or observer feels a qualitative shift in thinking, disturbance in the time sense, loss of control, change in body image, perceptual distortion, change in meaning, sense of the ineffable, feeling of rejuvenation, and hypersuggestibility. The deliberate pursuit of vertigo, self-loss, giddiness, through high speed is common in dance: the Balinese speak of "the other mind" that can be reached through music and dancing. Mihalyi Csikszentmihalyi conceives of *flow* as a pleasurable altered state of consciousness, which involves extraordinariness. The individual engages in an activity that provides immediate pleasurable feedback, a signal that all is well. Common to a variety of flow experiences is the "total involvement of body and mind with a feasible task which validates the competence, indeed the very existence of the action" (1975:157). Compared to experiences in normal life, this experience affords a relativizing perspective.

Of course, cognitive and affective functions are considerably intertwined. Dance tends to be a testament of values, beliefs, attitudes, and emotions. As Mills points out, the "cognitive and qualitative modes are banks of one stream of experience" (1971:85). Even if dance is mechanically performed and leaves the performer and observer unsatisfied or bored, these reactions are affective responses. And even mechanically performed dance, usually a stimulus-response pattern, retains its essence as symbolically transformed experience; it is this transformation which distinguishes cultural from natural movement (Williams 1972:24).

Intentional Rhythm

Rhythm refers to patterned, temporally unfolding phenomena. Similar elements are repeated at regular or recognizably related intervals; there are alternations of relative quietude and activeness. Such behavior as physical work, sports, playing instruments, and sometimes fear or anxiety responses are rhythmical. Thus dance must involve more than just rhythmical movement, the pulsing flow of energy in time and space.

Although "rhythmical motion" is mentioned as a characteristic of numerous western definitions of dance, *intended* rhythm seems to be implicit. A choreographer, who obviously need not be the dancer, may choose rhythmic variables which are then repeated; improvisation is also possible. Even in the pulse that modern dancer Merce Cunningham pursues, and other spontaneous, aleatoric, and improvisational choreography, one finds some intentional structuring of time. Sometimes this is based on deliberately breaking the cultural rules or parameters of dance rhythms to which the dancer has been socialized.

Dance can be viewed within several time perspectives. This is the duration of the performance itself; the duration of the interval during which the audience perceives, understands, and/or reacts to dance; and the interval actually portrayed in the dance itself which is based on the choreographer's conceptions of time. (For discussions of different views of time, see Leonard Doob 1971, Mary Douglas 1973, Edmund Leach 1971, and Richard Schechner 1969:89–93.) Rhythmic temporality in dance may be created by transformations of time itself (e.g., manipulating periods of quiet and activity) or by content (presenting motional configurations which represent events in time). The orientation of time may be toward the past, present, or future. Durations may be successive, circular (not in a causal pattern), oscillatory (discontinuous with repeated reversals, going back and forth, or inverted), or bracketed (succession and repetition not necessary and actions not related to each other occur). Furthermore, combinations of these, in what Schechner calls nodes ("a complicated circuitry capable of instant transformations and swift shifts of matrices" [1969]) may occur. Nigeria's Ubakala dance often reflects past, present, and future–the dancer, a reincarnated ancestor, will die and probably be reborn. Thus the dance represents the continuity of the lineage.

Dance can arrest time and offer to those with relevant predispositions and in an appropriate mood an opportunity to be in a particular time frame. This means that the principles ordinarily employed in judging the duration of intervals are suspended. Doob writes that "sometimes the arresting of time in art occurs because the audience is given the impression that it can master temporal intervals metaphorically and vicariously" (1971:382, see also 378–379). Dance may be rhythmically realized in different time frameworks. In "objective"

clock time, intervals of time are discretely measured and made mechanically regular through subjectively set registering devices. "Natural" time refers to ecological variables, such as the fluctuation of
the seasons, climatic variations, and the diurnal cycle. "Biological"
time centers on the human organism, for example, heart-beat, aging,
energy expenditure, and fatigue factors. "Historical" time is the recapitulation of a chronological period: it may involve an economic
expression (i.e., a ten-year period may be portrayed in one hour).
The Ghanian Krachi Abofac, a hunter's dance, is a funeral for an
animal about to die; at another time "it is both a celebration and a
means for the men to purify themselves and re-enter village life . . .
the dance isn't in 'ordinary time' because in it they recall what their
forefathers saw in visions about how to kill animals" (Williams, personal communication 1-20-74). In addition to a virtual condensation
of time, there can also be an extension. In this case, redundant expression could portray a second of time in a dance of greater length.
"Future" time may be presented as well as "psychological or subjective" time reflecting interest or boredom, high or low points. This
inner time involves recollection, anticipation, or expectancy; climaxes
or peaks of intensification are not necessary. A further variable is
"social convention time," time-reckoning as a conceptualization of
aspects of social phenomena, for example, market weeks, meal times.

In addition to performance duration, audience response time, and
the time expressed in the dance, through time alterations or content
references, and the various time frameworks within which to present
dance, there is also dance "motor" time, which consists of four elements: *Accent* is the significant stress, the relative force or intensity
with which energy is released. *Duration* is the relative length, the
amount of time, of movements, phrases (groups of related movements which have their own unity, perceptible start and stop, or climax), patterns, and performances. *Meter* is the underlying consistent
numerical grouping of beats and accents. *Tempo* is the rate or speed
at which movements follow one another. Each of these elements may
be simple or complex, uniform or variable within a dance; that is,
dance may be heterometric, meters changing within a dance or its
parts, and it may also be polymetric. Each element of dance motor
time can be arbitrarily demarcated.

Culturally Patterned Sequences

Dance is culturally patterned and meaningful. It is not universally
identical behavior, a proven innate, instinctive response, although

the raw capacities, materials or tools are. At some level, dance may reflect universal body structures, experiences, and structures of the mind, what Blacking calls the universal "collective consciousness" and universal "aesthetic sense" based on theories of evolution and biological development (Alexander Alland 1973 and Paul Byers 1972 discuss underlying rhythms). These issues will be discussed in the next chapter. An individual learns dance on the bases of innate capabilities, plus social interaction. Blacking writes that dance and music "combine in a unique fashion the expression of universal structures of the body with reflections of particular realizations of those structures in different cultural environments" (1973:9). Dance is a social phenomenon: it is an institution (Milton Albrecht 1968) and collective action (Howard Becker 1974). When we speak we are not always conscious of the syntactic and morphological laws of our language; as an individual creates verbal language and responds to it without being conscious of how he does it, so he may create and respond to dance. In this sense dance lives, develops, and persists as a collective phenomenon (cf. Claude Lévi-Strauss 1967:55–57).

Dance as a system of ordering movement, a cumulative set of rules or range of permissible movement patterns, is one of the elements comprising culture. It reflects other cultural manifestations and is a vehicle through which culture is learned. Dance is certainly not equally important in all societies. Within a sociocultural system, there may be classes of dance which are ranked in importance; within a class, a specific dance may be either a major or minor event. A class of dance may be a concomitant of another class or classes of events which assign rank to the dance: in the United States, ballet receives more recognition, financial support, and written coverage than other dance forms. Some ballet choreographers, for example, Marius Petipa and George Balanchine, are considered more important. When Balanchine choreographs a new work for a special occasion that is promoted as a benefit, it achieves major event status. The 1976 ballet "Union Jack" is illustrative. When there is an international arts festival and a dance is performed there, it takes on the status of the festival's importance.

Most behavior of members of a culture is, to some degree, patterned by that culture. The distinction here must be made between cultural patterning and such symptomatic behavior as an epileptic or hysterical fit, trembling from excessive excitation of the nervous system, or a child rhythmically rocking on all fours, excitedly jumping or otherwise instinctively, spontaneously, or idiosyncratically moving. The latter is what George Devereux calls "the straining of pure affect against pure (culturally structured) discipline" (1971:194). This cultural discipline has certain standards, certain criteria by which to evaluate the behavior socially, psychologically and/or choreologically (in terms of the intrinsic characteristics of dance movement). Motor behavior which is expressive but has undisciplined affect could be called dance only metaphorically (see Joost Meerloo 1960), or what Langer calls a "dance motif" (1953:172), or what *Webster's Third International Dictionary* includes in four of its sixteen distinctions. This means that movement styles (the particular and constant features, recurrent motifs, unique to a tradition, the way in which all the contributing elements are selected, organized, manipulated, and projected, and by which one may establish origin, place, and time) and movement structure (the appearance of the interdependent elements and values of space, dynamics, and rhythm) of dance do not occur randomly. Cultural patterning even affects the deliberate breaking of rules.

There are a virtually infinite number of possible combinations of movements that can be manipulated and the dramatic variants possible range from intense peaking or outstanding climaxes to the mere physiological change from repeating the same movement. However, dancers in a specific culture appear to use only certain combinations[3] within certain parameters or delimiting rules. The question arises, why is one form chosen or why does one evolve rather than another? Do functions determine form? Cultural patterning, within biological determinants or constraints, affects the way, if any, in which purpose and function create form; it determines what the minimal and maximal sequences and configurations (or syntax) of dance elements are. Cultural patterning affects the sequence of interpersonal interaction, that is, who dances and who interacts with the dancers and how, when the dance occurs, how often, how long, and why (Arensberg 1972). A dance may be a solo in privacy; sharing or interaction tends to occur as the performer, with or without awareness, draws upon his culture's inventory of stylistic movements. The individual dances to cope with loneliness, symbolically putting the self in contact with his or her people; becomes an audience to himself or herself in beseeching the self to move as he or she thinks appropriate; or perceives the self visually or kinesthetically as a detached observer, that is, the superego may stand for society. The private solo dance is similar to what John Dewey calls the inner dialogue or soliloquy, seemingly locked within the self but actually the "product and reflection of converse with others." For "if we had not talked with others and they with us, we should never talk to and with ourselves" (1922:171). Any number of participants may perform a dance for themselves or for another spectator or group of spectators.

A people's own inventory, borrowing or creation determine a cultural style. Moreover, psychological, historical, environmental, or idiosyncratic factors may shape that style. Thus a performer may project fantasies about social situations into the dance form with some aspect of the fantasy bearing a relationship to a real or desired situation or a social condition. Historical relationships may also be determining factors: a society's dance conventions may be elaborations of, or reactions against, earlier rules. The evolution of a style may reveal a pattern of enrichment in one direction, or impoverishment in another, or something new. Alland (1976) also speaks of breaking rules. The congeniality of a dance style of a neighboring group or other factors which lead a group to adopt a style by importation and imitation, why among a broad range of available variables culture A becomes the model rather than culture B, should be considered. J. L. Fischer points out that using known historical connections alone to explain the similarities in art styles of two distinct cultures or using general features of art styles to establish historical connections is dangerous (1961; see also Raoul Naroll 1973). The stimulus of forms in the natural environment may also determine style. Individuals who only cultivate tend to have some different movement vocabularies than those who fish, herd, or hunt. The weaver bird's courtship patterns are the model for the Sokodae dance of Ghana's Ntwumuru (Williams et al. 1970:30). The mandrill, with its vivid red, blue, and black facial colors and bold planes may have had an impact on the masked dancers found in West Africa, the mandrill's natural habitat. One group of Armenian dances is devoted to two types of trees, the pomegranate and apricot, both full of seeds and blood-like red juice, embodying the female essence, and the pshat and pear, embodying the male essence (E. Petrosyan 1973). The limitations of the human body, which vary by endogamous breeding populations in terms of body-limb proportions, may futher affect dance style.

It is most likely that styles evolve through the convergence of these factors plus the idiosyncratic. An individual's private nightmare or repressed desires may be expressed in a new style which is culturally congenial to what a group had heretofore found acceptable. If the new style is too unfamiliar, the behavior might qualify as dance, bearing traces of cultural conditioning, but would not be emulated and thereby perpetuated. In the United States, the development of white minstrelsy was based on the imitation of a black cripple's dance, but it blended the jig and shuffle of the extant Irish and Afro-American cultures and so became easily accepted by the dominant culture (Lynne Emery 1972:18, Marshall and Jean Stearns 1968:40).

Movement styles develop through psychomotor socialization patterns; they are largely dependent on observing dance, general motor activity, and dance practice and are subject to the forces of internal and external change. Such forces occur in relation to other aspects of culture, for example, work, economics, religion, and politics. While dance movement styles may require specialized training, the capability for mastering a style may develop through daily life experience. For example I observed, among a Nigerian Igbo people in the rural areas, the Ubakala dancers' ease in maintaining the common angular posture (upper torso inclined forward, pelvis tilted downward), knee flexibility, elisive hip rotations, sustained movement patterns, and stamina in dancing. This ease develops in such activities as traveling long distances in great heat, bending to fetch water, washing in a stream, crop cultivation, squatting to defecate, and carrying heavy loads on the head (which requires lifting high in the pelvis and subtly moving the hips). The common bending knee action gives elasticity to movement and helps to cushion irregularities in the ground surface. A dancer's projected strength is more than illusory: at an early age young people begin to participate in such family chores as yam-pounding, cultivating, wood chopping, and transporting heavy burdens. An individual's dance practice begins in his or her mother's womb, then on her back as she dances. Even before he or she can walk the child is encouraged to dance, and youngsters regularly practice. On the other hand, those Ubakala brought up in an urban industrialized environment use Anglo-Saxon styles of motor behavior for the most part. In contrast with the diffuse kind of movement socialization to dance in rural Ubakala, dance training in the industrialized, technological American culture tends to be, as with our other activities, relatively segmented and specialized. (This is not to imply an industrial/nonindustrial dichotomy, for a number of the latter cultures have highly specialized dance training.)

In the dance performance, we do not see the underlying structures, but merely the evidence of them. Dance style and structure may well be like a generative grammar. A grammar (syntax) of a dance language, a socially shared means for expressing ideas and emotions, is a set of rules specifying the manner in which movement can be meaningfully combined. There is a finite system of principles or conventions describing how the realm of semantic interpretation is related to movement realization (cf. George Miller 1973). Just as a key feature

2 Shaping: Noumenon from "Masks, Props, and Mobiles," the Nikolais Dance Theatre. Photograph courtesy of the Chimera Foundation for Dance, Inc.

of human speech is that any speaker of a language is capable of producing and understanding an indefinitely large number of utterances never encountered, so, in dance performance, new sequences of movement and gesture never previously encountered may be created by the performer and understood by the audience. Here it is necessary to distinguish between the choreographer-dancer (or improvisor) and the imitator-dancer who re-creates a dance conceptualized and choreographed by someone else. Choreography involves knowledge of grammar, relational rules for using a motor lexicon or corpus of movements and semantics. Imitation merely depends on learning a motor lexicon. Cultural patterning largely determines what Kealiinohomoku (1976:337) calls the parameters of must, should, could, and would. These parameters involve what is admissible according to the prevailing norms, what is preferred within existing values, what options are acceptable, and what conditionally is possible.

Nonverbal Body Movements Other Than Ordinary Motor Activities, the Motion Having Inherent Value

What is not ordinary is obviously relative to a particular society, as are the other characteristics of dance. Identifying and analyzing these call for a general knowledge of the society involved. An awareness of the human anatomy and physiology are also essential as a guide to the analyst in perceiving the ordinary/extraordinary distinction, because the human body as the dance instrument has natural kinetic parameters and extraordinary extensions (e.g., through exercise or drugs). It is necessary to examine the characteristic use of the body, the postural movements that activate or are largely supported through the whole body; gestural movements that involve parts of the body that are not supported through the whole body (e.g., head, hand, or shoulder movements used in isolation); and locomotor movements that involve a change of location of the whole body from one place to another as in the postural movements of walking, running, leaping, hopping, jumping, skipping, sliding, and galloping. The manipulation of the various dimensions of movement must be observed; these are subject to measurement and recording (cf. Rudolf and Joan Benesh 1956, Ann Hutchinson 1954, Adrienne Kaeppler 1967, Lomax 1968). One dimension of movement rhythm was elaborated above. The ordinary/extraordinary distinction in space, the area used by dancers, may be recognized by observing the following: Amplitude is size of movement, the relative amount of distance covered or space enclosed by the body in action. Direction is the path along which the body moves through space. Focus is the direction of the eyes and body. Level varies from high with the weight on the ball of the foot or elevated as in jumping; low with the body lowered through flexing knees, kneeling, sitting, or lying; to middle with the body in an upright position or bent at the waist. Shape refers to the physical contour of movement design created by the body or its parts forming angles or curves. Grouping refers to the overall spatial pattern of movement in relation to the dancers' interpersonal links either in free form or in an organized pattern that involves a couple, small group, or team with or without physical links.

The ordinary/extraordinary distinction in dynamics, the effort used by the body to accomplish movement, includes the following: Force is the relative amount of physical and emotional energy exerted. It involves the indulgence of minimum or maximum spatial use through "direct" straight lines or "flexible" curves and deviations. Effort flow is the change in expenditure of energy which qualifies movement on a continuum between degrees of uncontrolled to controlled movement; the kind of locomotion used contributes to dynamic patterns. Projectional quality refers to the texture created by the combination of elements and relative quickness or slowness of energy released in space. Movement perceived by dancer and spectator participants in a performance event, as well as by observers, can be extraordinary by cross-cultural agreement. Alternatively, what participants view as extraordinary might be considered ordinary by a cultural outsider. According to the specification of dance in this book, the movement must be extraordinary within the host culture. (See Figure 1.)

By using the concept of extraordinary motor behavior, we may distinguish dance from many kinds of behavior. Ordinary movement tends to be diffuse, fragmentary, and not self-aware in comparison with dance (in athletics and wrestling, for example, the overriding concern is winning). Dance is more assembled, interfused, and ordered. However, some work, sports, music-making, drama, ritual, love-making, and play (Edward Norbeck 1973 includes dance within this category) may also involve extraordinary body movements. These actions may have a *charismatic* quality, being extraordinary contrasted with the routine everyday world (cf. Rolf Meyersohn 1970), moving from an ordinary state of being to another realm of perception. Such activities may also involve special skill. As in dance, the human body may be the primary means of expression. In fact, the creator (dancer) and the thing created (dance) may be the same, as in some drama and love-making. Furthermore, these activities may be separated from, a prelude to, concomitant with, a postscript to, or even merge with dance.

The distinguishing characteristic which sets extraordinary nonverbal body movements in dance apart from other activities is the manipulation of ordinary motor activities within an aesthetic[4] domain; the emphasis is on the importance of movement (the fact of bodily action) and motion (illusion and residual action resulting from the kind of movement produced). Out-of-the-ordinary motor activities are transformed into dance configurations although ordinary movements may be incorporated. The extraordinary quality of dance allows it to set up a frame within which images can be scrutinized, and played with. As a frame for public reflexivity, dance may serve as a vehicle to comment on social structures, values, and roles.

Aesthetic Value

The philosophic connection between aesthetics and "beauty" originates in Western intellectual life. In cross-cultural studies the meaning of aesthetic must be broadened to include notions of appropriateness, quality, or competency from the dancer's perspective. The dancer's reference groups create expectations, which are significant whatever other values or motivations are associated with dance. These canons of taste, arising out of cultural conditioning, have a recurrent minimum way of deliberately manipulating, composing, performing, and sometimes feeling (cf. Kapila Vatsyayan 1968) the various elements for physically structuring and meaningfully presenting a dance. These actions constitute the rules of dance.

The aesthetic experience involves sensory elicitation of rapt attention and the contemplation of a phenomenon's immanent and/or transcendent meanings at the emotional-affective, cognitive, and behavioral-action levels. Performers and choreographers experience this with varying degrees of satisfaction, closure, or purpose. However, the audience(s) also has such an aesthetic experience; it differs from that of the dancer, although empathy with the creator may be intense. The spectator experience can provide a variety of feedback responses that affect future performances; responses that range from ignoring the performance to ecstatically encouraging a dancer and those who contribute to the dance production during or after the presentation. The variation in experience for creator and observer depends on such factors as age, dance and life experience, innate sense of form or what we call "artistry," and mood. In some cases, the response may be less to the actual artistic affect of a dance performance than to cognitive factors, such as the status of the dancer or the purpose of the performance (honoring a national leader, for example).

Inherently, dance has qualities which stimulate aesthetic awareness; it possesses noninstrumental features which exceed the requirements for work, magic, and other activities. Motion seems to have inherent value as a motivating force, the pleasure in doing or contemplating (the empathetic factor is operative here). Other psychobiological bases, which will be discussed in the next chapter, are relevant as well. The impact of dance is dependent not only on learn-

ing and knowledge, but relies also on "the direct and self-explana-
tory impact of perceptual forces upon the human mind" (Rudolf
Arnheim 1954:380). Theatrical dance, such as the work of the Alwin
Nikolais modern dance company, exemplifies aesthetic phenomena
that are explicitly and primarily designed, although not always so
realized, to provide an aesthetic experience in the observer and performer (Nikolais 1971). Features which stimulate aesthetic awareness
lie in the culturally patterned form and style of dance and, since it
is often difficult to distinguish form from content, content may also
stimulate aesthetic awareness.

The keys to extraordinary aesthetic motion having inherent value
are fashioning and meaning: Fashioning involves embellishment,
distortion, deletion, rearrangement, abstraction, contrast, miniaturization, and projection of personality. Kobla Ladzekpo (1973) writes
of the Anlo Ewe of Ghana: in all their dances, any movement, besides the principal motion or basic movement which a dance stands
for, must have *atsia*, which literally means "style" or "display." Meaning in this discussion is what a thing or an idea stands for. It is more
than the relationship between a sign and its referent; a disposition
to respond is involved (Charles Morris 1955). Roslyn Stone (1975)
speaks of awarenesses, patterns of data in the stream of consciousness which may be attended to, responded toward, or reported on.
Meaning is communication in contexts where the participants, dancers and observers, share semantic codes.[5] John Gumperz (1974:795)
points out that meaning may be referential (deals with direct propositional meaning); conveyed (includes referential meaning and a consideration of the intended effect of messages relying on social pre-
suppositions in the interpretation); and situated (social assumptions
constrain the interpretation of the message and consequent interaction). Further, there may also be nonpropositional types of meaning
such as those found in speech play. In this case the rules of communication may be played with and the shape of the message may
be the primary meaning (Barbara Kirshenblatt-Gimblett 1976). For
communication to be most effective, there should be shared knowledge about the form and familiarity with its use; shared notions
about when, where, how, and why messages are sent; and information sufficiently lucid to be perceived through distractions or impediments.

Communication occurs through symbols; a symbol is a vehicle for
conceptualization: it helps to order behavior and is a transformation
or system of transformations. As symbolic behavior dance creates an
illusion in that body locomotion and gesture, the raw material of

dance, and other dance materials, such as pantomime, plastic images, musical patterns, play, accidental and sociocultural forms found in the environment, become abstracted into what Langer describes as the "primary illusion of dance." Dance then is a virtual realm or "play of Powers made visible" (1953:187)–"not actual, physically exerted power, but appearances of influence and agency" (ibid.:175). Most symbols have a utilitarian purpose; for example, clothes frequently symbolize status; but they also protect the wearer against the elements. A Cadillac reflects high status and wealth, whereas a Volkswagen suggests the intellectual's disregard for wealth. Nevertheless, both transport the individual. Similarly, the imagery and illusion of reality in dance, and its utilitarianism, do not negate the reality of the performer and audience experiencing emotion and dance being–having an immediacy.

A symbol[6] itself is usually arbitrary. The degree of representational or abstract symbolization and the syntactic arrangement–the permissive groups of movements which refer to sequences of meaning–depend on cultural patterning. Substantive content may be realistically represented as in a mimetic hunt or work activity, or distorted as in a dance satirizing or idealizing a person. In addition, kinesthetic imagery (muscular) qualities may be employed, and the instrument of dance itself (the body) may be subjected to distortion as in the limbering demanded for the Kathakali dance of India, without which the dance cannot be properly performed. Time can be altered to convey meaning and scale offers further opportunities for manipulation and communication. A single concept may be elaborated in dance and thus magnified. Dance costume and masks (some as large as the Malian Dogon twelve-story house) are often used to enlarge movements, making them outstanding or formidable. The opposite abstraction, miniaturization, reduces the scale or the number of properties, thus decreasing formidableness (cf. Lévi-Strauss 1971:241).

Dance is considered meaningful behavior in three domains (Morris 1955):[7] pragmatics, semantics, and syntactics. Pragmatics focuses on the relation of signs to interpreters, the "real-life" level of antecedents, consequences, and ideology (see Becker 1974 and Pertti Pelto 1970 on event analysis). This domain deals with the origin and uses (purpose and occasion) and the effects (manifest and latent functions) of signs within the contextual ritual behavior or event in which those signs occur. Pragmatics concentrates on the participant users of the dance "language," on the encounter between dancer and spectator. It involves information transference (or the intent to communicate) on the part of the choreographer and/or performer. The "why" of communication addresses social structure, dance vis-à-vis groups in society, and the role of the dancer. The interdependence of semantics and syntax is seen in the pragmatic domain.

Semantics is the domain which focuses on the relation of signs to what they signify, information content, and the substantive nature of motional patterns. It may include syntax as noted below. Roland Barthes writes, "meaning is above all a cutting out of shapes" (1970: 57). Gary Shapiro (1974) argues that semiotic theories are deficient insofar as they are unable to give an account of the way a sign is representative of the object. Use of the grid, discussed below, may help to identify forms of representing and presenting. There are at least six modes or devices for conveying meaning that may be utilized in dance. Each device may be conventional (customary shared legacy) or autographic (idiosyncratic or creative expression of a thing, event, or condition). These are presented in a grid (Table 2, reading vertically), which is proposed as a tool in data collection and analysis. Developed in the course of analyzing dance field data, the grid is a step toward meeting the need Albert Mehrabian identifies: "The only comprehensive system of [dance] notation describes movements merely as motion, with no reference to what they signify (Hutchinson 1970). Such reliance on physical description alone for nonverbal and implicit verbal behavior is inadequate . . . it fails to provide guidelines for identifying socially significant implicit behavior" (1972:179).

(1) A *concretization* is a device which produces the outward aspect of a thing, event, or condition, for example, mimetically portraying an animal. It is an imitation or replica. (2) An *icon* represents most properties or formal characteristics of a thing, event, or condition and is responded to as if it were what it represents, for example, dancing the role of a deity which is revered or otherwise treated as the deity. The American Hopi Indians believe the masked *kachina* dancer is supernatural and treat it with genuine awe. The icon is a human transformation found among groups who believe in possession, the supernatural manifesting itself in specific human dancing patterns.[8] (3) A *stylization* encompasses somewhat arbitrary gestures or movements which are the result of convention, for example, pointing to the heart as a sign of love, performing specific movements as a badge of identity, or using dance to create abstract images within a conceptual structure of form, as in many of George Balanchine's "pure" ballets. (4) A *metonym* is a motional conceptualization of one thing for that of another, of which the former is an attribute or extension, or with which the former is associated or contiguous in the same frame of experience, for example, a war dance as part of a bat-

Table 2   Semantic Grid

DEVICES	SPHERES			
	Event	Body	Whole Performance	Discursive Performance
c	★	★	★	★
Concretization	— —	— —	— —	— —
a	★	★	★	★
c				
Icon	— —	— —	— —	— —
a				
c	★	★	★	
Stylization	— —	— —	— —	— —
a	★	★	★	
c	★	★	★	
Metonym	— —	— —	— —	— —
a	★	★	★	
c	★	★	★	
Metaphor	— —	— —	— —	— —
a	★	★	★	
c				
Actualization	— —	— —	— —	— —
a				

c = Conventional.
a = Autographical.
★ = Ubakala encoding.
    (see Chapters 3 and 4)

Specific Movement	Intermesh with Other Medium	Vehicle for Other Medium	Presence
★	★		
— —	— —	— —	— —
★	★		
— —	— —	— —	— —
★	★		
— —	— —	— —	— —
★	★		
	★		
— —	— —	— —	— —
	★		
★	★		
— —	— —	— —	— —
★	★		
— —	— —	— —	— —

tle. It might be thought of as a sample. (5) A *metaphor* expresses one thought, experience, or phenomenon in place of another which resembles the former to suggest an analogy between the two, for example, dancing the role of a leopard to denote the power of death (see Lincoln Kirstein [1970] for examples in ballet). (6) An *actualization* constitutes an individual dancing in terms of one or several of his usual statuses and roles, for example, Louis XIV dancing the role of king and being so treated.

Meaning usually depends on context; indeed, some scholars argue that all meanings are situational. The devices for encapsulating meaning seem to operate within one or more of eight spheres (reading the grid, Table 2, horizontally): (1) the sociocultural *event* and/or situation; (2) the total human *body* in action; (3) the whole pattern of the *performance*; (4) the *discursive* aspect of the performance (the sequence of unfolding movement configurations); (5) specific *movement*; (6) the *intermesh* of movements with other communication media (for example, dance meaning is inseparable from song, music, costume, accoutrements, and/or speech); (7) dance movement as a *vehicle* for another medium (as in background for a performer's poetry recitation); and (8) *presence* (charisma or performance magic). Singly, or in combination, the devices allow for a consideration of all message material in terms of possible relations to context.

The devices are signs (indications of the existence, past, present, or future, of a thing, event, or condition) that may function as *signals* when they are directly related to the action they signify, for example, a war dance to herald a battle (see Chapter 7).[9] They are mechanisms for encoding the meaning of a motor expression and may bear upon its kinetographic shape. Figure 2 presents a range of transformation possibilities from some kind of motor behavior through any one or more of the devices to a sign or signal. For example (reading the figure upward from the left), the motor action and concept of fighting may become associated with problems of land use. The dancer may convey this through a concretization and/or other device as indicated by the unbroken lines. Emotion, such as anxiety (reading upward from the right) may transform into the notion of flight or fight, which may in turn be conveyed as an icon, stylization, metonym, and/or metaphor as indicated by the broken line. Here the more concrete sensate makes accessible the abstract insensate (cf. Langer 1957:131).

Syntactics, the rules dictating how signs may be combined, is the grammar of how the realm of movement style and structure is related to the realm of meaning. Syntactics is critical to aesthetics

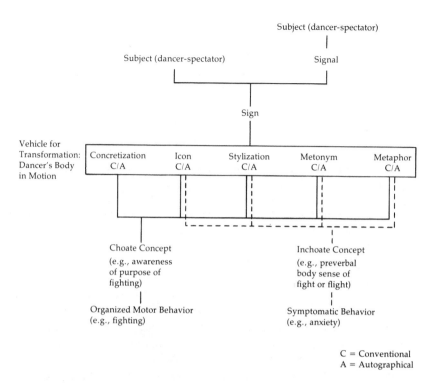

Figure 2. Transformations of cognitive-affective-sensori-motor behavior in dance available for sociocultural phenomena.

viewed as notions of appropriateness and competency. In this context, meaningful motor units are essentially synonymous with Laban's processual movement concepts, based on the architecture and function of the body. This discursive description and consequent analysis to identify dance structures comprises six dimensions (and their values) of space, four of rhythm, four of dynamics, and three of characteristic body usage (Laban 1974, Hutchinson 1970; see Movement Data Categories, Appendix 1). With the increase in movement studies, we may identify additional motor units or recognize a need to modify these categories. Units of meaning or structural units may be found in any movement or phrase–a wavelike motor pattern marked by alternations of activity and rest which cluster distinguishing traits–and its rules of combining motor units within itself and with other phrases. Syntactics governs not only the patterns of moving but those of rest and those exhibiting the intention to move.

Some linguists argue that semantics and syntactics may not be separable, that is, meaning is inherent in the rules of combination. Anthropologist Sherry Ortner (1975:166) refers to the "intertransposition of form and content." Nelson Goodman, a philosopher, also argues that subject is involved in style, the perceived regularities of an act of any time or place (1975). A property of a statement made, a structure displayed, or a feeling conveyed is considered stylistic when it identifies a work with one, rather than another, artist, period, region, or school. Style and structure are often referred to as form, the "how," so that a different way of saying something (how) may, in fact, be saying a different thing (what). For example, "minimal" dance with its use of everyday movement is used to refer to the subject of the common person (Marcia Siegel 1974) and to suggest that dance is not just for the elite trained performer.

The extraordinary nature of dance often makes it an attention-getting device, arresting or seductive. Thus it is useful as a medium of evocation, persuasion, and stimulation, for example, of work tasks. There is a distinction, noted above, between similar extraordinary nonverbal body locomotion and gesture in dance and other behavior. It seems likely that when movement is physically utilitarian, it may be considered to be dance if other, more efficient, physical means to utilitarian ends were available and not opted for. Where utilitarian purpose and the aesthetic and motion emphases are involved, one finds a fusion, a work dance such as that of the Nupe of Nigeria, during which women prepare a hut floor. The floor could be prepared more efficiently without the dance, with its stylizations and aesthetic, affective involvement. The center of interest is the process, the movement and motion, more than the goal, although it, too, is certainly significant. The dance apparently motivates and sustains the task (S. Nadel 1942:254–255, Kurath 1960).[10] Leach (1968:523) argues that "almost every human activity that takes place in culturally defined surroundings . . . had a technical aspect which does something and an aesthetic, communicative aspect which says something." In the same vein, Gordon Allport (1961) suggests that every single act a person performs has both expressive and adaptive (coping) aspects.

Comment

Although this chapter presents an analyst's definition of dance with cross-cultural applicability, the participants' labeling of behavior, the emic system of concepts, taxonomy, and exegesis, should not be

Table 3 Analyst's Check-list for Emic Concepts of Dance

	Purpose	Intentional Rhythm	Cultural Pattern	Not Ordinary Motor Behavior	Motion Has Inherent and Aesthetic Value
Participants conceptualize					
Different term					
Some Related Activities		Predance	During dance		Postdance
Spontaneous rhythmic movement					
Dissociation					
Mime					
Drama					
Ritual					
Work					
Song texts					
Music					

ignored. Table 3 lists some of the considerations: participants' perspectives provide valuable clues to inform the analyst's observations. More is learned about the universal phenomenon of dance when the categories in which it occurs, within a culture, are considered. The criteria by which a dance participant accepts or rejects activity as being "dance" may relate to purpose, function, occasion, audience relationships, use of movement elements, accompaniment, costume, or other factors. The analyst also examines systems of human action, the dance behavior and the interaction between participant and cocultural observer. The delineation and significance imputed by the participants (dancer, distinguishing between the leader and members of a group, and observer, distinguishing among sex, age, education, or political groups) as well as the dance behavior must receive attention in order to understand dance and modify the working definition.

This chapter offers a cross-cultural conceptualization, which attempts to synthesize much of what is known about dance worldwide and to distinguish dance from other behavioral phenomena. Thus dance is defined as human behavior composed, from the dancer's perspective, of purposeful, intentionally rhythmical, and culturally patterned sequences of nonverbal body movement which are not ordinary motor activities, the motion having inherent and aesthetic value. Obviously, specifying the meaning of a phenomenon is not an end in itself: The discussion of necessary and sufficient conditions first indicates the set of features that are referents for a concept and that provide a framework for the perception and description of reality with the rationale for associating elements of the description. Second, the discussion identifies some important variables in the hypotheses that will lead us to understand changes within dance and to explain and, eventually, predict and control the relationships of dance to other events. This would allow us to modify the outcome of a dance sequence by altering one or more related factors for educational and therapeutic purposes (Hanna 1978a). It is hoped that the conceptualization presented will lead toward a theory of dance. The set of interrelated propositions should lead to empirical tests of function, structure, change, semiotics, psychology, and culture acquisition and patterning. As there is further study of dance, it is likely that the definition will need to be refined to meet empirical and conceptual developments.

If humans dance, then the question arises, how did dance originate? The next section and following chapter deal with some of the relevant issues.

3   Creating stylized forms: George Balanchine directing Karen von
Aroldingin in "Vienna Waltzes." Photograph by Martha Swope.

Primeval Origins of Dance

There is no way of knowing the origins of dance or the developmental differentiation of the arts, although many books on dance, including those by respected dance scholars, offer suggestions (see Kealiinohomoku 1969–70 for a review of these in terms of false assumptions). Some peoples have handed down explanatory myths; rock art in some areas verifies the antiquity of dance; and there is a popularly held psychological theory of the origins of dance. Most of the dances of the Niger Delta are said to have been given to the mermaid "owu" goddess's victims in trance. Other dances supposedly were copied by ancestors who actually saw mermaids dancing on the river banks. The Kalabari believe that Ekineba, a village spirit hero, introduced masquerade dancing. Specific masquerade plays are derived from various anthropomorphic water spirits "associated with contemporary invention and creation; for people who introduce new dances . . . are often said to be relatives of water people or even incarnations of them" (Robin Horton 1962:200–201). Ikaki, the tortoise, one of the favorite Kalabari masquerade dances, is said to have originated from the desire of a few forebears to imitate Ikaki, a spirit who used to come out of the forest to dance "admirably" (Horton 1967:226–227).

Among the Dogon of Mali, dancing, often the "central liturgical action" in various rituals, has its origin in the Dogon cosmology, the first days of the world. God's son the jackal danced and tranced out the world and its future; and wearing the fibre skirt imbued with the first Word revealed by the Spirit to the earth, the jackal spoke the "Word that contained the designs of the celestial powers. So the first attested dance had been a dance of divination; it had told in the dust the secrets of the Word contained in the fibres won by the dancer. It was also a dance of death, for it was to honour and flout his father, whom he believed to be dead, that the jackal had invented it" (Griaule 1965:187). Ages passed and men appeared, according to Ogotemmêli's cosmogonic narrative. One of the Nummo spirits, the seventh, rose from the dead in a resurrection dance to the rhythm of the anvil and the bellows of the smithy who later found other rhythms corresponding to new dance-figures.

> "It was the seventh Nummo," said Ogotemmêli, "who taught men to dance." He had begun by repeating his first rhythmic movement in the underworld. He dances with the top half of his body, standing upright on his serpent's tail.

At first men danced on one spot, rotating on themselves or imitating swimming motions, but these movements were exhausting. Gradually they began to move their legs, imitating the slow walk of the chameleon, who has all the Nummo's colours, that is to say, the colours of the rainbow. Then the movements became more rapid. The *gôna* figure recalls the Nummo's vomiting in the tomb; later men took to leaping, raising one leg and then the other. The leg stretched out, while the body was lifted in the air, represented the tail of the serpent on which the Nummo stood erect (ibid.:188).

Apparently, dancing is an ancient cultural artifact. Early archaeology finds suggest dancing masked sorcerers or shamans and hunters in caves in Europe, e.g., Lascaux, Trois Frères, La Cueva del Civil, Marsoulas, Hornos de la Pena, and Altamira. In the Natal Drakensberg mountain range area of the Republic of South Africa, Harold Prager recently copied four thousand Bushmen rock paintings, most of which portrayed animals and people in movement. In one painting, six figures showed an entire series of movements in a Bushman dance-step. (Most of the South African paintings have not been dated; the archaeological deposits associated with them are generally of the period known as the Late Stone Age.) Jalmar and Ione Rudner (1970) point out that rock art in Africa has extended into recent times, and some of it is associated with population groups which still exist; thus it is an ethnographic document. The human figure is a favorite subject and, as Table 4 indicates, dance is the second most prominently displayed activity.

Perhaps in an effort to show that the importance of dance worldwide is rooted in its universal origins, the popularly held psychological (theological-magical) theories found in most books on the history of dance posit that dance evolved instrumentally, to cope with unknown happenings in the human's environment. These theories claim that early man had little awareness of the principles of nature or of his own human behavior. His existence was hazardous, unpredictable, and dependent upon the vagaries of the environment; his food supply and means of livelihood were precarious, often determined by factors and circumstances beyond human control. He was exposed to such imminent disasters as disease, beasts of prey, drought, flood, barren soils and pastures, and marauding invaders who stole land, animals, goods, and women. He was also confronted by thunder, lightning, and other natural phenomena. Spontaneous movement was one outlet for the emotional tension endemic in the

Table 4   Portrayal of Dance in Rock Paintings

	RHODESIA		SOUTH WEST AFRICA	
ACTIVITIES:	Mashonaland	Matabeleland	Brand-Berg	Erongo
Hunting	13	9	10	6
Dancing	5	1	2	1
War	1	1	–	–
Collecting	2	2	1	–
Sitting	5	1	1	1
Trekking	2	–	–	1
Meeting	2	–	–	–
Sleeping	1	1	–	–

(Adapted from Rudner and Rudner 1970:268)

perpetual struggle for existence in a baffling environment. Idiosyncratic motor reflexes developed into patterned movements for the individual and group. Emotion became symbolically transformed, formulated as a tangible, visible figure, to be dealt with by the total resources of the individual and his or her community. When a desired situation occurred, for example, the grain ripened, the game was caught, or the illness was overcome, after a patterned outlet of emotion in which dance was prominent (or a mimetic ritual, compelling a wish be realized through a symbolic body commanding a real body), dance was assumed to have causative power and life-giving force. Under these circumstances, dance became established to meet further exigencies, sublimate the strains of existence, and provide a psychic certainty. In this way, the secular dance and sacred beliefs intertwined, each relevant to the other. Thus dance, a pan-human trait, was, in part, motivated by desires to preserve the individual and the group, especially at critical junctures in their existence. Through dance, visual and dramatic expression was given to the will to live and to assure that the group would survive and continue, the gods and spirits would be placated, harvests would be abundant, calamities would not occur, social control would be efficacious, and evils would be expunged from the community. As humans began to control and improve the conditions under which they lived, their ideas and beliefs changed, and, as a result, the dance usually changed. Originally what was a primeval response often de-

| CAPE | | | | | TOTAL |
Southwestern	Southern	Eastern	Drakensberg	Northern Transvaal	
3	10	8	21	–	82
–	1	5	8	–	20
–	–	3	10	–	15
1	2	2	2	–	12
1	2	–	–	–	11
1	–	–	–	–	5
1	1	–	–	–	4
1	–	1	–	–	4

veloped into a different dance used to cope with new situations. Thus the dynamics of dance shift in relation to the dynamics of a culture, often as an index of its needs. Style and structure in dance evolve through such adjustments as the perception of supernatural revelation, mythical precedence, individual or special group initiative and contacts with other people. However plausible these theories may be, in the absence of historical evidence there is no way of validating them. They may well be a kind of "how-the-leopard-got-its-spots" explanation (see Evans-Pritchard 1965).

A suggestive example of the origin and evolution of a dance occurs among the religious Shaker sect which developed at the end of the eighteenth century in the United States. The Shakers believed that "the day of judgement was at hand, and that salvation was possible only by confessing and forsaking all fleshly practices." They "dance with the ecstasy of a chosen and exalted people," Edward Andrews reports (1940:4–5). "The first Believers were seized by such ecstasy of spirit that, like leaves in the wind, they were moved into the most disordered exercises: running about the room, jumping, shaking, whirling, reeling, and at the same time shouting, laughing or singing snatches of song. No form existed . . ." (ibid.:7). At first the movements were for the purposes of shaking off doubts and mortifying the lusts of the flesh (ibid.:144); later, the divine function of dance was recognized "to express outwardly and assist the inward reverence of the soul" (ibid.:146). With time, the nature of dance changed from individual impulsive movements to ordered patterns, the first of which was called the "square order shuffle." Successive development in the dance involved intricate and well-rehearsed elaborations of these simple patterns (ibid.:147–157).

Types of Dance

There are a variety of divisions of dance in the literature: one finds, for example, the oppositions of primitive versus theater, classical versus folk, social versus ethnic, ballet versus modern. The terms "ethnic" and "folk" have been variously defined (see, e.g., Kraus 1969:4, Lucile Czarnowski 1967:36, and Felix Hoerburger 1965:7–8) and are frequently used interchangeably. Kealiinohomoku summarizes her survey of how the term *folk dance* is used: "Variously, folk dance is traditional, but . . . not all traditional forms are folk dance; we learn that it is nonvocational, but that sometimes it is vocational; we realize that it is communal, but that this is not always so; we are instructed that it is and it is not ritually based . . . Also, we cannot consider the degree of competence to distinguish folk dance from some other dance form, because many folk dances are difficult to do, may require much rehearsing, and there are gifted folk dance performers who qualify as artists" (1972:385).

Dance is ethnic when it is explicitly linked to an ethnic group's sociocultural traditions; an ethnic group has a common cultural tradition and a sense of identity based upon origins; its members constitute a subunit within a larger society. It is folk when it is a communal expression; folk dance need not be ethnic, but both may be social, ritual or theatrical dance. The context of a dance clarifies its type and whether it is, in Hoerburger's terms, a first or second existence folk dance. A first existence refers to "dance as an essential part of life" whereas a second existence refers to a revival or arrangement, perhaps a stage performance (ibid.).

Categorizations of dance are not clear-cut: Kealiinohomoku (1969–70) describes ballet as ethnic dance. An ethnic group in the United States, for example, may perform its dance in a member's home at a holiday, as a social dance, or in a theater for a heterogeneous audience. Twyla Tharp combines social discotheque dance with classical ballet for the Joffrey Dance Company which is a ballet company; Yvonne Rainer's social sensitivity training of her colleagues is also presented on stage as theater dance (Robin Hecht 1973/74). Moreover, Blacking (1973) argues that such distinctions between "art," "folk," and "primitive" music are spurious, nonsensical, and merely serve the elitist class structure which insists upon them. This argument may be relevant to dance! Classification should obviously not be an end in itself. It might be useful to bear in mind when considering dance as human thought and action, distinctions[11] based on participation (purpose, recruitment pattern, motivation, and participation action); elements of movement and body emphasized (movement elements, body parts pattern of motion and pose and exhibition of intention to move, movement transformation); genetic classification (independently invented, imposed, borrowed voluntarily, elaborated creation); and consciousness (transcendental or temporal-cognitive, temporal/transcendental). These distinctions are presented in Table 5.

Table 5   Dance Classification Considerations

I. **Typology based on aspects of participation**
  A. Participant purpose
    1. Social dance (social interaction primary)
        a. therapy (self or group working through problems)
        b. ethnic-folk
        c. 2nd existence folk
        d. popular (dominant culture in a heterogeneous setting)

    2. Skill acquisition
        a. individual teacher
        b. class instruction
        c. informal observation

    3. Theatrical performance of one or more dancers for an audience.
        a. audience is distanced from dancer(s)
        b. audience has limited participation
        c. audience plays significant role

  B. Participation recruitment pattern
    1. Ascriptive
    2. Achievement

  C. Participation motivation
    1. Required
    2. Expected
    3. Voluntary

  D. Participation action
    1. Dancer initiated (doing)
    2. Dancer acted upon (becoming)

II. **Typology based on elements of movement and body emphasized**
   A. Movement elements: space, rhythm, effort
   B. Body parts: head, torso, chest, shoulder, limbs, etc.
   C. Pattern of motion and pose and exhibition of intention to move
   D. Movement transformation
      1. Change in spatial ground pattern through locomotion (doing)
      2. Change in body space/state through swelling, spreading, undulating (becoming)

III. **Genetic classification**
   A. Independently invented
   B. Imposed
   C. Borrowed voluntarily
   D. Elaborated creation

IV. **Typology based on consciousness—(related to participation purpose)**
   A. Transcendental (altered states of consciousness; purpose is to achieve extraordinary metaphysical-physical experience)
      1. Religious (associated with deities, spirits, essence)
      2. Secular (associated with self-extension and exploration)
   B. Temporal-cognitive (concern with explanation, prediction)
      1. Control (maintaining cultural patterns and managing tensions, attaining goals, adaptation, and integration; initiating and coping with change)
      2. Physical preparation (for work, war, etc.)
   C. Temporal/transcendental (one form leading to another, intermeshing, alternating)

This chapter examined the essence of dance and its necessary and sufficient components: human behavior composed, from the dancer's perspective, of purposeful, intentionally rhythmical, and culturally patterned sequences of nonverbal body movements other than ordinary motor activities, the motion having inherent and aesthetic value. This conceptualization of dance as both cognitive and affective communication is the keystone of the theory which informs subsequent chapters. A broad anthropological approach, requiring an exploration of psychobiological bases and evolutionary perspectives, is focused, in the next chapter, on the relationship between dance and psyche, soma, and society.

3   Psyche and Soma: Some Bases of the Human Phenomenon of Dance

HAVING IDENTIFIED OUR subject, we now draw upon physical anthropology and attempt to show that the configuration of human behavior that is called dance is significantly different from the behavior of other animals (including that which has been labeled dance). Human dance has its roots in phylogenetic and ontogenetic evolution; firstly, in predisposing psychobiological processes and, secondly, in social experience. I seek to identify both the basic psychobiological factors that may generate or modulate the many diverse forms found through historical time and across sociocultural areas, and certain processes that dance has in common with other forms of nonverbal communication, motor activity, play, artistic behavior, and altered states of consciousness. This is done in the hope that thereby more attention will be directed to those specific properties of dance that can help explain why it is a common attribute of temporal and transcendental behavior in the religious and secular worlds; why it is a component of sociopolitical manipulations; and why it has potential for individual and group therapy.

The following sections examine the interrelated psychobiological bases for each element of the operating definition presented in the previous chapter. The argument draws on a variety of perspectives; cumulatively, these may amplify our understanding of dance as thought and action.

Dance, I proposed, can usefully be defined as human behavior composed, from the dancer's perspective, of purposeful, intentionally rhythmical, and culturally patterned sequences of nonverbal body movements other than ordinary motor activities, the motion having inherent and aesthetic value. Within this conceptualization, behavior must meet each of the four criteria in order to be classified as "dance." That is to say, each behavioral characteristic is necessary, and the set constitutes sufficiency; the combination of all these factors must exist.

Dance as Human Behavior

Human dancing behavior emerges from an evolutionary process lasting millions of years. Therefore, presages might be found in other animals and in infants. On the basis of recent studies, there is a relatively thin behavioral barrier between humans and other primates. The phylogeneticism of dance is suggested in the rhythmic troopings of chimpanzees and the development of gesture. Nevertheless, although nonhuman primates carry the seed of those visual, motor, auditory, kinesthetic, affective, and cognitive patterns that are more fully developed in humans, certain incipient capacities in nonhumans are realized only in humans. The problem is to discover to what extent humans have a biologically based predisposition for dance as, for example, there seems to be a genetic program for language (Eric Lenneberg 1967, 1973).

It is true that a human can dance mechanically or perform a dance pattern conceptualized and created by someone else, in the same way that a nonhuman can be trained to perform a dance by a human. We have all seen "dancing" chimpanzees, horses, dogs, bears, parrots, or elephants. Through operant conditioning humans teach these animals movements within the latters' biological possibilities. Bears thus dance on cue; then music is added and modified to the movements which have been taught. However, differences between humans and other animals occur in symbolization, emotional expression, movements, and the ability to use syntactically novel forms without being trained in phrases of that form (Jerrold Katz 1976). The distinction within a species between fixed action patterns and selected action patterns is critical. The bases for these contrasts lie in the development of the human brain, as well as the increased dependency and socialization of human offspring.

Symbolic Capability

Evolutionary changes in the human brain are generally accepted to have had relevance in the development of the capacity for tool-making and the use of language (e.g., Norman Geschwind 1973), and to those we can add dance. The human brain evolved, expanding in size and becoming *restructured* in specific components (Ralph Holloway 1966). Changes occurred in the cerebral cortex to allow greater memory storage, a high order of multiple, fine, perceptual discriminations, coordination and integration, hemispheric specialization, and novel classifications. The more features of an information unit which an individual can detect and store, the greater will be the likelihood of his retrieving it at some later time. The limbic region makes up most of the cerebral cortex in the most primitive mammals, and it is apparently associated with emotional behavior necessary for species survival. In higher primates, areas of the cortex known as association areas have differentially expanded. The development of an "association area of association areas" in the parietal region, which has connections only with other association areas and not with primary sensory or motor regions or with the limbic system, is greatly increased in humans. The capacity for neurological cross-modal cortical connections allows relatively unlimited expansion of symbolization. Cross-modal perception is the capacity to abstract and exchange information between different sensory modalities. Symbols are at a distance (in relative terms) in time, space, and affect from what they represent. A neurophysiologist tells us that the "facts of physics and physiology show that perception is the end-result of a series of physical events, the last of which, a state of activity of the brain of the percipient, differs so completely from the events occurring in the object perceived that the qualitative feature of a percept can have no resemblance to the physical object which it represents . . . The physical world is, therefore, what we infer about the causes of our perceptions, and since it is a product of influence, it is a symbolic representation of the structure of events occurring in space-time" (Russell Brain 1959:10, 39–40). The capacity of neurological cross-modal cortical connections permits the appreciation of an object and the ability to associate it with a picture, label, or other element which denotes it. Nonhumans can learn to link a sound, object, or picture to some kind of behavior involved in reducing basic drives such as hunger, thirst, or sexual satisfaction. However, they lack the extensive neurological structures that would allow formation of links between sound and picture, between picture and object, or between picture and picture, which are required in symbol use (Howard Gardner 1973:90; cf. Gordon Hewes 1973:7). An adult human being can tactilely recognize an object after seeing it once, whereas a chimpanzee needs five hundred trials to perform the same task (Richard Davenport, C. Roger, and I. Russell 1973).

Nonhumans appear to lack the human level of synesthesia, the capacity to perceive and transmit simultaneously stimuli in several senses. Synesthesia also involves the appearance of a color when a certain sound is heard, that is, a person's visual sense being stimulated by auditory reception. The addition of a second sensory stimulus to the original increases the acuity of the first. Davenport (1976:

143) points out that "the sensory modalities of most human adults operate in concert as an integrated system of systems. Information received via one modality is coordinated in some manner with information from other modalities, and much of adaptive behavior . . . presumably depends to a large extent on this intermodality integration." Multimodal extraction of environmental information appears likely to result in more accurate perception (ibid.:147). In dance there is the sight of performers moving in time and space; the sounds of breathing, the impact of feet upon the ground, and other physical movements; the odors of bodily exertion or materials applied to the dancer's body; the feeling of kinesthetic activity (the dancing) or empathy (observing); the touch of body to body and/or performing area; and the proxemic sense.

What other animals communicate in motor patterns ethologists call ritual performances (or dances). Such performances seem to involve immediate emotion and drive (for example, fear, hunger, well-being, aggression, reassurance, submission, sexual arousal) and autonomic rhythms. Humans share these behaviors, but they can also voluntarily communicate abstract concepts, removed from an immediate stimulus, distanced in time and space and in deliberately chosen rhythms. On the basis of many studies in the human social psychology of emotion, K. Strongman (1973) concludes that recognition of emotion is determined by a very complex process of integrating many cues, from facial expression through body movement to the situation and the more static features of the individuals interacting. Humans are able to reflect self-consciously on emotional experience. (See Allen Dittman 1973, especially pp. 74ff. on the measurement of emotional information.)

In what ethologists call the bee dance, bees communicate to members of their colony, through motor patterns, the direction, distance, and richness of the pollen source discovered minutes earlier. It is perhaps less an immediate reaction to the environment than a relating of certain aspects of past experience (Edward Kilma and Ursula Bellugi 1973). However, humans have the capacity to project experience extrinsic to themselves, to alter feeling and thought, and to transform it symbolically through varieties of cognitive-sensori-motor-aesthetic patterns, using different devices and spheres of encoding messages (see Aesthetic Value in Chapter 2). In other words, humans can deliberately express or withhold an experience. Although, in common with nonhumans, some human movements may have universally shared meanings, such as approaching, fleeing or attacking, jumping with joy, or drooping with sorrow, most are semantically culture-specific (Kreitler and Kreitler 1972:181).

Humans can embed symbols within one another, use opposites and inversions, situational qualifiers, synonyms, neutralization, and interrelated symbol systems. A symbol may have a patent meaning, while its latent meaning may be contained in a constellation of symbols. One symbol may have different or condensed meanings; it may be continuously reinterpreted or it may change in intensity over time. The same symbol may have different meanings at different phases in performance, while metaphoric equations can operate in two directions at once. Humans also can combine media in the dance. They often interweave music, song, and movement, extend or otherwise sculpt the body through costuming and accoutrements (e.g., elongating it through stilts or masks, or creating illusions of foreshortening through body paint). They can "fossilize" or capture the motor-gesture patterns through objectification in lithic, ceramic, or painted form (Kurath and Samuel Martí 1964b, Lillian Lawler 1964, Vatsyayan 1968) or, more recently, in notation, film, or videotape.

There is, of course, a difference between cognition, or knowledge about dance, and behavior. One can know the grammatical rules for dance and appreciate its denotations and connotations with ideas about appropriateness and not have the skills or opportunity for performance.

Related to the human's greater range and complexity of symbolic behavior is the fact that no other mammal has a dominant left half of the brain, nor a dependency upon it for learning certain kinds of knowledge (cf. Geschwind 1973). The left hemisphere appears to be involved in abstract symbolic functions, sequential information processing, and complex patterns of movement. The right hemisphere seems to involve elementary perceptual tasks, nonverbal processing of spatial information and music, and emotional reactivity. Until the age of five the hemispheres are relatively equal. Rigid lateralization of brain function is precluded by the transfer of inputs to each side of the brain over the corpus callosum, the main body of nerve fibers connecting the two hemispheres. In adults, when one hemisphere is damaged, the other may take over new functions within its mode of information processing. Recent findings suggest that the two halves are not as highly specialized as was once thought. The human brain is a complex interacting system. Karl Pribram (1976:729) suggests that front/back (frontolimbic and posterior convexity) differences also contribute to the human use of symbols:

"Frontolimbic processing leads to the use of symbols defined as context sensitive construction, whereas posterior convexity processing leads to signs, defined as context-free constructions." Although the Broca and Wernicke areas, located in the left hemisphere, have been associated with language expression and comprehension, they may be equally important for creating, performing, and understanding complex patterns of movement (Jerre Levy 1974). The same brain structures generate both verbal and nonverbal language.

Moreover, a comparison of the design features of dance with those of verbal language described by Charles Hockett and Robert Ascher (1964) and others emphasizes the symbolic potential of dance (see Chapter 4).

Motor Potential

Both humans and animals have genetically programmed and learned locomotor-gesture patterns. However, humans have achieved a greater potential for generalization, which allows them to combine or isolate various locomotor and gesture patterns in different contexts (e.g., on land, ice, water, or air), using different parts of the body. Atypical of other animals is the human upright posture, requiring wakefulness and antigravitational effort, and bipedal locomotion. These two characterize most dance and are related to bimanualism and the dexterous gesture patterns exhibited in many Asian dances, as well as the elaborate costume and other accoutrements of dance. Humans can cling vertically, climb quadrupedally, move along branches, spring, brachiate, or knuckle walk in dance (e.g., Stephanie Evanitsky's Aerodance Multigravitational Experiment Group). Humans seem to have more control over innate[1] motor patterns, possibly through greater attention span and learning capability. On the other hand, nonhumans tend to move on the basis of urges, irritability, and external stimuli, that is, movement is reactive–symptomatic, or drive-motivated. Their dancelike behaviors are displays: they are stereotyped, usually repetitive, though not entirely arbitrary behaviors, which are ritualized in the biological sense that they have been subject to selection during evolution for their communicative values (cf. R. Anderson 1972:179, Erikson 1966, Alison Jolly 1972:140, 144–145). In human evolution, it seems that programmed action sequences were gradually replaced by those in which social learning and individual choice played a more important role.

Humans have a greater potential not only for motor variety, control, and learning, but also for creative manipulation of patterns with-

in rules (Julian Huxley 1966), so that different dance styles and structures can be chosen. Dance is an open-ended system, relational rather than just sequential, that tends to be cumulative within a culture.
The choreographer generates and expands themes and structural/sty-
listic patterns both to transform what is known and create new forms
through adding, deleting, and rearranging the various dance elements (cf. Yoshihiko Ikegami 1971, Williams 1978, Stephanie Woodward 1976). Although nonhumans may be trained to perform human-
like dances, there is no evidence that they can create meaning and
transmit to other animals dance sequences that are physically, affectively, symbolically complex. Nor can they leave something representing dance behavior that lingers beyond their lifetime.

Purpose in Dance

The second term of the working definition, purpose, will be discussed in terms of adaptation, and of cognitive and affective communication.

Adaptation

The phenomenological movement of dance may be its primary end
and reward. However, this pleasure principle does not automatically
negate the instrumental purpose, but rather subserves it. Dance may
have been, may still be, or may have the potential to be an adaptive
pattern spreading and differentiating at the expense of less efficient
precursors. Yet dance need not be adaptive to exist: one of the mechanisms of adaptation to an environment is natural selection, and
dance may be the result of processes which have been selected for.
Such purposes, according to Alland (1976), are exploratory behavior,
a sense of rhythm, metaphorisation, and the ability of the brain to
make fine distinctions. In some societies natural selection could even
favor individuals with dance skills. For example, in cultures where
choosing a mate is influenced by the skill exhibited in a dance that
incorporates qualities which predict success in life, the incompetent
may be excluded from procreation. Some war dance behavior (discussed in Chapter 7) might also confer a selective advantage if it
physically and emotionally prepares a childless warrior for battle success. William Irons (1974) points out that the pressure of warfare may
lead to natural selection favoring all patterns of behavior which increased military prowess (cf. Edward Wilson 1975:167). Females pre-

fer mating with males who compete successfully with other males over resources. Where social advantages of wealth and rank do not coincide with physical superiority, women often marry the wealthy men while taking the physically attractive ones as lovers (Van der Berghe and David Barash 1977:814). Alternatively, patterns of behavior originally developed to serve directly adaptive ends may recur through habituation even though they cease to be adaptive (Charles Darwin 1965:23). They may be so intrinsically rewarding that they become used for other purposes.

Purely exploratory behavior, pretence, the anticipatory working out of imminent problems, or experimenting with something new in dance, these may all in themselves be adaptive (cf. Kreitler and Kreitler 1972:330). There is evidence that the absence of such exploratory behavior has serious effects[2] (cf. Jolly 1972:231–235), though this has not yet been shown to apply to dance. Darwin, who may be said to have begun the modern scientific study of movement behavior, regarded motor behavior as subject to the same laws of natural selection, adaptation, modification, and extinction as are bodily structures (ibid.:xii). Innovations and variations in dance may arise, each one subject to selective pressures governing its survival and spread. For example, if a number of new movements are "auditioned" for a warrior dance, and certain ones attract members of the opposite sex, these will be incorporated into the repertoire, the others dropped.

Cognitive Communication

The survival of a species depends on its accommodation to the environment; and communication is one of the means to this end. Through communication humans solve crucial problems of social organization and regulation, discriminate sex, age, social background, group membership, emotional and motivation status, environmental conditions, and transmit culture to subsequent generations. Menzel and Johnson (1976:131) argue that communication systems ultimately secure "all of the requisites for the survival and reproduction of the phenotype. . . ." Dance is part of this cultural communication system in which information, valuable in adaption, is relayed to oneself and others. Dance can communicate information purposefully as well as offer an open channel that could be used. As pointed out earlier, shared knowledge about a form, experience in its use, and notions about when, where, how, and why messages are sent, as well as information sufficiently lucid to be perceived through surrounding distractions or impediments, all these are conditions for effectiveness. Dance may support or refute linguistic, paralinguistic, and other forms of communication. Its presentation may be through an interpersonal dialogue or a monologue in the presence of others. The power of dance lies in its cognitive-sensori-motor and aesthetic capability to create moods and a sense of situation for performer and spectator alike. (See above Chapter 2, "Purpose" and "Aesthetic Value.")

A people's basic cultural assumptions and orientations, their proscriptions and prescriptions, as well as the seeds of their destruction or alteration, may become locked into this mode of communication. On the one hand, dance may mirror or refract social and political structures and technoenvironmental factors; on the other, it may also be a generative force, a processual agent, reflecting "antistructure" (Turner 1974), even going beyond what Morse Peckham (1965) refers to as man's "rage for chaos," the individual's need to experiment with novelty within the safety of an artistic, "pretend" situation.

Clues to the basis of nonverbal communication and the use of parts of the body to create patterns that command attention are found in ontogenetic and evolutionary perspectives. Body language is as basic a means of expression as the cry, and it can be used meaningfully without verbal language, although it is generally analyzed in relation to verbal communication. In comparative studies of language acquisition, children of deaf signing parents began uttering two-sign sentences six to ten months earlier than children utter two-word spoken sentences (William Stokoe 1976:507). Hewes (1973) even argues that gestural communication was the first form of human predicative or propositional communication. However, John Lyons (1972:76–77) claims that there is no evidence from language to support the belief that language evolved from nonverbal communication; Roger Fouts (1973) suggests that vocal and gestural modes developed simultaneously. The question was discussed at the 1976 New York Academy of Sciences Conference without firm resolution. While Peter Reynolds (1976:164) argues for language as a phylogenetic derivation of the skilled motor system, I would agree with Holloway (1976) that there are some interesting yet unproved hypotheses. However speech developed, it clearly evolved in a matrix of extensive nonverbal communication (Nancy Tanner and Adrienne Zihlman 1976:474). What matters is not whether language or gesture is antecedent, but that both are conceptual vehicles and can reinforce and often substitute for each other.

In accounts of human learning in early childhood, written by such diverse specialists as Jean Piaget, Arnold Gessel, Maria Montessori, Gordon Allport, and Erik Erikson, the acquisition of communicative motor skills is viewed as critical to a young child's ability to cope with the world of persons, things, and ideas. In his study of the arts and human development, Gardner argues that it may be universal that somatic communicative involvement in children exists, although it is absent in many adults. "The possibility that this bodily reaction to symbols may at first be universal underlines the extent to which integration of feeling life and symbol may have an important adaptive function in human perception and performance" (1973:153). The human body instrument of dance is familiar to humans and thus useful for signification (cf. Douglas 1973, Leach 1972). The Kreitlers point out that "a shape created by a human body is spontaneously grasped in reference both to the habitual images of the body and the intimate experience we have of our own bodies" (1972:173).

Dance has the unique potential of having a greater impact than many of the audiovisual media. Walter Wittich and Francis Schuller point out that the normal learner gains understanding in terms of multiple impressions recorded through, for example, eye, ear, and touch. "Where sensory experience is involved, it should be as complete as possible" (1953:197). The communicative efficacy of dance lies in its capacity to fully engage the human being; it is a multidimensional phenomenon codifying sensory experience. Furthermore, it can lead to altered states of consciousness. Thus, there is a potential multisensory bombardment and saturation (see Berlyne 1971 on the psychological impacts of the arts which he believes primarily effect a rise and reduction in arousal). With its multisensory and flow or altered states of consciousness arousal, dance-ritual may promote change by circumventing the loading process, our habit of keeping our minds so busy with familiar ideation that unwarranted throught processes have no chance of intruding. The arousal process involves altering central nervous functions. Dance may be used as a driving technique to facilitate right hemisphere dominance, resulting in gestalt, timeless, nonverbal experiences. These are distinct when compared to left hemisphere function. The prolonged activation of ergotropic (energy-expending or stress) response ultimately leads to trophotropic (rest reactivity) response, including a shift to right hemisphere cognition, easing distress and providing pleasure. (This involves what is called central nervous system tuning [Barbara Lex 1975].)

While dance is used to communicate a variety of ideas and emotions, its meaning cannot be said to be intrinsic, that is, self-evident: it depends primarily on the meanings that are assigned or associated with it in different societies. Thus dance may transmit norms, values, and cooperative skills involved in procuring food: it can teach coordination, concepts, problem solving, and the discrimination of elements which develop those skills necessary for hunting, agriculture, or war. Dominance-submission hierarchies and other differential statuses may be communicated through homologous dance patterns. Individuals often assert territorial possession through dance as a conceptual boundary marker; and sometimes dance is a means of asserting ethnic or class identity or aspiration in a heterogeneous situation. Then there are, of course, instances where the values and meanings that are assigned to dance may coincide with a significance that is biological. For example, dances designed to exhibit the physical being may be functionally, as well as stylistically, similar to the display behaviors of other animals.

Affect

Affect generally refers to that conscious subjective aspect of emotion, considered apart from bodily changes. In dance, affective and cognitive communication are intertwined; as John Spiegel and Pavel Machotka (1974:24–25) points out, in body communication the contrast between emotion and cognition is not clear.[3] Physical movements associated with affect may stimulate or sublimate a range of feelings (cf. Thomas Alloway et al. 1972, Manfred Clynes 1978),[4] and may be elicited for pleasure or coping with problematic aspects of social involvement. Mehrabian (1972) argues that only a few basic dimensions of human feelings and attitudes are conveyed nonverbally: like-dislike (anger), dominance-submissiveness, and responsiveness (change in activity brought about by adapting to a changing environment). It may be that adults find succor and release cathexis in culturally permissible motor behavior, including dance, that is reminiscent of the nurturance and protection of the prenatal and infancy stages and thereby imitates the satisfaction of childhood behavior (Alice Kehoe 1973:7). The extraordinary potency of dance may be associated with heightened body activity and emotion, for example, eating, elimination, and copulation (cf. Erikson 1963).

Urban immigrants, for example, may find stability and solace in a heterogeneous, transient milieu through familiar dance performances. Similarly certain aspects of Balinese child training create feelings of frustration and the need for symbolic security which is apparently fulfilled in the rhythmic actions of the dance drama (Mead 1940:344).

Alternatively, dance may provide and communicate a kind of excitement.[5] Peckham (1965) argues that art forms provide protected situations, categorized by high walls of excited insulation, in which "disorientation" or the "discontinuity of experience" can be savored. Man's drive for order, he believes, prevents him from changing his orientation, even when the conditions within which that orientation functioned have changed. Art thus permits humans to experience chaos symbolically and without danger; it provides the novelty which is necessary to break up old orientations. Many psychologists, psychiatrists, and dance therapists recognize that dance may serve as a psychological defense mechanism embodying psychologically or socially unacceptable impulses, and so gratifying or deflecting needs. What is made sensorily perceptible in dance, such as anxiety and fear, is thereby also made accessible to purposive action by individuals or groups. Dance may therefore function like play, exploratory behavior, rituals of rebellion, or cathartic outlets for deviance, in which a segment of the psyche or world is represented in a nonthreatening manner in order to understand or cope with it. Anticipatory psychic management, or desensitization, describes the process of coping with a feared object or event by associating it, through speech or dance, with familiar situations. Young Ubakala girls' dance-play themes focus on imminent marriage, which involves leaving one's natal village to live among strangers (the husband's family), to conceive and bear children.

Dance, like many other forms of intensive physical activity, "often provides a healthy fatigue or distraction which may abate a temporary rage crisis and thus allow *more enduring personality* patterns to regain accendancy" (Ruth Munroe 1955:630). A specialist in African psychodynamics put it this way: "The rhythm, vigorous movements, their coordination and synchronization, tend to induce some degree of catharsis. . . . The essential psychological function of the dance, in fact, is the prevention of depression and accumulation of other psychic stresses" (T. Lambo 1965:41). Benno Safier (1953:242) points out that rapid motion in dance is especially intoxicating, altering the state of consciousness and "facilitating an orally regressive state of perception and feeling tone without attendant loss of acuity in intellection . . . which gives the feeling of bliss and elation." The Dogon of Mali describe the rapid *gòna* dance movement "as a relief, like vomiting" (Griaule 1965:188). It is well known that exercise, especially activities using long muscles, such as those involved in running, is helpful in alleviating depression. Dance also allows an individual to become, once again, impulsive after the weariness of conformity. Safier writes that "Convention dictates which postures, stance, carriage or gait we assume in this or that area of life. Dance is perceived as an escape from this restraint although dance brings with it its own bondage: in the stylization of movements. At least, dance movements are different from the movements of routine living. Thus dance encourages relaxation both in reality and in illusion" (1953: 242). And, in 1928, Mead noted the reversal of the pattern of conformity of Samoan society in the dance where the individual is given a chance to exhibit his or her own individuality and skill. Similarly, Charles Keil (1967:33) describes a high degree of role differentiation and organizational complexity in Tiv dance groups, which run counter to other institutions. Altered states of consciousness may be induced by socialized responses to the contextual situation; by autosuggestion; and by physical behavior, such as energetic dancing, which may change brain wave frequencies, adrenalin, and blood-sugar content. These changes induce giddiness through high speed or sensory rhythmic stimulation in more than one sensory mode. Kinesthetic stress, overexertion, and fatigue also increase susceptibility (Andrew Neher 1962).

Dance Is Culturally Patterned

Birdwhistell (1970) hypothesizes that expressive body movement is a culturally determined channel of communication learned through social experience, so that patterns of movement are commensurable with social roles, age, sex, and class. Alternatively, other scholars argue that some expressive movements are universal (cf. Clynes 1978, I. Eibl-Eibesfeldt 1972:307, Paul Ekman and Wallace Friesen 1969). However, in dance, these patterns of movement may be manipulated and combined and seem to be assigned a particular significance in culture. Movement styles, structures, and purposes reflect patterns of group interaction. Of course, there is also great variability in the creative potential and output of individuals who have an impact on a culture's dance patterns: an individual's dance is shaped both by cultural involvement and a unique set of experiences within the patterns of group behavior.

However, this cultural patterning is constrained by psychobiological bases and propensities, which interlock with historical-cultural and environmental factors to create conditions for a particular dance pattern.

Unconscious Mental Structures

As with much linguistic behavior, in which an individual creates sentences and responds to them without being conscious of how he or she does it, dance processes sometimes operate without an awareness of their mechanics. Entirely novel sequences of movements may be performed without the creator being conscious of how the creation occurred, and yet an audience may understand these sequences. There are, of course, underlying lexical, syntactic, and stylistic rules of movement which lead the initiated dance observer to distinguish among different forms of dance: Ballet, for example, has codified five basic positions and numerous steps and transitions and within ballet there are distinctions among such schools as the Kirov, Bournonville, or Balanchine. In modern dance, Martha Graham, Erik Hawkins, and Alwin Nikolais, for example, can each create a new dance that will be identified and understood. Generally speaking, one can recognize Graham by movements with percussive contractions and releases and a dramatic psychological story; Hawkins by lyrical vocabulary and thematic abstraction; and Nikolais by relatively balanced arrangements of human movement, sound, light, and visual and kinetic objects.

Such dance movements are not to be confused with symptomatic behavior, which includes epileptic or hysterical fits, a child jumping or trembling from excessive nervous excitement, and similar spontaneous movements. Spiegel and Machotka (1974) define these as responsive behaviors in contrast to the "presentational" behavior of dance. Figure 3 suggests that there are deep structures (*langue*) for dance–species-specific capabilities which are acted upon by the culture and specialized in a dancer–and surface structures (*parole*), the choreography and imitative dance performances.

Maturation

Individuals learn dance through social interaction within the constraints of general psychobiological maturation. Psychologists recognize that our primordial experiences with the body have an impact on later motor behavior. Such remembered experiences determine our body image, which is rooted in sensory experience and pro-

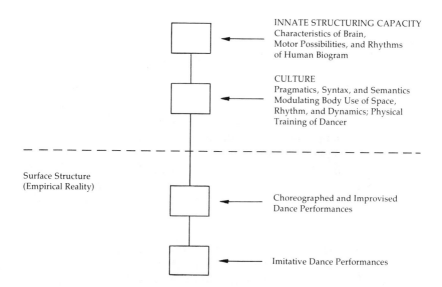

Figure 3.   Surface patterns and deep structures in dance (modified from Lane 1970:15).

prioception, and affect the attitudes toward or expectations about the personal body.

Gardner (1973:101–109), a proponent of neoteny, builds upon Erikson's theory of human development and posits that three early developmental stages, in which the individual resolves the conflicts that pervade a young child's functioning, form a substratum into which all later experience is initially assimilated. In the first stage, which focuses on the oral sensory zone, the characteristic mode of approach is getting and taking in or biting and grasping. Some vectoral properties include quick versus slow speed, regular versus irregular time, and narrow versus wide space. The predominant mode of response during the anal period is retention and expulsion, with the associated vectoral properties of ease versus strain, hollow versus full, and thick versus thin. The modes characterizing the genital state of intrusion or inception-inclusion are associated with the vectoral properties of open versus closed, and directionality, force, depth, comfort, and texture. The resolution of these developmental stages, with fixations and regressions sometimes occurring, matches certain common elements discerned in the symbolic media of the arts.

Physical Equipment

The human body works through the complex interactions of the skeletal, muscular, and nervous systems, which impose constraints on culturally patterned dance. Body build affects speed, power, elevation, the ballet "turn out," and double-jointedness. Differential body size, strength, pelvic structure, and fat deposit are usually sex-related. Coordination, balance, endurance, flexibility, speed of reaction and movement, sensory acuity, level of excitation: all these affect dance performance. While the human body's bilateral symmetry and sensory frontal plane equipment lead to innate forward, upright, and bipedal movement, Valerie Hunt (1968:62) claims that the ability to discriminate the side space of the body must be learned.

The capabilities of the sensory system limit the orientation mechanisms of the body in relation to features of external space: vision is important in maintaining a stance; information from the inner ear, ankles and feet, also contribute. The ratio of complex nonvisually to visually based choreography, which includes imitation within and between dance cultures and individuals, may be related to the proportion of innate or learned reliance on the left or right hemisphere of the brain. On the one hand, choreographing set dances and improvisation within a style both require a knowledge (usually tacit) of relational rules for using a motor lexicon. These rules are left hemisphere functions, emphasizing digital, analytical, and sequential information processing. On the other hand, imitation merely depends on learning a set pattern, which is a right hemisphere function, involving analogic and spatial abilities.

Although genetic programs, body structure, and early life experiences impose limits on cultural patterning in dance, humans often attempt to defy these with lengthy training, as in western ballet, Indian Kathakali, and Balinese ritual dance. Sometimes peer pressure achieves similar results: Youngsters teased individuals who moved their pelvises and torsos. Until the twist appeared in the 1960s, American modern dance teachers struggled to free their college-age students from "up-tight" rigid body patterns.

Intentional Rhythm

Intentional rhythm in dance refers to the organized flow of energy in time and space which contrasts with the autonomic-interactional rhythms of other human and nonhuman motor patterns. Intentional rhythm in the creation or performance of dance seems to be rooted in the alternations of quiescence and activity which are immanent in our experience (cf. Doob 1971). Humans can harmonize with the rhythms they recognize, or they can attempt to counter them. Psychobiological bases of intentional rhythm in dance may be found in sensorial reaction to natural time, which refers to ecological variables, such as the fluctuation of the seasons, climatic variations, and diurnal or circadian rhythms (Eliot Chapple 1970). Gay Luce (1971) concludes that "Invisible rhythms underlie most of what we assume to be constant in ourselves and the world around us. Rhythmicity," she suggests, "may have been one of the first forces of natural selection since organisms that timed their activity and life processes in accord with the changing light, temperature, humidity and other factors of the environment would have had an edge in survival" (ibid.:145). Time structure may be crucial to health: there is evidence that inconsistent light-dark circadian rhythms seriously perturb certain diurnal psychological rhythms in humans (Edward Foulks 1972: 83). Virtually all physiological functions in all living creatures show periodical fluctuations, which affect mood, memory, and sensory and motor capacities.

Biological time centers on rhythm in the human organism (A. Solberger 1965): all automatic functions of the body, such as brain waves, muscle contractions, heart and respiratory rates, hormonal tides, and peristalsis are rhythmic. The human foetus experiences intrauterine rhythms, the maternal heartbeat and its own in synchrony or counterpoint (L. Salk 1962), and the mother's rapid eye movement cycle (Luce 1971:36). Peter Wolff (1967) has analyzed the rhythmical repetition of the human neonate, its crying and sucking, indicating that these apparently simple motor patterns are organized in complex time sequences. The human central nervous system instigates motor rhythms and can influence anatomically unrelated motor activities; motor rhythms of different frequencies interact, one driving the other. Judith Kestenberg and her colleagues (1972) maintain that there are, from birth, individual differences in congenital motor rhythm which persist throughout a child's development, although the rhythm becomes more complex. They found that tension and shape, flow rhythms, planes stressed, and control over spatial dimension are correlated with body image, ego organization, and patterns of cognitive development. Analyzing taped conversations from eight languages, Byers (1972:90) finds speech to have an underlying biological rhythm; and in a sample of three Eskimos and two Rhesus monkeys, he notes that the interactants share a common rhythm in their movement behavior matching that cited for speech. Thus he concludes that there is a rhythmic structure in social interactions and a rhythmic structure which interrelates internal organ systems. Furthermore, Gardner notes the ubiquity of a 2:1 ratio in musical rhythmic patterns, a basic material form in folk verses, and a correspondence between literary forms and seasons, sensations and life rhythms (1973:266).

The three time dimensions of dance (duration of performance, intervals portrayed in the dance, and dance motor time), which affect the perception of the dance, can be related to natural and biological rhythms. Thus they can be manipulated to provide security or novelty and to arrest attention. We could hypothesize that intentional rhythm in dance is homologous to the biological rhythms that all humans experience and/or to individual congenital rhythms when the purpose of dance is to provide affective security and consistency. Alternatively, these may be modified in dances that attempt to manipulate the environment for some other purposes.

Dance Is Extraordinary Nonverbal Body Movement, the Motion Having Inherent Value

What is ordinary in one society may be extraordinary in another. However, the distinguishing characteristic of extraordinary nonverbal body movement is the manipulation of ordinary motor activities within an aesthetic domain; the emphasis is on the importance of bodily movement, the illusion and the residual action that results from the kind of movement produced. Thus ordinary movements are transformed or incorporated into dance configurations. For a signal to be effective, among animals it must be distinguishable from ordinary instrumental activity; for example, animals must manifest social attention before they engage in social behavior (cf. Michael Chance and Ray Larsen 1976, Rappaport 1971). Dancing attracts attention.

Motion is one of the defining characteristics of life; it is inherent from inception and developmentally progresses from the generalized to the more specific (cf. Yasuhiko Taketomo [1969] on generic aspects of action). The intrinsic merit of motion may well correspond to the growth and development of the individual, particularly in mastering the environment. It is a basic means of expression after the cry. The infant, in the first few weeks of life and early phases of perception, responds to motion and contrast and discriminates objects by their movement. Motion involves the anticipation, continuation, and cessation of exploratory behavior: there is pleasure and power in the mastery of body movement as a child learns to turn, sit, crawl, hold and operate (grip development), walk, coordinate eye-hand motion, such as rocking, swinging, and spinning. Moreover, Lois Bloom (1976) speaks of the importance of movement in language acquisition. The first names that children learn include objects that move, such as persons, pets, and balls. They use semantic-syntactic structures to encode action events prior to encoding stative events. Furthermore, they talk predominantly of their own intentions to move, for example, to "eat cookies." In their first two years, children learn about the ways in which objects move and relate to themselves and to each other. This pattern seems to have its analog in the origins of language: in the creation of "new" languages, such as pidgins and Creoles, the encoding of movement aspects of events predominates over static aspects.

Even without being extraordinary, motion has the strongest visual appeal to attention (Arnheim 1954:361, 1969), for it implies a change in the conditions of the environment which may require reaction. Used extraordinarily in the dance, motion is potently related to the experience of arousal and motivation. The Kreitlers point out that "the intimate relations of meaning to characteristics of motion greatly expand the experimental potentialities of dance movements. Meaning of the perceived dynamics may not only accentuate contrasts, such as that between fast and slow or circular and angular movement, but provide possibilities for the creation of new contrasts, such as that between animate and inanimate motions or pursuing and approaching" (1972:183). Using a refined model of motivational dynamics, they argue that the focal point of the arts is pleasure, which includes altered states of consciousness. These states can be induced through the driving technique involved in repetitive rhythmic movements and central nervous system tuning. Couched in social situations generating energy and releasing inhibitory mechanisms, dance may automatically affect the human body.

Aesthetic Dimension in Dance

Aesthetic parameters for movement style and structure, meaning, and situation specify how dance should achieve its purpose within a particular culture or subculture. The psychobiological bases of aesthetics lie in the human capability for reflection and action. Cultural patterning contributes to the selection of those mechanisms that transform affect and cognition into meaningful patterns of body movement, which arrest attention both because they are intentional and extraordinary.

Conclusion: A Model of Dance Communication

There are, then, psychobiological factors which seem to generate dance and certain properties which may help to explain why dance is a component of temporal and transcendental behavior, sociopolitical manipulations, and mental health therapy. Dance appears to be the result of processes that have had a selective advantage as being potentially adaptive. Phylogenetic and ontogenetic perspectives focus on the distinction between human dance and other animal nonverbal communication: Table 6 summarizes the distinctions. As

Table 6 Comparison of Dance and Nonverbal Communication of Other Animals

	DANCE	NONHUMAN NONVERBAL COMMUNICATION
Purpose		
Affective and cognitive motivation	- - -	
Social bonding, territorial possession	- - -	Mostly displays
Courtship and mating	- - -	
Dominance-submission, reassurance, aggression	- - -	
Child care	- - -	
Exploratory behavior	- - -	
★ Coordinate actions from immediate and distant context, assert continuity in defense of threat of mortality		Coordinate approach, withdraw, follow in relatively immediate or limited context
★ Express, evoke and transform emotion		Express and evoke emotion
★ Multipurpose		Food, fear, and sex motivational states mostly energize and drive organism

Intentional Rhythm

★ Choice of rhythm in harmony or counter to psycho-biologically based rhythms	No deliberate choice

Culturally Patterned

★ Open (productive) system of movement, semantic, syntax	Limited intraspecies variation
★ Complex movement, semantic, syntactic systems; modifiers and context important	Relatively simple systems; response to relatively few simple perceptual cues; reactive motility
★ Learned arbitrary forms	Learning, but not of deliberately chosen forms

Extraordinary Nonverbal Movements, Motion Having Inherent, Aesthetic Value

Extraordinary movement and gesture	- - -
Motion has inherent value	- - -
★ Aesthetic values, notions of culturally based rules of performance	Recognition of naturally based performance

Innate Bases

Motor gesture potential great	Limited
Cross-modal perception	Limited
Cognitive generalizations	Limited
Memory capability	Limited

- - - Refers to continuity across species.

the human brain evolved, expanding in size and restructuring specific components to allow greater memory storage, a high order of multiple, fine perceptual discriminations, coordination, and novel classifications, programmed action sequences were gradually replaced by those in which social learning and individual choice played a more important role. Even though unconscious mental structures, maturation, and physical equipment impose constraints on cultural patterning, individuals and groups attempt to counter these. One form such opposition takes is human dance, a form of thought and action which, compared with other animal nonverbal communication forms, serves a wider variety of purposes with greater complexity in open, lexical, semantic, and syntactic systems. Although the ability to dance and to understand dance might be said to reflect human competence in general, there is a dearth of systematic research on the impact of dance or the relative salience of what is universally or culturally determined.

Implicit in the foregoing discussion is a processual model of dance performance in a sociocultural context. Dance can be analysed into many parts which function together in a pattern, forming a system. While components may be studied in isolation, they can be fully understood only within the overall system. The model for this system suggests the interaction between human endowment, sociocultural context, and the dynamics involved in what is dance and what is assigned to dance. This perspective is schematically presented in Figure 4; illustrative commentary is drawn from a study of Nigeria's Ubakala.[6] Of course, effective communication also depends upon shared knowledge and the interplay between skillful dance expression and sensitive perception. The model is an imaginative creation of a segment of the real world: it summarizes, in an interrelated set of propositions, what we can apprehend through the senses or infer from sensory cues. For a dance performance there is a *catalyst* (Figure 4A), determining who dances, why, where, and how (vis-à-vis cultural values, society, polity, economy, and religion). For example, a village market, family birth or death, or festival makes participation in an Ubakala dance-play virtually obligatory for performers and spectators. The dry season or a moonlit night provokes the memory of the pleasure of a dance-play, the enjoyment of the performance per se and its related communality. Individual or group initiative to conserve social patterns, introduce change, or to cope with the behavioral exaggeration of a contradictory principle in the Ubakala ethos stimulates yet another dance-play performance.

Selective perception (Figure 4B) is the extraction of information from sensory stimulation, on the basis of memory and cognitive structures (relatively permanent functions of mind that act on information to transform it), emotion, hereditary capabilities, learned communication skills, and in general sociocultural experience. The motivations, incentives and desired rewards of participating in an Ubakala dance-play include the fear of being shamed for not meeting expectations; pleasure (aesthetic involvement, alleviation of boredom and desire for arousal, and the opportunity for cathartic experience); social approv-

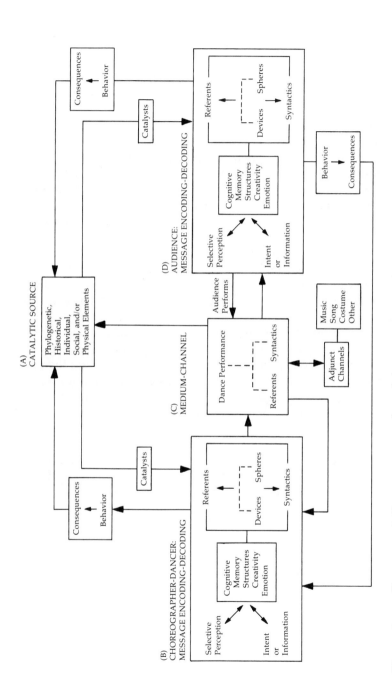

Figure 4. Dance semiotics: a processual model.

al and prestige and/or money received for a praiseworthy performance; and/or the need to keep informed of current events in order to pursue individual and group goals. Furthermore, once a dance-play performance is successfully underway, it commands attention.

The dancer, an incumbent of a social role, selectively perceives the situation and makes movement choices with some *intention* (Figure 4B) to inform, evaluate, prescribe, and/or affect; or without specific intention, but with the possibility that information transfer may occur. Intent becomes transformed through the communication medium or *channel* (Figure 4C) of dance-play performance. The Ubakala send messages, clarified and dramatized, about values (fertility, egalitarianism, innovation, respect, and reciprocity), beliefs, and norms. Rules about what is required, preferred, or permitted govern the combination of dance elements (space, rhythm, dynamics, and body usage). Dancers encode messages through *devices* which operate, in one or more *sphere*, within rules governing the combination of these elements through the channel of dance performance. The dance performance is the product of motional configurations and sometimes includes *adjunct channels* (Figure 4C), such as music, song, and costume.

Communication and systems theories include the concept of *feedback* (the arrows in the dance model indicate feedback possibilities) to refer to introducing information about a performance into the performance system. Feedback may be positive (serving to reinforce performance in its current pattern as does a western audience's applause) or negative (serving as a disincentive for the current pattern as does an observer's refusal to buy a ticket to see another such performance). Feedback, whether immediate or delayed, involves multiple relationships or elements linked by reciprocal influences: A performer may block out feedback or "noise" may preclude it. Interference may be caused by natural events such as rain, the circumstance of a loose animal, a fight, or the presence of outside government officials. Interaction—a series of messages exchanged between individuals—in the dance-play performance may involve dance group participants interacting among themselves, particularly in practice sessions and leader-group or dancer-musician exchanges. Audience-performer interaction (Figure 4C, 4D) may involve individuals and/or groups, the latter not necessarily being homogeneous in their response. If there is no interference, the audience decodes messages of intrinsic form, what Armstrong (1975) calls the "affecting presence," and/or extrinsic reference and makes some assessment with selective perception (Figure 4D). The audience reaction may have a recognized or unrecognized, or no effect. However, the performance may have implications for the dancer, observers, and/or external event structure, the catalytic environment (Figure 4A). Performers, sensing something inappropriate in a performance, may alter or terminate it. They receive feedback from their own kinesthetic proprioceptors and other internal sources concerning their bodies' response to expression. Among themselves, dancers respond to the unfolding, intrinsic properties of movement style and structure as well as the qualities of other channels. The audience's praise may provoke further improvement or continuation of a performance; their denigration may lead to a change or termination. Feedback related to the outcome of a performance occurs through performers' or spectators' thoughts and actions.

If dance is rooted in basic human capabilities for comprehension, choreography, and performance, how do we account for the varieties of dance in similar environments and the absence of dance in some times and places? It appears that a natural tendency to dance becomes repressed, inverted, or otherwise culturally modified, as Ekman and Friesen (1969) argue is the case of the smile for joy, in which people learn to mask emotion, and Leach postulates for a variety of phylogenetically evolved predispositions (1972b:339). Although somatic expression is natural and spontaneous, from about the age of four onwards, the individual becomes self-conscious, aware of traditions and expectations (Gardner 1973). Out of alternative means of communication, a kind of sociocultural selection may operate, so that those means perceived as useful are preserved. Significant forces affecting dance performance have been Christianity, the French revolution (Kern 1975), and totalitarianism (Mary Swift 1968). In the United States, where verbal modes of expression have been dominant because of a bourgeois, puritanical, and technological heritage, we now have dance study, performance, and observation (particularly to counter disillusionment with an impersonal society [cf. Margaret Theeman 1973]), reflecting a trend toward greater involvement with nonverbal communication. The contemporary sense of novelty and transience emphasizes the need to devise creative ways of adapting to the changing environment. The persistence of dance through the ages, of cave paintings and archaeological artifacts, is evidence of its versatility; the diversity of such creative, potentially adaptive expression might diminish in the face of a "shrinking" homogenizing world. This is not to argue that dance is an adaptive strategy, but merely to suggest the possibility. Obviously such a strategy is limited to certain spheres of life in a modernized, technological environment.

Thus far, the material presented in this book suggests an overview of some of the possibilities and limitations inherent in dance with its instrinsic and extrinsic dimensions and cognitive, sensorimotor communication. The following chapters will elaborate on a few of the potentialities of the human phenomenon of dance.

4 Dance Movement and the Communication of Sociocultural Patterns

HUMAN GROUPS IDENTIFY themselves and maintain their boundaries by various means. They create social taxonomies by using signs already in existence, producing new ones, and/or destroying old ones. In this context aesthetic expressions are often part of a culture's inventory of signs and demarcate and convey we/they social groupings. Mental categorizations may be transformed into dance, signs of visual motional configurations, to transmit information about and for social interactions. Such signs may promote self-identity, prescribe and assert social values and roles, and mediate between persons and their situations; they may also evoke emotion and rally people to action, as did the twelfth century heraldic forms. Dance may function in the same way as speech, concepts of plants and animals in totemism, and economic products in caste social organization (Lévi-Strauss 1967).

This chapter, which proceeds using a sociolinguistic perspective, focuses on associations between movement and social relations which appear in the dance-plays (*nkwa, nkwa di iche iche* [plural]) of the Ubakala Igbo of the former Eastern Region of Nigeria (in what is now Imo State). The Ubakala are a patrilineal, patrilocal, achievement oriented agricultural group of about twenty-four thousand; they are one of about two hundred formerly politically autonomous Igbo groups in Nigeria. Agriculture is the primary occupation involving men and women, and there is a sexually based division of labor, in part biologically determined by the exigencies of reproduction and strength. Reincarnation and ancestor honor are key tenets in the traditional polytheistic religion, which persists to some degree even among converted Christians. It is not sufficient merely to point to the relationships between the dance-plays and other social patterns: it is also important to know how the relationships were discovered and to suggest how they operate. The chapter discusses the data collection methods used to analyze the dance-play movement and presents some research findings on the relationships between text (movement) and context (sociocultural setting). These two considerations are set within the theoretical, explanatory framework presented in the previous chapter.

Data Collection and Methods

Data for the study of relationships among dance movement and social relations and structure include participant observations, including dancing where possible, nonparticipant field research notes, interviews probing the dance-plays and related subjects, 16mm motion picture films, slides, music-song transcriptions of dance-plays, ethnographic studies by other students of Igbo culture, and official government documents.

What the Ubakala say, what they actually do, and the association of meanings, in the dance-play, with meanings in other sociocultural spheres of Ubakala life lead to conclusions about the meaning of movement in the dance-plays. A grid of devices and spheres for encoding meaning guides the semantic analysis (see Table 2; it is elaborated in Hanna 1978c). The categories used to describe dance style and structure are essentially those of Rudolf Laban's movement concepts, comprising six dimensions and values of space, four of dynamics, four of rhythm, and the characteristic body usage (see Appendix 3). A ten-minute documentary film (16mm black/white, 24 frames per second) focuses the analysis for validation and reliability. Film is used in much the same way as a linguist uses tapes: on the basis of observations, learning dances in a variety of contexts, and verbal and written reports, the dances filmed seemed representative of dance-play performances at the time the film was made.

The dance sample is based on a competition judged by a consensus of representatives from each of the thirteen Ubakala village groups. The Ubakala world view encompasses the notion of competition. A common saying is, "no one knows the womb that bears the chief." Thus Ubakala presented those dances which expressed their aesthetic; that is, notions of appropriateness and competency or what the democratically chosen leadership considered were groups of dancers following the appropriate rules.[1]

For the description and analysis of movement, an ideal perform-ance model describes the movements of each group's leader, whom the group selects on the basis of achievement. In linguistic terms, movement description centers on the idiolect (individual pattern of speech) of the dance leader. Such description is a lexical transforma-tion from visual imagery on film, viewed through a projector run at various speeds, as well as through a hand regulated, four-inch moviscope, which permits single frame analysis. The movement transcript does not reflect every movement exactly as made each time the dance is performed; some variation is permitted by different dancers, as well as within an individual's performance. The model is an instance of a well-accepted version at a particular point in time.

A verbal rather than a graphic transcript is used: notational ideo-graphs, representations in graphic symbols, are a shorthand for data, as is academic jargon—meaningful and rapidly used by a small coterie of "experts." Mastering the concepts for notation, or the actual no-tation, sharpens one's observational ability to discern minute varia-tions in movement patterns and qualities. The four major dance no-tation systems (Laban's notation and effort shape, Benesh, and Noa-Eshkol) do not specify the meaningful structural units beyond the corpus of what is notated for dance reconstruction, the purpose for which the systems developed. Moving to contrastive patterns and to digital coding for computer analysis to show quantitative patterning, clusters, and correlations is as easy from verbal as graphic tran-scriptions (Martin Tracy 1974).

The Ubakala dance transcript is the basis for examining distinc-tive features, contrastive structural elements. An examination of movement traits as features in themselves (see Ubakala Dance-Play Profiles, Appendix 2), as well as phrases[2] in each dance-play revealed the relationships between movement and social patterns.

Theoretical Underpinnings

What are the grounds for suggesting that dance messages might have some impact on social relations? The secret may lie in dance's cyber-netic potential, languagelike features, multisensory modalities, a composite of persuasion variables, mechanisms for encoding mean-ing, and homology of movement patterns and sociocultural phe-nomena.

Cybernetic Potential

Cybernetics refers to elements within a communication system which affect each other as messages are sent and received. (See the dance model, Chapter 3, Figure 4.) A sociocultural system, following Walter Buckley (1968), is not primarily a stable or homeostatic system like a clock or organism, but a complex, open, self-directing system of interacting and interpreting individuals who adapt to external and/or internal change. Cybernetics concerns power, when defined as the ability to influence others' predispositions, feelings, attitudes, beliefs, and/or actions. In dance, power is exercised through interaction–the exchange of messages between individuals, such as between dancers, dancers and spectators, and either of the latter with other individuals in society.

Languagelike Features of Dance

To understand the communication potential of the dance-plays, a comparison of the design features of dance with those of verbal communication (following Hockett and Ascher 1964) is useful. (See Table 7 for a summary.) Both forms of communication require the same underlying cortical faculty for conceptualization, creativity, and memory. The comparison of verbal and nonverbal is clearer if one conceives of dance as more like poetry than prose. Dance and language have directional reception; interchangeability (a sender and receiver may be the same person); arbitrariness (many characteristics have no predictability); discreteness; displacement (reference can be made to something not immediately present); productivity (messages never created before can be sent and understood within a set of structural principles); duality of patterning (a system of physical action and a system of meaning); cultural transmission; ambiguity; affectivity (expression of an internal state with the potential for changing moods and for changing a sense of situation); and a range of sizes of potential communicating participants. Productivity, it should be noted, involves grammars, which are theoretical statements of what performers know about the inherent structure of the communication form and of their competence in a linguistic/or dance movement. It is knowledge of the *langue* of movement. In transformational theory internalized rules recursively generate new expressions; but these expressions are not new in the sense of falling outside the genre, as defined by its specific rules.

There are six distinctions between dance and verbal language:

Table 7   Comparison of Design Features of Language and Dance
(X = shared features)

	LANGUAGE	DANCE
Directional reception	X	X
Interchangeability	X	X
Arbitrariness	X	X
Discreteness	X	X
Displacement	X	X
Productivity	X	X
Duality	X	X
Cultural transmission	X	X
Ambiguity	X	X
Affectivity	X	X
Range of sizes of potential communicating participants	X	X
Channel	Vocal/auditory channels predominate	Motor/visual-kinesthetic channels predominate
Time and space	Temporal dimension	Time and space dimensions
Feedback	Speaker can hear self	Dancer cannot see self
Involvement	Total involvement in communication act is not necessary	Fuller involvement required in dance
Minimal units	Minimal units of phoneme and morpheme agreed upon by linguists	Lack of agreement about minimal units
Complex logical structures	Greater ease in communication	Greater difficulty in communication
Syntax	Detailed syntax governing sequences exists for many languages	Syntax exist for few dances

First, in dance the motor/visual-kinesthetic channels predominate instead of the vocal/auditory channels. (The auditory-olfactory-prox-emic-tactile channels may be relevant to both forms of communication.) Second, language exists in a temporal dimension, whereas dance involves the temporal plus three dimensions in space. Third, the degree of language feedback, the speaker's ability to perceive most things relevant to his speech as an acoustical phenomenon, is not possible in the multisensory mode of dance wherein, for example, the dancer cannot see his or her own image. Fourth, specialization in language, the fact that someone can speak and be doing something else, is not generally applicable to dance which requires fuller physical involvement in the communication act. Fifth, dance has greater difficulty in communicating complex logical structures than verbal language does. Sixth, there are differences in the study of dance and verbal language: Linguists generally agree that the minimal units of verbal language are phonemes and morphemes. However, agreement about minimal units in dance does not exist. This lack of agreement seems to be more a result of the relative lack of studies rather than a phenomenon inherent in dance. The kind of detailed syntax governing language sequences is yet to be worked out in dance. Such syntaxes in the channels through which speech, including the nonverbal concomitants, is accomplished, also remain to be addressed in the study of "the ethnography of speaking."

Linguists have shown that language asserts social relationships. However, there are numerous nonverbal variables that function in a similar capacity. For example, Mehrabian and J. Friar (1969) report on distance and posture, Michael Argyle and R. Ingham (1972) on the orientation of the body and eye direction, and Nancy Henley (1973) on touching. "In general," writes Susan Ervin-Tripp, "the findings suggest that when there are discrepancies, the information in the nonverbal channel may be more important than its verbal counterpart" (1976:142). As is the case for learned speech acts, there are imperatives (sometimes with modulators such as polite greetings), imbedded imperatives, need statements, and hints. Ervin-Tripp (ibid.:145) discusses the social utility of developing elaborate indicators of social differences in language, and, we might add, dance, when those differences are often quite apparent. She suggests that some of the meanings, from one set of contrasts, carry over to another, as a kind of metaphor. Metaphorical thought, which uses nature to refer to social relations, grounds the relationship in an order larger than itself. Dance communication may reveal actual or claimed features of social relationships without making these assertions focal or topical, imply more extensive features connotatively through metaphor or other devices, and/or suggest shifts in obligations. As is the case for verbal language, there is polysemy in nonverbal forms, that is, multiple meanings for single forms, which may be situationally invoked.

Multisensory Impact

The efficacy of dance-play messages on social relations may arise from their being multisensory. Education specialists recommend that to change opinions and attitudes sensory experience should be as complete as possible. It may approximate what Antonin Artaud (1958:92) called "a genuine enslavement of the attention," of the total being, mind and body, but without the violence he advocates. People may, in fact, be seduced through dance. Those not interested in attending to the communication as such often "unavoidably perceive it because they are attracted to another stimulus which thus serves as seducing bait" (Doob 1961:247).

A variety of such seductive stimuli operate in the dance-play: there is movement, the feeling of kinesthetic activity or empathy; the sight of performers, and sometimes the audience, moving in time and space with effort; the touch of body to performing area, to the performer's own body, or to another's body; the sound of physical movement, the impact of the feet or other body supports on the "stage," heavy breathing in high energy presentations; the smell of physical exertion and perhaps the smell of food and drink digestion which accompanies the dance event. It is noteworthy that the *nkwa* performers' costumes are most often yellow, orange, and red, colors which are highly conspicuous to humans (Chapple 1970:256). R. Gregory (1973:48, 77) points out that yellow is the color to which the eye is maximally sensitive. Furthermore, patterns of color create signs of long duration at minimum energy cost (Wilson 1975:239).

The dance-play incorporates certain qualities found to evoke arousal. *Surprise*, and the excitement of an unboundedness, exist since the performer moves in a unique way each time he or she performs. Ubakala expect individualism and *innovation* as well as the self-regulation required to unite with a group. Furthermore, there is the preparation and anticipation, prelude or psychological set, for a euphoric experience and then the performance. Preludes to enjoyable dance performances are prayer, wine drinking, birth, marriage, and death.

The *complexity* and *ambiguity* lie in the design features of dance and the performer-audience interaction. Dance can lead to some degree of altered state of consciousness or flow; Ubakala spoke of feeling pleasure and the young were further excited by courtship possibilities. Palm wine is an additional adult intoxicant and, of course, the energy expended, heat, and perspiration affect everyone.

Composite of Persuasion Variables

Relevant to this analysis of how the dance-play operates to ensure its impact are some findings from psychology on how opinions and attitudes are changed. Marvin Karlins and Herbert Abelson (1970) summarize these. In presenting an issue, strong appeals are more effective than mild ones when communicated by highly credible sources; pleasant forms of distraction can often increase the effectiveness of persuasive appeals; and the impact of a persuasive appeal is enhanced by requiring active, rather than passive, participation. Audience participation helps overcome resistance to opinions and attitudes. In time the effects of a persuasive communication tend to wear off but repetition and/or active participation contribute to persistence over time (ibid.:73–79). Since, according to Claus Mueller (1973:42), political perceptions develop and are reinforced in large groups, and cognitions can be generated in popular dramatic participation, the dance-play could be effective. It is strong, pleasant, active, involving a repetitive appeal manipulated by a credible authority in a striking setting for a dramatically participating large public with a degree of consensus about shared meaning.

The repetition phenomenon warrants comment. Song text, movement, costume, and semantic redundancy occur in the dance-play. This redundancy may eliminate the risk that a solitary message might be missed or misinterpreted, it may yield new information (Alfred Smith 1966:9), and it may clarify conflicting or changing messages. Also this redundancy modifies the audience's selective perception, retention, and comprehension. Audience decoding of the multichannel Ubakala dance-play in settings buffetted with noise external to the performance (goats, chickens, crowds, and other attractions in a market or other festive setting), may change with each successive repetition of a unit or the whole. Repetition may have an arresting quality. Wilson (1975:200) suggests that the employment of multiple signals that are different in form but redundant in meaning sustains a state of arousal. He also proposes that redundancy in some cases may prove to be more apparent than real.

Encoding Meaning, Movement Patterns, and Sociocultural Phenomena

There are conventions for encoding meaning in the dance-play. Table 2, Chapter 3, suggests a range of possible forms as well as those used by the Ubakala, for whom meaning appears to reside in the *spheres* of dance as a sociocultural event, total human body in action, total pattern of discursive performance, specific movements, and the intermesh with other communication modes, namely song and music. Occasionally the message is transmitted in the sphere of specific movement using a concretization *device* (the production of the outward aspect of a thing, event or condition), such as mimetically cradling an infant in the dance-plays celebrating birth. Married women with offspring joyously celebrate the birth of a child and communicate the news to a new mother's kin, at the same time as they identify themselves as mothers—a woman's prestige is related to the number of her progeny. Moreover they reinforce their identity as a group which wields informal yet powerful influence. This concretization device is also found in the enactment of a battle in the men's second burial *nkwa* (a ceremonial dance following some time after interment). Such a dance often heralded the beginning of a physical, or otherwise, confrontation among men. Another form in the sphere of specific movement is a stylization device (a somewhat arbitrary movement which is the result of convention), for example, a youth moving the pelvic girdle and upper torso vigorously to highlight secondary sex characteristics and to create energy for imminent social, political, and economic roles. The youth and warrior shoulder shimmy or shudder may be traced to erectile shoulder hackles which is one of the main mammalian modes of increasing height and enlarging the body as a threat display to ward off an attacker (R. Guthrie 1976:53). Women symbolize fertility stylistically with undulations and hip shifts to mark status advances with the birth of a child (rebirth of an ancestor) and a woman's elevated prestige.

In terms of semantic devices, Ubakala dance seems to be a pervasive metonym, that is, a motional conceptualization of one thing for that of another of which the former is an attribute or with which it is associated or contiguous in the same frame of experience. As specialized cultural motion, dance is metonymical to the motion of life and the Ubakala ethos of action. The processes of reproduction and recreation in the human-supernatural cyclical pattern of reincarnation merge and the ancestors continue their existence in the dancers' bodies. In the spheres of event and total performance, there

4   Coping with death: the Nkwa Ese, Ubakala, Nigeria. Photograph by William John Hanna.

is a vivid presentation of the unity of lineage, past and present (cf. Jan Vansina et al. 1964:372–373). At the death of an elderly respected woman who has borne many children and achieved other forms of wealth, her relatives dance to help her effect her passage to the ancestor world. Similarly, at a man's second burial, dance assists his transition. Dance as metonymical to the ethos of action is further exemplified in the use of the dance-play to communicate world view and order social relations.

A concretization device occurring in the first six spheres is the presentation by men and women of anger at the death and physical absence of a beloved one by dancing with weapons. Women and youth use the stylization device in the spheres of event and whole body, performance to convey an attitude of respect toward the "life-charged," mystically controlling, and retributive earth, thought to be the basic genus and grave of life. Posture is forward-oriented, and the focus is most commonly downward. Their movement appears to receive vitality from the earth, and in turn to nourish it. Ubakala honor their land: Ala, the earth deity, is all merciful mother; food and clothing come from the land; and ancestors are buried in the earth to await later reincarnation.

Dancing to celebrate the birth of a child serves as a metaphor (in all but the vehicle for other medium sphere of encoding meaning) for safe passage to different villages, achieving wealth and prestige, and fruitful parent-child and husband-wife relations. (A metaphor expresses one thought, experience, or phenomenon in terms of another, which resembles the former, thus suggesting an analogy between the two.) In the past, one obtained protection to visit and trade in villages other than one's own through marriage. Strangers were liable to be captured and sold into slavery or buried to accompany a prestigious deceased individual in the journey to the ancestor world. The dance for the newborn celebrates an increased labor force and the potential for wealth. Furthermore, the dance confirms the family bonds: a parent properly cares for a child so the child may in turn play a reciprocal role in the parent's old age, second burial, and reincarnation (requiring the child's marriage and procreation). Married women from the same natal village dancing together as in the *Nkwa Umunna* ("Outsider" Relations' Society Dance-play) is a metaphor for their support of each other against the bonds of blood which bind their husbands. Women often unite to "sit on a man," to sing and dance about apparent infringements of their customary rights or subversions of their economic rights; thus they suggest that remedial action be taken. Response to the performance is, in part, generated by the history of the unheeded dance-play message of 1929 and the consequent Women's War. Inattention to the women's danced grievances about the possibility of being taxed and the abuses of indigenous representatives of the colonial government led to subsequent violence. This had local and international repercussions: the women moved the mighty British to alter their colonial administration of Eastern Nigeria.

Women's and youth's dance-plays may be metaphors (in the spheres of events, whole performance, specific movement, and intermeshed with song) for anarchy, revolution, or violence. The dance-plays sometimes present veiled threats, reminding authority to keep within its appropriate bounds. Leadership is competitive, achievement oriented, and in flux. Women have successfully united against those whom they perceive to have abridged their rights. Young men soon become adult participants in the leadership councils, and youth dances metaphorically refer to the dancers' energy and endurance for adult roles. The young girls' parodied waltz dance is a metaphor (in the spheres of whole performance, discursive performance and specific movement) for colonial penetration (the pierced shell of traditional autonomy), rural-urban interaction, and modern and novel behavior patterns.

In the sphere of specific movement, the circle appears as a metaphor for safety, solidarity, stability, and the never-ending cyclical characteristics of agricultural societies and the process of reincarnation. The circle can be found in dance-plays expressing peace and fertility.[3] Conversely, since venturing far beyond the home village was dangerous because of the perils of war, slavery, wild animals, and the unknown, the use of relatively large space and angular lines in the men's warrior dance suggests a metaphor for engagement in the wider, dangerous, and unstable world. Because clockwise movement is believed to be the path of the dead, it may also metaphorically indicate sorrow or the displeasure of the ancestors; counterclockwise movement expresses pleasure.

Contrastive movement patterns are metaphors for distinct social roles.[4] There exist a number of principles which seem to generate Ubakala dance-plays for warrior men, women, and youth. For example, as illustrated in Figure 5, "Deep and Surface Structures in Nkwa Ese," tension, rapid tempo, and linear noncircular spatial patterns

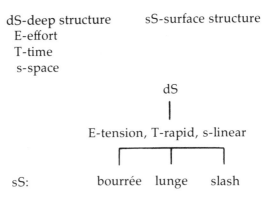

Figure 5.   Deep and surface structures in Nkwa Ese.

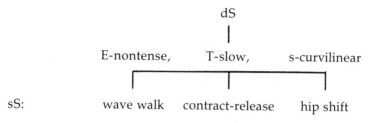

Figure 6.   Mothers' deep and surface structures.

characterize this dance-play. These deep structures can be realized by bourrée (tiny rapid steps on the ball of the foot), lunge, and slash movements. Figure 6, "Mothers' Deep and Surface Structures," illustrates that nontense effort, slow tempo, and curvilinear space generate the wave walk (the upper torso undulates up and forward with one step and scoops down and backward with the next step to create a wavelike quality), contract-release (with the torso nearly at a right angle to the ground, the spine curves upward making the torso convex and then creates a concave shape), and hip shift (hips and buttocks shift from side to side during locomotion or movement in place and may also rotate making two small circles when shifting from side to side).

The Ubakala dance movement patterns which I studied show a relationship to the social organization, specifically the age and sex role differentiation patterns. These seem homologous and conservative. In Figure 7, "Dance Style and Structure in Relation to Age–Sex Role Differentiation," the axes for age (vertical) and for the greatest sex role differentiation (horizontal) are drawn to illustrate the distribution of features and patterns. Young people of both sexes have relatively similar dance movements in terms of their use of time, space, energy, and body parts. At the other end of the age continuum, elderly men and women have similar dance patterns. Figure 8, "Tension Distribution in Ubakala Dance-Plays," presents another way of viewing the differences.

When the two sexes are relatively similar in age, but very different in biological and social role, the dance movement patterns diverge most markedly. There is a strong contrast between women as life-creating and nurturing and the men as life-taking warriors, actually or symbolically, in the domains of movement and social structure. There are distinct rules for differential behavior as well as actual be-

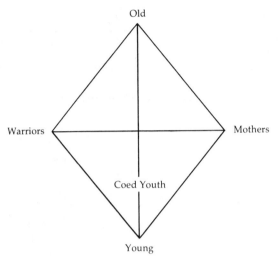

Age = vertical axis
Greatest Sex Role Differentiation = horizontal axis

Figure 7.   Dance style and structure in relation to age–sex role differentiation.

havioral differences.[5] Social differentiation, at what Turner (1967) calls the emotional and ideological poles, is symbolically manifest in the movements of each *nkwa* genre, as well as in its participation criteria, the substantive content of the movement, and song.[6]

Contrastive movement occurs most notably when both sexes are physically capable of distinct behavior. (Life/death is the ultimate binary structure for humans.) These dance movement structures are presented in Table 8, "Age-Sex Contrastive Patterns in Ubakala Dance-Plays." Furthermore, men's directional changes are more angular, with marked succession and segments; body shapes are more varied and complex. Whereas men dance in a circle extrusively, stepping in and out, leaping up and down, and moving on the ball of the foot, the women use the circle intrusively, have a more homogeneous spatial level, and more predominantly on the whole foot. Rapid speed and varied spatial use suggest destruction just as slow speed and limited spatial use suggest construction. The warrior's killing thrust is swift: he ventures abroad. The woman's gestation and suckling period of about two-and-three-quarters years somewhat restricts mobility.

Social patterns of leader-follower dynamics manifest themselves in the dance with the leader demonstrating and then the group following, but with some individual variation. Different members of the group may emerge to direct the performance. A soloist may present movements rhythmically counter to, merging with, or overlapping group movements. Innovative movement patterns, as in the waltz dance, correspond to innovations of a cultural order.

Ubakala movement patterns mark changes of status. They indicate the time for crossing social frontiers, gradually switching categories. Movement labels and categorizes performers in much the same way

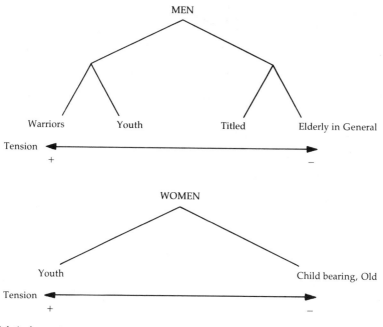

+ Relatively greater
− Relatively less

Figure 8.   Tension distribution in Ubakala dance-plays.

Table 8   Age-Sex Contrastive Patterns in Ubakala Dance-Plays

	SPACE			
	---	---	---	---
	Direction	Amplitude	Level	Grouping
WOMEN (mothers, life-creating)	— counter-clock 0	— small	— middle	unison
	face line of direc.		low	pairing in gp.
	face center 0			leader in 0
MEN (warriors, life-taking)	+ vertical line	+ small	+ high	+ unison
	horizontal line	large	middle	soloist moves apart from group
	diagonal line		low	
	forward/ backward			

+ Relatively greater variability.
− Relatively lesser variability.

as does costume, speech pattern, and identification with animals in totemism or economic products in caste systems. *Nkwa* performance often refers to various phases of transition and the division of labor. For example, the Nkwa Edere of young girls from about eleven to sixteen years of age focuses on a girl's imminent marriage, leaving her own home to marry and live among her husband's kin, and as reflected in the shimmy movements of the upper torso, which emphasize adolescent mammary gland development. Coed teen dancers also shimmy.[7]

Movement patterns reflect and order patrilineal and patrilocal social organization. An Ubakala woman leaves her kin at marriage to live among strangers; she gains status by bearing children. Her hus-

	DYNAMICS			RHYTHM	
Spatial Flow	Locomotion	Projectional Quality	Tempo	Duration	Accent
− minimum indulg.	− walk	fluid	slow	long	
	step	continuous			weak
free flow					
+ maximum indulg.	+ walk	tense	rapid	short	
curves	step	sharp			strong
	hop				
lines	lunge				
free and bound flow	bourrée				

band gains safe passage to his wife's town. When a child is born, the women in the father's compound perform a dance-play. Singing and dancing along the roads, they wend their way to the compounds of the mother's kin to inform all of the joyous event. Group dancing, especially when the movements are performed in unison and in the circular spatial pattern (symbolizing unity), often fosters a feeling of solidarity; it is congruent with the song text. The couplet of the accompanying song most often repeated is "Ubakala, we are coming. . . . Peace be with you as we come together." At one level, moving together depends on solidarity; on another, it creates solidarity, as in the case of lineages united to celebrate the birth of a child and the change in a woman's status.

In contrast, the men's warrior dance fosters intragroup unity; it has less uniform movement and linear spatial patterns. The dance-play is more often the occasion of intergroup hostility than cooperation. Dancers vigorously portray as warriorlike the deeds, exploits, and prowess of the deceased or his ancestors in order to bestow praise and honor upon him and his descendants. Since an important man was a heroic warrior, the reminders of his heroism would invoke the wrath of individuals attending from other areas whose relatives had been his victims. In the past, a murderer was killed by the son of the deceased in a manner similar to that by which his father was murdered. Obviously, references to old scores not settled create tensions, particularly under the influence of the tropical heat, palm wine, and performers gesturing with machetes or fighting sticks.

The discussion in this chapter explored some of the relationships between the movement (text) of Ubakala dance-plays and social relations (context), within a theory of dance as communication. It seems reasonable to conclude that Ubakala dance-plays, in terms of movement components, and who does what with them, when, how, and why, are about social relationships made visible through structural congruences and interweaving. Movement style and structure serve to identify social groups and individuals, differentiate roles and statuses, and promote group linkages. The movement channel in the *nkwa* communication medium appears to be congruent with song texts (roles of wife, mother, husband, father, and grandparent are delineated) and participation criteria for the different dance-plays. Dance may be selected as a medium of communication because it is "good to do" and "good to think." Religious and moral proscriptions have not made this kind of motor activity improper here as they have elsewhere. Dance provides pleasure, allows a special kind of license prohibited in everyday life, guards against the misuse of power, and produces nonviolent change in Ubakala society. The next chapter continues this discussion of the association of dance movement and cultural beliefs and social relations, in the context of the sacred.

5 Dance in Religion: Practicality and Transcendentalism

DANCE HAS THE POTENTIAL to be part of that human process by which meanings are exchanged through a common set of symbols. The communicators may reside in the same world or, as in some belief systems, different realms. References to dance's association with indigenous and syncretistic religious systems abound in scholarly reports from subsaharan Africa.[1] And yet they rarely discuss the reason for dance being a prelude to, concomitant of, or successor to other elements of ritual behavior. Usually "then they danced" suffices.

This chapter explores why humans commonly relate to the supernatural through the nearly universal form of dance. I present a range of danced religious practices using African ethnographic illustrations, set within the perspectives of social and cultural anthropology and the communication theory sketched in the beginning of this book —what dance is and how it works. Ultimately the question is whether there are any apparent governing regularities in the various manifestations of religious dance. The categories reflect more than a taxonomy of religious forms: they tell something about the potential of dance in human religious experience and about its practices and practitioners.

My comments are heuristic, for the data base, my own field work and an extensive survey of the literature, is a restricted and problematic one. Some dance examples are from relatively old reports and may no longer be performed. Some reports on African dance were written within the context of colonialism and its legitimization or paternalistic defense of native institutions. Others were written by self-reflective indigenes. Questions that should have been asked were not; behavior that should have been observed and recorded is missing. It is not clear whether ethnographies rely upon the well-informed informant, or reports from the actual performer, or from various members of the audience. Thus it is difficult to know whether the differences and similarities found, and the absence or presence of a phenomenon, are valid or rather the artifact of the trends of anthropological study which guide data collection and analysis.

Religion and Dance

Religion is a system of beliefs and practices encapsulating the ultimate values of a people. This system involves tension or conflict arising from social relations and anxieties, fears, and bafflement about the self and natural environment. Religion is also a system of social interaction; for many African ethnic groups, the corporate lineage continues beyond human life into the supernatural realm. Here the deceased joins deities and spiritual entities who actively respond to their living kin's behavior. And religion is a system of symbols which establish "powerful, pervasive, and long-lasting motivations" in humans (Clifford Geertz 1968:8).

Magic, manipulating supernatural forces for profane ends, is viewed in this discussion as part of religion, as is prayer or sacrifice (Dorothy Hammond 1970:1355; cf. John Mbiti 1970:12). From one perspective, religion "institutionalizes optimism, makes predictable the unpredictable, and attempts to bring under control those things that knowledge and science have yet to control" (Paul Blumberg 1963: 158).[2] The validity of such magical belief may lie in the child's experience in physical self mastery and his or her subsequent maneuvering with peers and superordinates (cf. Erikson 1963, 1966:348 on the ontogeny of ritualization). Magical formulae (sacramental utterances, exorcisms, curses, and blessings, sometimes in dance form) set in motion some supernatural entity or transcendent power, and thus have an impact on the individuals involved. The efficacy of religious practice depends upon the performer's and spectator's beliefs. Because the line between public (communal welfare) and private (individual therapy) is tenuous, distinctions will not usually be made (cf. Hammond 1970:1350–1351 on Warner's work challenging Durkheim's differentiation).

Because dance is extraordinary, it is an attention-getting device, arresting, and seductive. Its departure from ordinary behavior emphasizes the distinctiveness of dance and makes it memorable (cf. Arnold Van Gennep 1960). Thus dance is useful as a medium of evocation and persuasion, it focuses attention by framing experience (cf. Douglas 1966:79). As ritual, "it does not merely externalize ex-

perience bringing it out into the light of day, but it modifies experience in so expressing it" (ibid.:80).[3] Jakobson's discussion of cona-
tive function in poetics also applies to the dance: "There are messages primarily serving to establish, to prolong, or to discontinue
communication, to check whether the channel works . . . to attract
the attention of the interlocutor, or to confirm his continued attention. This set for contact, or in Malinowski's terms phatic function,
may be displayed by a profuse exchange of ritualized formulas, by
entire dialogues . . ." (1960:355).

It is through the process of symbolization[4] that we may be able to
understand the dance-supernatural relations. Three classes of data
are necessary: the dance, interpretations of specialists and lay persons, and the context. From the ethnographic data it is often difficult to determine whether individuals believe the dance is symbolic
action or realistically instrumental. Unless otherwise specified, we assume the primacy of the former.

Evans-Pritchard recognizes the necessity of associations in religion
to link inchoate concepts "to visible objects which enable the mind
to hold them and keep them apart" (1956:142). Fernandez argues that
the sources of these associations lie in "(1) the primary experience
of corporeal life with its inner 'textual' sensations of events and (2)
the secondary life of the self in the external (structural) world (prin-
cipally in the society of others) in the causal-functional context of
social contiguities and discontiguities. The succession of . . . [sym-
bols] in any expressive event will be found . . . mainly to be calling
successively into focus different aspects of primary and secondary
experience" (1974:129). Thus people use dance symbolically because
the human body as the instrument is intimately familiar, and, onto-
genetically, an important communicative mode (cf. Gardner 1973,
Kreitler and Kreitler 1972:173). If we accept Fernandez's proposition that humans engage in religion because it is emotionally gratifying, it seems that the involvement of bodily action, rather than just
cognitive action can more fully realize such an endeavor. It is to
Marett's credit that he conceived of religion as danced, the motion
and affect involved being significant (1914:xxxi).

The efficacy of dance lies in its cognitive-affective-sensori-motor
power to effect change (see Chapters 3 and 4). The creation of symbolic action forms is like other innovations, the province of the few,
the visionaries, the artists. However, the knowledge and understanding of these creations is differentially distributed in a society.

In considering how the kinetic symbolism of dance works, the
principles of contrast, or opposition, and mediation merit attention.

Cognitive anthropologists, French structuralists, and other scholars of symbolic behavior have found binary opposition to be a common way of conceptualizing. Dance also offers examples of this phenomenon: different qualities seem to be the simplest way of inducing arousal (Berlyne 1971:141).

Dance may be a "mediating" device, connecting the apparently unconnected and bridging gaps in "causality" as we seek identities and activities to concretize the inchoate, to "fill the frame in which we find ourselves," binding "the past and the future together" (Fernandez 1974:126), perfect and imperfect, powerful and powerless. It may be the desire to accommodate the idea of the singular which tempts humans to mediate the contradictory forces they perceive. The concept of dance as mediator is acknowledged in western modern dance and ballet: describing the approach and basic premise of modern dancer Erik Hawkins, Lucia Dlugoszewski, composer and musician for the Hawkins company, writes:

> For him, the purpose of having art as well as nature is to help man. Nature is already perfect, but the function of art is a ritual to help "imperfect" men become identical with this perfect nature. We are only beginning to learn that while perfect nature is always aesthetic, meaning fully alive, man is often inaesthetic, meaning not experiencing directly, really unalive, enslaved by the thinking and feeling diseases of his psyche. . . . The aim is to present man, not man instead of nature, but man identical with perfect nature, that is man at his very best, real, alive, and free. (N.d.:38)

Dancer and choreographer in the Aerodance Multigravitational Experiment Group, Stephanie Evanitsky, writes about the group's search for the "bird in man": "Certain of our experiences with the air touch a realm of consciousness so seldom reached that we feel open to another reality. Our theater explores these psychological states of existence off the ground: a 'theater of translucence' whereby an event is lived and realized not only as a thing in itself, but also as a thread to a different order of experience" (program note, The Hudson River Museum, November 11, 1973). Classical ballet expresses the potential for domination over the forces of nature, over the dancer's own weight in exultant leaps, over gravity in joyously sustained balance, and over muscular limitations in the high leg extensions. The nineteenth century further defied gravity by attaching dancers of aerial roles to wires by which they could fly and dance

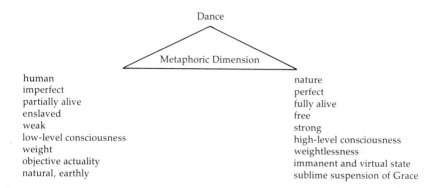

human	nature
imperfect	perfect
partially alive	fully alive
enslaved	free
weak	strong
low-level consciousness	high-level consciousness
weight	weightlessness
objective actuality	immanent and virtual state
natural, earthly	sublime suspension of Grace

Figure 9.   Dance as mediator.

on toe or *pointes*. Grace is a gift of God and the supernatural destination of the soul, and thus, through gracefulness, the dancer achieves a sublime presence (David Levin 1973:42). Figure 9 summarizes some of the oppositions which dance appears to mediate.

Adaptation: Extraction or Procurement

The concept of adaptation[5] is immanent in dance vis-à-vis the supernatural in Africa. The function of adaptation is to link a social system and its environment, specifically extracting goods and services from the environment for the society. Chandler Norse calls the problem of adaptation one of "properly perceiving and rationally manipulating the object world for the attainment of ends" (1961:114). I use the term "functional" in its constructive (eufunctional) sense and do not consider the ways in which dance may be disfunctional or nonfunctional to a society or an individual. Although dance in Africa is sometimes used to assist humans in extracting resources from the natural habitat, as in a hunting or hoeing dance in which motor skills are developed and motivation stimulated, and although it is often a money-saving activity, it appears especially to contribute to adaptation to the supernatural environment, including that inhabited by ancestors, spirits, and gods. Adaptation involves individual and social adjustment and coping. If dance seems efficacious to the participants, this feedback leads to its continued use. Dance, as adaptation to the supernatural, assumes the actors' perspectives and beliefs. Otherwise, the dance behaviors I describe fall only and variously into such classifications as maintaining cultural patterns (particularly managing tensions), attaining goals (in the sense of motivation), and achieving integration (group solidarity). It is important to point out that not all African peoples believe they play an active role in adaptation (e.g., see Evans-Pritchard 1956:316–317 on the Nuer who are passive and submissive toward their god).

This discussion is, necessarily, tentative since dance has received little attention. However, certain defining characteristics of the relationship between dance and the supernatural can be observed.

Dance in religious expression, communication, and instrumentalism fall within four broad categories, which are neither exhaustive nor mutually exclusive: worship or honor, conducting supernatural beneficence, effecting change, and embodying the supernatural. The last category has several types, which accounts for the more extended discussion of this grouping than the others. Bourguignon describes two alternative "ways of achieving convincing impersonation": possession, "an inner transformation, a change in the impersonator's essence," and masquerade, "an external transformation, a change in the appearance of the actor" (1968:13–14). It is also possible, of course, that a masked dancer might become possessed. I distinguish four types of possession: the first three, invited, invading, and dream, involve personalized entities; the fourth embodies a supernatural essence or potency.

In most African cosmologies a supreme being and lesser spirits concern themselves with the affairs of the local community and its environment. The complex spirit world responds to supplications through various formulae, many of which include dancing. Besides placating the supernatural, common appeals are made to enhance general and specific well-being, improve a group's or individual's malaise, promote fertility, and enlist support for social control. In addition, supplications may be for something specific, such as information about the best time for an activity or the solution to a problem.

Worship or Honor

At regularly scheduled seasonal times, or at critical junctures, or spontaneously, dances are parts of rituals that revere; greet as a token of fellowship, hospitality, and respect; entreat; or placate (cf. E. Parrinder 1969) deities, ancestors, and other supernatural entities. Furthermore, as Edmund Ilogu notes, the music and dance may be "in agony and sorrow, as an act of penitence" (1965:336), for example, after a plague.

The mediation of dance brings human and supernatural into a communication system. Mbiti claims that people in nontechnological societies envision a time orientation, governed by the present and past, which dominates their understanding of the individual, community, and the universe: "Time has to be experienced in order to make sense or to become real" (1970:23, 34; see Mircea Eliade [1959] for a more general discussion of this concept). Dance content links the present and past and the sacred and profane. Through the kinetic symbolism of dance, a performer musters the dynamic forces at his or her physical, intellectual, and affective command. Dance may be part of a group's technology for overcoming risk and misfortune in much the same way as the power of words brings into being events or the states they stand for (Horton 1967:157–158). At critical junctures, dance is a remedial vehicle to propitiate or beseech; at other times, it is prophylactic–honorific and reverent to preclude disaster.

In many Ghanaian groups, J. Nketia points out, "public worship does not take the form of a quiet and solemn contemplation but rather that of action–verbal action, musical action or bodily actions" (1957:4).[6] In the sphere of total human body in action, dance functions as a conventional sign of reverence. Thus, when the ritual leader among the Gogo of Tanzania conducts the annual ritual for good rains and fertility, a major part of the cycle is the *cidwanga* dance, a public act of propitiation to the spirits of the dead (Peter Rigby 1968:453). Dance may function as a metaphor for human efficacy in working with the supernatural. The operation of dancing sets off an operation at another plane, an exemplar of sympathetic magic. It may serve as a signal for the deities' intervention. Horton reports that the "Kalabari say, 'It is men who make the gods great.' Fervent worship will add to a god's capacity to help the worshippers: and just as surely the cutting off of worship will render the god impotent or at the very least cause it to break off contact with its erstwhile worshippers. This fact has more than once been used to put an end to the influence of a god which has started to act maliciously towards its congregation" (1960:15–16). Among Nigeria's Efik, the worshippers of the sea resident Ndem, clothed in the requisite white, dance in a circle at the deity's shrine. The brisk dynamic quality of dance metaphorically expresses the affective intensity of a wish directed toward the supernatural, which has the potential to grant it. A childless woman may ask for a child from Ndem; another dancer may

5   "Aerodance" by Stephanie Evanitsky. Photograph by Ric
Schreiber.

request a safe journey. The Efik believe that the brisker the dance, the more likely Ndem is to grant requests through her priestess (*Nigeria Magazine* 1957:166).

The regular performance of dance may metaphorically convey the continuity of the lineage; Ubakala dancers are, in fact, reincarnated ancestors. Dance is thus of a metonymical order, mediating the diachrony and synchrony of the lineage, creating a timeless totality. Frequently a concomitant of public rejoicing, along with libations and food offerings dance, as offering of the same sort, serves to emphasize and renew the link between the natural and supernatural, humans living and departed, visible and invisible, to mediate these polarities and create a semblance of unity. Because dance honors and propitiates the respected living, it is not surprising that the departed and other supernatural entities are so treated. Some deities, such as the Yoruba's Shango, love to be entertained and can be best placated with good dancing (Sam Obianim 1953:306). That dance is enjoyable for participants and spectators makes it therefore appropriate as entertainment for the deities and ancestors (the former often personified and the latter viewed as an extension of the lineage). Like the human creatures they basically are, the Dahomean ancestors or the other spiritual entities who are given anthroposocial attributes, are believed to love display and ceremonial. Trained dancers must be costumed richly and each step must be performed properly (Melville Herskovits 1938:I, 217). Thus both the living and the spiritual entities watch a dance performance, and both categories of spectators may even join the dancers, the latter often doing so through possession.

Horton (1960:16) reports that the Kalabari explain the effect of worship on the god by analogy with human beings, whose spiritual existences become strong and forceful, or ineffectual and apathetic, in proportion to the approbation they receive from their peers. However, for the Kalabari, since their gods are greater in every way than men, "the scale of entertainment due to them is correspondingly greater than anything due to one's fellow human beings; and so it is that many religious rites are at the same time the most elaborate and flamboyant recreation periods of the Kalabari year" (ibid.:70).

Dance in these cases is greeting behavior. Firth points out that "forms of greeting and parting are symbolic devices . . . of incorporation or continuance of persons in a social scheme" (1972:1). Expressed in this behavior he sees three major social themes, each connected with the concept of personality: attention producing, identification, and the reduction of uncertainty or anxiety in social contact. He notes that "confrontation without communication is threatening, and even the most casual greeting gesture tends to remove an element of uncertainty from the encounter" (ibid.:30–31). Firth is discussing interpersonal interaction, but his points seem applicable to human-superhuman interaction, in which humans attempt to immobilize potential superhuman aggression and create a bond through symbolic action. Esther Goody, in a discussion of functions attached to greeting in Gonja, claims that greeting is status enhancing, a mode of entering upon or manipulating a relationship in order to achieve a specific result (1972:40).

Okekan Owomoyela supports Firth's position that greeting behavior reduces anxiety. He argues that "supernatural powers become involved in festivals simply because of man's desire to placate them before and during the revels so that the revellers would be left in peace" (1971:122). Similarly, Horton notes that the Kalabari too, take various precautionary measures to ensure that no accidents mar a play (1960:33). Even the childless deceased, the despised and embittered denizens of the supernatural world, must be "collectively entertained, lest in their bitterness they upset the feasts of their better-favoured companions" (ibid.:27). Supernatural beings, then, have attributes which are projections from attitudes, ideas, and behavior developed in the context of ordinary life.

In Western Nigeria, Eshu Elegba, the Yoruba trickster, or god of mischief, is "universally recognized and appealed to by all Yoruba regardless of their affiliation to other cults" at an annual ritual festival (Joan Wescott 1962:337). Honoring the spirited, jocular, and abandoned Eshu metaphorically mediates contradictory phenomena in a stable social system with noncontradictory norms and provides an explanation, and perhaps an excuse, for conflicts and disruptions that occur. It is noteworthy that while "Yoruba dance consists of a gentle shuffling, in Eshu's dance there is much side-stepping, high kicks, and sudden and violent contractions. The intricate steps and displays of agility are not a characteristic of Yoruba dance generally, nor is the Eshu dancer's exuberance and flamboyance . . ."(ibid.:344).

Conducting Supernatural Beneficence

Dance is often the medium through which an individual (through self or other, as masked or possessed) takes on the role of a mediator and becomes a conduit of extraordinary power. Dancing, the individual iconically conveys supernatural essence, and the abstract becomes more concrete. Among the Baganda of Uganda, parents of twins, having demonstrated their extraordinary fertility, and the direct intervention of the god Mukasa, "go through the country performing dances in the gardens of favoured friends," acting on the belief that dance may supernaturally transmit human fertility to vegetation (James Frazer 1929:I, 137–138). Twins among the Yoruba of Nigeria are supposedly spiritual beings with special powers. Mothers carrying their twins, dance in return for alms, paid in equal amounts for each child, promising their blessings on all those who are generous to them (Marilyn Houlbert 1973:20, Robert Thompson 1971:10). In these cases the mediating process works through the motional dynamic rhythm and spatial patterns of dance, transfering to objects or individuals desired qualities; dance, as spell, activates wished-for results.

In the symbolic sphere of specific movements, the erotic *phek'umo* rites of Tanzania's Sandawe have as their purpose "making the country fertile" by appealing to the magic of the moon, a supreme being believed to be "life-giving and beneficial or destructive and polluting" (Eric Ten Raa 1969:38). Men and women dance by moonlight and, identifying with the moon and its fertility, adopt moon stances, stylized signs; they embrace tightly and mimic the act of fertilization, in concretizations. "The magical result," says Ten Raa, "is based on similarity." The moon is associated with the role of the seasons in the fertility cycle of the country, women's menstrual cycle, and the sexuality of human beings: thus the dance metaphorically conducts supernatural beneficence (ibid.).

Dance appears metonymically to effect the ascendance of life and health forces over those of disease and death, manipulated by elders believed to be sorcerers. The conceptualization of this conflict occurs through dances which mock disease, death, and witchcraft. Dance is metonymical to life movement and signifies positive motion versus its absence, life versus disease and death. Thus, the Tiv use concretizations and metonymy.

> *Ingogh* parodies "dropsy"; at a signal a normal dance pattern is interrupted, the dancers distend their bellies grotesquely, take on idiotic grins, cross their eyes, dangle their arms, presenting a picture of complete affliction. Another signal and the situation returns to normal. At one point a dancer rolls over on his back, feet stiff in the air, dead. But he is quickly revived by his fellows. In Agatu, a masked elephantiasis victim is featured, a soccer ball slung beneath his loin cloth. Onlookers come forward to kick his inflated testi-

cles and put money in his hand. The climax of the dance is
a drama in which a sorcerer slays a "doubting Thomas"
with his "juju." The victim is also miraculously resurrected. (Keil 1967:33–34)

Effecting Change

Dance metaphorically enacts and communicates status transformations in rites of passage, death ceremonies, curative and preventative
rites. Dance mediates between childhood and adult status in the *chisungu* girls' initiation ceremony of the Bemba of Zambia. Each initiate
must be "danced" from one group with its status and roles to another. "The women in charge of this ceremony," writes Audrey Richards,
"were convinced that they were causing supernatural changes to
take place in the girls under their care" (1956:125). Among the Wan
of Ivory Coast, a man must dance an initiate (Ravenhill 1978). The
dancer and the danced form a picture of opposites. Dressed in finery
the girl is carried aloof, cool, and almost immobile except for smooth
and fluid movements on the shoulders of the dancer who is dressed
in working clothes. He dances, gets hot, sweats, provides locomotion, and moves sharply and brusquely with restricted movements
as he suffers from bearing the girl's weight. During the initiation
cycle of an ancestral cult, the Fang remove religious statues from
their usual place and dance them as puppets "to animate them, vitalize them, give them life" (Fernandez 1966).

The Ubakala of Nigeria perform the Nkwa Uko and Nkwa Ese
dance-plays to escort a deceased aged, respected woman and man,
respectively, to become an ancestor residing among the spirits, later
to return in a new incarnation. The spirit of the deceased exists in
limbo between living and ancestral states—perhaps wreaking havoc
upon living kin instead of joining other ancestors—until the performance of final mortuary rites, called "second burial," which feature
these dance-plays. These physical and spiritual forms are similar to
the dances in the Christian church to enable one to enter heaven
(Backman 1952). The sociocultural event of second burial is a metaphor for appropriate child-parent relations in which the parent is
motivated to have and care for offspring in order to be honored. Second burial participants are the deceased's children. It seems that
these dance-plays may signal the release of the living from the psychic tensions imposed by the death in a way that is minimally disruptive and may give the living an opportunity to anticipate, and
thus better manage, their own deaths, reconciled to an inevitable

fate. Victor Uchendu notes that despite the universality of death, its rationalization, and the Ubakala belief that ancestors are the continuation of a lineage's living representatives, considerable anxiety still exists (1965:12). However, through dance, it is metaphorically dissipated.

Among the Dogon of Mali, death creates disorder; but through the dance, humans metaphorically restore order to the disordered world in a like-equals-reality conception. Symbolically spatializing things they have not seen (see Michael Watson 1972 on the semiosis of proxemic behavior), the Dogon illustrate the representation of heaven on earth, their cosmic image conventionally reflected in arranging villages by pairs, one representing heaven, the other earth, their fields cleared spirally as the world is believed to have been created. So, too, at the time of death, the mask dance occurs to help the community cope with the psychic distress and spiritual fear of the dead. Order exists in the dancing with its specific symbolism and patterns in the spheres of sociocultural event, total human body in action, organic and discursive performance, specific movements, and other communication, particularly costume (see Griaule 1965). The Dogon conceive of the body as an image of the cosmos: "The human being appears with a material frame, the body distinct from the external world but in close osmosis with it thanks to the circulation of common elements through both" (Douglas 1968:19). Eliade discusses the human body as ritually homologized to the cosmos, the body being a system of rhythmic and reciprocal conditioning influences that characterize and constitute a world (1959:172 ff.).

The funeral dance of the Nyakyusa in Tanzania begins with a passionate expression of anger and grief and gradually becomes a fertility dance. It mediates between the passionate and quarrelsome emotions felt over a death and the acceptance of it, between the uncontrolled and controlled. Confronted with the death of a kinsman, a man's "passionate grief is made tolerable in the dance; it bound his heart and the dance assuages it" (M. Wilson 1954:230–231). Through the concretization device of participating in chaos and violence and expending energy, the Nyakyusa recognize metaphorically various tensions arising from altered social relations and create peace and order anew. Figure 10 summarizes the discussion in this section: transformation as a consequence of mediation.

Dance does not necessarily accompany ceremonies related to death. If dance is viewed as a metonym for life, extraordinary motion within the same frame of experience as ordinary life movement, one can understand the Lele of Zaire forbidding dancing for three

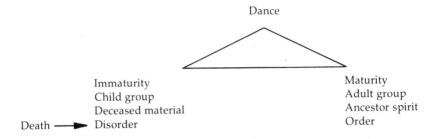

Dance

Immaturity   Maturity
Child group   Adult group
Deceased material   Ancestor spirit
Death ⟶ Disorder   Order

Figure 10.   Dance as transformer.

months in a village where a man has died (Douglas 1954:12), as a form of mourning. Symbolically, all life has ceased in this sense. Similarly, the Marghi of Nigeria cry but do not dance at a funeral except for that of a very old person (James Vaughan 1973:186).

Among the Gogo, dance metaphorically effects a supernatural change in a curative and preventative rite, through role reversal behavior in dance; this contradicts Durkheim's belief that since in ordinary life one sex is charged with certain tasks, it is also the one to perform rites (1947:355). The women's dance performance instigates action on another plane to counter ritually dangerous conditions. Men have ritual responsibility for controlling human and animal fertility. When they fail, disorder reigns and women become the only active agents in rituals addressed to righting the wrong. Dressed as men they dance violently with spears. Rigby points out that "A major element in all the rituals is dancing (*kuvina*), and the women are said to 'dance away' (*kuvinira*) the ritual contamination. In fact, the dancing is the primary 'curative' aspect of the ritual, and no other 'medicines' (*miti*) are used" (1972:240).

Embodying the Supernatural (Inner Transformation: Personal Possession)

Diviners, cult members, and medicine men are frequently among those who participate in *invited spirit mediumship* possession dances as acts of communion. These dramatic forms are consistent with, what Nketia claims is a commonly held view of the gods "as beings that do themselves act dramatically. . . . The drama of worship, therefore, is in effect, an elaboration of the dramatic implications of the behaviour associated with the gods. It is an attempt to provide a convenient medium by means of which men, taking the initiative, can meet their gods" (1957:4). The worshipper lends his body to the tutelary spirit when there is an indication that it wishes to communicate with the living or when the devotee desires to meet and consult with it. Bringing into play the powers inherent in the spirit, the dance is symbolic action signifying through sensori-motor images. As a sign, the dance may indicate the deity's presence or a leader's legitimacy; as a signal, it may be a marker for specific activities; as a metonym, it may be part of the universe; and as a metaphor, it may symbolize human self-extension or social conflict. To dance the deity is to evoke its powers. "Sacred power means reality and at the same time enduringness and efficacy" (Eliade 1959:12).

Devout belief, autosuggestion or autointoxication usually caused by frenzied, specific musical accompaniment,[7] audience encouragement, and sometimes also drugs, induce possession. A possessed devotee may achieve a consciousness of identity or ritual connection with the supernatural iconically metonymically, and/or metaphorically cross the threshold into another order of existence. Possession represents "the point of intersection of the human and the divine" (Raymond Prince 1968:v). Possession experiences may so overwhelmingly alter somatic states that they cause collapse (see Bourguignon 1968a:15). It should be noted that although there may be authentic abandonment and submission to possession, the specific characteristics of the seizure are culturally determined; children often grow up playing at possession.

The supernatural possessor usually manifests itself through the dancer's performance of identifiable and specific patterns and conventional signs, thereby communicating to the entire group that it is present and enacting its particular supernatural role in the lives of humans. Thus fear of the supernatural entity's indifference is allayed. Alternatively, people, such as the Kalabari, disown ineffectual entities.[8] Possession dance metaphorically mediates the polarities of the living and the supernatural and is a phenomenon in which they are both manifest. The "mission of metaphor" is to provide identity for the supernatural and help resolve problems.

The Kalabari symbolically manipulate the total body, specific movements, and costume to signify the deity's presence, "bringing the gods as guests into the village" (Horton 1960:20). The Kalabari conceive of their universe as body, or material with definite locations in space, and as the spiritual or immaterial which may come to a specific place and stay there or be anywhere and everywhere at once (ibid.:15). In possession, a god takes over control of a man's body from his own spirit. The community considers successfully dancing the gods to be an admirable achievement. Usually the cult group appoints a medium after divination to ascertain the god's choice; the medium holds this position until death. He dresses in clothes symbolizing the world of spirits. Masquerade dancers may become possessed, and in some cases the performer is expected to await possession before dancing. In possession dances the ability of Water People to materialize as pythons is accented as the god "turns from acting like a man to writhing on the ground and even slithering about the rafters of houses as the great snakes do" (ibid.:50). Kalabari possession dance is a device to force the gods to show their hands to humans. "The God who refused to come to the medium's head when called would be a portent of major trouble requiring immediate divination and diagnosis. . . . his reception when he arrives owes to this an intensity of feeling seldom paralleled by the other two modes [mime and masquerade] of dramatization" (ibid.:34, 51).

For the Kalabari, *oru seki* (spirit) dancing is part of the ritual to solicit some special benefit ("prosperity, peace, children, money") or appease a spirit whose rules for human behavior have been infringed. First, there are enthusiastic praise-songs for the spirit, an empassioned lengthy invocation "calling it temporarily into a sculpture which symbolizes it," a succession of offerings, and a signal of their acceptance ("the thrashing of an animal's body in rigor mortis after the invoker has cut its throat"). In the second phase, there is vigorous praise-singing and drumming the special dance-rhythms of the spirit so the invoker might dance and present the spirit in a conventional or iconic sign in the midst of the congregation. Possession provides assurance of the spirit's continual presence and power and his acceptance of the invocation and offerings (Horton 1969:17–25, 1970:194).

When a dancer is possessed by a god, ancestor, or other spiritual being, he may ascertain and interpret its will. Among the Ga of Ghana, possession dance is a crucial element of the new year's rituals requesting supernatural help for the well-being of the tribe in the coming twelve months. The Ga ask for such needs as rain, fish, crops, and health. Through mediums, whose state of possession is induced by dance, the god signifies its presence by delivering messages prophesizing the coming year's events and suggesting how to cope with them (M. Field 1961:54). The meaning of dance vis-à-vis the supernatural lies in a system of repeated analogues, each ritual performance carrying the semantic and structure of past and present ones, as in language or the culinary medium (see Douglas 1972). This serves to distinguish order, economize expression, and enrich

6   ''Aerodance'' by Stephanie Evanitsky. Photograph by Charles Dexter.

meaning. Possession frequently legitimizes leadership. Among the Fanti of Ghana, possession is an important attribute of the priesthood. Because the deities love to dance, the priests assemble drummers, become possessed, and then speak with the power and authority of the deity (James Christensen 1959:258, 261). The *ntsham* society members of the Kaka people in northwest Cameroon dance through the heat of the day at the termination of their initiation rites in the hope that some members will become possessed. "Public display of possession gives status to the possessed, for he is believed to commune with the ancestors while in the trance, and thus, is deemed worthy to preside over the society until next year's annual dance" (Paul Gebauer 1971:11).

Possession dances may metaphorically symbolize what is and is not desired at the sociocultural level and thus become a mechanism for stimulating change. They may become a medium for individuals to transact relationships more favorably, affect the dynamics of a corporate group, and sanction correct relations. The Kalanga of Rhodesia, for example, believe that "troubles are . . . the immediate cause for a [spirit] host to dance while possessed. There is a dogma that for the sake of health and good crops a host ought seasonally to dance while possessed at the year's end and before first hoeing and at first fruits. . . . the guardian spirit may be divined to have brought affliction merely out of hunger for offerings, and of love for the ritual's dance" (Richard Werbner 1964:220–221). During the possession dance "charges of treachery, and complaints of maltreatment, of personal suffering, of hatred secretly harboured by people who ought to love the host, all these are made in the ritual to reprobate those who could become the enemies of the host and the values she represents" (ibid.:222).

A second kind of possession dance, *the invasion*, usually a metaphor and signal of social pathology or personal maladjustment, indicates that a supernatural being has overwhelmed an individual causing some form of malaise, illness, or personal or group misfortune. Dance may then be used as a medium to exorcise and appease the being, thus freeing the possessed individual and ameliorating his or her irksome ascribed or situational position. At one level of analysis, the individual is in a passive state; at another, the individual's manifestation of malaise, which requires procedures for coping, is an active step. Meeting the wishes of a spirit as part of exorcism frequently imposes obligations on those related to the possessed: a neglected wife, for example, becomes the center of attention, or receives gifts, or works less. Thus possession contributes to adjustment through the processes of adaptation. Possession dance closes the distance between human and the supernatural, like an inversion of the parent-child relationship–the adult in this case incorporating the supernatural. Dance here again is a metaphorical linking of time and space, sacred and profane; it also links human to human.

The messages dance encodes often derive from such patterns of social relations as hierarchy, inclusion-exclusion, and exchanges across social boundaries; these relations may be part of the cosmology as well. The predication of a spiritual entity upon a person evokes certain behavior, and this metaphorical identification makes that person different in the eyes of others who then respond accordingly.

Alifeyeo Chilivumbo describes the *vimbuza* healing dance of Chewa and Tumbuka societies in Malawi as a socially sanctioned means for expressing those feelings and tensions which, if otherwise broadcast, would be disruptive of family or community social relationships. The dance is a medication for the *vimbuza* disease, which causes terrifying dreams or visions, the eating of unusual meat or the uttering of a specific groan. The dance is performed at night, sometimes on several consecutive nights, in a hut belonging to either the *vimbuza* healer or the patient, and both current and former patients may take part. A frustrated wife may complain about her husband's neglect: "Why have you rebelled? Is it because you have married another wife? If so, then I am bidding you farewell. But time will come when all the graces of your other wife will have gone and that will be the time when you will remember me." An annoyed husband may vent his aggression against a lazy wife: "When I ask you, my wife, to prepare food for visitors you always say you cannot cook because you are ill and hence you must sleep. But when another woman prepares some food for the visitors you get out of bed and extend your long, clumsy, lazy fingers to the dishes" (1969:III, 4). Trances, orgies, and possession often occur in the dance (cf. Michael Gelfand 1962:30–99, 117–178).

Dream possession is another way of linking humans, the supernatural, and dance. For the Gola of Liberia, artistic creativity comes from the artist's special relationship with a tutelary, a *jina* (spirit of the sky, forest, mountain, or waters who is friendly to humans). The archetypical Gola artist, Warren d'Azevedo reports, is a dreamer who creates external forms that project the "ideas" given to him as a gift of love by his spiritual companion (1973:336). Ritual involves mass participation in dancing, although there are some "artistic," virtuoso dancers whose style is highly individualized, agile and dexterous (ibid.:313). Their expertise is a sign of a *jina*'s involvement.

Not only may individuals be possessed by supernatural entities, but they may also experience *essence possession* by a religious or supernatural potency, an impersonal supernatural. For example, among the Lango of Uganda, *jok* is liberated or generated notably in dancing[9] (Edgar Castle 1966:52). Similarly, among the !Kung Bushmen of Namibia (South West Africa), dance activates *n/um*, that "supernatural potency from which the medicine men derive their power to cure" and which may overwhelm an individual enabling him to protect the people from sickness and death (Marshall 1969:347). The possession signifies a human ability to control the environment. Richard Lee points out that the medicine dancer goes into trance and in this state may communicate with spirits although not be possessed by them (1968). Crisis situations call for the ceremonial curing dance or it occurs spontaneously; the dance is redressive and prophylactic (Marshall 1962:148). For a medicine dance to occur, every person in the vicinity must be present. "The !Kung feel that they should all be together when strong *n/um* is present, as it is at the dances" (Marshall 1969:347, 349–350, see also 1962:248). Lee's research among the Botswana Bushmen provides substantiation: living men transmit healing power whereas the spirits of the dead and other forces external to the living cause illness and misfortune. Thus the Bushmen, as do the Yoruba, seek benevolent powers within the social body, but project on to external causes blame for malevolence (1968:51). The medicine dance is a conventional metaphor for well being and collective solidarity; it mediates contradictory forces.

Embodying the Supernatural
(External Transformation: Masquerade)

Sacred masquerade dances, part of a people's intercourse with the spirit world, make social and personal contributions through symbolic action that are similar to those made through honorific, change-effecting, and possession dances. The *midimu* ancestor masked dancing of the Yao, Makua, and Makonde of Tanzania and Mozambique marks the presence of the supernatural in the affairs of the living. The ancestors come all the way from the dead to rejoice on the occasion of the initiate's return from their training camp (J. Wembah-Rashid 1971:44).

The metonymic and metaphoric use of dance to capture the sense of continuity and oneness with the total universe and to function as a model for the belief system is illustrated by what we know about the Dogon through the work of Griaule and his colleagues. In the spheres of sociocultural event, total body involvement, and specific movements, the masked society dancing patterns depict this Malian group's conception of the world, its progress and order. The mask or woven hood also allows broad representation of all people, ages, animals, spirits, activities, and things: "The whole complex constitutes a picture of the smythy beating out the rhythm of the movement of the universe" (1965:189).

Not only does dance symbolically recapitulate beliefs, but it mediates nature and culture. The Nyau society of the Chewa-speaking peoples of Malawi has dance performances which "in cosmic terms . . . may be interpreted as a re-enactment of the primal co-existence of the three categories of men, animals and spirits in friendship, and their subsequent division by fire. Fundamental to the religious significance of the cult is the belief that underneath his mask the dancer has undergone what might be called a 'spiritual transubstantiation' to become a spirit. The spirits and animals come in from the bush and a temporary reconciliation with men is enacted as they associate with the people in the village around pots of beer, as in the Chewa creation myth they were first united around the waters which came with them from heaven" (Matthew Schoffeleers and I. Linden 1972:257).

Masked dancing enlists supernatural support for a society's and individual's well-being and appropriate behavior and metaphorically presents key concerns. In Nigeria, the Yoruba's Gelede society masquerade figures appear annually at the start of the new agricultural year to dance in the market place and through the streets. They honor and propitiate the female *orisa* (deities) and their representatives, living and ancestral, for the mothers are "*orisa egbe*–literally the 'gods of society' and their children are its members" (Henry Drewal 1973:149–150); all animal life comes from a mother's body. Only men dance the female and male masks, which portray the appropriate sex roles for each, although both men and women belong to the Gelede cult to seek protection and blessings and assuage their fear of death. Mothers have both positive (calm, creative, protective) and negative or witch dimensions (unmitigated evil affecting fertility, childbirth, functioning of men's sexual organs). The Yoruba concept of *ase*, "vital life force, energy, mystical power and potential which is present in all things in varying amounts and differing manifestations," is involved. Powerful *ase* resides in the *orisa*, and mothers have *ase* which ultimately stems from the Earth mother. Man can have *ase*, most fully when he is spiritually united with an *orisa*. Drewal writes that "The act of symbolically externalizing these vital life forces in dance is the spiritual reinforcement devised by the male to: (1) assert his virility and freedom in the presence of the powerful mothers and (2) recognize and honor their powers, thereby appeasing them to insure that they utilize their *ase* for the benefit rather than destruction of society" (1973:177). Drewal describes the voicing of *ase*, publicly spoken prayer which is felt to be efficacious and powerful (ibid.:76). It seems that Gelede dancing may well be another form of voicing (cf. Durkheim 1947:359), beseeching beneficence, and at the same time activating and conducting strong *ase*.

In the Ivory Coast, the Nafana Bedu masked dancers appear almost nightly during one lunar month of the Nafana year to bless and purify the village dwellings and their occupants. The Bedu spirits, which live in the masks, metaphorically absorb "all evil, misfortune, difficulties, and negativity." They take and remove them from the community, "so that the next year is started fresh and clean" (Williams 1968:20). The Tyi Wara masked (antelope headdress) dance of the Bamana of Mali represents the god of agriculture, a supernatural being, half animal and half man, who first taught men how to cultivate the soil. The performance invokes the blessings of Tyi Wara on man's agricultural effort as part of the ritual supporting a difficult yet essential undertaking for survival–farming poor savana land (Pascal Imperato 1970). The Tyi Wara's public presence in a concretized form makes appeals more understandable to the young. This mask metaphorically brings the god's attributes of beneficence and knowledge into man's presence and effort. In the animal masked dances, the performance reminds man that he has some of the same characteristics as animals, and these are positively or negatively responded to in a demonstrative way. The masked dancing distances human foibles and is a metaphor or metonym for them, so that they can be examined without threat.

Masked dance communication is a metaphor for normative behavior: Under auspices of religious dance, a communicator, via sacred separation and distancing from the profane, is freed from restrictions and thus able to present secular messages and critiques couched in mutually understood religious ritual. The masked dancer (as the possessed dancer)[10] "often has freedom for comments on [social] relations and for actions, that if unmasked, would produce social frictions or hostilities. By their very difference, the actions of masked dancers serve to make clearer the desired qualities of everyday behavior" (Simon and Phoebe Ottenberg 1960:68; see George Harley 1950).

In Nigeria's Nsukka area of Igboland the council of elders employed masked dancers, representing an *omabe* spirit cult, whenever there was difficulty in enforcing law and order (Tekena Tamuno 1966: 105). The Zambian Wiko *makishi* masqueraders representing resurrected ancestors and other supernatural beings patrol the vicinities of the boys' initiation lodges to ward off intruders, the women and non-Wiko (Kafungulua Mubitana 1971:59). Among some groups, as in northeast Liberia, the masks embody the authority of local chiefs who appear masked in public appearances. Sieber notes that, in general, masks are "symbols or foci for the spiritual forces that loaned their authority to the edicts and acts that emanated from the masks" (1971*b*: 435; cf. Peter Weil 1971:277).

At the domestic level, the Chewa peoples' male masked *nyau* dance is an initiation dance which is also performed at funeral ceremonies, weddings, absolution of ancestral spirit dreams, and merely for entertainment. A man residing with his wife and mother-in-law often uses the mask to mediate between himself and his mother-in-law. "Constant demands on him by parents-in-law, especially the mother-in-law, to perform countless duties: cultivate garden, construct baskets, build a house, make fences and execute sundry jobs, impose on the son-in-law tensions." However, "in his plaited mask transformed as *chirombo* [beast], he indulges in obscene language directed at the source of his tensions such as the mother-in-law. Although he may be recognized no action against him can be taken for in his mask he enjoys the immunity of *chirombo*. However, as a result, the mother-in-law may change and reduce her demands on the son-in-law" (Chilivumbo 1969:II, 8).

Socially sanctioned ritual abuse is permitted in the Bedu masked dance winter festival of the Nafana people of Ivory Coast. "Many of the movements and gestures used . . . are highly ribald and lewd. The abuse is seriously meant, and the atmosphere highly charged. At the same time, there seems to be humour and an underlying feeling that these acts are socially acceptable and that through them participants will be purged of whatever negative emotions they may be harbouring. The fact that the social hierarchy, the 'pecking order,' is dissolved at least once a year is in itself significant" (Williams 1968:20).

Masks often inspire in spectators a sense of dignity and mystery for the deities, spirits, and ancestors whom they conventionally depict; or, they may simply evoke a sense of awe toward the unknown.

7   Defying the forces of nature: Mikhail Baryshnikov in "Le Sacre du Printemps" by Glen Tetley. Photograph by Martha Swope.

The masked dancer is often an iconic sign, revered and experienced as a veritable apparition of the being he represents, even when people know that a man made the mask and is wearing it. Richard Hull reports that the Chokwe mask and its wearer were a spiritual whole both in life and death: when a dancer died, the mask was buried with him (1972:151). When he dons his masquerade costume, the dancer undergoes a transfiguration; his identity is concealed or lost and a new one revealed. This is not to say that he cannot also provide fun and amusement with zany clowning. In some cases no sharp distinction is drawn between sacred and profane, awe and humor, and the masquerade serves both spheres simultaneously. According to Claude Tardits, the masks bring religious ceremony into everyday life, "as if mediation between the supernatural and human beings should be accomplished partly through entertainment" (quoted in Maquet 1972:143). In other instances, there may be different masquerades for each realm.

Summary and Conclusions

Because the study of religion has neglected the structural and processual importance of dance, some uses and effects (manifest and latent functions) of kinetic symbolism vis-à-vis the supernatural have been explored. These are part of the larger question of what dance is and why, among alternative modalities of expression and communication, humans dance. African dance appears to contribute to the individual and his society through the religious dance practices of worship and honor, conducting supernatural beneficence, effecting change, impersonating the supernatural in possession or masked dances, and embodying a supernatural essence or potency to gain supernatural goods and services. These may be supportive and/or displacement/redirective ritual behaviors in Kehoe's terms. The former, nurturant and protective, with parental behavior possibly as the underlying model, reduces "anxiety by communicating the acceptance and integration of an individual into a group with those values he wishes to identify." The latter, stressing the efficacy of the behavior, may reduce "physiological tension in the group as a whole" (1973).[11]

The perceived efficacy of dance sheds light on the persistence of dance through historical time and geographical space (see Andrew Greeley 1972). Is there, then, a deep structure, an underlying principle, to dance? A basic assumption of the psychoanalytic tradition is that people everywhere share unconscious biological attributes and urges which come into conflict with social constraints. The Lévi-Strauss structuralists claim that there is an unconscious a priori structural determinant beneath observable patterns (cf. Jerome Kagan and Robert Klein 1973:960).

Common ideas appearing in the examples of symbolic action through dance are: self-extension, loss of self in being, transcendence, life as a process of becoming, and asserting continuity in defiance of the threat of mortality. Perhaps this is part of a universal aesthetic or aesthetic sensibility if either exists. Theorists of religion argue that its basis lies in the biology and psychology of man (cf., e.g., Michael Banton 1966, William Lessa and Evon Vogt 1972). We may find these are also the bases of dance. Dance as kinetic symbolism vis-à-vis the supernatural in Africa appears to fall within what I call one of the universal genres of dance: transcendental dance. (There seems to be a temporal genre and a combination of transcendental and temporal.)

Dance, as with totemic ideas and myth, appears to be part of a cultural code or logical model enabling the human being to order experience, account for its chaos, express isomorphic properties between opposing entities, and explain affective and cognitive "realities." Dance and religion merge in Africa to permit the articulation into a semantic system of sensory experiences, diffuse and disorganized emotions, and personal and social conflicts. Dance often mediates between individual and society, human and supernatural, time and space, good and evil.[12] The properties of extraordinary nonverbal body movement motion having inherent and aesthetic value, separate dance from ordinary motor behavior which occurs in actual time and space. With its hedonic and cognitive coupling, dance has the power to create a second world, one of virtual time and space.

Fernandez argues that among the Fang the status of an art rises with its ability to impose order upon a fundamentally disordered society (1973:216). "Malinowski refers to culture as a seething mixture of contradictory principles. . . . art is a major way of ordering this seething mixture, of giving this seething mixture that coherence which sets one culture apart from another. Sometimes art is the only ordering process whose complexity matches the complexity of what is to be ordered. There are two reasons why art, as distinct from discourse, is capable of doing this: the complexity of its symbols, and its capacity for engaging all sides of a human being" (Mills 1973: 405–406). Thus dance can be viewed as adaptive and as a conceptual tool in the reasoning process, not a mere epiphenomenon of the facts of society, polity, economy, and religion.

The reason for the choice, in Africa and elsewhere, of kinetic symbolic expression among alternative modes is partly found in the intrinsic properties of dance, the values ascribed to them, and their psychobiological bases. Why high value seems to be ascribed to dance within some societies and not others is the subject for another research; the personal and cultural experience of the individual, social and historical factors, and "noise," in communication terms, are obviously pertinent.

A researcher should be acquainted with the common idiom in which a society expresses its affect, conation, and cognition. Maquet points out that a society does not maintain an equally intense aesthetic interest in all things within its borders (1971:11). In Africa, one of the predominant idioms is the dance. Furthermore, dance represents two characteristics which reveal the essential and distinguishing characteristics of human nature: it is a form of abstract language and it is an element of religion. It is hoped that in the future scholars will not continue to overlook the role of dance as symbolic thought and action.

Thus far in our odyssey into the potential of dance, we have explored some of the ways in which people comment through dance on values, beliefs, and social interaction in the secular and sacred worlds. Chapter 6 examines ways in which dance can also organize and mediate social relations in the political realm.

6 Dance Rites in Political Thought and Action

WESTERNERS RECOGNIZE THAT dance provokes a sense of personal and group power for performer and observer alike: "Dance will bring the dead world to life and make it human," writes Herbert Marcuse (1970:132). Langer argues that dance makes the world of powers visible (1953, 1957b). Many nonwestern peoples also attribute special power to dance. In Africa, Nyanga epic heroes escape danger by dancing (Daniel Biebuyck 1973:89). The Fang dance religious statues belonging to the ancestral cult to animate and vitalize them (Fernandez 1966). The Bemba must "dance" an initiate from one group with its status and roles to another so that she becomes magically protected and given the promise of fertility (Richards 1956: 125). Siva is the Hindu "Lord of the dance" who dances in the sheer joy of overflowing power: he dances creation into existence. Conversely, his frenzied Tandava dance represents the destruction of the world (Homer Custead 1972).

Humans equate dance with the vitalization of animate and inanimate powers and both positive and negative energies. In this sense dance is power, a form through which life forces are made manifest and communicated. It seems, then, not unlikely that dance messages may significantly influence a performer's mind and body and an audience's responses. This chapter heuristically explores the relationships of dance to power over self and others. The latter concept focuses on dance as symbolic of power relations and actual political strategy: the validation and re-creation of leadership, competition for power, social control, coping with subordination or its threat, constraints on the exercise of power, and redress and transformation. As in the case of all the chapters in this book, part of the justification for asserting the potential communicative potency of dance lies in its cybernetic process, languagelike features, psychobiological patterns, and persuasion dynamics. The typological survey will suggest a range of possibilities; two case studies, which provide more social and cultural contextualization, amplify the relationship of dance to (1) ethnic integration through symbolically engendered perceptions and beliefs and (2) paradox mediation and social drama. The first study treats some concerns in archaeology, the second, social and cultural anthropology. Before proceeding, it will be useful to summarize the concepts of ritual and power which inform the discussion.

Ritual describes an extraordinary event involving stylized, repetitive behavior. In Firth's terms, it is a "symbolic mode of communication of 'saying something' in a formal way, not to be said in ordinary language or informal behavior" (1973:176). Dance is often a set of operations to ensure a certain type of communication. *Power* refers to the ability to influence others. This includes their predispositions, feelings, attitudes, beliefs, and actions. Power is inherent in social relationships (cf. Abner Cohen 1969, 1974, Anton Blok 1975). Influence can be effected through coercion, actual or threatened physical force, reciprocity or negotiation, ideology, and persuasion. Hugh Duncan (1962, 1968), Murray Edelman (1972), and others speak of the manipulation of significant symbols to affect individual and collective attitudes which in turn affect behavior, what Fernandez (1974) calls "the mission of metaphor." *Politics* is the exercise of power in economic, religious, and authority domains, involving who gets what, when, where, and how. It concerns differential roles and the allocation of resources or access to them. People who operate in dominant roles must have ways of communicating these in order to validate and renew their statuses. Power tends to be in flux, challengeable, and characterized by obvious or subtle conflict. F. Bailey (1969) views politics as a game in which leaders mobilize supporters within rules governing the competition procedure. Those who win power must legitimize their roles by norms and values perpetrated within a society; decisions must be enforced and impediments to maintaining the system overcome. Actual or potential losers in political encounters make accommodations and adaptations, while constraints modulate the politics of those in power positions. When losers consider the constraints ineffective, they often engage in redressive or transformative efforts.

Viewed as a "language" of command and control, dance may be a significant symbol and medium of power and politics. This potential in part explains the utility and persistence of dance through historical time and geographical space. Legitimization of dance as part of a religious belief system further reinforces its tenure.

The Bases for Dance as Political Thought and Action

Body Power, Image, and Symbol

The simplest form of power is the individual's own body. Onto-genetically each person experiences the discovery and mastery of the body in time, space, and effort patterns. Initially there is incorporation with the mouth and eyes, sensory power of sight, smell, touch, and sound. Then follows an increased body awareness and mastery and physical control of the environment through various manipulations, weight exertion, and speed and strength in gesture and loco-motion. There is a drive to overcome helplessness (cf. Gardner 1973, 1976, Frank Caplan and Theresa Caplan 1973): sight and movement are specific ways of entering the relationships with objects. Humans express life experiences through their own bodies prior to using other material objects. "To move one's body is to aim at things through it" (M. Merleau-Ponty 1962:137). Volitional body movement is the manifestation of the interaction of four sources of force: mental energy, muscle strength, force of gravity, and momentum developed in the moving body or any of its parts. Because sexual intercourse is seen to be life generating, the body is equated with potency, and this potency is often taken as a symbol for efficacy in general. Thus we can see that one's body, as an object of viewing or instrument of expression, communication, and other action, becomes an important experiential context which introduces order and meaning into our relations with others. For example, among the Ankole, when the physical powers of the king waned through approaching age or through sickness, the kingly powers were believed to wane with them. No king therefore was permitted to age or weaken; his magicians would prepare his poison (K. Oberg 1940:137).

Rooted in sensory and internal experiences, the body image comprises the memory of the individual's body phenomenology and the cultural attitudes toward or expectations about it. Not only is the human body an instrument of actual power; it often becomes a symbol of power in a variety of domains. Many people use the body metaphor to objectify and communicate. Bodily imagery suffuses the language of power, government, and authority (Ralph Nicholas 1973, Douglas 1973, Albert Scheflen 1972).[1] We speak of the "body politic," the "head of state," the long arm of the law." In social relations we use the expression of "stepping on someone's toes" or "stabbing a person in the back." Drawing upon the concept of sympathetic magic developed by Sir James Frazer, Brenda Beck (1975) suggests a sense of secret sympathy between the human body and other spheres of experience. The immanent energy of the body is externalized and transmitted through the dance. Energy is, after all, the ultimate source of social control and with the body as an instrument, dance may signify power and/or be charged with it. People use dance images, institutions, and behavior to send messages about themselves to themselves and to each other.

Psychobiological Bases

Some reasons for the efficacy of dance as political thought and action (what appears to make dance "work") are related to dance as a multisensory phenomenon; the importance of vision, motion (as body energy, arousal, aspects of time), and the emotional impact of body symbolism; and the interplay of communicative expressive skill and distinguishing ability. These and other psychobiological bases of dance were discussed in Chapter 3.

Persuasion Variables

Some of the findings of social psychology also help to explain the efficacy of dance in power relationships. These were summarized in Chapter 4. In his *Politics as Symbolic Action: Mass Arousal and Quiescence*, Edelman supports the findings of Karlins and Abelson (1970) on the importance of the credibility of the persuader for changing opinions and attitudes. He notes that in the United States, government has a legitimacy derived from early childhood socialization and the legitimizing rituals of elections, appeals for support, justification of government actions as reflecting the will of the governed, and myths defining leaders as benevolent protestors of their constituents. And Mueller (1973:42) points out that "if an individual has spent most of his lifetime in a political system dominated by directed communication, his language and consciousness will be shaped accordingly." Political perceptions develop and are reinforced in large groups and cognitions can be generated in popular dramatic participation. This phenomenon is particularly relevant to dances of Aná-huac. Nancy Munn (1973:584) points out that through symbols, the individual internalizes the imperatives of his or her community. Discussing art and political leadership, Douglas Fraser and Herbert Cole suggest one of the characteristics of leaders is their ability "to commission, control, and distribute works of art and to inform them with meaning" (1972:295). The significance of this lies in the potency of art as a socializing and integrating mechanism (ibid.:312, 325 and *passim*; see Stefan Morawski 1973).

In sum, the efficacy of dance communication in political thought and action appears to lie in the actual power of the body instrument, body image, symbolism, psychobiological bases, communication system characteristics, and composite of variables psychologists found to be persuasive.

Dance as Self-Mastery

Specialized dance involving a trained body is actual power for a performer as well as a symbol for this individual and the observer. Dance, as in ballet, conveys self-control, dominance, and ascendance (similar to man's conflict with nature in Spanish bullfighting). As Kern (1975:93) puts it, "The will to power has been marshalled over many years to discipline the haphazard and instinctive movements of the body and to create the control necessary to make artful . . . moving forms." The development of unique motor skills of flexibility, strength, and endurance surpass the ordinary human capability and overcome susceptibility to the effects of ill health, poor nutrition, negative body image, and the helplessness of infancy and old age. Some dance forms require the individual to gain control over the body in order to win freedom to use it in a particular way.

American modern dance apostle Martha Graham views the dancer's body as "something of the miracle that is a human being, motivated, disciplined, concentrated" (S. J. Cohen 1974:136). Aesthetics ("beauty" or other rules of appropriateness and competency), informs the physical effort. The dancer's body becomes free from the usual limitations upon human motion and victorious over nature and the ordinary. There can be motion in any direction without the loss of equilibrium; instead of simple backward or forward or sideways motion, the body creates oblique or rotating spatial shapes. Unaided, the human body attains victory over gravity and captures lability. The accomplished dancer transforms into a unique being, an instrument of precision. Daily rigorous exercise to avoid lapsing into an ordinary human state is mandatory, especially if the dancer has an unquenchable thirst to surpass previous accomplishments (Joseph Mazo 1974). Power means "to become what one *is*" (Cohen 1974:140).

Whereas the ballet dancer usually wants to make weight disappear and defy gravity, the modern dancer often uses it actively, exaggerating the downward pull of gravity upon the body. From the European ballet tradition, Fokine speaks of the need for the dancer to "conquer his or her own body" (ibid.:106). The dancer's body, perfectly formed according to a particular beauty norm, exquisitely tuned, and performing extraordinary feats, metaphorically communicates freedom from mundane function and ultimate deterioration and decay of the body; symbolically transcending the human condition, the dancer's performance symbolizes power (Kirstein 1970). Qualitatively extraordinary, dancers may disclose an ideal structure of heightened potentialities of posture and movement. The dancer may exult in achieving what others want to do, try to do, but cannot do well.

Dance can also lead to mental self-transcendence, altered states of consciousness, what the Balinese call "the other mind" (Beryl de Zoete 1953), what the Turkish whirling dervishes achieve (Ira Friedlander 1975). Depersonalization, weightlessness, absence of tension, a soaring, oceanic sense of oneness with the universe, and euphoria occur. (See Hendin and Csikszentmihalyi 1975; Ludwig 1969, Robert Ornstein 1969.) Dance may be considered the expression of divine knowledge or power or secularly achieved power. Indian dance is imbued with the sacred, and among the !Kung Bushmen of Namibia, dancing activates the supernatural potency from which the medicine men derive their power to cure (Marshall 1969:347).

As Philip Phenix points out (1970:11), the dance owes its special aesthetic impact to the viewer's awareness that the dancer's potentialities are also his or her own because they are embodied in persons with basically similar bodies. Dancers often dance for themselves, for others, and in place of others. Professionally and/or religiously motivated, dancers achieve what others may want to do, try to do but cannot or may not do.

Dance as Power over Others

One kind of power (such as the physical or symbolic self) may be used to secure another (over others) through an individual dancing, or others dancing, as proxy. Dance articulates, creates, and recreates power relations: Frank Hatch (1973) argues that the function of dance is to control and organize social interactions. A. Cohen points out that political man is also symbolist man: "Ceremonials of authority do not just reflect authority but create and recreate it" (1974: xi). Herbert Gans, following Marxist and Weberian perspectives on the arts, claims that "all cultural content expresses values that can become political or have political consequences" (1974:103–104) in the struggle for power. Mao Tse-Tung, of course, denied the possibility of an "art" being independent of policies (quoted in the *New York Times* 2-19-72, p. 32). (See Don Dodson 1974 on art as an object and agent of control, also Gloria Strauss 1977, Hanna 1973.) Peacock (1968:40, 219) points out the significance of the Indonesian government's recognition of the impact of art forms. In his study of the Venda, Blacking notes that a system springing from the needs and nature of the body may be harnessed to establish and maintain the interest of a dominant group (1962; cf. Maurice Bloch 1974). Plato associated the illusion of the arts with deliberate deception and found them vicious on moral and metaphysical counts. He feared the uncontrollable "Dionysian dance" popular with women and lower classes who had little escape from their work (Frank Ries 1977:52).

Totalitarian governments consistently attempt to control the arts, fearing their independent exercise. The elusiveness and ambiguity of artistic forms permit their use for politically stabilizing functions or politically innovating ones. Jeffrey Goldfarb (1976) argues that political expression in the theater is potent because it is difficult to censor the methods of the performer–the subtle gesture, ironic tone, and/or well-timed pause. And there is an implicit awareness of the delicate boundaries between play and nonplay. Play and the arts permit the expression of what Peckham (1965) calls man's rage for chaos, what Brian Sutton-Smith (1974) refers to as the possibility for anti-structure or protostructure, and what Berlyne (1971) refers to as the satisfaction of the arousal need through novelty and other "collative" variables. In these realms the "unsafe" can be explored without the consequences of such a thrust in the "real" world; there is the possibility for distancing, safe examination of problems, and the separation or merging of serious and nonserious. Play, Schechner (1973) argues, on the basis of primate studies (Caroline Loizos 1969), maintains a regular, crisis-oriented expenditure of kinetic energy which can be transformed from play into fight energy. In her discussion of play as an aesthetic concept, Hilde Hein notes that although play distinguishes between the present activity of play and the ordinary sense of reality, the differentiation may be collapsed (1969:71). This issue is taken up later in the section on redress.

The political dance rite communication patterns are not all found in every time or place nor are they mutually exclusive. The six relationships described below represent some of the range of human phenomena:

Validating and Re-creating Leadership

Body power exercised in dance may communicate sociopolitical statuses and roles. If dance is extraordinary activity, associated with vitality, and if charismatic authority is based on personal powers perceived to be extraordinary, then it follows that the fusion of this authority, or its symbolic manifestation, with dance increases the potency of a charismatic leader. For example, the King of Onitsha in the former Eastern Region of Nigeria was by custom required at the annual Yam Feast to dance before his people outside the palace high mud wall. He had to carry a great weight, generally a sack of earth, on his back. Dancing with the weight was symbolic proof that he was still able to support the burden and cares of the state. "Were he unable to discharge this duty, he would be immediately deposed and perhaps stoned" (Frazer 1929:I, 200).

Possessing power over life and death, warriors generate energy through dance to sustain particular leaders and political structures. The Swazi believe their warrior dance to keep the king alive and healthy by their own movements; and, at certain times, the king himself dances (Hilda Kuper 1969:206–209). In Nigeria, Uganda, Kenya, and Tanzania, people dance before their leaders to honor them, sometimes singing their praises and wearing costumes with their pictures. Through these dance rites the people communicate support for their leaders. Similarly performers entertain the president of the United States and other political leaders. By accepting an invitation to perform at the White House, or by refusing it, performers make a political statement.

Moreover, signs can establish and maintain social stratification. For example, Ivory Coast's Nafana men assert their dominance with dance movement. Power is measured by the differential amount of activity and movement present between the male and female dancing masks, the male exhibiting the greater amount (Williams 1968:72). The ability of the individual to mobilize popular energies around the dance communicates evidence of the political and economic power he or she holds. In the highlands of Bolivia, not only does sponsorship of a dance group (paying expenses) express the authority of political office, but it also establishes the vendor's right to sell in the market (Hans Buechler 1970). South Africa Venda's headmen or prominent leaders send dance teams of boys, girls, boys and girls, or men to each other to dance for a few days. These expeditions consolidate bonds between rulers and their families who are separated spatially (Blacking 1962).

European royalty understood that "art in all its forms could contribute to the establishment of power and could strengthen the 'cult' surrounding a class or men who could exemplify the state" (Jean Duvignaud 1972:120). In the ballet, "La Délivrance de Renaud," Louis XIII's performance as a demigod was a metaphorical message of the triumph of his orderly, exalted monarchy over anarchy (Kirstein 1970:62). Catherine di Medici of France commissioned a lavish production of "Ballet des Polonais" in 1573 to impress the Polish ambassadors who were arriving to negotiate a royal marriage: sixteen ladies of the court, representing the sixteen provinces of France, performed. Politics also motivated France's next major dance venture. The goal of the 1581 "Ballet Comique de la Reine" was to enhance the glory of France. The performance promoted the national image before an audience of invited dignitaries as part of marriage festivities. Officially the ballet was to honor the liaison; more importantly it was a message that the queen's treasury was not bankrupt. In such an instance, the symbolic presentation of power in a competitive display may lead to the additional gain or loss of power. Ballet was also harnessed to glorify the power of the Russian state and then, subsequently, the Soviet Union (Swift 1968).

Competition for Power

Dance is often used as a symbolic arena in which men compete for power. The following examples are of dance as a preparation for competition, setting for competition, and competitive mode through which the winner, dancer, or dance sponsor, achieves power. The Maring massed dancing of visitors at the *kaiko* special entertainment is an example of dance as a preparation for competition. This dancing communicates to hosts, during a peacetime truce, information about the support they may expect from the visitors in later aggressive activities. The size of the dancing contingent indicates the number and strength of warriors whose assistance can be expected in the next battle. One kinsman extends dance invitations to another: invitees urge coresidents to "help them dance" (Rappaport 1971b:62).

Among the Zulu, the warrior's dancing the powerful king's dance was metonymical to the king's power. The Zulu believed such action led to successful battles (Eugene Walter 1969). The performers communicated to themselves and to each other their increased strength for a serious competition. Warrior dance may create an affective state, a nonplay context, in which the individual is able to commit acts of violence which are normally taboo. Message and reality merge. Often warrior dances work up to a frenzy and an ecstatic delirious state: the unusual motor qualities of swift movement through space and vigorous accelerating activity may distort and attenuate perceptions and imbue the individual with an alien quality and a superior source of energy. Seymour Fisher (1973:33) describes this as boundary loss, the submergence of the self in a flow. The violent change in the state of one's body may help instigate or cushion the effect of what is considered to be a radical change in the social state of affairs.

The BaKwele exemplify the use of dance as a setting for competition: leaders vie with each other to present gifts in "sponsoring" a mask dance in a direct contest of wealth. Those who present the most gifts humble their peers (Leon Siroto 1969:149). Paying an entertainer ostentatiously as a reward for service is important in the existence of specific masks, for example, *buol* maskers with the spectacular massive helmet mask (ibid.:230). The display of wealth could determine new alignments: lesser leaders gravitate to the winner. A prospective leader must be diplomatic and influential to sponsor *buol*. He has to collect a quantity of wealth on short notice, to recall debts and borrow, but not excessively. Other means of achieving power are through abducting raids, unredressed harassment of other leaders through masked *gon* performance of certain virtuoso dances, and having one's home achieve the status of a cult center by attracting resident specialists in ritual and entertainment (ibid.:150).

Not only is dance a setting for communicating who is most powerful, but the dance is a vehicle for earning wealth, one of the few bases of leadership. Both wealth and power are normally in flux. The BaKwele borrowed and harnessed *beete* cult precepts and dances to solve nonreligious problems. A masked dancer receives gifts, the better ones receive more. The maskers who win acclaim in lesser roles are encouraged to learn dances and buy masks of more important spirits (ibid.:244). As a dancer's wealth increases, so does his responsibilities and the need for greater wealth. By becoming a big man, one of the village leaders, he has to attract followers by having women to offer. As the demand for wealth outran the incidence of *beete* rites, the *buol* dancer eventually had to perform outside (ibid.: 247). Political strategy was involved; the decision to appear extra-ritually required assessing the situation properly. Too frequent a performance could lead to overfamiliarity as well as a charge of venality against a dancer (ibid.:277).

Competitive dance teams were the vehicle through which political figures competed for positions of power and authority among the Venda (Blacking 1962), Tutsi (Pagès 1933:170), and a number of Malawian groups (Chilivumbo 1969). The size of a group and the innovative dance patterns were usually aspects of the contest. The manifestation of social energies coalescing around the dance also conveys evidence of power among the Kaoka speakers of Guadalcanal (Hogbin 1914:67–69).

Social Control

Dance may be both the object and the agent of social control. Since it may enculturate and maintain political and religious values, implement norms and enforce juridical functions, the powerless and powerful seek to control aspects of the dance phenomenon. The Chinese Communist Army, occupying Nanking and Yangtze Valley, introduced the Yang Ko dance to the large coastal cities to promote the conversion of the population to their way of thinking (*Dance News* 1949). Strauss (1977) argues that the Chinese government uses the demanding energetic European ballet dance form as a symbol of the "great leap forward" and the social equalization they promote. In the past, only the elite studied ballet and women were socially subordinate; now everyone participates in ballet and the dance portrays women as active and equal or superior to men. The Russians, too, use ballet to communicate their egalitarian, patriotic values. In the 1920s, pointe work symbolized metaphorically the ballerina's aloofness from material reality and was reserved for corrupt, aristocratic characters; folk dance steps symbolized the idealized proletarian heroes (Roger Copeland 1978:9). The distinctive style of Russia's ballet derives, in part, from incorporating the acrobatics of mass entertainment; thus, the dance has a broader appeal and, as Lenin proposed, art serves the workers. Through symbols, individuals internalize the imperatives of their communities: for the Nazis, dance (aesthetic gymnastics) was part of the "cult of the body" designed to foster discipline and comradeship and restore the body wearied by industrial labor.

While coping with basic survival, nationalizing industry, redistributing farmland, and abolishing illiteracy, the small underdeveloped country of Cuba appropriated about $200,000 to found the eighty-five member Ballet Nacional de Cuba and has been supporting it ever since (Copeland 1978). Castro, following Mao, has transformed the originally aristocratic art form into a metaphor for egalitarianism, harnessed body sensuosity and energy, and the anticapitalist ethic of planned obsolescence. Whereas in the pre-Castro era only the wealthy studied ballet, now approximately four thousand students throughout the country study ballet at government expense. "The upright carriage of a ballet dancer's body seems to reflect the sort of pride exuded by a once-colonized people now 'standing tall' and exerting an impact on international affairs that seems totally disproportionate to their actual size or military might" (ibid.:13). Admission prices are within the reach of the average Cuban; furthermore, the ballet travels with portable stages to remote areas of Cuba. The prerevolutionary Cuba had been "America's whorehouse," a hotbed of exotic, Latin sensuality to be exploited; it had the image of "passive, lazy, undisciplined happy-go-lucky celebrants of the here and now." Ballet is a metaphor for a transformed Cuba. This dance form requires hard work, discipline, regimen, postponed gratification, and channeled bodily sensuality and energy. Participants and observers can identify with the metaphor of superhuman transcendence and continuity with history as dancers defy gravity and the ordinary constraints on physical behavior and engage in unanticipated accomplishment. For the proletarians who do not attend performances, they see dancers in the famous balletic poses captured on Cuban postage stamps and public posters. Through the nonverbal symbolism of ballet, Castro illustrates that communism can take capitalist traditions and use them in more "productive" ways. Traditions can persist and products can be created without being deliberately designed to become outdated. The government's implicit goal is that ballet will propel individuals to self-extension in the wide range of tasks necessary for national development.

The Spanish used dance-dramas, especially those depicting the struggle of the church against its foes, to demonstrate the Christian faith to the illiterate Indians they hoped to convert. The pageant of Moors and Christians was a common presentation (Nancy Saldaña 1966). Muslim slaves used indigenous attachments to the old Yao initiation dances to gradually introduce another dance which was regarded as an initiation into Mohammedanism (Edward Alpers 1972:188).

American modern dance is also didactic. For example, in the 1920s, Doris Humphrey depicted the conflict of humans with their environments; in her 1938 "American Holiday," she celebrated the American struggle for independence in order to communicate the values of life, liberty, and the pursuit of happiness in a democracy.

As well as enforcing political belief, dance can also proclaim new government or political state. In Kikuyu tradition, the effective way to promulgate a new constitution is to call for war dances to be held in every district. Song phrases and sonic and danced media embody the words of the drafted constitution. On the appointed day, the constitution is announced, and the warriors dance brandishing their spears and shields to welcome the newly introduced government (Jomo Kenyatta 1962:186, 197, 200). At the 1963 ceremony marking Kenya's independence from Great Britain, Kenyatta, the first president and a Kikuyu, perpetuated and extended the tradition by calling for dances in every district to promulgate the new constitution. Ethnic groups from all parts of the country came to the capital of Nairobi to dance. Throughout Africa, nations similarly celebrate anniversaries and in doing so reaffirm the political continuity.

Dance conveys messages of unity[2] among the BaKwele. Their ethos of self-help and autonomy, as well as an unstable sociopolitical structure where the freedom of choice allows for village fission and opportunism, works against the direct provocation of an attack of litigation. The belief in the spiritual essence and magic of the *beete* cult and the animation of the mask dance (which means the village echoes the excitement of people dancing together) helps to solve nonreligious problems. The BaKwele believe *beete* averts evil and restores health and harmony (Siroto 1969:176). Furthermore, dancing makes the individual "hot," rendering a person less susceptible to illness. Therefore, mothers make their children dance in order to shake off certain illnesses. Because of the autonomous nature of the village segments and interpersonal conflict, an unaffiliated, unhuman dance leader is necessary. Thus the masked dancer–*ekuk*, a thing of the forest–is the answer. One or two masked dancers encourage the villagers to dance together of their own accord (purportedly only *beete* initiates know the identities of the dancers). The dance is part of the process to cohere disaffected village segments, thus preventing a potential conflict from reaching the point of attack or litigation which would tie up the village. The preparation and participation in cult activity, such as at the death of a notable, divert violent conflict. All unite for the common good in an endeavor apparently leading to what is an altered state of consciousness, the transcendence of potential personal antagonism (Siroto 1969:280, 314, 1972).

Although dance in precortesian Mexico was intended to honor gods and thereby assure agricultural success, its performance and, later, its representation in artifacts (double-encoding) apparently served contemporary sociopolitical designs: namely, it was used as a communicative symbolic system to create, reflect, and reinforce social stratification and a centralized, integrated political organization encompassing diverse, geographically dispersed ethnic groups. The theoretical orientation for this argument has already been elaborated; it is supported by the development of a stratified society in general, the stratification in Anáhuac, and the seeming relationship between dance, stratification, and integration. As in the case of Louis XIV and his courtiers dancing in a strict hierarchy of assigned roles (Kirstein 1970:86), so too, the Anáhuac leadership manifested their ideological stratification in motional configurations. Dance was a code to help establish and maintain control. (See the discussion of Anáhuac dance below.)

Ritual makes special use of all kinds of languages to create an unusual aura; many options in form, style, lexicon, and syntax are reduced with stylization. Bloch (1974) investigates the effects of singing or dancing something rather than saying it or moving normally. He argues, from his work among the Merina of Madagascar (a society Weber characterized as traditional and one in which leadership is continually challenged) that ritualized, invariant dance, the formalization of ordinary motor activity, is a form of power or coercion. As the range of choice in communication decreases, the potential for challenging the status quo decreases. Messages conveyed through body language in dance become "ossified, predictable, and repeated from one action to the next, rather than recombined as in everyday situations when they can convey a great variety of messages." The formalization of body movement in dance implies control of choice: "argument and bargaining with bodily movements are replaced by fixed repeated fused messages. The acceptance of this code implies compulsion. Communication has stopped being a dialectic and has become a matter of repeating correctly" (ibid.:72).

Besides being a medium of enculturation, dance may be a vehicle for enforcing values. When a dancer is possessed by a god, ancestor, or other spiritual being, or when he dons a mask, he may ascertain and interpret its will. Such dancers often have the freedom to comment on social relations and gain religious sanction for aggressive actions that, if not possessed or masked, would result in hostilities. Thus they can directly communicate norms and act as policing agents. Tamuno reports that the Igbo council of elders employs masked dancers representing the *omabe* spirit cult whenever there is difficulty in enforcing law and order (1966:105). Among the BaKwele, the *gon* mask institution is a way of forcing restitution, since the *gon* have access to village livestock which cannot be given away, even in time of need. Furthermore, the *gon* killing of livestock could end privation (Siroto 1969:256–258).

It is noteworthy that adults foster dance activities as a form of youth control. The Ngoni of Malawi had *ingoma* dances as the main village recreation for young and old. For the young, the dances were a severe test of physical strength requiring energetic leaping, stamping, and singing. The older men affirmed that the dancing made young men obedient and self-restrained. Channeling energies in the dance, as Americans do in dance, soccer, and baseball, leaves little time and energy for challenging the status quo (Margaret Read 1938:10).

Coping with Subordination

While the last section discussed dance from the perspective of superordination, this section focuses on dance performance as a response to actual or potential subordination. Dance may release and neutralize socially produced tensions and thereby perform a politically stabilizing function. However, dance may often be a vehicle of self-assertion symbolically establishing identity as a counter to colonialism, a dominating power, or a competitively heterogeneous situation. Bernard Siegel (1970) refers to "defensive structuring" in which members of a society attempt to establish themselves in the face of felt, external threats to their identity and so create a feeling of self-worth. Dances of the conquerors or elite are often imitated by the conquered or masses as if power and prestige would follow.

Third world countries make use of indigenous dance forms, competitions, schools, dance companies, and world festivals to assert their political and cultural independence (Hanna 1965, 1974, with W. Hanna 1968a, Owomoyela 1971). Milica Ilijin (1965:89) claims the performance of traditional dance becomes a symbol of Yugoslav resistance and revolution. In his study of the Beni, a popular, versatile team dance (*ngoma*), T. Ranger (1975) describes the dance as an indigenous form which selectively borrowed from the powerful colonizers as an accommodation rather than a submission. With its elements of mimicry and mockery, the dance conveys the essence of a sequence of alien intruders. The dance is a mode for the display of self-respect and self-confidence in communal values; it expresses the pride of groupings based on locality, ethnicity, moiety, or class in a continuing tradition of communal dance competitions. These groups have elaborate ranks, displays of military skills, opportunities for innovation, achievement of high rank, and the exercise of patronage for high status.

The Mexican dance groups, popularly known as "concheros," "danza Chicimeca," "danza Azteca," and "danza de la conquista," originated in the states of Queretaro and Guanajuato as a response to the Spanish conquest in the sixteenth century. Gabriel Moedano (1972) describes the groups as "crisis cults," syncretistic attempts to maintain cultural identity and find new forms of social integration. The groups are at the low end of the socioeconomic scale, heavily represented in the laborer and shoeshine occupations. Group members adopt the nomenclature of the Spanish military hierarchy, as do participants in the dances of the conquest (derived from the Moors and Christians). In the *conchero* groups, however, participation in the warlike dance involves women, aged, and children, as well as men. (See Claude Meillassoux 1968, J. Mitchell 1956, James Mooney 1965.)

Dance may symbolically define a group within a competitive, heterogeneous urban context. The dominant local group in Bandung are the Sundanese; in vehement opposition to the Javanese, who have overwhelming national political power and numerical superiority, the Sundanese assert their identity to themselves and others through promoting their own dances (Edward Bruner 1974). In the city of Juchitan, Oaxaca, Mexico, privileged upper-class groups cling to their dance as a symbol of cultural identity in a milieu which has become heterogenous and threatening (Anya Royce 1974*b*). Guardians and promoters of everything Juchiteco (a Zapotec tradition) are two wealthy old families from the town who have been prominent since before the 1860s. Most of the best traditional dancers belong to these families, and the expensive fiestas are occasions for proud demonstrations of their position as upholders of a superior tradition; this is particularly true when there is threat from outsiders –one-fifth of the population of approximately forty thousand, comprised of Mexicans, Spaniards, Japanese, Lebanese, and other Indian groups. Outside threats frequently take the form of marriages between locals and outsiders. The Juchitecos do, however, perform Mexican popular dances amongst themselves.

Constraint on Political Power

Dance is sometimes a vehicle for constraining the excesses of political leadership; it presents veiled threats of alternatives. Dance may instruct the rulers and impress the ruled. Frederick Errington argues that the dance performances of the mortuary rituals of the Melanesian Karavar are messages about big men and power–an ordering activity and restraint upon the exercise of power and energy (1974). Among the Karavars, women once owned the female dance masks that men now control. However, men coopt women in the mortuary ritual to uphold, rather than subvert, the contemporary order of that ritual and daily male-dominated political life in a matrilineal society. A man's followers are his matrilineal kinsmen whom he attracts in a shifting power situation.

Participation in rituals of rebellion and reversals of class or sex, symbolic chaos, may not be merely cathartic for participants. Max Gluckman (1959) argues that order is created anew after the recognition of the tensions and balance of power. He suggests that rituals of rebellion among the Zulu and Swazi proceed within a system in which the dispute is about particular distributions of power and not about the structure of the system itself. In the Zulu girls' *nomkubulwana* ceremonies, there is prescribed, socially approved, inverted, and transvestite behavior which is believed to be for the common good. Although Zulu beliefs and practices ordinarily stress the social subordination of females, in this ceremony girls dress as men, assume their dominant cattle-related authority roles and dance in a manner considered immodest and obscene. In the Swazi *Incwala* ceremony enacted at first fruits, there is inverted behavior–commoners and rival princes sing songs of hate, rejection, and treason, and taboo behavior is directed toward the king, who appears nude among his councillors. Thus the tensions of national life, the polarities of king and state versus the people and king versus royal kin, are defused and the king emerges strengthened from the trials. The patterns of role inversion among the Zulu and Swazi may be more than catharsis: they may be boundary maintaining mechanisms which impose constraints on the occupants of high status positions. Indeed, they may present a threat of anarchy or rebellion. If we accept Munn's (1973) notion that messages are created to suggest possibilities inherent in the ritual situation, Berlyne's (1971) theory of arousal value, Peckham's (1965), Sutton-Smith's (1974), and Turner's (1974) assumptions that certain phenomena can be considered as protostructure, a creative source of new behavior and structure, it may well be that these representations are offered as a latent system of alternatives. This reminds individuals and groups of their responsibilities.

Colonial records document government awareness that play could become nonplay. Therefore Europeans constrained or proscribed dance in order to eliminate subversive messages. The East African *mbeni* dance threatened some Europeans not only because of its mimicry and mockery, but also because of the extensive social network that developed as part of the process of dance instruction and performance. Pacification virtually eliminated warfare and thus the need for war dances as physical and affective preparation for violent encounters. However, performance of warrior dances, along with large assemblies of people in the charged atmosphere of a dance event, symbolized independence, self-assertion, and pride. Such playing is, of course, antithetical to the colonial state of dependency imposed on a subject majority by an imported European oligarchy. Unregulated by the Europeans, warrior dance could become a metaphor and instigator of revolution, ousting European occupants from office and installing Africans.

Redress and Transformation

In the 1930s Jane Dudley, Sophie Maslow, and Anna Sokolow were among the Americans who viewed dance as a weapon of social protest. They wanted to bring dance to the masses to expound upon poverty, exploitation, and the rising evils of fascism (Margaret Lloyd 1949). Moving people to redressive action was the goal. Kurt Joos' 1932 antiwar ballet "The Green Table" is an overt communication about diplomatic duplicity, its path to war, and death. Periodically, dances focus on the holocaust. Antony Tudor choreographed his 1963 antiwar, anti-Nazi ballet entitled "Echoing of Trumpets" in memory of the massacre of the inhabitants of the Czechoslovak village of Lidice and in hope that people will act to prevent such events. More recently, such choreographers as Alvin Ailey, Tally Beatty, and Eleo Pomare have been presenting commentaries on the black experience. Ailey's "Masekela Language" has an accusatory tone reaching beyond the specific locale of the South African jazz trumpeter-composer. A world of barely repressed violence eventually and horrifically surfaces in this ballet to make its audience ill at ease (Anna Kisselgoff 1977). Anna Sokolow's dance "Opus 65" derives its title from the year of its composition, the era of social protest by an alienated youth against the tensions of big city life and the loneliness in the crowd (Kisselgoff 1976). Similarly, Theeman (1973) describes the "urban celebrations" performed in the streets: participants were drawn from the artistic avant-garde, radical theater, architecture, city planning, marginal academia, and New Left radical groups, all in some way alienated from institutions. Through dance they tried to warn about and to act against certain aspects of social conditions. Many dancers hope the messages in dance will move observers to social action in the Brechtian tradition.

Among some groups the deprived use possession dance to increase their own power through identification with a deity who demands redress (Chilivumbu 1969, I. Lewis 1971, Werbner 1964:220–221). Ranger (1975) points out that dance societies played a role in the 1935 riots on the Copperbelt. The women's dance-play of Eastern Nigeria, used to express grievances which if not ameliorated can lead to serious consequences, achieved its greatest notoriety in the so-called Women's War of 1929 (Aba Riots).

The Ghost Dance is another example of a people's adaptive response to intolerable stresses of poverty and oppression. Many American Indians, unreconciled to reservation life, were receptive to ways of altering their situations. The Pvaiotso traditional belief in the eventual return of their dead, encouraged by dances and their shaman's influence, provides the contextual receptivity to their prophets' efforts to revitalize local Indian communities and restore traditional ways. The revelation that the dead were soon to return at the same time that the white people's culture would be destroyed had a strong emotional appeal that accompanied the rapid diffusion of the Ghost Dance religion. This disturbed American authorities and contributed to the Sioux outbreak of 1891 and subsequent Wounded Knee battle (Mooney 1965).

Summary and Conclusion

I have tried to suggest that dance, using the human body with its actual and symbolic energy, can exercise power over self and others. Dance is actual power as exemplified in the strength required by such dance forms as ballet or an instrument of power as manifest in the Indian Kathakali masked or possession dances which unite the human with divine power. Communicating power relationships and strategically playing a role in politics, dance validates and creates leaders and is a vehicle of competition for power, social control, coping with subordination, constraints on the exercise of power, and redress and transformation. The efficacy of dance in communicating political thought and determining political outcomes appears to lie in the combination of two factors: One is that dance has cognitive dimensions. Second, dance is an autonomic system with multisensory immediacy that causes excitement, fear, and pleasure for performers and observers. Dance is couched in social situations and belief systems generating energy and releasing inhibitory mechanisms. There is the hedonic coupling of somatic and emotional indulgence with beliefs, values, and attitudes. Of course, the potency of dance in the political domain varies in different times and places. For example, the overemphasis on the verbal and technological in the United States underevaluates dance for the population at large. However, as a consequence, many subcultures exist which overvalue dance precisely on this account. Dance has been a part of most societies through historical time and geographical space. Surely the time has come to consider the significance of the human body, in the dance realm of specialized nonverbal communication, to move and otherwise influence individuals and groups. This chapter calls attention to a neglected area of study in the sphere of art and politics and suggests a few propositions within a theory of dance communication and political symbolism and action. It is hoped that this will catalyze further work.

Case A. Dance of Anáhuac: For God or Man in Prehistory?

Having presented an overview of some relationships between dance and politics, I will present two illustrative studies in greater detail. The first elaborates on dance as social control and draws upon the perspectives of archaeology. The second explores constraints on political power and process of redress and transformation; this study draws upon perspectives in social, cultural, and linguistic anthropology.

What is the relationship of politics to religion in the Anáhuac dances of Mexican prehistory? This section assesses the use of dance representation–the objectification of an ephemeral phenomenon in ceramic, lithic, or painting–as correlative data in understanding processual change in time and space. My argument is based upon the conceptualization of dance (identifying the properties and processes of dance that allow it to function as an affective and cognitive semiotic system) presented in earlier chapters, and the dynamics of persuasive communication, sociopolitical change (stratification and integration) in general and in Anáhuac, and art iconography.

Kurath and Martí (1964) admirably attempt to reconstruct the May-an and Aztec dances[1] within the framework of their relationship to other aspects of culture. (Anáhuac is the Nahuatl name for what is now the Basin of Mexico.) In the reconstruction of extinct dances, the study of sculpture, painting, prehistory documentary descrip-tions, and ethnographic analogy, must substitute for observation. The authors convince us that music and dance were vital forces among the early Mexicans. With the evidence from artifacts and pre-history codices, no one can doubt the extent and development of these expressive forms, nor that combining several techniques of re-construction and analysis will provide, "despite some obvious pit-falls" (ibid.:150), some insight into precortesian dances. The discus-sion of contemporary live dances (ibid.: Chapter 11) does not quite "help to visualize the early dances as whole" (ibid.: 150), as sug-gested, since we are only given fragments, but the discussion does give us clues to continuity and syncretism. We are made aware of the interrelations of dance with the belief systems. Although we are given descriptions of the ecological, social, and political systems, and the dances related to these, the authors' conclusion is that *dance was primarily harnessed to agrarian needs: it was part of the invocation of the gods*. Martí describes the setting of precortesian ceremonials as the product of agrarian civilization, and indicates that dance was directed toward successful cultivation and hunting victory in war, and the ancestors' beneficence. Sacrificial rites involving dance were one means of identification with a deity. Dancing was meritorious like deeds of charity and penance (ibid.: 25). Kurath and Martí sug-gest that the Aztec political goal to unify various city-states into a powerful nation was the reason for the "fanaticism, hieratism, and formalism" that typify Aztec art. Such was the rigid ceremonial pre-scription in dance that one who deviated in performance was pun-ished. The section entitled "complementary hypothesis" explains why the authors' view of the purpose of dance may be too limited.

The authors also investigate the development of dance. They ex-amine the distribution of dance "evidence" within the three great eras distinguished by Pedro Armillas (1958:18–19). The first era, pre-agriculture (probably 25,000 years ago to about 3000 B.C. and the beginnings of plant cultivation), offers no dance representation; the second era, protoagriculture (3000–500 B.C., characterized by plant cultivation, animal domestication, and new processes of technology), provides a few representations; the third, High Civilization (a con-tinuous development from 500 B.C. to 1500 A.D. and associated with increases in productivity from intensive agriculture), is rich in numbers of dance representation. It seems, then, that an increase in dance representations corresponds to the development of agriculture.

The authors argue that militarianism might have had an impact on dance. During the militaristic era, religion continued to be important for social control and dance, part of religious practice, appealed to the deities not only for success in agricultural endeavors, but also for victory in war. A change in dance style also occurred as the Aztecs incorporated the practices of the local peoples they dominated: there was an interaction of dance styles from the various petty states of Anáhuac. Moreover, the authors demonstrate how dance disappeared in the postconquest era, when the theocratic structure was destroyed.

Their concentration upon the religious purpose of dance, rather than a religious *and* sociopolitical intent as I propose later, is perhaps a function of the book's place within the history of archaeology. Viewing the volume in this light, we can see a concern with historical reconstruction—what the authors call "archeochoreography." Such a concern is evident in the archaeology predating Walter Taylor (1948): there is an interest in diffusion, a comparison of elements throughout a regional area and between different regions. Taylor's focus on "conjunctive" archaeology, a holistic approach, is reflected in Kurath and Martí's discussion of the cultural subsystem of dance in relation to other subsystems within the total system. Dance is explicitly related to religion, agriculture, and warfare, but its relationships to other subsystems are not explicitly analyzed. Agricultural needs and, later, militaristic success seem to be the "independent" phenomena while dance is dependent upon them. Thus the focus is upon dance as a content and reflection of culture, not as a variable in the creation and organization of society.

The new archaeology, developed after the book was written, is concerned with process, how a society develops from one era into the next; it analyzes a system at one point in time and place and determines how that system is afterwards transformed into a different system in the same area. Comparing systems, rather than their individual traits, provides data for understanding trends and comprehending regularities. Paul Martin (1972:11) points out that "comparing forms and systematizing . . . data were not leading to an elucidation of the structure of social systems any more than did the ordering and taxonomy of life forms by Linnaeus explain the process of organic evolution" (ibid.:8). The processualists are less concerned with "the Indian behind the artifact," the representation of dance, than "with the system behind both." They are interested in dynamic articulations of the various components of the generative systems and attempt to isolate the conditions and mechanisms which bring about cultural changes (Kent Flannery 1972:105).

Kurath and Martí's book typifies the approach of the cultural historian: analogous behavior in a known ethnic group is used to suggest that a prehistoric behavior served the same purpose. The process theorist proceeds differently: using the analogous ethnic group, the theorist "constructs a behavioral model to 'predict' the pattern" of an artifact. "This model is then tested against the actual archaeological traces of the prehistoric culture, with the result that a third body of data emerges, namely the differences between the observed and the expected archaeological pattern" (ibid.:105).

Complementary Hypothesis

A different conceptualization of dance, along with the theories and findings in persuasive communication research discussed earlier, lead to an alternative explanation for the purpose of Anáhuac dances. This explanation includes certain assumptions of the new archaeology which focus on processual change and Robert Adams' hypothesis, which deemphasizes the primacy of agricultural development in favor of the growth of social organization (1966).

Martí points out that dance was devoted to the deities: "As in Oriental cults, one is aware of a complete surrender to mystic contemplation and to ethical and spiritual problems, while paying meager attention to material problems" (ibid.: 192). Furthermore, Martí notes that the Aztec hierarchy manifested a monotheistic trend as part of its policy aimed at forging a unified state, with one official language and religion; he states that "the fundamental idea of this political evolution was associated with the cult of rain, the earth, and the deities of vegetation" (ibid.: 193). The authors point out, in the chapter on symbolism, that the philosophical doctrine of Nahuatl was expressed in languages, a different one for different social strata –the people, the lords, and the religious leaders. Furthermore, pictorial representations varied in terms of forms used: "idols were for the laymen, color or hieroglyphs for the priesthood, mathematical-astronomical-calendric forms for the initiates" (ibid.: 199).

Could not dance also be considered as a symbolic communication system, a paralanguage used for everyone? There is constant evidence of its manifestation by social strata. Different groups have different movements and different spatial levels at the temple for performance. Also, spatially dispersed strata periodically assemble at the central temple. The audience comprised the commoners and depressed classes: the serfs and slaves. Could not dance, a dynamic process in time and space–the body in motion, with an arresting seductive appeal to attention, and then its representation–the result of action, but a reminder of the process, serve to say something? Might not dance communicate the authorities' viewpoint in order to promote and maintain the system? The authors point out that ceremonialism was used for social control, but not that dance could be a symbolic system in its own right, one of "the techniques of the body assembled by and for social authority" (Marcel Mauss 1935).

I hypothesize[2] that *although dance in precortesian Mexico was devoted to religious deities and agricultural success, its performance and later representation in artifacts (double-encoding) served sociopolitical designs: namely, it was used as a communicative symbolic system to create, reflect, and reinforce social stratification and a centralized, integrated political organization encompassing diverse, geographically dispersed ethnic groups.*[3] Stratification refers to the ranking of people in a society by its members into higher and lower social positions which produce a hierarchy of respect, prestige, or power. Integration refers to the linkage through emotions, perspectives, and the interaction of otherwise autonomous individuals and groups to form a goal-attaining unit. The latter concept serves as a point of departure for analyzing the loyalty a political system enjoys (Mueller 1973:5). It may be that the more authoritarian, rigidly stratified, and ethnically heterogenous a society is, the greater is the need to use shared symbolic communication to bind that society.

This theoretical explanation for the relationship between dance and society is not meant to be a substitute for the religious purpose suggested by Kurath and Martí, but rather to complement it. Their explanation of behavior patterns does not by itself account for the complexity of the dance phenomena. It does seem probable that dance was harnessed to agrico-military religious purposes, but it also appears likely that for people to dance, and then to present this activity in long-lasting artifactual substance in one particular era rather than another, involves something more. (We cannot retrieve evidence of the dance process itself in prehistory except by inference.) If one uses a systems processual model, then one expects a change in one of the subsystem components to cause a change in another. Thus, if there is a change in a society's political organization and population density, one might expect dance purpose and function to also change over time and in space. These changes do not negate the possible continuity of dance as part of religious behavior. Indeed, the latter can be used to validate the former.

THEORETICAL BASIS FOR HYPOTHESIS.   In proposing a socio-political role for dance, it is necessary to examine symbols in politics and dance as a symbolic system; to investigate how opinions and attitudes are changed, how a stratified society in general develops, and stratification in Anáhuac; and to explore the possible relationship between dance, stratification, and integration. Students of socio-political organization have examined the persuasive role of symbols in coordinating action, in integrating society. Such persuasion was particularly evident in efforts at war mobilization during World War II.[4]

A society which becomes hierarchically ranked and stratified utilizes mechanisms to promote and maintain the system, motivating members to carry out activities necessary to its survival (cf. Morton Fried 1967:186). When everyone shares similar roles and statuses it is unnecessary to have distinguishing emblems and boundary markers. Of course, symbols are not the only means of binding a society politically; others include the use of force or threat of it, economic control, religious sanctions, diplomacy, intrigue, marriage alliances (Ronald Spores 1974), and the manipulation of interest groups. The advantage of using symbols in persuasion in a large society is that other means, particularly force, may be more difficult, inflexible, and dissipate resources (cf. Michael Coe 1962:148, Elman Service 1962:181). It is generally agreed that each political system must continually sustain its legitimacy unless it relies on coercion. Mueller suggests that legitimacy can be successfully effected in a noncoercive policy if material needs are met, the political system decisively influences public communication (transmitting and regenerating values which permit a minimum degree of solidarity among its members), support is available from cultural strata, and the supportive values of the population at large can be regenerated (1973: 145). It is therefore to the advantage of the political leadership to manipulate the repertoire of symbols; if competitive communications can be inhibited, the articulation of conflict can be diminished.[5]

It seems certain that dance could function as part of this political repertoire. It is a potential semiotic system, part of a society's ideational domain which can transmit information, values, beliefs, attitudes, and emotions within and between strata and intergenerationally. In this context, "dance" refers both to the dynamic process in time and space *and* its visual representation, a transformation and concrete form of a behavioral phenomenon, which is a reminder in the absence of the behavior, and may have a redoubled impact when observed contemporaneously with that behavior.

FACTORS CONTRIBUTING TO A STRATIFIED BEHAVIOR.   There are interrelated conditions which contribute to a stratified society and its integration. Such conditions include agricultural development and the managerial imperatives of utilizing gross surplus, territorial aggrandizement, commerce, population concentration and pressure, increase in population heterogeneity, and new ideas. William Sanders and Barbara Price are among those who argue for the primacy of ecological processes in population growth, cooperation, and conflict in a microgeographically complex environment (1968:171, 187, 209–210). They believe agriculture brings into existence, and is maintained by, new forms of social organization and different views of the world. For example, irrigation agriculture, requiring primary and secondary canals, depends upon a cooperative effort, planned, organized, and undertaken on a large scale.

Adams places greater emphasis on ideas within a culture contributing to social stratification. He argues that a change in social institutions precipitates change in technological subsistence and religion (1966:12). Systems of centralized authority are first rooted in primarily religious institutions, which become transformed and result in structures of authority, basically secular and militaristic. "The growth of social stratification seems to have been preeminently a politically induced process associated with royal largesse in the distribution of lands and tribute" (ibid.:65–66). This stimulus complements that which results from ecological pressures within the community (ibid.:59).

Whichever position one adopts does not diminish the potential importance of a symbolic system promoting and maintaining stratification and integration. (The issue of how people are initially differentially stratified is not addressed.) Paul Wheatley argues that primacy should not be accorded "to any one of the functionally interrelated components involved in the cumulative process of change. . . . But, validating the augmented autonomy resulting from each institutional adaptation, providing the expanded ethical framework capable of encompassing the transformation from ascriptive, kin-oriented groups to stratified, territorially based societies, and from reciprocative to superordinately redistributive economic integration, was a religious symbolization, which itself was becoming more highly differentiated and developing" (1971:477). Thus religious concepts may be the bases and rationale to legitimate a system.

Representational art reappears with a complex society (Adams 1966:30, 96, 124); it seems likely that it functions as propaganda. "It was the emergence of an elite–whether secular or sacred makes little difference–that promoted those aspects of individuality for portraiture became necessary as an enduring symbol and monument" (ibid.:124). Flannery points out that competitive ethnic groups with internal social ranking in early Mesoamerica were preoccupied with status iconography (1972:222). Coe notes the coincidence of art and social cleavage (1962:103) and remarks that the kind of art produced by the early civilizations "reveals the sort of compulsive force" which held them together: "a state religion in which the potential leaders were the intermediaries between gods and men" (ibid.:82). Miguel Covarrubias (1957), Coe (1965), and Sanders and Price (1968: 117) argue that the spread of a sophisticated, specialized art style and its accompanying concepts was a catalyst in the transformation of simple societies into complex ones.

The possibility that dance and its representation serve as a semiotic mechanism is supported by George Kubler's analysis of the iconography of the art of Teotihuacan: "The entire repertory of pictorial expression . . . supports the view that painters and sculptors were seeking forms of logographic clarity and simplicity. They were less interested in recording appearances than in combining and compounding associative meanings in a quest for viable forms of writing" (1967:5). Supportive evidence comes from Tatiana Proskouriakoff's analysis of inscriptions at Piedras Negras, Guatemala (1960). These form a pattern of discrete sets of records, a pattern which has qualities one might expect of a historical narrative with reference to lineage or dynasty rather than place. Phrases of hieroglyphics are groups of appellatives referring to rulers or their associates; furthermore, stela depictions manifest rank. This analysis counters the view that only religious and astronomical matters appear in the representations.

Ethnographic data suggest the communicative potential of dance and its relationship to religion, stratification, integration, and change. There are many illustrative examples: Griaule describes how in Mali the Dogon dance team and masked society dancing patterns depict the Dogon conception of the world, its progress and order. The mask or woven hood allows the broadest representation (of all people, ages, animals, spirits, activities, and things) and order exists in dancing, that is, each mask has its associated patterns, rhythms, and procedural routines (1965:189). The public performances of Hopi dance are ritual enactments of the mythohistorical basis for society and power. The dances are a character for clan and society, the dance culture is "an epitome of total culture" (Kealiinohomoku 1974a).

Achieving excellence in dance may assure individuals of high status for a short time, and sometimes, for a lifetime (e.g., Field 1961, Peggy Harper 1968, Otto Raum 1940, Nadel 1942). Dance communicates or legitimizes nondance ranking by displaying one's own rank and by honoring the rank of others. Among the Yoruba, chiefs often express the authority of their office in the Olosorope dance. Among the Yakö, only those warriors who returned from military action with the heads of slain enemies could take leading parts in the fighters' dances (Daryll Forde 1964:148). Richards points out that the Bemba commoners dance for their chief, a young man for an older person, a senior man for a senior woman or her family (1956:59).

The occasion of the dance may be the integrative device. Among the !Kung Bushmen, nothing but a medicine dance assembles all the people into a concerted activity (Marshall 1969). For the Lugbara of Uganda, death dances are important occasions for the greatest gathering of kinsfolk (John Middleton 1960:203); and the Venda of South Africa have a national dance which brings diverse social groups together (Blacking 1965:35, 1971). Mitchell (1956) and Hanna and Hanna (1968a) provide insights into the integrative purposes and effects of dance on urban and national levels.

Hanna (1965, 1973, 1974), Peacock (1968), Royce (1974b, 1977), and L. Vidyarthi (1961) discuss the interrelations of dance and change in heterogenous societies in Africa, Indonesia, Mexico, and India, respectively. Marjorie Richman and Gertrude Schmiedler relate changes in the popular Israeli *hora* dance to changes in patterns of relative peace and guerrilla warfare which necessitated individual initiative coupled with strong group unity. Peacetime was characterized by a close circular formation and steady rhythm; in the active fighting period, stamping replaced hopping, and a dance leader emerged who signalled the group to stop, sway back and forth in unison, and then resume the circular movement at a more rapid tempo (1955).

STRATIFICATION AMONG THE AZTECS.   Coe (1962), Kurath (1964b), and Sanders and Price (1968:151–153) provide us with the general pattern that developed among the Aztecs. The basin of México was divided into about sixty semiautonomous sociopolitical units, each with a hereditary ruler with despotic powers. All paid tribute to and were politically dominated by one of these centers. The pattern at Tenochtitlan illustrates the stratification system: There were two main levels of society, the leaders, with hereditary status, and the commoners. Within the former, a professional priesthood dominated religious ceremonials. Politically, the priesthood had power equal to that of the nobility. Both groups had a complex organization with a head, the king being the ultimate religious authority. Each organization had upper officers and councillors, and the professional priesthood had a rank system to minister to the various cults in the pantheon of deities. Certain priests trained noble youths who entered either a school for priests or one for singers and dancers. The royal household was polygynous; the line of divine descendants married daughters of lordly chieftains who, with their servants, attended the royal court and were supported from the state treasury. The king received tribute from subjugated towns and had estates at his disposal (Adams 1966:110), while nobility was landed and controlled the production and distribution of goods through market and taxation systems.

The other level of society, the commoners, were ranked by occupation. Professional warriors and merchants enjoyed the most prominence. There were also professional craftsmen and peasants, who comprised the bulk of the commoners and provided the agricultural produce, craft goods, and labor necessary for warfare and construction. There was some mobility within the social system, for important professional warriors could become priests or nobles while a nobleman could also fall to a lower status.

In addition to the leaders and commoners, there were three depressed classes: serfs worked the nobles' lands, owed tribute and labor services; a temporary slave class included indebted individuals and those who had committed crimes; and slaves were war captives. This social structure involved interdependence. There was "consensual power," that is, "compliance is exchanged for understanding that, at some future time, the compliers will be able to gain favorable decisions from the power holders" (Marc Swartz et al. 1966:15). The upper echelon ruled, served as the supernaturals' representatives on behalf of man, provided peace and security, and made land available. The prominence of religion in the everyday life of all groups was reflected in the ubiquitous household altar (Muriel Weaver 1972: 129). The nobility surrounded the primary altar—it was to the temple that all directed their efforts for it was the symbol of the distribution of beneficence, the "point at which divine power entered the world and diffused outwards" (Wheatley 1969:14). Wheatley points out that the ceremonial center was a "ritual paradigm of the ordering of social interaction at the same time as it disseminated the values and inculcated the attitudes necessary to sustain it" (1971:478). The lower echelon received supernatural intervention, well-being, and land to farm in exchange for its labor, produce, and obeisance. With the rise in the power of militaristic groups, the ceremonies and beliefs of an area that were retained took on new meanings in new contexts. The temple became "the key redoubt of [that society's] political autonomy and military resistance" (Adams 1966:133, 148).

DANCE, STRATIFICATION, AND INTEGRATION.   If we postulate (on the basis of the preceding discussion of properties of dance, persuasive communication, and mechanisms of stratification and integration) that dance is a phenomenon which might have contributed to the stratification and political integration of a complex, heterogeneous society, we could expect to find evidence of the performance of dance and its objectification covarying with evidence of stratification and complexity.[6] Such evidence should be both quantitative and qualitative, that is to say, change in dance should correlate with change in other subsystems.[7] The distribution of dance material used by Kurath and Martí (1964b:2) is suggestive. Covariation, it should be noted, does not tell us about causation; it does not distinguish between four possible explanations that society influences dance, dance influences society, that there is a mutual dance-society interaction, and that exogenous intervention is a determinant. The argument for dance contributing to stratification and political integration would be strengthened if we could show that change in dance preceded change in society.

The use of dance to promote fertile plant and animal life, for example, or to bring rain is likely to be a preagricultural phenomenon: such is the evidence from cave paintings in Europe and Africa and hunter and gatherer ethnographic analogies. Dance may have been used to integrate society in the preagricultural and protoagricultural eras, but what we predict to be new is actually "fossilization" through ceramic, lithic, and painted representation, coincident with agricultural, social, and religious complexity. Thus we would expect to find a correlation between the number of representations and greater stratification and sociopolitical complexity as suggested in Figure 11. Not only would we expect to find greater quantities of dance objectification in the third period during which there seems to be increased population densities and stratification, but we would expect to find dance participation based on ranking-stratification. It seems

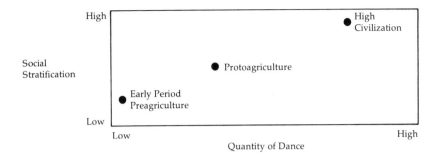

Figure 11.   Expected artifactual and documentary evidence of dance.

that the location of the dance objectification would also be related to these patterns.

Martí notes (Chapter 3) that among the Maya, dance was part of public and private festivities and had varied patterns according to its context. For the great feast celebrated at Maní, the citadel of the reigning Xiues dedicated to the Mayan Quetzalcoatl called Kukulcán, peoples from all over the peninsula flocked to compete in their offerings and observe dances. The Dance of the Standards was performed by eight hundred or more individuals. At other times, there were Okotbil dances for priests, a dance for women, and a dance of the Fire Ceremony where the most fervent faithful continued to dance over burning ashes. We have some indication of differential participation, but nothing of the order of the Aztec era. This may be because the Maya civilization was more homogenous, the population less dense, or that we have less information on Mayan music and dance.

Aztec dance, as reported by surviving members of the Aztecs to Fray Bernardino de Sahagún, and preserved in the Codices, reveals a definite indication of differential dance participation homologous with social stratification. These differences are revealed in who dances (participation criteria), what (meaning), and in the way they dance (form and style). Kurath writes that "the dichotomies of nobles and commoners, old and young, male and female, found choreographic expression. The two military orders symbolized the conflict of sky and light (eagle) against earth and darkness (ocelot or jaguar). These warriors also enacted the drama of sacrificer and victim, as aggressors against inadequately armed captives. The supreme drama of sacrifice was enacted by the priests in an active role, with slaves or captives in a passive role. Thus the lowest social rank played the most crucial part in the ceremonial drama along with the highest rank, and closed the circle of gradations" (1964b:83–84). Although Kurath distinguishes between religious and secular dances, I am not sure of the criteria for this separation in a theocratic state and thus do not make that distinction. The ritual organization was identified with the political: priests planned and orchestrated the various activities, and everyone participated according to predetermined hierarchical roles (ibid.:81). The high priest who personified Ilamatechuhtli had a special dance in which he stepped backwards and kicked up his heels. A slave, impersonating the "Ancient Lady" or "Mother Earth," performed a rather different, anguished dance before her death (ibid.:55). Higher officials, the ruler and his four upper officers and nobles, performed special dances during the calendric festivals, such as the elegant, slow Lordly Dance, Netecuitotlio, held every four years during the feast of Tititl, in Month 17 (ibid.:56). Nobles solemnly danced for the gods of earth and sun during Month 5 (ibid.:77). Kurath quotes Sahagún who informs us that the lords conscientiously prepared the feasts and dances: they counseled their sons to be conscientious about the dance and its accompaniment to please the deity who was everywhere (ibid.:62). Sometimes more than one thousand knights gathered to dance in the temple (ibid.:63), to participate in the serpentine dance, or during Xocotl Huetzí, to be paired with captives and, at other times, with ceremonial harlots. "A more unusual formation was the nobleman's dance in two rows. Representatives from Tenochtitlan and Tlaltelolco came together, facing each other; all danced very slowly; the dance proceeding in harmony. Sometimes Moctezuma joined them along with neighboring princes" (ibid.:82).

Seasonal ceremonies saw the nobles representing the conflict between summer and winter, sky and earth, light and dark, joined by women in a serpentine phallic dance to show the awakening of nature. Youths lept and performed elaborate footwork to symbolize the impregnation by the deities; women performed an ecstatic trance dance impersonating the goddess (ibid.:70, 72). There were also age grades–young men and women danced (ibid.:47); elders had other roles. There were even professional dancers, respected by rulers and rewarded by them, who performed.

At the next level of the social structure, the merchant guilds held separate ceremonies to special deities. For example, they performed a narcotic dance as part of ceremonies held before and after a trip, or merchants and feather workers danced with sacrificial slave captives "in frenzied circlings" in Panquetzaliztli (ibid.:82, 76). At the lowest level, sacrificial war captives impersonated deities before their sacrifice. Plebeians and serfs were the audience for the dances of the nobility. On some occasions, however, all strata of society danced together; for example, the plebeians joined the serpent dance of the nobles.

Festivities were held in which three to four thousand people participated; some of the dances were in praise of a ruler or great hero or principal. In such festivals, the nobility, priesthood, neophytes of seminaries, and general population participated; Martí cites Hernández's report that all sang and danced uniformly. Other festivities were organized to entertain the people, principals, or a visiting dignitary (ibid.:63). More than ten thousand Indians took part in the Mitote dance in which the elders, principals, and more important people danced in the middle, barely moving around a central altar; others, arranged in pairs, danced around them; the latter's pace was more rapid, and their steps and leaps were different (ibid.:65; see also Alfonso Caso 1958:78).

The setting of dance is significant for the argument that dance promotes and maintains stratification and integration. We are told that horizontal and vertical space designs have symbolic signification relating to the rain and sun deities and their directions and positions. Wheatley speaks of the ceremonial center as being a focal point for communication (1971:478). Dance images are created in the temples to emphasize the symbolic force of god and man, and the natural shape of certain men. In addition, the spatial levels of the setting for the performance enhanced the dramatic effect. Moreover, they also depict social structure: the rounds of nobles and commoners coursed along the level of the plaza and at the foot of the pyramids, while victims ascended the stairs. The stone representations at the temples are enduring, sometimes larger than life, and spaced with visible distinction (cf. Berlyne 1971:137 on the overpowering effects of size). From the architecture of Monte Alban (Ignacio Bernal 1969: 153–156), we know of the old Temple of the Dancing Figures or *danzantes* which cover the building. Bernal suggests these figures belong to Olmec II period at a time when writing was unknown. The figures have been interpreted as captives, testimonials to successful campaigns. Representations on ceremonial vessels and pots in homes are more frequent reminders, providing repetitive communication. Thus the human-made "landscape" was purposefully shaped (cf. S. Giedion 1960, Gyorgy Kepes 1972).

Conclusion

Were dance and its concomitant rites, and then their representation in enduring form, meant to influence god or man? Archaeological data, prehistory documents, theoretical conceptions of dance, persuasive communication, and sociopolitical change and ethnographic analogy appear to indicate that the Kurath-Martí argument of dance developing as an agrico-military aid vis-à-vis the divine may be too limited, that dance may indeed fulfill other functions. I hypothesize that the dances of Anáhuac were a vehicle to create, reflect, and reinforce social stratification and a centralized, integrated political organization encompassing diverse, geographically dispersed ethnic groups. The dancers were also re-created images of motional configurations set up in temples and at the home altar to emphasize the symbolic force of the human elite who were legitimized by divine sanction. Tests are called for to assess this hypothesis.

The examination of dance representation in time and space could be used as corroborative evidence of continuity, change, and process in other subsystems, particularly the sociopolitical; and thus to elucidate social systems. Flannery points out that "change in terms of quite minor deviations in one small part of a previously existing system . . . once set in motion . . . can expand greatly because of positive feedback" (1972:234). As an archaeological artifact, dance representation stands for human events and activities and is the result of human creation and is in dynamic association with other variables. Where we notice quantitative and stylistic change, we are encouraged to seek antecedent and successive phenomena. Change in dance may lag behind change in other domains or may be the forerunner; ethnographic data support both possibilities. This position counters that of Adams who argues that

> Art focused on myth and ritual creates special problems
> of distortion in the study of sociocultural change. It tends
> to deal mainly with traditionalized, symbolic themes, which
> probably always were most resistant to change. In so doing,
> it avoids representation of other activities, particularly in the

political and economic sectors, which we might expect to find most sensitive to the trends at the core of the Urban Revolution. Useful and important as representations in art are, therefore, their primary contribution is not to the interpretation of broad institutional patterns but to the fuller understanding of the same limited range of ritualized activities that the remainder of the archeological record already tends to overemphasize. (1966:30–31)

He fails to understand that art, myth, and ritual can take on new meanings. Viewing dance within the perspectives of nonverbal persuasive communication, semiotics, and symbolic interaction, its representation could be used in conjunction with other evidence, as a subsystem to expand archaeology's data base and to help solve ideational and behavioral problems.

This case study has explored the relationship between two important domains of human life, religion and politics, and the reliance upon common symbolic imagery to create and maintain the sociopolitical system. The next case, Ubakala dance-plays, focuses on the role of dance in conflict mediation.

Case B. Ubakala Dance-Plays: Mediators of Paradox

The Ubakala Igbo of Nigeria perform dance-plays that generate pleasure, reinforce shared perceptions and values, reaffirm social bonds, and assist in dissipating tension. These are functions generally ascribed to dance in the anthropological literature. However, the dance-plays are also a vehicle to introduce innovation, mediate paradoxes in anticipated or actual expressions of the Ubakala world view, and encapsulate phases of social drama (in Victor Turner's terms, marked disturbances in social life). This study will focus on the dance-play as a mediator of paradox.[1]

As in all societies, the fundamental values of the Ubakala catalyze social action. However, the pursuit of one part of an antinomy to the exclusion of the other creates dilemma and social drama. In this context, the dance-play can adjust imbalances, working through the dialectics of social life. This is expecially true for the women and youth groups who are excluded from formal, societywide decision-making structures. When a world view is expressed such that it violates another equally valid tenet and threatens an individual or group, the dance-play can contain, modify, or reverse it. The dance-play mediates between persons and their situations in much the same way, as Dell Hymes notes, that speech mediates between persons and their situations; the dance-play serves as a political lobby in the American sense.

This study examines, first, the five world view principles which seem to embrace Ubakala existence and describe their expression in the dance-plays, which are media for socializing individuals to share values and for ordering social relations, including managing those tensions which do not arise from marked disturbances in social life. Second, the study explores the dance-play's potential for encapsulating phases of social drama and mediating paradoxes generated by contradictory Ubakala values. Third, it focuses on some factors which might explain the dance-play's potential, namely, memories of un-heeded dance-play communications, a dynamic concept of play, and the cybernetic potential of dance with its languagelike properties, multisensory components, and clustering of variables which have been shown to be persuasive.

World View Principles

The Ubakala world view, like most general conceptions of order, permeates many fields and situations. It is condensed in the dance-play which synthesizes and circulates meaning from many domains and specific contexts. Five general principles seem to embrace Ubakala existence: At one level of abstraction, the dance-plays symbolically represent (1) fertility and continuity, (2) egalitarianism and an orientation toward competitive achievement, (3) innovation and group advancement, (4) respect and seniority, and (5) reciprocity. From another perspective, they are continuity, competition, innovation, respect, and reciprocity. The dance-play, *nkwa*, contributes to the ordering of social relations (cf. Firth 1973, Gluckman 1954) through communication in song texts and dance themes about the limits and contours of social roles; through the participation criteria for different dance-plays; and through the correlations of movement style and structure, music, and costume to social roles.

The primary Ubakala value is fertility and continuity. Ubakala emphasize birth within the context of marriage and the child's anticipated behavior. According to the Ubakala, an individual, having received the gift of life from his parents, has the moral obligation to pass this gift along in order that reincarnation may occur and future generations will not die out. Therefore, women's dance-plays celebrate birth, young peoples' *nkwa* anticipate it through references to marriage and child-bearing, and the *nkwa* for second burials help to assure fertility and continuity by sending the deceased to the other world so that they may be reincarnated. When a normal, healthy child is born, usually in the father's compound, the women perform the *nkwa* to rejoice. Then, after about three hours, they sing and dance their way to the compounds of the mother's kin to inform them of the joyous event through the dance-play, gathering additional dancers as it moves from compound to compound. In this *nkwa*, in which only married women who have given birth perform, the dancers highlight procreative body parts, birth exercises, and child care gestures. The song texts stress normative sex, spouse relations, and parental roles.

The dance in Nkwa Oñu Nwa entitled "Ubakala, I am Coming" celebrates the birth of a child and includes the phrase "Praise to the expert in bearing children." Thus the women dance in honor of those who bear children and thereby achieve high status and prestige. In "Dimle Dimle" from Nkwa Oñu Nwa, the women's group sings, "Whether or not I know how to behave, exercise patience and live with me"; and in the "Mna Nwayi Aruola" of Nkwa Umunna (Outsider Relations' Society dance-play), performed by a village's married women from the same natal village, the song text, "An old woman whose beauty is fading away is not seen," suggests the proper behavior of husbands after the beauty of youth has passed. Participation criteria reflect descent and affinal groupings. For the Nkwa Oñu Nwa, the father's womenfolk first dance and then join with the women's relatives in their compounds. In Nkwa Umunna, the married women from the same natal village seek each other but not only to celebrate the fact that they have issues in common but also as an attempt, as outsiders, to counter the bonds of blood that unite their husbands.

Nkwa Edere (Young Girls' Shimmy dance-play), and other *nkwa* for youth, with their vigorous upper torso shimmy and pelvic movements, direct attention to pubescent body changes, the energy and strength for procreation and nurturance, and the emergence of a new generation with its own innovations. These dance-plays are performed on festive occasions such as market days, moonlight nights, the New Yam Festival, and the Christian holidays of Christmas and Easter.

Nkwa Uko and Nkwa Ese focus on the reward for productive and nurturant roles: ancestor honor and reincarnation. These dance-plays are performed on the occasion of "second burials," feasts which eulogize, propitiate, and show respect for the respected deceased as well as help move the deceased to the world of the ancestors. The participants are the deceased's mature kin. Emphasis is placed on the need for lineage continuity and the themes of fate and destiny. Thus the "Uwam le He" soloist in the Nkwa Uko sings repeatedly, "I have remembered my fate, my fate." Nkwa Ese also features the deceased man's protective role: attention is drawn to the history of lineage, bravery, and cooperation.

Ubakala dance-plays further contribute to fertility and continuity by enhancing group or societywide emotional bonds. The dance-plays insure courtship opportunities and motivate men and women to create a nuclear family; they rank units to facilitate a division of labor and organize various other activities; they mark changes from one social status to another; and they manage potentially disruptive tensions. When lineages unite to celebrate the birth of a kinsman, the group dancing, especially when the movements are performed in unison and in a circular spatial pattern, often fosters a feeling of solidarity. The song text reinforces this: a frequently sung couplet is "Ubakala, we are coming . . . Peace be with you as we come together." The Ubakala facilitate courtship by providing an occasion, the dance-play event, to which everyone is usually attracted. The holiday performances of youth are especially conducive to the initiation of interfamily integration. Dance-play participation criteria, style, and structure distinguish individuals on the bases of age, sex, and achievement. This social differentiation facilitates a division of labor and a chain of command which further helps integrate society. For example, when the age of both sexes is relatively similar but the biological and social roles are the most different, namely, when the women are life-givers and the men are life-takers, the dance movements, in terms of space, time, and effort diverge most markedly. The male warriors' tension, rapid speed, and varied spatial use signify destruction just as the mothers' relaxed movement, slow speed, and limited spatial use signify construction. Further, excelling in dance-play performance provides one of the few ways young men and women gain public recognition.

The dance-plays which accompany social transitions–birth, imminent marriage, and death–symbolize and display status transformations and new ranking, besides celebrating, anticipating, and working through issues related to major life changes. *Nkwa di iche iche* are parts of rites of passage in Van Gennep's (1960) and Victor Turner's theories. The transitions in terms of many ritual forms of separation, transition, and reaggregation are not, however, contained within a dance-play performance event as they are in an initiation rite of the

Zambian Ndembu people. *Nkwa* performances refer to various phases of transition and the division of labor. Changes in movement mark the crossing of social frontiers.

Marriage involves the separation of the bride from her natal village; giving birth marks the reincarnation of an ancestor in an infant's sentient existence and a female's qualifications to join women's groups. Nkwa Edere focuses on imminent separation, a girl leaving her own home to marry and live among her husband's kin. Dance-plays for youth point to the transition to adulthood, courtship, and marriage: a girl leaves her own home to marry, live among her husband's kin, and have an independent economic life; males participate in ritual and political life. *Nkwa* for a second burial of an aged man or woman marks the transition to the ancestor world and the realignment of social and political relations. In order to take a title (see Onuora Nzekwu 1963, 1964), become a member of a cult or age-grade, or attain majority, an individual may be required to go through certain initiation rites that involve dancing (see Rems Umeasiegby 1969:23).

Furthermore, dance-plays promote Ubakala continuity since participants can cope with psychic tension through "anticipatory psychic management" (Hanna and Hanna 1968*b*) and "catharsis." Anticipatory psychic management, one method of achieving socialization, prepares an individual for a threatening experience by rehearsing it until its potentially destructive emotional impact is reduced to manageable proportions.[2] Usually, repetition, to manage or assimilate a situation or feeling, is of a past traumatic event. However, repetition can also help manage anticipated events. Among the Ubakala, anticipatory psychic management apears, understandably, to most commonly relate to the tensions of adulthood, for example, birth and death. Typical of anticipating womanhood is the Nkwa Edere for young girls. In several of the specific dances, the movement refers to anxieties and emotional occasions in the life of an adult woman, for example, heterosexual relations, becoming a wife and living among strangers, being fertile, and giving birth. Such anxieties find symptomatic expression: "When a small girl is put into a womanly state, she doesn't know if she'll be able to deliver, and she begins to be afraid" is an illustrative dance theme. Aspects of both Nkwa Uko and Nkwa Ese can be interpreted as anticipatory psychic management because they familiarize participants with the rituals accompanying death, reminding them of their own deaths and their opportunity to eventually achieve ancestor status (cf. Stan-

8   Socialization through dance begins early in Nigeria. Photograph
by William John Hanna.

ley Keleman 1975). Such is the message of the Nkwa Uko dance entitled "The Deceased are Blessed."

Catharsis is the experience of reducing anxiety or conflict through the release of energy and frustrations; distressful emotions are discharged. The dance that results in cathartic experience, averting harmful alternatives, is similar to the tension reducing rituals of rebellion or dramatized conflicts reported by Gluckman (1954) and Norbeck (1963). Enervating movements, deviant movement patterns, and/or transgressive criticism characterize cathartic behavior. The dance-play serves as a legitimate vehicle for otherwise prohibited or inappropriate social commentary, criticism, joking, or aggression.

Dance, like other forms of intense physical activity, "often provides a healthy fatigue or distraction which may abate a temporary rage crisis and thus allow *more enduring personality patterns to regain ascendancy*" (Munroe 1955:630). An African psychiatrist put it this way: "The rhythm, vigorous movements, their coordination and synchronization, tend to induce some degree of catharsis . . . The essential psychological function of the dance, in fact, is the prevention of depression and accumulation of other psychic stresses" (Lambo 1965: 41).[3] The Ubakala Nkwa Oñu Nwa and Nkwa Umunna appear to provide catharsis for women's empathic fears about the uncertainties of a successful birth, sanctions for failure, and pain related to marriage and childbirth. Similarly Nkwa Uko and Ese are outlets for some of the emotional stress that accompanies the loss of a loved one and fear of the deceased's spirits.

A second principle of the Ubakala world view is egalitarianism and an orientation toward competitive achievement. Everyone is assumed to have a chance to gain prominence. It is said that no one knows the womb that bears the chief. So in the dance-play, skill, innovative capability, and persuasive proficiency are the bases for *nkwa* group leadership and a dancer's acclaim. Young people's dance-play groups operate relatively free of parental supervision; herein they have the opportunity to compete with each other and develop political experience. Through the dance-plays, agricultural and trading success, wealth, old age, and other achievements are encouraged as personal goals and as bases for respecting others. These may be limited to the dance group, but they usually have larger social implications related to the third principle of innovation and group advancement. Wealth is the theme of "Omara Mma N'ibi Akwukwo Ego" from the Nkwa Umunna; the leader and the group sing, "Zik, a young man is good at printing currency notes. When you look at him you will be convinced." Zik is the nickname of Dr. Nnamdi Azikiwe, former president of Nigeria and leader of the nationalist movement that obtained independence for the country in 1960. The Nkwa Ese emphasizes competition and achievement in the dramatic portrayal and commemoration of an individual warrior's great feats.

Related to achievement is the third principle of innovation and group "getting up," enhancing its status vis-à-vis other groups. Group formation, it should be noted, is situational. In the dance-plays, performers allude to people who do things which retard innovation endeavors and prevent the acquisition of power and material goods. Braggadocio about success and the presentation of new dance movements which arouse admiration reflect progress. Each generation is supposed to effect some kind of innovation for the improvement of society. Individualism exists, but it is rooted in group solidarity. Competing kin are supposed to assemble in the spirit of amity from time to time, for example, at the dance-play performances for the birth celebration and religious propitiation service of the second burials; and villages will unite in contests with other clans. All members of a village are expected to be present in support of its market.

Dancers symbolically portray group cooperation for common goals when they form a circular spatial pattern. An increase in a group's population indicates its "getting up." In the women's Nkwa Oñu Nwa, the lead singer asks the members of the dancing group and audience to "rejoice with me, rejoice because my child gave birth to a child."

Innovative, deviant movement patterns[4] occur in the Nkwa Edere Waltz dance. Through parody, the girls mime the heterosexual physical contact found "abroad," which, from the Ubakala perspective, is immoral behavior. The girls suggestively caress each other, a less threatening event than boys and girls behaving similarly in public— even in the *nkwa* medium. New patterns of social interaction are thus presented in the "traditional" (cf. Hanna 1965, 1974) vehicle of the *nkwa* and thereby the strange is made familiar. The *nkwa* does not try to match reality, but to create a model for it, providing individuals with an opportunity to be aroused, amused, and develop a new consciousness for possibly accepting such patterns. For those who may leave the village to live in the urban areas, an opportunity is provided to anticipate and learn to cope with a different kind of behavior which is acceptable there.

A fourth principle of the Ubakala world view is respect for au-

9   Dance reflects and influences culture: the Nkwa Edere, Ubakala, Nigeria. Photograph by William John Hanna.

thority which is largely based on seniority. Ubakala reveal this on the occasions of *nkwa* performances in deciding who is entitled to a second burial and in the participation criteria for the dance-plays for birth and death. Only the preeminent elderly are entitled to a second burial, and those who have a family and have thereby gained a certain measure of prestige are the key performers. The themes of youth dance-plays about chiefs, men's yam productivity, and properly greeting one's elders and chiefs also manifest respect. In "Una Ahula Eze Ayi Nabia" from Nkwa Umu Oma (Teenage dance-play), the leader sings, "You have seen our chief coming"; "Come respect him; come greet the chief, come pet his neck." The Ubakala perform *nkwa di iche iche* in honor of living leaders as well as former leaders who have died.

The fifth principle is reciprocity. The *nkwa* event and performers, with their participation criteria and song and dance themes, mirror the interacting relationships of the child and parent, of the family and its connections, and of the living and the dead. Dance-plays celebrate child birth and good parental care: children contribute to work, protection, and parental old-age security. Furthermore, children are the key participants in their parents' second burials to insure their journey to the world of the ancestors. Besides, there is within the dance-play another expression of the value of reciprocity: the performer expects hospitality. For example, if not received in a friendly manner when performing their *nkwa di iche iche* to communicate "important news," Ubakala women express their displeasure through the dance-play medium by singing of the misdemeanor for all to hear. Thus they register the violation of the reciprocity code. The dance-play call and response patterns also reflect interpersonal reciprocity.

Thus far in the discussion of dance-plays, I have suggested that the *nkwa* has a confirmatory intent in promoting cultural values and ordering social relations through performance occasions; purposes; participation criteria; messages about the limits and contours of age-sex and other roles in song texts and dance themes; the correlation of movement style, structure, music, and costume with social roles; integration; and tension management. The dance-play seems to be reflective and refractive, having clarifying qualities that stress values in a gentle and pleasurable didactic mode. It seems to provide a safety-valve for strong emotion. Now I would like to turn to the redressive potential of Ubakala dance-plays. It should be noted that the confirmatory and redressive functions are not mutually exclusive.

Turner points out that Radcliffe-Brown viewed symbolic behavior as a dependent phenomenon, whereas he tries to give it ontological status (1974:57). In pursuit of this, he points to fields where paradigms are formulated, established, and become social dramas—marked disturbances in social life. Turner's view of the social world as a dynamic process is compatible with the Ubakala world view and is consequently useful in analyzing the dance-plays. Dance is what Turner (1977) calls a "well-developed subjunctive mode of cultural flow-reflexivity." The subjunctive mode includes desire, supposition, hypotheses, and possibility, that is, positing models for future thought and action. Dance can comment on systems of thought, sustaining them or undermining them through critiques of institutions, policies, or personages. In contrast to the subjunctive mode is the indicative mode of everyday life. These modes overlap and interdigitate in concrete sociocultural action. I would add that at times of crisis a subjunctive dance mode may become indicative.

Mediation of Paradoxes and Social Drama

The dance-play functions in much the same way as a shaman who mediates unbalanced forces in a healing ritual. Mediation involves exhibiting indirect causation, effecting, or reconciling by action. This process includes inciting to action and creatively transforming potentiality into actuality. The dance-plays mediate social relations and political situations through encapsulating the issues and phases of social dramas. The four phases are (1) a breach of the norms of a social group, (2) a mounting crisis, (3) a legal or ritual redressive process, and (4) public and symbolic expression of an irreparable schism or conciliation (Turner 1977:38). The *nkwa* may communicate the breach, foment the crisis, ameliorate the conflict (or at least hold it in suspension so that it is visually present, viewable, and ponderable), and proclaim the schism or celebrate the reintegration.

In examining the Ubakala world view, one can identify opposing principles which catalyze social action. First, an individualistic competitive achievement orientation is juxtaposed with the need for cooperation and interdependence (community spirit, group solidarity, and sharing the wealth: personal aggrandizement is not emphasized). Second, the desire and expectation of change often run counter to the principle of respect for authority which is largely based on seniority; thus, innovation generally involves criticism or rejection of what those older than oneself have established. Third, the principle of respect and obedience to leaders is opposed to the egalitarian distaste for assertive authority and the norm of bringing things into the open. The latter is what Uchendu calls "transparent living," a pattern which sometimes leads to irreverence and mockery. The dance-plays contribute to mediating these three paradoxes and maintaining a delicate balance. The *nkwa di iche iche* also contribute to mediating the Ubakala oppositions of in-group versus out-group, male versus female, and descent versus affinity. The ambivalence around these conflicting values creates potential hostility.

The occasions for many dance-play performances provide a virtually captive audience. Ubakala allow a special kind of license in the dance-play which protects the individual and group from libel. Mead (1946) speaks of expression in "counterpoint": dance permits emotional communication prohibited in everyday life. Dance-plays are a kind of ritual of rebellion (Gluckman 1954). In the *nkwa* women and youth can speak publicly, venting strong emotions without breaking those norms of etiquette related to interactions with males and seniors. They can assert themselves in those arenas of adult, male-dominated, formal public affairs from which they are otherwise excluded. Thus, there are digs at the conceited, protests against the overbearing, and movement and song text novelties for the community. But the *nkwa* has the potential for more than catharsis and unification of the group: it can guard against the misuse of power and produce social change without violence. However, *nkwa* messages are often implicit; and a symbolic system is a weak vehicle of control unless enforcement is implied. The *nkwa* is a political forum of coercion in a shame-oriented society. Energy (force), the ultimate means of social control, is symbolically represented.

The *nkwa* has an element of "liminality" which Turner (1974:253) characterizes as a temporary dissolution of the usual structural statuses and customs and an unusual introduction of egalitarianism. In this period thought and bodily energy are liberated. A potentially unlimited series of alternative social arrangements can be played with, existing programs undermined, and new ones generated. Contrary ways of acting and thinking, perhaps ultimately unworkable or with disastrous consequences, or new ways with positive impact, may be prevented. Criticism and challenge in some circumstances can provoke retaliation and revenge. The *nkwa* is a mechanism for distancing the accuser from the offender in much the same way as joking relations among nonkin, witchcraft, masking, and possession behavior. It is a vehicle for negotiating separate personalities, individual biographies, into a shared entity, transforming personal experience and thus creating a certain degree of anonymity.

How does the dance-play work in the mediation of paradox and social drama? Relevant considerations are the memories of unheeded dance-play communications which generate contemporary responses to dance-play messages, a dynamic concept of play, and the cybernetic potential of dance as a language with multisensory components and the clustering of variables which have been shown to be persuasive.

1. The famous 1929 "Women's War" in which the dance-play communication went unheeded illustrates the potential of the *nkwa* in social drama and change. Repercussions were widespread both on local and "international" levels. Contemporary politicians and leaders frequently refer to this notorious episode of feminine protest; they remember how the women moved the mighty British to alter their

10   Women in praise and pursuit of power: Ubakala, Nigeria. Photograph by William John Hanna.

colonial administration of Eastern Nigeria. (Harry Gailey 1970 provides one of the fullest accounts.)

Judith Van Allen (1972) and Caroline Ifeka-Moller (1975) point out that women have traditionally had autonomy and power based on their solidarity, expressed in their own political institutions. Meetings held when needed (with women of wealth and generosity taking leading roles), market networks, kin groups, and the right to use strikes, boycotts, and force can effect change. Mazi Njaka (1974:122) argues that women's intrusion in the affairs of the state and their imposition of sanctions makes them the custodians of the "constitution." Because women marry outside the village group into which they were born (their own *umunna*), their kin organization cuts across the units of any one level of political structure and often beyond it. The organization is thus integrative and powerful in its representation of numerous groupings behind any single member. The women's boycott is sometimes called "sitting on a man." The aggrieved gather at the compound of an offender and dance and sing to detail the problems (M. Green 1964). Movement presents a dynamic image and emphasizes the argument as well as releasing physical and psychological energy and tension. The accompanying song with its potent ridicule and satire serves as a vehicle for specific social criticism.

The British government was generally aware of the potential for public disturbance in this cultural expression. Thus its native council was empowered by the 1901 Proclamation, Section 36(3) to regulate "native plays . . . a gathering of natives in any public street or market, or in any house, building, or in any compound adjoining a public street or market for the purpose of dancing or playing native music" (C.O. 591/2 in Samuel Nwabara 1965:188–189). In some areas licenses and permission from the District Commissioner were necessary to hold plays.

The first phase of the Women's War began with a *breach* of understanding between women and the colonial government. In 1928 the British government introduced taxation applicable to men. Late in 1929 women believed incorrectly that this tax was to be extended to them. This misunderstanding signaled the beginning of an example of the "sex solidarity and political power which women can exercise when they choose to do so" (C. Meek 1937:201). They viewed taxation as an infringement upon their economic competitive patterns. Since women had not become representatives of the colonial government, they did not see the benefits from the imposition of taxes. The women's economic and political grievances coalesced: they were aggrieved by what they considered abusive and exortionist practices of many government appointed warrant chiefs (e.g., some obtained wives without paying full bride wealth; others took property improprietously).

In the midst of a depression era, the spark igniting the conflagration was supplied by a young assistant District Officer in Bende Division. (This was the same division where the District Officer, A. L. Weir, deceived the people in 1927 about the purpose of the initial tax census.) Because census registers were incomplete and inaccurate, the administrative officers were supposed to revise the initial counts in their spare time. In October, Captain John Cook, who had taken over from Weir, decided on his own authority to obtain information on the number of men, women, children, and livestock.

The massive protest was incited when the Warrant Chief Okugo, of Oloko Village near the town of Aba, employed a school teacher, Mark Emeruwa, to take charge of the census. Inquiring about Nwanyeruwa's (a local woman) possessions, the messenger engaged in argument and physical scuffle with this angry woman who reported the incident to her village women's meeting. The second phase of the social drama was a mounting *crisis* as women gathered to discuss what had occurred. The alarmed women sent palm leaves, symbols of warning and signals of distress, to women of neighboring and distant villages (including those in the Umuahia area), summoning them to Oloko to join the protest. Women from far and near, even pregnant women, met in the Oloko square on November 24.

The third stage was the potentially *redressive* process of "sitting on a man" which usually works to resolve conflicts. (The *nkwa* medium serves as a vehicle to express strong sentiment which, in turn, has the effect of catalyzing action to ameliorate the cause of dissatisfaction.) The irate women trooped to the mission that employed Emeruwa, the chief's messenger, to demonstrate against him. They camped in front of his compound at the Niger Delta Mission and "sat on him"–the man was kept from sleeping and carrying out his usual tasks. They danced and sang outside the mission compound all night, eating, drinking palm wine, and singing that Nwanyeruwa had been told to count her goats, sheep, and people (Nwabara 1965: 231). A song was quickly improvised to meet the situation and the women sent their message. However, no satisfactory response was forthcoming.

The next day, with the problem still unresolved, the social drama reached the *schism* phase. The women became more excited and went to the chief's compound. They beseiged Chief Okugo at his house and demanded his cap of office. He escaped to seek refuge on the Native Court compound. Captain Cook met over twenty-five thousand women in the market to assure them they were not to be taxed; however, the women insisted that Chief Okugo and Emeruwa be arrested and tried. Skeptical of government assurances that they were not to be taxed, the women's rampages began to spread. Late in December, the women forced the Umuahia warrant chiefs to surrender their caps, symbols of authority. In Aba, women sang and danced to no avail about their antipathy toward the chiefs and the court messengers. Then they proceeded to attack and loot the European trading stores and Barclays Bank and to break into the prison and release the prisoners (Margery Perham 1937:208).

The riots spread, involving about ten thousand women in two provinces. Destruction was directed primarily toward the warrant chiefs and buildings representing this detested authority. The most extreme violence was triggered by a car accident and heated pas-

sions. In one of the worst episodes, in the town of Opobo in Calabar Province, the police opened fire: thirty-two women were killed
and thirty-one wounded. (See *Nigerian Government Reports* 1930*a* and
1930*b*, Perham 1937:206–220). The women's rapid mobilization was
possible because of their strong society organizations and effective
communication networks based on concentration in the markets and
dispersal along the trade routes. Colonial government reorganiza-
tions in 1930 and 1931 followed the reports of two commissions of
inquiry and anthropological study. The women succeeded in their
destruction of the warrant chief system. The cost would have been
less had the *nkwa* audience been more attentive initially. Thus the
contemporary women's dance-play performance serves as a metaphor for their power.

   2. Related to memories or stories about dramatic instances of unheeded dance-plays is a dynamic concept of play which may help
to explain the role of the *nkwa* in conflict management. Schechner
(1973:28–36), building upon Johan Huizinga (1955) and Loizos (1969),
rejects Huizinga's exclusion of function in the concept of play and
accepts the possibilities of play as a school or practice: it is a safe
arena for exploring beyond the known or working through problems,
an exercise of mental or physical faculties, and/or having survival
value in being a derivation from life situations of flight, fight, sexual,
and eating behavior. Schechner points out that play maintains a "regular, crisis-oriented expenditure of kinetic energy" which can be
"switched from play energy into crisis or fight energy." Answering
the question of how animals (and persons) tell the difference between
play and "for real," he suggests the following: "Ritualized behavior,
including performances, are means of continually testing the boundaries between play and 'for real.' The 'special ordering of time and
place' most observers note in play–even animal play–are signals that
the behavior[s] taking place within such brackets are 'only play.' Even
so, confusions happen, and placative gestures, or the presence of a
referee, are necessary to keep the play in hand" (ibid.:33). Colonial
administrators settled the issue of whether dance-plays and other
similar performances were real by banning such public assemblies
in urban areas; missionaries helped the suppression in the rural
areas.

   In performing the dance-play, the serious and nonserious, reality
and fantasy, and visible and invisible situationally intermingle, separate, and merge. This is especially true when dance-play messages
do not evoke what performers feel to be a satisfactory response.
There is pleasure in a synesthetic medium with its motion and rhy-

thm related to ontogenetic and other psychobiological bases. For the Ubakala, playing is somewhat improvisational, strategic, futuristic, and often crisis-oriented. They take a gaming perspective: the *nkwa* is a rational attempt to gain an optimal outcome in a dynamic situation. However, the course a dance-play takes is uncertain, for it deals with humans in an emotionally charged setting. A dance-play performed to maintain cultural values or to mediate a paradox may indeed stimulate a crisis.

3. Another consideration in the dynamic sociopolitical role of the dance-play is the processual communication model of dance. It suggests the cybernetic potential of dance, its languagelike properties, multisensory components, and clustering of persuasive variables. (See Chapters 3–6.) Here the concept of flow or altered state of consciousness is relevant for the Ubakala spoke of feeling pleasure through the dance. The young are further excited by courtship possibilities, and palm wine is an additional adult stimulant. The energy expenditure, heat, and perspiration affect everyone.

In this study of Ubakala dance-plays, I have tried to illustrate some patterns and functions of a dance form in the conduct of a particular group's social life. My concern is much the same as the sociolinguists in their study of spoken language in social interaction. The dance-play is a symbolic instrument operating in changing fields of social relationships. As conservative and innovative ritual, the Ubakala dance-play promotes shared perspectives and ordered social relationships; it also mediates paradoxes arising from contradictory values and encapsulates phases of social drama. Infused with social values and political situations, the dance-play is a form of information processing and social action involving an interplay of mind and body. The dance-play is part of the Ubakala ethos of movement: "My brother, my sister, try hard," they say.

However, social and political conflict may be expressed through a more obvious concretization–physical attack. The next chapter examines the involvement of dance in symbolic or actual aggression.

7   Warrior Dances:
Transformations through Time

THE SYMBOLIC REPRESENTATION of confrontation in dance may lead to actual assaults or interweave with the dynamics of social relations, religion, and politics. One such symbolic encounter occurs in warrior dances. This chapter explores the relationship of dance to the warrior tradition over time in Africa: its multifarious manifestations, the Eurocolonial impact on warrior dances, and the transformation of "traditional" warrior dance in the postcolonial independence period. The warrior tradition has been characterized as capturing such aspects of human organization and symbolism as the idea of adulthood and related notions of self-reliance and the concept of manhood linked to violent valor and sexual virility (Ali Mazrui 1975).

First, some preliminary qualifications and comments on why the dance form of human behavior is so commonly a part of the warrior tradition. There are problems with the concepts, "warrior," and "tradition." The concept of "tradition" in dance has been misunderstood. From the evidence we have, dance seems to be characterized by change. The concept of "warrior dance" refers to dance which is performed by real or symbolic warriors. "War" will be used broadly to include national battles, group raids, dyadic affrays, and the isolated manslaying to prove manhood. There is no full study of the relation of dance to the warrior tradition. Rather than a historical thread within a single ethnic group, woven from precolonial through colonial times to independence, one finds scattered and often superficial descriptions of warrior dances in the literature. By the time many scholars were on the African scene, pacification had occurred.[1] Some colorful descriptions refer to mock attacks, frenzied leaping and charging, wild plunging and thrusting of spears, savage weapon brandishing, abandoned gesticulating faces, eyes transfixed on invisible enemies, dilated nostrils, perspiring bodies, nervous trembling, unflagging vigor, blood-curdling shrieks, roars of defiance, and exhilarating throbbing sonic accompaniment. However, these phrases are hardly useful to the serious social scientist. Warrior dance description and discussion of its purpose, function, and the relationship between dance behavior and other sociocultural phenomena are also limited because of the underdeveloped status of African dance studies.[2] This discussion of African dance and the warrior tradition must therefore be incomplete.

It is important to point out that on the African continent with its eight hundred to one thousand ethnic groups, not all have a "warrior tradition" (cf. Claude Welch 1975). Sometimes entire groups migrated or parts seceded from a group in order to avoid confrontation; others surrendered to preclude confrontation. The Lala were not alone in their behavior in the event of a raid: they would desert their villages and seek refuge in the nearby hills until marauders had left (Norman Long 1968:80). Through conquest or voluntary submission to a warrior tribe or nation, some groups were forced to acquire the warrior tradition.

The notion that warrior tradition encapsulates adulthood and self-reliance must be qualified. Warriors achieved the physical characteristics of adulthood and usually an increased detachment from their parents' nuclear family. However, in many instances, the warrior tradition was a "liminal" (Turner 1967) transitional status toward adulthood and social power. The Samburu gerontocracy forbid the young warriors age-set (*moran*) from marrying and kept them in a state of delayed adolescence until they could be replaced by a new age-set, the creation of which the elders determined. Among the Zulu, Shaka's warriors were by no means independent; they were a symbol of his independence. He controlled nearly every aspect of their conduct and careers, extending the time they remained unmarried and determining the sequence of age-grades that was previously regulated by the natural progress of the life cycle (Eugene Walter 1969:148, 190).[3]

Warriors are usually thought of as having the ability to take life and to give life (sexually and in not killing). Dance, and especially warrior dance, may be a symbol of power representing, expressing, and communicating self-control and dominance. One kind of power, such as the physical or symbolic self, may be used to secure another (over others) through the dancing self or others' dancing, a substitution of proxy for self. Symbolism in warrior dances is linked to the notion of play, borrowing or adopting patterns that appear in other contexts where they achieve immediate and obvious ends. The mimetic fight is divorced from the original motivation and is qualitatively distinct. There may be exaggerated uneconomical motor patterns, the sequence may be reordered with more repetition than usual, sequences may be fragmented, or not completed. The warrior dance is a playing with the body, with ideas, and emotions, and this play allows a safe examination of problems and the separation or merging of the serious and nonserious. Play, Schechner (1973) argues, maintains a regular, crisis-oriented expenditure of kinetic energy which can be transformed from play energy into fight energy. The boundary between play and reality may, of course, dissolve.

Dance in Pre-European Independence Era

Evidence from the oral histories reported in the ethnographic literature suggests that, in the precolonial period, warrior dances were status markers for groups and individuals; vehicles for sexual display; physical preparation for war; affective readying for violent encounters (incitement, communion, we/they distancing); religious behavior; displacement; and political behavior. These categories are neither mutually exclusive nor necessarily independent.

Status Markers

Dancing makes manifest and communicates many social and cultural categories and value concepts and distinguishes the ordinary from the extraordinary. It marks status changes, including the passage from childhood to youth or adulthood. Dances are frequently part of rites of passage in which separation, transition, and reaggregation occur. Moreover, in the transitional period, dance is usually an educational medium for adult male physical and moral behavior. Military training and discipline in dance are frequently the mode of status change, while emergence dances celebrate the new maturation level and are an emblem of the successful status change.

Although the Shilluk had no elaborate and prolonged rites of passage for youths to acquire manhood status, participation in a *cong bul* dance for warriors and their partners was the measure of achieving adult status and a symbol of reintegration with the community after a short period of segregation (P. Howell 1941). In Ruanda, the Tutsi kingdom had several years' training for the young men, the *intore* or chosen ones, who lived at the court of the *mwami* (king) or a chief allowed to recruit an army. The *mwami* asked his clients to bring their sons to his court for training. One hundred and fifty to two hundred young men, chosen on a wide territorial base, learned the qualities of manhood–self-mastery and military courage–and received instruction in war and raiding through warlike dances. They memorized and recited the poems exalting the extraordinary bravery and boldness of their warrior forbears (Maquet 1961:109, 117–119).

Among the Ndembu there were special high status cults with specific dances for killers. Hunting men or animals epitomized masculinity in a society jurally dominated by the principle of matrilineal descent. Part of the prayer at the onset of the *wuyang's* ritual, "We want a man who can sleep with ten women in one day, a great . . . hunter," points to the associated qualifications of virility and a disregard for the usual norms for a blood shedder (Turner 1957:29, 59, 203, 380). The *mukanda* initiation rite for boys inculcated these values with the dominant symbol, *chikoli*, a strong hard tree, signifying strength, an erect penis, and the masculine virtues of courage and skill. During circumcision, dancing occurred near the tree (Turner 1967:354) and, on the last day, in the rites of return, each boy, holding an axe, performed the *ku-tomboka* solo war dance (ibid.:259–260) signifying aspiration to the high status cult for killers.

Dance is also an indicator of individual achievement and prowess during victory celebrations. At the *nwole* feast of the Nuba, only the youths who killed an enemy could take part in a special dance in which they displayed symbolic trophies to proclaim their feats–a shield or spear for every man killed, a gourd for every woman (Nadel 1947:141). For the Lele, *tamo* referred to ferocity and courage, and a youth had to prove his manhood by killing a man or man-slaying animal, such as a leopard, and bring back proof of the dead. This allowed him to make a triumphal dance around the village to the beat of the special *nkoko* drum played only to celebrate mankilling (Douglas 1963:187). Sonjo warriors were given prominent roles at most major rites; they were the principal dancers at the harvest festival during which they gave exhibitions of strenuous dancing (Robert Gray 1965:55). The Boran displayed their achieved strength and skill through dancing, carrying trophies of raids to further emphasize their patriotism, and prestige (P. Baxter 1965). Raiding was the surest way of obtaining a large herd of cattle and thereby achieving or validating social status.

The influence of an Igbo "town" was measured by the strength of its able-bodied warriors. The Edda and Abam, famed for their war-making power, had strong age-grade organizations: they required taking an enemy's head as a precondition for manly status (Victor Uchendu 1965). When an Igbo youth took a head for the first time, he joined in a public dance performed by all headgetters, holding the head in his left hand, his machete in the right, and sporting an eagle feather on one side of his head, a parrot feather on the other (C. Meek 1937:49). Man-killing warrior societies, on certain occasions, performed their own special dance, with a distinctive drum covered with human skin. They would bring out the heads of people killed and place the skulls on a tray which was balanced on the head. Holding the machete between the teeth, they danced with deliberate steps or tiny rapid ones on the ball of the foot while the shoulders quivered and vibrated (M. Green 1964:67). Meek reports that formerly at Ngbwidi, the title of Ogbute was conferred on any man who had killed and decapitated an enemy in war. A dance was held to announce the feat. The head was buried for about three weeks to clean it of flesh after which it was dug up and a dance of all headgetters was held in the market place (ibid.:172). About some of these warriors, Nzekwu writes, "their ruthlessness was fed fat by the realisation that at the welcome dance held in their honour on their return from each campaign, they were to display the human trophies they had won" (1963:17). Similarly, among the Yakö, only those warriors who returned from military action with the heads of slain enemies would take leading parts in the fighters' dances. The men danced around the ward squares with the heads before throwing them in the latrine. Later the teeth were removed to decorate the dancers' special fibre caps (Daryll Forde 1964:148, 155).

Sexual Display

Women discriminate among men in terms of their dance performance vigor and endurance. In *Song of Lawino*, Okot p'Bitek (1966:33) writes about Acholi dance: "A man's manliness is seen in the arena,/ You cannot hide anything,/ All parts of the body/ Are clearly seen in the arena,/ Health and Liveliness/ Are shown in the arena!" (P'Bitek is a social anthropologist and a dancer.) Nadel's description of the Nuba Tira tribe characterizes much of the continent. In the *habodha* dance, young men recited their exploits in raiding and mimed their skillful actions, their pugnacity, and endurance. "In this dance, male pride and sexual stimuli are inextricably mixed. For by means of these self-praises the young men try to attract the attention of girls, who standing in the centre of the ring formed by young men, will pick out one or the other, and throw themselves against the partners they have chosen" (1947:248).

The *duñuba* warrior flagellation dance of the Kouroussa was designed to test strength and courage. Holding a small war axe or saber in one hand and a short whip made of the plaited membrane of a donkey's penis in the other, each man whipped the man in front until blood ran. Those who could not bear the pain left the dancing group amidst the jeers from the crowd. When about four or five of the original fifteen youths remained, they danced and were nursed by the women. After they retired to rest, women and girls danced and sang their praises (Meillassoux 1968:93). Mazrui sums up the dynamic: "The dancer, the warrior, the lover, become indistinguishable where the heritage of imagery draws no distinction between valor and virility" (1973:20).

Physical Preparation for War

For the Zulu, according to G. Mahlobo (1934:184), the different regiments compete with each other in their dancing, exercising mind and muscles. Shaka's success was attributable in some measure to the warrior training in physical endurance and effecting mass movements (Walter 1969:142). The "Old Style" of fighting was highly individualistic, a campaign was an "unorganized swoop" (ibid.:122–123). However, Shaka led his dancers in the royal kraal; the men danced in drill units with mass attack strategies at the different camps. The tactics may have been the revival of practices that had died out or that derived from indigenous hunting procedures. A crescent was formed, and the "horns" of the warrior unit encircled the enemy killing everything within the circle.

Kikuyu warriors performed the *kebata* and *nguro* dances to display their physical fitness and dexterity in handling spears and shields and their ability to jump high and broad while carrying their weapons. This training was necessary to prepare the youths to meet any danger with confidence and to help the men become good runners; in the absence of mechanical travel, running was an important talent in pursuing an enemy or dangerous animal (Kenyatta 1962:93, 197). War dances were often reviews at the opening of the campaign season as among the Chamba of Donga (Meek 1931:I, 349).

Affective Readying

Dancing in preparation for a physical conflict has a scientific foundation as do "warm-up" exercises for athletes prior to a game. Furthermore, physiological research at Harvard suggests that palm and sole

11 Promulgating the new constitution: the Kikuyu, Kenya Independence Day. Photograph by William John Hanna.

sweating in response to stress, exercise, and heat may be part of the "flight-or-fight" reaction that prepares animals, including humans, to cope with danger by running away. Sweating increases the coefficient of friction and enables animals to run better (*New York Times* 1976). Warrior dances often incite men to action, signalling a forthcoming raid. Boas (1955) notes the intense emotional value of music and dance and their implied heightened effects which, in turn, call forth an intense emotional reaction, exciting the passions. When the Chaga had to prepare for war, hundreds of warriors were called upon to perform the *rosi* war dance personally supervised by the chief. The dancers advanced in a semicircular formation and then closed in upon each other engaging in sham duel. The simultaneous feet stamping, surging forward of the far-flung battleline, and thunderous roars were assumed "to arouse the spirits of all and make concerted action possible" (Raum 1940:222). Part of the incitement to action involves the preparation for the dance as well as the dance itself. For the Turkana *akimumwar* dance, all the men elaborately mud themselves with multicolored ochre in intricate patterns and colors, fasten bells around the knees, stick ostrich feathers in the headdress, and carry fighting sticks (Pamela Gulliver 1953:75).

The creation of solidarity through group dancing is generally reported in the literature (scholars also recognize that fights often break out at occasions for the dance and during the performance). Langer (1953:176, 190) speaks of the individual partaking of a feeling of strength in group rally and bonding, promoting combative readiness although the actual combat may be through individual skirmishes; Franklyn Wepner (1973:82), of dispelling or forgetting anxiety through a greater expenditure of energy and higher fever of involvement; and Alvin Zander (1974:2), of team spirit as a "potent and invigorating tonic." He finds that group success is not a permanent trait of individuals, but a motive that develops in particular group situations. The Swazi man called Sobhuza explains: "The warriors dance and sing at the *Incwala* so they do not fight, although they are many and from all parts of the country and are jealous and proud. When they dance they feel they are one and they can praise each other" (Kuper 1969:224). Often the precursor of war waged against external enemies, this annual ritual promoted solidarity and fortified the warriors for attack. The Zulu danced as a communal group in the image of the king, reflecting his personal disposition in the style of movement. Walter argues that the Zulu felt the state should be the body of the despot, "responding to his emotions and controlled by his will" (1969:256). Dancing the king's dance was metonymical to the king's power, expressing, communicating, and revivifying sentiments which sustained the combative extraordinary behavior. The encouragement and communion evidenced in dances retelling stories of successful warrior encounters motivated continued achievement by focusing on tested and proven skills. The power of dance as a stimulus and sanction (shaming) is a potent weapon in many African cultures (see Gluckman 1960).

We know that Shaka conquered a number of groups and incorporated them into his kingdom and regiments. It is possible, therefore, that battle unity and group integration were promoted by incorporating movements from these different groups into a full corps' performance. However, there are no movement analyses to support this hypothesis. (There is evidence among the Anáhuac of Mexico that the dances and deities of heterogeneous conquered groups were incorporated.)

Part of affective readiness involves setting apart the fighting from the nonfighting group and the friend from enemy; adjusting behavior from one sphere of appropriateness (e.g., thou shall not kill) to the opposite, through altered states of consciousness, or distancing. Anthony Wallace (1968) calls this a shift from a relaxed to a mobilized state, necessitating a releasing mechanism. For many African groups the war dance serves as this kind of mechanism since it is a special language code with kinetic graphic symbols evoking a disciplined response, a motivational state. Warrior dance is similar to the use of masked or possession dance which separates and defines differences between an individual's role in ordinary life and his role in another domain, sanctioning extraordinary behavior and freeing him from libel and similar repercussions. Thus warrior dance may create a frenzied, delirious affective state in a nonplay context; the individual's violent physical change may help instigate or cushion the effect of what is considered to be a radical change in the social state of affairs. In this way the individual is able to commit violent acts which are usually forbidden.)

The discussion thus far has suggested that when a group goes to war there are frequently processes of separation and distancing, transition and preparation, and reaggregation and victory celebration which are marked by warrior dance (cf. Van Gennep 1960). An example of closure is found in the Acholi performance after a battle when the warriors danced the *bwola* backwards into a hut. As they entered to return the spears, a woman repeatedly poured water onto the roof above the doorway wetting them and so terminating the mobilized state (p'Bitek 1971).

Religious Behavior

Dance is often a form of prayer (see Chapter 5) to praise, thank, and invoke the deities, and to reenact cosmological events. In southwest Nigeria's Benin kingdom, there was a war ritual to honor *Ogu*, the god of iron. The warriors proceeded through Benin City and then, suspended from the trees, performed an acrobatic dance enacting the mythical war against the sky (R. Bradbury 1957:58).

Warrior dance is often a form of sympathetic magic. The dance becomes a kind of transformer transmitting currents of bodily energy. Dance activates a supernatural essence the !Kung Bushmen use to cure, the Lango to release *jok*, and the Bemba to transform girls. Thus the shaking movement of the Samburu warrior dance makes a man irresistible in battle; it also reflects anger, self-assertion, and manliness (Paul Spencer 1965:263–264). For some peoples who believe in reincarnation, reenacting the ancestors' celebrated maneuvers activates their power and skill.

Dance is, of course, metonymical to life. The transmission of life forces through dance is seen in the most important of all Swazi national ceremonies, the *Incwala* ritual for the hereditary king who shares power with his mother. Held annually at the time of the southern summer solstice, it expressed the symbolic meaning of kinship (fertility, authority, and order). The people who contributed bride payment for the king's mother "made" the king and they sustained the regime. Nearly every male Swazi has at one time or another participated in the *Incwala*. Through this warrior dance the power of life or death was harnessed to promote the common good. With regiments stretching beyond the boundaries of clan and principality, warfare was essential to the Swazi to sustain the kind of society that had developed. Sometimes initiated by warriors to provide the opportunity to display their courage, loyalty, and strength, war was the vehicle for commoners to achieve power, wealth, and fame (Kuper 1969:123). For the especially richly costumed warriors to abstain from dancing in the *Incwala* was to withhold the power which bestowed strength and life (ibid. 1968). Held in the royal cattle byre, the dance acquired "perfect performance" by long hours of practice. The Swazi emphasized that the dance itself strengthened the king and the earth at the *Incwala*; here more than at any other stage the people kept their king alive and healthy by their own vigorous movements (ibid. 1969:218). Officials urged the people: "Dance! Dance! The *Incwala* was not a thing of play. Dance" (ibid.:290). And at specific times during this drama of kingship, the king himself was expected to dance with his men (ibid.:209, 218), for dancing the *Incwala* secured the monarchy.

From Ghana there were a number of reports of married women, whose men had gone off to battle, pantomiming war through dance as an imitative charm. The women painted themselves white, adorned themselves with beads and charms and carrying guns, sticks, and knives, they hacked paw-paw fruits as if they were enemy heads. Carrying long brushes made of buffalo or horse tails as they danced, singers made the point verbally explicit with such phrases as "Our husbands have gone to Ashanteeland, may they sweep their enemies off the face of the earth" (Field 1940:103, Frazer 1929:26).

Displacement

From a psychological perspective, displacement is essentially the expression of a dangerous impulse in a comparatively harmless way. Dance performance may reduce anxiety, emotional tension, or surplus energy by acting out frustrations or expending energy. Dances have been viewed as an outlet for sexual and aggressive feelings. Thus, the Ngoni use the strenuous leaping and stamping *ingoma* dances to dissipate energy and emotion. Young men were continuously being told by older men "to dance strongly, *usina namandla*." *Ingoma* were supposed to make a youth "obedient (*wamvera*) and self-restrained (*wadziletsa*)" (Read 1938:10).

There seems to be evidence, however, that like play, warlike activities sometimes lead to aggression.[4] The competitive warrior dances of display and courtship were often the occasions of fighting. There was tension between the graded Samburu age-sets over relationships with girls, honor, and prestige. Spencer notes that the course of a dance is uncertain: it either becomes a safety-valve reducing tensions and inhibitions through a release of pent-up energies in a harmless way or it becomes a fray (1965:125). Performance of the Ubakala Igbo Nkwa Ese sometimes led to violence at an elderly, esteemed man's second burial. Usually an important man was also an heroic warrior, as were some of his sons and other kin who are the designated participants. The dance-play reenacted the heroic deeds of the deceased, and reminders of his heroism would invoke the wrath of individuals attending from other villages whose relatives had been his victims. Among the Zulu, Gluckman saw men lock in armed combat because one bumped into another or became agitated in the excitement of the dance (1959:9). P'Bitek writes that "a man's manliness is seen in the arena/ No one touches another's testicles" (1966:33).

There are distinctions between warrior dances which are playful and those which are instrumental in provoking violence. Among the Ga, for example, there were two distinct patterns in which the Nungawa Asafo military body grouped itself. One formation was used for going to war, to honor a new leader, or engage in public works; the other formation was created for what was called "play–drilling, training, dancing, singing, and funerals" (Field 1940:171). Such distinctions often become blurred. In Accra, many quarrels and fights derive from ancient rivalries and battle behavior boasted about in the play dance competitions: Gbese people danced "the War of the Skewer," with a fish-hook meaning, "This is very shallow water," or "These Jamestown people are valueless and negligible." The

Jamestown people retorted with a dance involving a bell: "You left your bell in the war, and your power is now our power."

Political Behavior

As suggested earlier, warrior dances sustained particular leaders and the political structure within a religious perspective. Warrior dances were also politically important symbolic behavior, praising and honoring government leaders. Among competitive groups, success in warrior dance competitions accrued to their chiefs. For example, the Tutsi chiefs, like the king, entrusted their pages to the care of highly paid dancing teachers who secretly instructed these youths in new movements and rhythms. The leaders derived honor from hearing their warriors were the best trained (Pagès 1933:170).

Dance was the vehicle to proclaim a new government among the Kikuyu and calling for war dances to be held in every district the effective way of promulgating a new constitution. Words from the drafted constitution were put into song phrases and embodied in sonic and danced media. On the appointed day, the constitution was announced, and the warriors danced brandishing their spears and shields to welcome the newly introduced government (Kenyatta 1962:186, 197, 200).

Gluckman calls attention to "rituals of rebellion" in Africa, in which behavioral inversions occur. Women, usually the subordinate sex, engaged in socially approved inverted and transvestite behavior which was believed to be for the common good. Girls dressed as men, assumed their dominant authority roles, and danced warrior dances. When the Gogo men who hold ritual responsibility for controlling human and livestock fertility fail, disorder reigns, and the women assume the men's ritual roles and become the only active agents permitted to redress the wrong. They dress as men and dance violently with spears (Rigby 1966). Warriors mock and attack their leader in dance. At an Anuak headman's installation, the village men arrive at his homestead carrying spears and rifles and stage a mock attack; sometimes they shout words of rebellion, miming an attack on the dance drums which the headman controls and which, when seized, mark a successful rebellion. The headman's permission is necessary for the drums to be brought out for a dance which possesses principles of communal order (Godfrey Lienhardt 1957).

In these instances, I do not think it is catharsis, the controlled release of tension in which the powerful allow a contest or reversal against themselves so that they might order the state of affairs more effectively, that is at issue. It may be that the temporary public sharing in high status behavior and then its loss serve to emphasize the holder's superiority, to reinforce the maintenance of the system, and to create order. Alternatively, the rituals of rebellion may be boundary maintaining mechanisms which impose restraints on the occupants of high status positions. Perhaps these representations of conflict through role reversal and behavioral inversions are offered as a latent system of alternatives, if contingency so warrants: a role reversal in fact, revolution or anarchy. The inverse, conversion into the opposite, can be used to present a veiled threat and prophylactic, portraying what might happen if normative bounds are violated and power abused. Thus individuals and groups are put on their mettle to act appropriately and receive support (see Chapter 6).

European Impact

European penetration of Africa caused more warfare due to the increased slave trade and refugeeism. Initially, dances were part of war behavior among African groups and then, later, between African groups and Europeans. This contact with Europeans also set in motion a series of social, economic, and political changes.

Religion, Morality, and the "White Man's Burden"

The introduction of Christianity into Africa had emasculating consequences on many forms of dance. Europeans recognized that dance was intertwined with indigenous religion and morality, and so, even though African dances often had universal themes and origins comparable to those of European folk dances, their performance was seen as the manifestation of savage heathenism and antagonistic to the "true faith." African dance was found too licentious for the "civilized" Victorian Europeans. Geoffrey Gorer, who observed many dances in West Africa in the 1920s, suggested that the European perception of African dances as orgies could be traced to the perfervid daydreams of sex-obsessed missionaries "who [could not] see anything in negro manifestations except illicit copulation" (1962:175–176). B. Malinowski thought that the early missionary was frightened of dance without ever coming near it (1936:500). Furthermore, some Christians came to Africa as missionaries in order to escape what

12   Warrior dance demonstrating personal prowess: the Suk,
Kenya Independence Day. Photograph by William John Hanna.

they considered the decadence, often including dance, in their own
societies. Europeans had often perceived Africa as a "dark continent"
immersed in barbaric gloom and the African mentality childlike at
best. To some, the people of Africa resembled the simian genus more
than European humanity, and therefore had no culture. Indeed, the
"white man's burden" was to spread western civilization to "primitive" peoples.

Political Behavior: Order and Defiance

Order was a primary concern of the European administrations. With
pacification, warfare was virtually eliminated and thus the need for
war dances, as physical and affective preparation for violent encounters, terminated. Consequently, members of the Sonjo group changed
their patterns: they would leave the home area to work in the urban

area or mines where they performed their warrior dances (Gray 1965).

The colonial situation stripped to its essentials is characterized by a state of dependency imposed on a subject majority by an imported European oligarchy. Thus warrior dances could be viewed as a symbol of independence, self-assertion and pride; they suggest a kind of potential disorder antithetical to the dependency complex. From the European perspective it was a metaphor of revolution or, at least, decreasing European influence. The Bemba believed in their rulers' omnipotence and arbitrary action (Richards 1940:111) and Shaka maintained complete dominance over his nation (Walter 1969). In this light, dances which praised African leaders were unacceptable and so, throughout Africa, warrior dances were usually crushed as were other dances that might loosen the colonial grip through their expressions of communal life.

Containment or proscription of dance is widely documented: As early as 1901 in eastern Nigeria there were proclamations about regulating "native plays" defined as "a gathering of natives in any public street or market for the purpose of dancing or playing native music" (Nwabara 1965:188–189). Licenses and permission from the District Commissioner were often necessary. Northern Rhodesia Township Regulations proscribed the organization or participation in any dance "calculated to hold up to ridicule or bring into contempt any person, religion or duly constituted authority" (cited in Mitchell 1956:12). As pointed out earlier, dances were often the occasion of fights; Europeans feared that these might have broader repercussions as they did in the 1929 "Women's War."

The *Beni* dance, performed by a number of ethnic groups in East Africa, is an interesting example of dance perceived as defying the European presence. In 1919 an administrator commented: "The obtrusive simulation of a superior race by the specious elegants of the youth was not an effect that was lacking" (Ranger 1975:37). The term *Beni* refers to a popular, versatile team dance (*ngoma*) with urban origins which had recognizable features of modernity (a brass band and European dress), organization (military drill and a hierarchy of officers with European titles), and competitiveness; it also had a continuing tradition of communal dance competitions, elaborate ranks, and displays of military skills. The missionaries so disliked and feared the *Beni* that some turned to supporting traditional dances which they had earlier tried to abolish. Europeans were dismayed at the widely dispersed Tanganyika dance society network which was centrally controlled during its early development. Communication between groups occurred through the flow of migrant labor. The potential threat to European domination in the degree of coordination was not overlooked (ibid.:44, 123). The European perception of the sense of solidarity the dance association members developed, the African mockery directed against the colonialists, the impatience dancing bred with authority, and a revolutionary conspiracy spearheaded by Islamic and coastal Arab culture concealed within the dance led the disconcerted Europeans to prohibit government clerks from joining dance groups and to impose high fees to obtain licenses for publicly held dances (ibid.:88, 92, 124, 130).

However, the warrior tradition persisted in *Beni*, even providing physical and affective military training for the African *askaris* who fought in World War I. European participants in the East African campaign admiringly described an *askari*'s dancing in the battle-line to rally his men, although reporters sometimes displayed "uneasy astonishment that the suffering and death in East Africa would be responded to by a dance" (ibid.:55). African support personnel were able to identify with military power and prestige by performing *Beni*. In both war and peace times, it was a status marker displaying characteristics of the elite class and modernity. Although *Beni* was a mode of identifying with European military prowess, Ranger emphasizes that it was not a submission to European power but an accommodation to power in a traditional vein. He explains *Beni* as an indigenous dance form to display self-respect and self-confidence in communal values and express and communicate the pride of a group based on locality, ethnicity, moiety, and/or class against others in a tradition of dance competitions. These dance groups traditionally had elaborated ranks, displays of military skills, opportunities for innovations, achievement of high rank, and the exercise of patronage to achieve high status. This form, historically sensitive to changing power relations, selectively borrowed from the European military and settlers in a combination of mimicry and mockery.

Not all administrators agreed to the policy of wiping out traditional culture. Destruction of traditional institutions countered the romantic conservatism of those colonial service members who believed Europeans and Africans were destined to be culturally separate and that most worthwhile resources of the Africans inhered in traditional institutions (Helmuth Heisler 1974:7). In the 1920s, local traditions in Tanganyika which seemed consistent with morality were encouraged by the missionaries, although earlier they had wanted to save Africans from their traditional culture (Ranger 1975:126–127).

Secular Factors

Europeans also had a convenience or "efficiency" reason for banning African dances: the "noise" of these often disturbed the sleep or work of Europeans or distracted the attention of Africans who might be enticed away from their jobs to join the dances. Furthermore, Africans might spend their resources on the related feasts and clothes and consequently be unable to pay their taxes (ibid.:88, 110). The new technology of education and mechanization tended to somewhat diminish the importance of actual physical power. Gunfire, hell fire, and book power destroyed or suppressed the pre-European warrior tradition. For example, the Bemba saw that Christian supernatural power meshed with other western resources surpassed the indigenous supernatural power of Bemba leaders (Richards 1940:114) and the complex in which it was embedded.

Nationalism

In the nationalist period, educated Africans sponsored the growth of "traditional" consciousness in Africa. They formed ethnic groups and unions to mobilize support in competition for the scarce resources which became the goals of modernization—land, jobs, trade, and education. Africans resurrected warrior dances in nostalgia for the lost grandeur of kingdoms or a pre-European dominated way of life. They symbolically represented aspirations rather than hard and fast rules of conduct or direction of aim. In South Africa, Hugh Tracy claimed the performance of war dances was merely for the love of movement (1952:2). However, it seems difficult to overlook the prideful recapitulation of history as a source of reference and set of models for current aspiration, however much stifled: the formerly dominant Tutsi of Ruanda continue to perform their *intore* nobles' dance in exile. Some groups espouse the warrior tradition in order to identify with contemporary prestigious groups which pride themselves on it. Paul Makgoba, for example, a Sotho professional dancer, singer, and actor from Johannesburg, grew up with Zulu children and observed their tribal dancing in the black townships on Sundays. He, as many others, was most impressed with Zulu dance—its "virile, manly grace"—and developed Zulu warrior dance teams (personal communication). The Ndau of Rhodesia adopted the war dance of the Nguni who dominated them from 1830 to 1900 (Tafirenyika Moyana 1976).

  Bakary Traore (1968) points out that theater arts simultaneously permit recreation and transcendence—incarnation of and escape from reality. In the 1930s, however, Tanganyikan protonationalists viewed dances such as *Beni*, competitive in terms of locality, moiety, or class, as divisive, making Africans easy prey to colonialism (Ranger 1975: 96).

Postcolonial Independence Era

Reemergence of the Warrior Dance

With political independence, African leaders seek sociocultural independence and integrity by mediating modern and traditional influences, choosing selectively from an ancestral heritage, often regenerating ennobled patterns. The revival or invention, as may be the case in some instances, of warrior dances is an aspect of negritude or authenticity. Both concepts lead toward an increased consciousness of indigenous cultural values as a counter to the imposition of colonial values with its consequent denigration of indigenous ones (Kenneth Adelman 1975). Negritude and authenticity are most valuable to those who experienced cultural disruption and separation. These may be a reaction, vengeance, or more likely, a positive affirmation of self-instilling pride, obtaining inspiration from the past rather than returning blindly to it (e.g., in Zaire there is an official rejection of fetishism and tribalism). Leaders and parties may romanticize the past as a strategy of coping with change (cf. Alvin Toffler 1970).

Political Behavior

Warrior dance continues as an aspect of political behavior as it was in the pre-European contact era. While traditional offices tend to be eclipsed, new political leaders often use the traditional symbols of power (P. Lloyd 1966:35). Authority is legitimated in the eyes of traditional masses by employing symbolic forms of independence and power, such as the warrior dance. Adelabu's way to power was "to dance in the streets to the strains of Mabolaje songs that celebrated his name" (Richard Sklar 1963:299). Dances celebrate and pay homage to political leaders in Uganda (to Obote and now to Amin) on their visits around the country. Moreover, the ability of a local individual to mobilize popular energies around the dance is evidence of the power he or she holds. Thus Kenyatta, Kenya's first president and a Kikuyu, perpetuated his ethnic group's tradition of calling for war dances in every district to promulgate a new constitution.

Status Markers and Sexual Display

Besides the warrior dance being a status marker of national independence, it continues to recognize individual and group achievement. I witnessed the traditional Igbo war dance C. Meek (1937) and M. Green (1964) described in the colonial era. The dance now celebrates a feat considered equivalent to manslaying–obtaining a law degree. With "heads" placed on a tray and balanced on his head, machete in his teeth, shoulders quivering, a dancer lauded a kinsman who had just returned from his legal training in the United Kingdom. Virtually every African dance team or national company has its warrior dances, memories of the positive aspects of historical times, deeds immortalized in repetitive performances. These dances continue to permit the communication of self-assertion and sexuality.

Dance has become a symbol of ethnic identity in a heterogeneous nation. It is a we/they boundary marker in independence celebrations, school competitions, national dance companies, the military, and urban areas (Hanna 1973, Meillassoux 1968, Mitchell 1956).

Physical Preparation and Affective Readying

Even with European pacification and national laws since independence, dance and war are still related in some areas which had a warrior tradition. The dance continues to provide physical and affective preparation for violence for a number of pastoralist groups. Samburu raids are still expected; girls bait the youths at the dance and egg them to lawlessness as a counter to the social order. They too feel suppressed and controlled by the elders in the gerontocratic system and partake in vicarious rebellion (Spencer 1965:122, 125).

Conclusion

In order to understand the relation of dance to the warrior tradition in modern Africa, we have taken a diachronic perspective. The significance of dance appears through an examination of some of its various manifestations, interlaced with other sociocultural phenomena, in different historical eras. (These are not fixed categories, for behavior often extends beyond the boundaries of historical events.) During the pre-European independence era there was a pervasive but not universal dovetailing of valor and virility with prestige in African societies. These qualities permeated the warrior dances which were communicative status markers for groups and individuals, vehicles for sexual display, physical preparation for war, affective readying for violent encounters (incitement, communion, we/they distancing), religious practice, displacement, and political behavior.

Then, the European impact constrained warrior dances: Christians found them antagonistic to the "true faith" and immoral; missionaries and administrators considered them a challenge to their dominance and also an inconvenience. The Africans themselves saw the alternative to the physicality of the warrior tradition, and its dance, in western education and technology, and they defected. With nationalism and independence warrior dances rise phoenixlike when their symbolic value becomes apparent. And there are transformations in style and structure or, alternatively, continuities in different contexts, such as the battle of barrister training and its celebration, or illegal raids for female approbation. It appears that the warrior dance as a display of strength and self-affirmation, as a status marker, and as political and symbolic behavior are pervasive structures.

The introductory chapters of this book outline the properties of dance underlying the product and process of the dance-warrior tradition interaction. The power of dance lies in its cybernetic communication process, its multimedia thought, emotion, motor, and aesthetic capability to create moods and a sense of situation for performer and spectator alike. The manipulation of the body through movement in purposeful, intentionally rhythmical, attention riveting, discrete cultural patterns presents a dramatic, powerful statement which can influence predispositions, attitudes, beliefs, and actions.

Thus far we have addressed manifestations of dance in certain key realms of human existence: sociocultural socialization and organization, religion, politics, and war. Many of the illustrations have come from rural areas. The next chapter extends the discussion of change and focuses on urban areas and examines the interplay between dance and a form of human-structured environment: what happens to the catalyst, concept, process, performance, and impact of dance as a result of specific urban conditions?

8 The Urban Ecosystem of Dance

It is the city which has been, and to a large extent still is the style centre in the traditional world, disseminating social, political, technical, religious, and aesthetic values, and functioning as an organizing principle conditioning the manner and quality of life in the countryside. (Wheatley 1969:7)

The city, as Lewis Mumford and Robert Redfield note, is a locus, an index, and a generative force for change in much of the contemporary world. Although the globe is not fully organized into cities, urban agglomerations, for the most part, are increasing in number and population; they continue to have a significant impact in a broader context upon the people within and beyond their boundaries.

In what ways do urban areas and dance patterns affect each other? This is a question which has rarely been addressed. Dance, a nearly universal form of human behavior, is a living system which is reflective, constitutive, and conditioning of socioculture. As the processual model, Chapter 3, suggests, dance interacts with other aspects of socioculture and the physical environment (the catalyst, Figure 4A) to carry on aspects of social and psychological life. As an institution, dance constitutes a set of roles, and as a medium for people relating to each other (Figure 4C-D), dance may be symbolic interaction. It is frequently a way of blending harmonious principles and mediating contradictory ones in culture and society (cf. Ubakala case study). As affective-cognitive-sensori-motor communication, dance has the capacity to engage the human being, performer and spectator alike, quite intently. With the potential cybernetic flow between dance and the sociocultural system, it might be possible to gain some mutual understanding of each. As is the case with other patterned expressive-communicative phenomena, dance study provides barometric readings of situational and structural dynamics. In the urban area these readings may have significant policy-making implications for politics, education, and mental health. Dance manifestations reveal urban-rural continuities and identify a range of facets of urbanism and urbanization.

Main Proposition, Caveats, and Concepts

The main point is that *in the urban area, sociocultural factors are the primary determinants of dance concept, process, product, and impact, but these are influenced and modulated by the constraints and opportunities (substrate) of relatively high settlement heterogeneity and density, and the concomitant minimization of friction space.* This proposition, also applicable to nondance activities, is derived from L. Wirth's theories of urbanism (1938) as *reformulated* by Claude C. Fischer (1975), human ecologists (cf. Robert Netting 1971), and communication specialists (Hymes 1974, Everett Rogers and F. Shoemaker 1971). The organization of space is assumed to have an important bearing on human interaction and its dance manifestations. But the physical environment alone cannot explain urban phenomena (cf. Manuel Castells 1972), including dance patterns. Between the environment and dance lies the interface of socioculturally patterned and adaptive individual and group responses. Dance is culturally learned thought and behavior which is transmitted through imitation and/or instruction in much the same way as one learns native and second languages. Competence (knowledge about dance), and performance (the actual dancing), and ways of responding to dance are guided by the dynamics of reference groups.

The purpose of this chapter is to illuminate the significance of dance as reflective, constitutive, and generative in the urban area and to begin to spell out the conditions under which certain dance patterns appear to be operative. Just as there are specific phenomena common to humans as members of an animal species (see Chapter 3), there appear to be some structural dynamics (reoccurring processes affecting a variety of dance forms) which are similar irrespective of time and place, by virtue of commonalities in human creation.

I will posit three sets of *probable* relationships that appear to exist between dance and the urban area. Dance illustrations drawn from ethnographic and other reports which led me to these propositions and suggest their plausibility in the real world, will be presented.[1]

Several caveats are warranted. Many things can diminish the strength of the propositions, for example, totalitarianism restricting individual and group choice. The "postindustrial" phenomenon of the megalopolis in which a metropolitan area and its hinterlands merge into a single sociocultural unit may also diminish the strength of the proposition. Second, although there have been some studies of various aspects of dance in the urban area, dance is not always performed within such an institutional framework that keeps written or pictorial records. The sources in the literature are scattered and fragmentary, due to the nascent state of social science dance studies, and the locations of described dances are not always specified (cf. Martha E. Davis 1973, who laments the neglect of urban contextual description in Latin American studies). Consequently, the data base has limitations. Third, the exemplary material is deliberately extended beyond a single case, "culture area," or city type to direct attention to those relationships between dance and the urban area which appear to be widespread historically, geographically, and cross-culturally (cf. Edgar Borgatta and Jeffrey Hadden 1970). Of course, the specifics of the illustrative cases cannot, necessarily, be universally extrapolated and generalized through time and space, and a contradictory case does not disprove a general tendency.

It is impossible to speak of *the* dance in urban areas viewed through time and space. Dance has its variations as does language or other cultural phenomena; categorizations of dance as social or popular, ethnic, sacred, and theatrical are obviously not clear-cut. For our purpose here, it is unnecessary to distinguish between fine arts and primitive forms, formal and informal dances, the role of dance in western and nonwestern societies, and the multiple roles of dance (e.g., social recreation, ceremony, fine art). It is postulated that processes in the urban area affect processes in dance role, function, and form regardless of the dance category. Indeed, many of the distinctions which are made by western scholars reflect the absence of comparative study and the presence of ethnocentric, elitist, and egocentric conceits. My participant observation in African villages and towns, Latin American towns, and New York City studios and theaters reveals more basic similarities than differences in such aspects of dance as cult activity, training, audience role, and relation to society. Whether a ballet series at Lincoln Center in New York City or a performance for a New Yam Festival among the Ubakala in Nigeria, dance may fulfill the same kinds of functions for dancers and observers: it may provide group identity, create self-esteem for the dancer and those identifying with the dancer's reference group, reflect on social concerns, be autotelic, or generate income. There are more similarities than differences to be found in Balanchine's students' devotion to a dance form, intragroup competition, and cooperation and that of an Ubakala's youth group (cf. Mazo 1974 and Hanna 1976). Of course, differences may be found in the degree of distribution of a dance role and function among a society's populations: more of a total population may engage in a dance activity in the Ubakala clan area than in New York City or Dallas; yet, in some African societies, only special classes of people dance.

If one takes a broad historical and contemporary world view in looking at the relationships between dance and urban areas, the criteria for "urban" should likewise be nonrestrictive. Thus in considering different time periods and discrete environments, I will use the concept of "urban" as a land settlement which has a relatively dense population, social and occupational differentiation, and stratification.[2] D. Dwyer (1972) argues that implicit in an urban concentration is "the elimination ["minimization" may be a more appropriate term] of friction space," the reduction in distance (what Wheatley, 1971: 477, calls "a creator of effective space"). The urban area is viewed as an "ecosystem," which relates individual and interacting, interdependent people to the total sociocultural and physical environment. It is the complex reciprocal, cybernetic effects of all factors (cf. Otis Duncan 1969, Kepes 1972, Netting 1971, Rappaport 1971a). The central theme running through ecological research and commentary is interrelatedness.

Three derivative sets of propositions emanating from the primary argument suggest the conditions of the urban area-dance interaction. The first set focuses on the urban area as a stimulant to dance innovation and diversity; the second set, on dance as a manifestation of urban contingencies; and the third, on urban dynamics and the restriction of some dance forms.[3]

Proposition Sets

1. *The urban area tends to be a reservoir of ideas and catalyst* (Figure 4A) *for creativity* (used here interchangeably with "innovation"), unless inhibited by sociocultural factors (described in the third set of propositions, below).

Creativity may not be inferable from the end product alone, but to some degree it is perceived by a group and is nonimitative in one or more of three intrinsic dance properties: form, function, and meaning. Creativity may be subtle and evolutionarily cumulative, or the opposite. I agree with Mueller, who states in his discussion of creative communicative possibilities, that there can be entirely new forms or a combination of old ones in new basic ways, new encoding possibilities (new human meanings or technical refinements), and new perceptual meanings–all of which lead in some way to new insights or perceptual experiences (1967:92). In discussing innovation, no qualitative judgement is intended. Identifying the point at which one dance or component becomes "new" is often difficult for both participant and analyst. Systematic studies of the minimal characteristics, that is, the rules for what are essential features, and the generative structures for a dance form and style have been made for few dances–ballet (Cecchetti, Russian School, British), classical Indian (Bharat Natyam), and Tongan dance (Kaeppler 1967) have some degree of codified rules. Within these, however, interpretation varies. Motivation to innovate also varies; it may be intentional, spontaneous, or combinations of these factors.

H. Barnett (1953:39–59) points out that, while all innovations are finally initiated by individuals, they arise from a cultural background which provides certain *potential* for innovation. The size and complexity of the available cultural inventory, including the state of knowledge and degree of its elaboration, tend to be greater in urban areas than rural ones and thus establish a broader generative base. Urban areas tend to be relatively heterogeneous and to provide a range of possible social networks and an arena for possible interaction among different cultures. Fischer (1975:1324, 1328) argues that the association between urban residence and unconventionality (which tends to encompass receptivity to innovation) is persuasive. Besides, the more urban a place, the higher the rate of unconventionality. Georg Simmel (1970) speaks of the intensification of nervous stimulation, fluidity, and choice, and Fischer (ibid.:1320) points to the congregated numbers of persons or the "critical masses" sufficient to maintain unconventional subcultures which may generate innovation, or result from it. Not only do urban areas encourage innovation, but innovations may also increase exponentially: existing ones constitute an ever-increasing base upon which future developments can build (cf. Richard Appelbaum 1970:74).

Arguing that the urban area is a crucible for creativity does not deny the occurrence of creativity in rural areas, urban-rural interaction, or rural heterogeneity. In both urban or rural areas, dance develops through planned or spontaneous change, via individual or group inspiration and contacts with other groups through trade, migration, military conquests, and the various communication media. Dancing was a standard attraction of the periodic country fairs in eighteenth- and nineteenth-century England, for example. These fairs brought dispersed villagers together (Robert Malcolmson 1973: 54, Frances Rust 1969). In the rural areas of southwestern United States various Indian groups (e.g., Pueblos, Navajos, Apaches, Cohoninos, Supai, Hulapai, Mojaves, Pimas, and Papagos) still frequently interact and seek diversity in dance events (Kealiinohomoku, personal communication, April 2, 1974). However, the urban area has the potential for linking more extensive and diverse groups and geographic areas, opening up more communication channels (personal in situ, full-length observation of a performance; second-hand reports and face-to-face gossip networks; impersonal radio, newspaper, film or TV presentation; and personal or group instruction), and stimulating an accelerated, exponential pace of creativity.

In some situations it is difficult to determine whether the urban dynamics per se are responsible for the inventory potential and technology of innovation, rather than other factors such as colonialism or industrialization. What we can say is that the urban area does serve as an arena for the acting out or mingling of other dynamic environmental factors (see Owomoyela 1971).

1a. *Greater exposure of diverse dance phenomena probably occurs in the urban than rural area.* (In the United States, which has about a ten percent rural population, suburban areas should probably be grouped with rural areas.) One tends to find a multiplicity of old, new, and syncretistic dance forms in the urban area. Two assumptions can be made: among inhabitants, such exposure is differentially experienced and perceived, and the possibility for learning through contact exists. Television, of course, brings some diversity to rural areas in industrialized countries, but it is mass communication most often catering to a common denominator which limits diversity.[4] (Although some U.S. rural college campuses have become havens for choreographers, functioning as impresarios for concerts and classes, exposure to diversity is somewhat limited by the economics of a relatively small audience.) In less industrialized countries, TV reception tends to be limited to the urban areas.

Exposure to dance diversity is greater in urban areas on the occasion of independence celebrations in many African nations. Governments bring groups from throughout the nation to the capital to perform their dances. For example, in 1963 William John Hanna and I observed (and filmed) dances performed in Nairobi, Kenya, by the Kikuyu (the group whose homeland includes the capital), Giriama, Luo, Curia, Kisi, Malagory, Kipsigi, Kalenjin, Turkana, Masai, Nandi, Kamba, Digo, Samburu, Suk, Tende, Embu, Thoraka, Taita, and Arabs. Some of these groups are traditional enemies and would not

13   Immigrant's dance performance in an urban area: Umuahia, Nigeria. Photograph by William John Hanna.

otherwise have seen each other's dances. On another occasion, in Kampala's stadium, the Tutsi, Ganda, Bunyoro, Lango, Soga, Bake-di, Acholi, and Iteso were among the groups we filmed dancing to celebrate Uganda's independence. Large cities often host regional dance competitions. For example, the 1962 Enugu Festival of Arts was filmed, but only other urban areas received the TV transmission and exposure to these geographically dispersed dance groups.

In a week's visit to Port-au-Prince in 1967, we observed a range of local dance phenomena also seen by inhabitants in a variety of ways, from participating to being a "peeping tom." A "native dance" show and social dancing for tourists was a Monday night feature at Hotel Olaffson. The show choreographer Lavinia Williams Yarborough, an American, first came to Haiti to teach ballet at the behest of the Bureau of Tourism; she now has a dance studio where various forms of dance are taught. A Haitian friend took us to join the social dancing of elite Haitians at Djoumbala, a Petionville suburb club featuring the country's top bands. Nonelite Haitians engage in social dancing at informal, physically modest haunts such as Aux Palmist and Palladium. The open-air Théâtre de Verdure presents the Troupe Folklorique Nationale (designed to appeal to local residents as well as tourists). And because it was *rara* (the "Mad Carnival," or peasants' version of Mardi Gras), we encountered dozens of peasant groups, in and around the city, in shuffling procession to the homes of prestigious wealthy residents where they and the kings (dancers skilled in rapid footwork and *jon*, baton twirling) perform in return for money or food or drink. Similarly, in the town of Umuahia, Nigeria, on Easter day, perched on the verandah of one of the wealthy townsmen, we watched seven different ethnic groups dance and saw many others on the roads throughout the town. In the surrounding villages, one would see fewer ethnic groups. Indeed, outsiders were sometimes not welcome.

Urban areas were the seat of actors' guilds in prerevolutionary China. At first theatrical performances were only for the court—performers were invited from the countryside by an emperor and often enjoyed his personal patronage (John Burgess 1928). When merchant classes developed, they created a demand in the urban areas for the theatrical styles with which they were familiar in their native homes (Colin Mackerras 1972:19). There were at least two hundred forms of regional theater in China (ibid.:v).

In ancient times, the ceremonial center (Wheatley 1971), and more recently the king's court, were the places where one came into contact with the dances of peoples dispersed beyond the center's immediate bailiwick. Today, of course, New York City is the paradigm par excellence: one need look only at the newspapers or *Dance Magazine Annual* for documentation of the diversity of dance phenomena from the nations of the world, different schools, and various subcultures. And informal networks lead one to even greater opportunities for dance experiences (Theeman 1973).

Even when ethnic groups are relatively segregated spatially and socially within a city, as in the Addams area of Chicago, there is exposure to diverse popular, social dance phenomena (Gerald Suttles 1968). The black teenagers were almost invariably ahead of the provincial Italians in what they were dancing; the Mexicans and Puerto Ricans were in the middle. However, between April 1962 and June 1964, at least ten different dance styles passed through the Addams area. The urban blacks, less rooted to organizations than the other groups, were less restricted to their own local business places, churches, and ethnic section and thus spent time in non-neighborhood establishments and institutions. Consequently, they were exposed to diversity and better able to borrow from the wider society. Within their own area, cross-ethnic contact occurred when individuals changed residence but maintained contacts in their former neighborhood and when they attended school and church (1968:70, 227). These examples suggest that individuals and groups in urban areas have access to a wider pallet of dance experience than is available in rural areas.

1b. *Within the urban milieu, there tends to be more opportunity for a creative element to develop because of the minimization of spatial impediments and potential exposure to diverse dance phenomena, economic base, and location and nature of religious authority.* In the city people may gain more from the efforts of others through greater exchange at less cost. Possibilities exist for a collaborative effort or exposure to effort in which several creative individuals simultaneously explore similar venues. This happened with the use of film "light shows" and strobe effects in social and theatrical dance in U.S. cities. The New York City "Electric Circus" club epitomized this combination in rock dance while the Alwin Nikolais Company illustrates the merger of light shows and movement in modern dance.

Economics contributes to the development of creativity: the urban area tends to be the most important locus for patrons and to support a critical mass to encourage innovations. This is true even for the preindustrial literate city.[5] Gideon Sjoberg points out that "In feudal China, Japan, India, Medieval Europe–artists of various kinds concentrate in the capital," and that they, and other members of the aristocracy, subsidized the work of dancers (1960:203). Geertz (1963:103) refers to the upper class role as art patron in Tabanan, Bali. Cities became important centers of dance in China because the merchants possessed the largest amount of capital of any group in the empire (Mackerras 1972:51). Furthermore, the economic endeavors of the towns and cities were less dependent upon the needs of crops and the vicissitudes of the elements than those of the rural areas, and therefore individuals in the urban areas had more flexible leisure time to indulge in the arts (ibid.:41).

There is also an important relationship between the location and nature of religious authority and the opportunity for creativity in the urban area. Specialized theocrats in some ways determined dance behavior in the early ceremonial centers in Shang China, America, Mesopotamia, Egypt, South and South East Asia, the Mediterranean realm, and the Yoruba territories. These centers are regarded by Wheatley as essentially urban in character and a functional and developmental stage in the urban process. He describes the ceremonial center as affording "a ritual paradigm of the ordering of social interaction at the same time as it disseminated the values and inculcated the attitudes necessary to sustain it" (1971:478). All submitted to the authority of the deity, represented by ritual initiates, who managed the earthly affairs and interests of the populace. (The analysis of Anáhuac dance discusses the relationship of dance and religion in early Mexico.) The ancient cities of Greece and Italy were also loci for divinely inspired dance innovation (Lawler 1964:13). Sacred dances were part of the sacrifices and festivals of the city (Fustel de Coulanges 1956:221–222).

The general decline in the importance of religious authorities in western societies has been accompanied by an increase in the tolerance of many dance forms. Previously religious authorities acted as powerful guardians of morality and body use; where there is strong religious adherence, as in the fundamentalist south of the United States, there tends to be less exposure to contemporary ballet themes and costumes (or lack), modern theater, and social dance.

1c. *The urban area both acts upon traditions brought to it and spawns new forms* (Redfield and Milton Singer 1954). In many cities, one finds a clash or coexistence between old and new, as well as syncretistic blends and original forms reflecting heresy, heterodoxy, and dissent. Andrei Simíc points out that the urban area experiences "peasantization, since rural folkways are brought into the city as part of the baggage of migrants" (1973:12). In Belgrade, for example, one can see the traditional Serbian *slava* (celebration of the patron saint) in which circles form, and the *kolo*, a line dance of endless variants, commences. Or one may see dance from different regions in a park or "a Gypsy wedding party serpentine along the street, dancing to the asymmetrical shifting rhythms" (ibid.: 70).

The *gūbe*, an urban originated dance association in Bamako, Mali, represents a modernization of the village *flā-to* dance groups. As in the rural areas, it recruits neighboring youths of the same age from all castes, has disciplinary rules, structures boy-girl relations, and has an adult supervisor. However, in the urban areas, ethnic background is, according to Meillassoux (1968:124–126), irrelevant to participation criteria, and the dance movements and songs are inspired by the charleston, beguine, rumba, mambo, cha cha cha, merengue, rock and roll, and twist of the west.

The city is often host to visitors from varied hinterlands and also from other cities or countries who seek out the kind of dance they have at home (cf. Mackerras 1972) or perhaps cannot find there. The stimuli and economics of trade, tourism, or immigration foster diverse and new dance developments. In such large African cities as Lagos, Ibadan, and Accra, the African elite mingle with foreign businessmen and tourists in the large hotels. They learn the foreigners' social dances and then merge some of the elements with their own indigenous forms. And thus was born, in English-speaking West Africa, the popular "highlife" (Hanna 1973, Sylvia Kinney 1970). The style and steps are seen in traditional village dances–the form of a ballroom couple waltz position is a European import. This dance spread throughout the cities of black Africa. The European waltz, observed in the cities and carried to rural areas by urban residents visiting their ancestral home or by returning migrants, took a different turn among the Akan, according to Eva Meyerowitz (1962). In Bisease, near Kumasi, she saw its common manifestation: a funeral dance.

In Java, "fading urban forms 'coarsen' and 'sink' into the peasant mass and elaborated rural forms 'etherealize' and 'rise' into the urban elite" (Geertz 1960:228). Ilijin (1965) describes the reciprocal rural-urban influence in Yugoslavia: countryside traditional dances adopted by the town become enriched and are returned to the countryside. Dances composed on a stranger model also penetrate the countryside where they undergo some modification (cf. Lange 1975 on the Polish case).

Theatrical classical ballet drew upon the dance steps of rural peasant ethnic groups, systematizing elements of traditional dance cultures (Pierre Beauchamps in the seventeenth century is recognized for such codification). Provincial patterns were originally transformed in the image of the royal court. Furthermore, ballet creatively incorporated exotic dance patterns observed and reported from the age of exploration. Later, America's and Europe's "modern" dance developed as a rebellion against the ballet traditions.

In the growth of American social or popular dance (what the Stearns [1968] call vernacular or jazz dance), large numbers of blacks migrated with their dances from the south to the northern cities during World War I. The styles and structures of African and European dance forms influenced their dances. In the cities, new styles with different combinations and permutations were elaborated, legitimized, and assimilated into dominant American culture. It was in the urban areas that black dance gained artistic distinction (John Suess 1969) and became part of the resource repertoire for social and theatrical innovation for various other groups. D. Braun claims that twenty-four of the twenty-eight U.S.-originated popular music and dance phenomena he studied between 1920 and 1968 (including such dances as the charleston, black bottom, varsity drag, dancing marathons, truckin' shag, lindy hop, big apple, boomps-a-daisey, lambeth walk, square dance, congeroo, Susi-Q, be-bop, rock and roll, twist, discotheque, and go-go) came from very large cities (over a million population) and only four originated in rural areas (1969:157). More than half originated in New York City (cf. Hilton Kramer 1978).

1d. *Urban residents tend to be relatively more receptive to a variety of new dance forms than nonurban ones;*[6] *heterogeneity, tolerance, and cosmopolitanism are determining factors.* The heterogeneity usually found in urban areas tends to correlate with relative tolerance of different moralities and deviant behavior (cf. Vytautas Kavolis 1968:32, 41–51, 72–91). A climate is created where ideas and behavior can surface and grow (see Jerome Bruner 1962 on conditions for creativity). Orientations toward change tend to be more favorable, education levels higher, and contact with outsiders easier and greater. This constellation is cosmopolitanism. Also, because of employment opportunities related to population density and other urban properties, better educated individuals of high modern status tend to be located in urban areas, and these people tend to be more receptive to new ideas (William Baumol and William Bowen 1966; see also National Research Center of the Arts 1973).[7] Thus there are more potential recipients or supporters, financially and morally, of a variety of artistic forms and styles. The urban area not only spawns innovation, but serves as an arena for its acceptance by hosting a variety of different participants and audiences. It is difficult to identify the consequences and antecedents in a temporal sequence of innovativeness and cosmopolitanism. Both variables are probably interdependent, a small increment in one leading to a similar increment in the other– which in turn influences the first, and so on (cf. Rogers and Shoemaker 1971:92–93). When creative impulses need expression, these take on formal style and structure congenial to images already conceived by artist and audience (Bruner 1962).

The urban/rural contrast in receptivity is illustrated by examples from the United States and Africa. Under the Puritan influence, dance in the United States was castigated for its exposure and use of the body in public. Heterosexual torso-to-torso couple dancing– the waltz evolving from the slow turning circle dances of village Landler peasants–as opposed to group dancing with couples merely holding hands gained its ascendancy slowly in the 1890s. The waltz captured the attention of the Viennese in 1840 and created a stir in London and Paris. In the United States the waltz first entered the repertoire of urban areas: it took many years and much preliminary experimentation for it to penetrate and to be accepted in the rural areas (Dudley Ashton 1951:174), even though, William Johnston argues (1972:129), "the dance appeared anything but erotic because whirling couples had to lean away from each other in order to keep balance."

In the United States popular dance forms which succeeded the waltz from the charleston to the twist, and its evolved forms, were also held in check from too rapid an advance into the morally conservative rural areas. And theater dances like John Butler's sensuous and tension-ridden "After Eden" are still more likely to be seen in large cities than smaller ones where the "Nutcracker" reigns supreme.

The West African urban highlife, a dance incorporating the ballroom position in which a man and woman publicly clasp each other (behavior considered highly immoral among a number of traditional societies in this part of Africa), has met opposition, particularly in the rural areas. "Our highlife dance is naive, embarrassing, immoral shufflings and gyrations reminiscent of ambling gorillas in a mating session," exclaimed Nigerian newspaper writer Chigbo. "Traditional" ethnic dances are most commonly circular or performed inside a circle of spectators; they do not involve cross-sexual close body contact. (Cf. the study of Ubakala dance-plays.)

Two qualifications to the generalization that urban residents tend to be more receptive to dance innovation than nonurban ones must be mentioned. To the extent that innovation reflected in dance threatens an actor's privileged status, it becomes unacceptable. On the other hand, there is also resistance to innovation on the part of the underprivileged who cling to dance forms which symbolically anchor them within a familiar, comfortable frame. (These situations are discussed in Section 2 below.)

1e. *Dance innovations which originate or are observed in urban areas are more likely to be legitimized by style setters and diffused to relatively large numbers of people than rural innovations which do not get urban exposure.* Obviously not all innovations are accepted everywhere. If one hundred different ones are conceived simultaneously, only a few spread; probably ninety or more are localized and often forgotten. Acceptance, or what Rene Bravmann calls "artistic mobility" (1973), depends upon observability and awareness of the innovation's existence, the status of the source and promoter of the idea, relative advantage or utility factors, whether the innovation is part of a larger entity being accepted, compatibility with established forms, complexity, and personality orientations toward change (cf. Appelbaum 1970,

Arensberg and Arthur Niehoff 1971, Paul Meadows 1971, Rogers and Shoemaker 1971, Rothstein 1972). In a discussion of folk tradition and its absorption and modification through universalization, Nicholas Hopkins (1972:52, 54) suggests that cultural forms may be subject to some kind of up-or-out principle: if an innovation does not begin the path to diffusion it will be superceded by ones that do. Fischer (1975:1327) states that the more urban a place, the more numerous the sources of diffusion and the greater the diffusion into subcultures.

"Old" forms introduced by immigrants, may be accepted as innovations by other groups in the urban area; they may be accepted as they are or modified. This has occurred with black dance in the United States as southerners became immigrants to northern cities. The urban area is the node, in recent times, of TV broadcasting, filming, record players, juke boxes, discotheques, nightclubs, dance halls, restaurants, studio parties, Y's, schools, theaters, and theater surrogates. Sharon Clark (1973) attributes much of the development and diffusion of rock dance in the United States in the decade of the 1960s to the urban-based television and record industries. In the urban United States, businesses subsidize the arts as a "public service," to gain publicity (on the assumption that a potential market can be reached through the arts), and to decrease taxable income by making donations to nonprofit organizations.

If ever realized, the potential of the mass media and rural university to disseminate dance may lessen the need for direct contact with the urban environment. On the other hand, it is the urban area which encourages the simultaneous presentation of many teachers, interaction among different professionals, and multiple quantitative and qualitative performances. Moreover, receptivity to and development of innovation usually correlate with characteristics normally found in the urban area. Visitors to urban areas take home dance forms which urban style setters expose and legitimize. John Caldwell's systematic study of rural-urban migration shows that with nearly half the rural population having at least seen and had brief experience in the larger urban centers (most trucks arriving in the village bring some urban envoys), the urban area strongly influences the countryside (1969:210, passim). The rural population, especially in contemporary times, is made up not only of isolated farmers and hunters, but also of people living in large villages and market towns, some who have lived in cities, worked abroad, or served in the army; others have relatives, friends, and business connections in the city. Thus the West African highlife is found in small towns and from there introduced to the villagers. For example, among the Ubakala clan of eastern Nigeria, a young girls' traditional dance group has a dance number called "Come Waltz With Me," in which they break the traditional circle and body contact dance patterns to form couples and parody the waltz by clasping each other's heads, necks, shoulders, waists, hips, backs, and buttocks (Hanna 1965, 1976a). Elizabeth Colson (1971:168–170, 238–244) describes how Gwembe Tonga villagers thought in terms of urban entertainment. Between 1956 and 1957 young people danced the *mankutu*; it was supplanted by *cilimba* in the early 1960s and, by 1965, the twist had taken over.

1f. *The urban area tends to be the locus of legitimization by style setters and of institutionalization of dance forms.* It has the most influential dancing schools, community centers, religious headquarters, folklore institutes, and similar institutions which sustain innovations and perpetuate a society's cultural repertoire, codifying new dances and steps. This generalization holds particularly for primary cities, courts (particularly dictatorial ones), and ceremonial centers. David Sutherland (1976:42) reports that in Federico's 1966 sample of 146 male and female dancers belonging to twelve ballet companies in the United States, none of the dancers in prestigious companies studied outside a medium or large city (i.e., under 50,000), and only six percent of the dancers from less prestigious companies acquired training in small towns.

Historically, in England, the London schools set the standard for proper dancing: masters were sent to the provinces, or provincials visited the city to acquire the latest forms and styles (cf. Dennis Brailsford 1969). From the nineteenth century onwards, the larger Scottish towns had permanent dancing academies. Sometimes the teachers in the urban schools also served the smaller towns and villages around them (J. and T. Flett 1964:7–8). In the Balinese town of Tabanan, Indonesia, court dancing was often the paradigm for village dancing. Talented boys and girls from the countryside went to live in the town where as servants at the court they could study with the great teachers (Geertz 1963:103).

New York City, where dancing masters and teachers have been a part of the cultural pattern since the eighteenth century, has been the pinnacle of legitimization and institutionalization of dance in the United States. The teaching of social dance, alone, has become a million-dollar business. Professional dance organizations in New York hold day-long sessions two or three times a month to give teachers an opportunity to learn the latest dances and combinations. These organizations represent several hundred teachers who teach hundreds more (Don Begenau 1972:60). New York is also the dance capital for theater dance. Through her work as a university professor of dance and with the Artists-in-the-Schools Program, College Dance Festivals, and Massachusetts Arts and Humanities Foundation, Jeanne Beaman concludes that U.S. theater and educational dance have a flourishing, virtually dictatorial, New York City based corps of "priests and assistant priests" disseminating doctrine and fostering its adherence (personal communication, 9-25-75). Of course, there are also numerous regional and local urban loci of legitimization and institutionalization of dance forms. And in Croatia, Yugoslavia, urban members of the national dance company LADO, which presents traditional dance forms that were "all but dead," resuscitates them through the efforts of urban folklorists and choreographers using urban dancers trained in the idiom. They "are hired to teach dance routines in the villages near the city so that the villagers may dance in public folklore presentations" (Anthony Shay 1974:9).

In conclusion then, the first set of propositions attempts to suggest that, compared with rural areas, urban areas tend to be greater reservoirs of ideas and catalysts for dance creativity (innovation) through a qualitatively and quantitatively different population density, sociocultural context, and physical infrastructure. The second set of propositions focus on some results of this dance-urban area interaction.

   2. *Because dances tend to be an integral part of their host sociocultural systems, dances in urban areas manifest urban patterns of social differentiation and interaction.* These patterns are evident in the occasion of dance, its purpose, participants, consequences, and style and structure. Dance, as pointed out in Chapter 4, is often part of a culture's inventory of signs used to demarcate and communicate we/they social groupings. Through dance, people represent themselves to themselves and to each other. (Claude Lévi-Strauss and Hugh D. Duncan are among those who have given much attention to nondance symbolic expression and social role and structure.) In heterogeneous, fast-changing towns, the need for classification of individuals who are potential social partners or competitors for different purposes is necessary (Mitchell 1956). Signs can stand for social relations in abstraction and also be instruments of social control or emblem-rallying calls to action.

   2a. *Dances in urban areas often provide adaptive vehicles for coping with personal or group need.*[8]

   2b. *Dances may provide stability*[9] *by presenting symbols of identity and vehicles for integration.* Migrants from a rural area, small town, or foreign country who perform "traditional"[10] dances in urban and suburban areas during nonworking hours may experience a sense of belonging and relief from the tensions of an alien, heterogenous, sometimes hostile, urban environment. In what Theodore and Nancy Graves (1974:39) call an isolating mechanism, dance acts to reduce stimuli and the problems of disjunctive life styles. As a nostalgic counterforce to the new environment, dance may be less a reactionary than an anchoring, stabilizing phenomenon (cf. R. Nayacakalou and Aidan Southall 1973:392, 398). Examples of such a mechanism can be found in Africa, the United States, Latin America, the Balkans, and the Pacific. In Bamako, Mali, people seek security in spontaneous, popular or traditionally patterned associations which have dances as part of significant life event celebrations (Meillassoux 1968: 75, 105). James Hirabayashi et al. (1972) describe the U.S. Indian urban powwow as an important adaptive social mechanism for coping with the transformation from rural life. The dance performance is a symbol of identity (cf. James Howard 1976) and a means of maintaining the Indian social network. In the early years of the relocation program in the San Francisco bay area, few Indians had costumes or knew how to dance, but the powwow system created a structural interaction network for mutual interests and communication. It operates throughout the western states and involves reciprocal participation among individuals in the various areas so that visitors' costs are partially defrayed by the hosts.

Paul Doughty describes the Saturday night dances, fiestas, and performances of special dance groups (scissor dancers, *Negritos*, *pallas*, and others) among the highland migrant groups in Lima, Peru, as rites of intensification par excellence: they are a periodic revitalization of existing patterns of interaction. The institution of dance performance, sponsored by clubs, organized by regional place of origin, helps to maintain social networks which are related to traditions of reciprocity. "'Affective' and expressive human interaction are the items of exchange: the elaborateness of the social form maximizes opportunity for it" (1970:39). The dances help maintain the functional integrity of the extended family in an urban environment in which people live in dispersed areas, and they provide the opportunity for migrants to find suitable spouses among the *gente conocida*, the familiar, trustworthy people (ibid.:49). Similarly, the fiesta system in the northern highlands of Bolivia serves to link the cities, towns, and peasant communities and thus provides some continuity for the migrant to the city. "Dance group formation in voluntary associations shows that La Paz is not a closed system, for these associations maintain intimate ties with the home town of their members" (Buechler

1970:70). Another illustration of dance as a mechanism to cope with urban transience is found in the Mexican dance groups discussed above in Chapter 6. The group, its members coming from different communities, unites periodically in religious festivities to dance, eat, and discuss discordant ideas. The dance performed in Mexico City "responds" to the urban environment: its rhythmic pace has been accelerated and its costume has been modified. Because the Aztec group is more prestigious than others, the *conchero* participants like to call their dance Azteca and use Aztec costumes rather than reflect its Chichimeca roots (Moedano, personal communication, 1974).

In Belgrade, migrants interact heavily with friends who have a common ethnic and geographic origin. During the summer, these friendship groups spontaneously dance and sing on the upper terrace of Kalemegdan Park. "Balkan dances are performed, for the most part, in lines or circles, which can effectively delineate one group of dancers from another. The participants are thus able to differentiate themselves on the basis of region of origin" (Simić 1973:135).

Dance may reflect acceptance of the lack of social mobility. Meillassoux argues that some of the dance associations dating from pre-independent Bamako, for example, *jarawara* and *duñuba*, may have positive consequences in the short run, but are ultimately maladaptive to the performers' integration into urban life. The associations are linked with rural origins, low social status, and the age-set system which perpetuates stagnant conservatism, particularly in maintaining and promoting rural particularism or the traditional caste systems (1968:93–96, 112). The *koteba*, a Bamana traditional farcical street-theater which includes dance, mainly "caters for those inhabitants . . . still attached to village customs and for those who rarely go to cinemas or dances either because of their status (like the women and young girls) or because of their meagre resources" (1965:33). The *segu-ka-bara* is danced by nonaristocratic Bamana from Ségou, who, not having the educational and other resources for upward mobility in the urban milieu, perhaps "tend to look to ancient values as a way for promotion within a limited and backward present social sphere"; they offer a means of coping with an apparently insurmountable handicap (1968:106).

The pattern in Chicago's taxi-dance hall (also called dime-a-dance hall, stag dance, and monkey hop), an urban institution of the 1920s also found in numerous American cities and in an equivalent form at other times and places, exemplifies a form of "marginal person" behavior (cf. Thomas Cottle 1966, Kenneth Little 1974:102–103). The taxi-dancer, so-called because she was publicly for hire and paid according to the time spent and services rendered, usually came from a disrupted family life and had no social or vocational opportunities to find satisfactions in more conventional ways (Paul Cressey 1968: 54–83). The taxi-dance hall arose to meet the demands for feminine company from homeless and lonesome men crowded into rooming houses. The polyglot patrons included Chinese, Sicilians, Hawaiians, Scandinavians, Mexicans, Russians, Filipinos, Poles, Greeks, American Indians, Hindus, and Anglo-Saxons of varying age and physical fitness who did not have the opportunity to interact with women of their own group in the city and were denied free social contacts with the dominant group (ibid.:190–194).

2c. *Dances may socialize new urban area participants to urban norms.* The Bisa tribesmen's *kalela* dance in Zambia permits urban learning and adjustment. Mitchell (1956) reports that in this superficially traditional dance even the songs of self-praise are more urban than parochial; they are composed in town for the amusement of townsmen and deal with events and situations familiar to town dwellers. Mitchell found the *kalela* dance to display in microcosm the two most important determinants of social relationships in multiracial Zambia: the degree of westernization and tribal membership. *Kalela* modern dress and European titles are clues to the importance of the European way of life and its significance in the social stratification. Thus by performing the *kalela*, dancers seek to participate vicariously in the westernized upper levels of African society from which most are excluded due to lack of such qualifications as wealth and education (ibid.:15). They may be assimilating values which then affect the success of their children in upward mobility.

Similarly Bamako's *sogoñi-kū* dance association imitates the European hierarchy with positions such as *président, vice-président, secrétaire,* and *trésorier* (Meillassoux 1968:100. See also pp. 112–116 on traditionally based associations for the young unmarried which perpetuate traditional customs and lore while adapting to new needs. These include teaching the "socially useful" skills of the latest modern western popular dances.) According to Banton, the new class of literate tribal immigrants with Creole skills and living standards who lived in Freetown, Sierra Leone, had no recognized place in the tribal society which tended to exclude them. Thus the use of nontraditional status titles and syncretistic movement patterns in their dance behavior (1957:173) is partly a response to the need for role differentiation in a confusing situation of an emerging new structure of roles and statuses (ibid.:182, 162–174).

The urban West African highlife, as with many traditional secular forms, permits self-expression and encourages improvisation and creativity. It is a medium for unpretentious yet wisdom-filled commentaries and gossip on the trials and tribulations of everyday living and thus may be cynical, ironical, and cathartic. Its themes, that is, problems of "good-time" girls, need for proper behavior and morals, religious precepts, and nonparochial values, reaffirm some traditional norms and clarify and create new urban norms (Hanna 1973, cf. Norman Whitten and Aurdio Fuentes C. 1966). This dance genre, regularly found in the large urban centers of Nigeria and Ghana, is also popular in small towns. Musical accompaniment may be provided by visiting name bands, local aspiring groups, or electric or battery-operated record players. This informal urban highlife dancing to the music of local radio stations has even diffused to some village bars. In the urban areas even youngsters not old enough to participate in the couple dance, and people who cannot afford to pay the admission fee, are often found in the streets outside the hotels and nightclubs dancing to the music of favorite bands. The highlife serves much the same function as a newspaper with its criticism and praise of current events, and, as with newspapers and magazines, some highlife numbers may be censored or banned.

The Javanese *ludruk* theater, of which dance is an integral part, contributes to the participants' (spectators and actors-dancers alike) urban world view, according to Peacock. The importance of *ludruk* is reflected in the number of performances: between 1962 and 1963, Peacock estimated that three hundred troupes performed simultaneously on major holidays in local communities and in commercial theaters (at that time there were five theaters in Surabaja, Indonesia, the second largest city and capital of the Province of East Java). *Ludruk*'s persuasive influence is compounded by "the fact that Javanese are trained so much through bodily imitation (as opposed to verbal instruction)" (1968:159). The symbolic *ludruk* form, described merely as entertainment, may also have a subliminal impact "by inducing empathy and imitation" in contrast to religious influences which are overt, everyone being aware of them and thus on guard against them (ibid.:244–245).

Ludruk finds its followers among certain kinds of proletarians who do not seriously follow the rules of Islam, are of family-raising age (between twenty and fifty years), are underemployed and poor–the artisans, construction laborers, road sweepers, petty traders, and minor clerks who live in *kampungs*, urban slums or shantytown neighborhoods within and on the outskirts of the city.

Ludruk disseminates common multiethnic images and introduces functionally specific relations of urban life as opposed to the socially diffuse ones of village life. It enhances homogeneity (as it replaces a local rite which perpetuated traditional values) and prepares the individual for the incorporation of *kampungs* into city and national government (ibid.:219). Peacock argues that the most important effect may be the vicarious experiences of individuals who cannot change their situation and the way their children are raised (ibid.: 250). *Ludruk* helps individuals to cope with the onslaught of ideas and ideals which run counter to their traditional belief systems: "Because daily actions must take place under conditions not totally of the actors' choosing, the actors cannot totally express their ideals through their daily actions. But on the *ludruk* stage, they can construct, in fantasy, any conditions which they wish, so they can construct conditions which allow them to express their ideals in rather pure form" (ibid.:236–237). Peacock notes that "Many *ludruk* goers are too old to embark on real-life 'quests' from *kampung* to extra-*kampung* realms, but the experience of vicariously enjoying the quest of *ludruk* heroes helps them glamorize the 'quests' on which their children or their neighbors' and relatives' children have embarked or will embark. In this way *ludruk* diminishes elders' tendencies to inhibit youths' ambition to rise from the *kampung*" (ibid.:219).

Recently in the United States, the arts have been viewed by some dancers, educators, psychiatrists, and government officials as a "challenge to poverty" or what others have called "behavior control" in the "inner city" (Gilbert Geis 1968, Judith Murphy and Ronald Gross 1968). The poor in these urban areas can be viewed as immigrants— not necessarily from rural to urban areas, but from parochial to dominant urban culture with its emphasis on work achievement and conformity to certain norms. In this context, attempts have been made to harness dance as a medium of socialization.[11] The assumption is that it rechannels energies "off the streets" and provides a "bridge" out of the inner city for the talented dancer (Hanna 1970).

2d. *Dance may be a vehicle for criticizing the urban condition.* Illustrative of this proposition are the highlife in Africa and in the United States the "urban celebration," a subcategory of expressive body movement activities. Traveling across the United States as a participant-observer, Theeman (1973) reports on the experience and culture of these dances. Individual awareness is one of the goals, to discover and experience truth about oneself, to tear away masks. Some presentation of subject matter, improvised and personal, is involved. Participants in "urban celebrations" are drawn from the artistic avant-garde, radical theater, architecture, city planning, marginal academia, and New Left radical groups, all in some way critical of and alienated from institutions (ibid.:342, 463). The performance group is open and usually short-lived; however sometimes it evolves into communal small-group theater depending on paying performances for its precarious existence. Movement is used as a form of social criticism "to highlight, to celebrate, to warn about and to act against aspects of perceived social conditions" (ibid.:332). There is interest in novel environments and juxtapositions in order to change traditional spatial relationships (e.g., those between the audience and performer, student and teacher), to confront critically the mores of dominant culture so that its rhythm, absurdity, and chaos is experienced: to change through participation and perception (ibid.:345).

2e. *Dance behavior may correlate with urban sociocultural status aspiration, acceptance, or defiance.* As suggested earlier, dance is a form of self-presentation, what Suttles describes as "essential expressive interludes when group members reestablish each other's confidence in the coincidence between subjective and objective realities" (1972:264). Ethnic groups have differential rates of adaptation and attitudes toward change. Some find relatively insulated enclaves and tend to maintain traditional practices. For others, there is often an association between (a) time spent in the urban area and (b) adaptation to extant socioeconomic structures and the filling of available niches in the opportunity structure. (Migration studies show that rural home proximity to the city and migration regulation negate motivation and need for urban adaptation; cf. Heisler 1974, J. Jackson 1969.)

The *concheros* identifying their dance with a prestigious group and the dynamics of the *kalela* and *ludruk* dances illustrate vicarious participation in a higher class and upward aspirations. A low status group often ceases to perform its ethnic or class dance when it assimilates to a dominant group. Erving Goffman, utilizing the metaphor of theatrical performance, tells us that upward mobility commonly "involves the presentation of proper performances and that efforts to move upward and efforts to keep from moving downward are expressed in terms of sacrifices made for the maintenance of front" (1959:36). In San Lorenzo, Ecuador, the marimba, ridiculed as a primitive curiosity by the mestizos, was danced by blacks in rural areas and in the cities. Whitten and Fuentes C. note that "one of the marks of an upwardly mobile kindred is that members cease to dance the marimba" (1966:169). This pattern is further discussed below in Section 3 and presented in Figure 12.[12]

Dance may be a vivid assertion of self for migrant, settler, and indigenous resident in a competitive plural society. Siegel (1970) refers to this as "defensive structuring": members of a society attempt to establish and present cultural identity in the face of felt external threats to that identity. Thus, dance functions as a boundary maintaining mechanism (cf. Fustel de Coulanges 1956:25). Conservatism in dance is not just a characteristic of low status groups such as those mentioned before; on the contrary, upper class privileged groups may cling to their dance as a symbol of cultural identity in a milieu which becomes heterogenous and changing. The Juchitecos from Oaxaca, Mexico, discussed above in Chapter 6, illustrate this principle (Royce, 1974*b*, 1977).

Redfield encourages us to look for creative patterns of interaction between different social constituencies (1953), for example, defiance. Low status groups may parody upper status group dance forms or styles, belittling them to make the status group less appealing. *Mbeni*, the forerunner of *kalela*, and the case of Sundanese expression and communication of defiance have been discussed above in Chapter 6.

Colonialists and indigenous aspiring leaders had their most intense interaction in the urban area, which therefore became the locus for the revival of dances as a symbol of national identity in the pursuit of cultural independence after political sovereignty was achieved. Manjusri Sircar (1972) describes the nationalistic development of dance in Calcutta, a large city with a climate of receptivity to change and an audience to support the performances. Similarly, in Uganda, a national theater was created in the city of Kampala to assert the identity of the Ugandan population. Drawing upon performers throughout the country, the ethnically heterogeneous Heart Beat Company was based at Kampala's national theater or stadium (Hanna and Hanna 1968*a*). Likewise, one finds national dance companies burgeoning in major cities throughout the Third World. In San Juan, Puerto Rico, the tradition of the Fiesta de Cruz had declined, but was revived, acquiring new functions–namely, asserting sociocultural identity, symbolically presenting a bygone way of life, and institutionalizing folklore as a reaction against change, modernization, and the tourist impact (Martha Ellen Davis 1972).[13]

To review, the second set of propositions about dance and the urban ecosystem focuses on urban transience and such dance functions as anchoring, identifying, socializing, integrating, innovating, and defying.

3. The third set of propositions considers some conditions which preclude the urban area functioning as a stimulus to increased diversity (Proposition Set 1) and shows a culmination of some forces in the urban environment which manifest themselves in dance (Proposition Set 2). *The less a dance conforms to the norms of urban decision makers or high status groups, the less likely it is to survive unmodified and/or to be widespread in an urban area.*

3a. *Some urban regulations inhibit certain public dance behavior.* Urban laws, particularly those concerning moral, traffic, nuisance, and safety behavior, may affect the dance traditions of rural, immigrant, or avant-garde groups in terms of such factors as performance space, time, lighting, setting, duration, song texts, costume, use of drugs, sounds of musical accompaniment, and number of performers congregating. In Bamako the Chef de Canton forbade the *sabar* dance in 1947 because of its alleged lewdness: "Some of the figures," according to Meillassoux, "required that dancers of the opposite sexes lie on top of each other or display their private parts" (1968:118). Councilmen in Paraná, Argentina (Ruben Reina 1973:30–33, 123–125), feeling highly responsible for public morals and *cultura* (refinement and urbanity), constantly argue over the moral implications of public carnival festivities. Street fiestas require permission from the president of the municipality and must meet regulations of time, noise, language, and respect for performers and patrons. Fines are imposed on those whose dances are considered indecent or insulting. Many of the morality laws in urban areas are the result of Christian influence. Although the Bible discusses two kinds of dance, that of propitiating God through prayerful dance (e.g., the Israelites demonstrating through pious dance that no part of them was unaffected by the love of God), and that of immoral dance (Salome's dance, e.g.), it seems that the latter drew more attention and concern, and as a result, dance has been periodically proscribed (E. Backman 1952, H. Clive 1961).

If a dance form is staged in a theater, such further constraints as production skills, improvisation limits, rent, and lighting costs may exist. And the dance must be familiar enough to sufficient numbers of people who are willing to pay for theater seats, or at least show up. These points lead to the next hypothesis.

3b. *Some economic conditions constrain dance.* Some dance forms may be stifled in urban areas because of the economic predicament of the performing arts. In the United States the costs of live performances continually escalate and performances no longer pay for themselves. An important factor is the relatively strong unionization which exists in the cities; this is linked to such nonurban phenomena as the rising productivity per man hour in other spheres of the economy and technology in performing arts which permits little in the way of labor-saving devices. Furthermore, competitive salaries for dancers in an inflationary economy is necessary to encourage their continuance in the arts (Baumol and Bowen 1966:390).

Another stifling effect occurs when patrons (individuals, groups, or governments) or urban based performers become tastemakers and support a standard repertory with little room for innovation or support only narrowly selected creative artists (Suess 1969:274). The Harkness Ballet exists when Rebecca Harkness wants it to exist—patrons can and have taken away monetary support (i.e., disbanded a company).

3c. *Some dances are eliminated or significantly modified by processes of group (immigrant or class) sociocultural assimilation to the dominant urban culture or other reference group behavior* (cf. Robert Merton 1957). Does the adoption of an expressive form precede structural change or vice versa? It may be that both forces are operative and that behavior is situational with push-pull factors relating to opportunities which present themselves or are sought out by dissatisfied individuals. The case for dance appears to be similar to that argued for language: the choice of language made by individuals in a multilingual urban situation reveals not only personal identity but more generalized principles of society (Joseph Greenberg 1965). Sociolinguistic studies over the past ten years have demonstrated how linguistic behavior changes as a person's social position changes.

Figure 12 illustrates simplistically and linearly that, with education or luck, a person in Situation A may enter a new social condition, Situations B and C, and find their former world view no longer workable; an adjustment usually occurs. As an individual in the urban area becomes involved in another culture or subculture through upward or lateral mobility, change tends to occur in the idiom of cognitive-affective-sensori-motor expression, adoption of a new dance repertoire, or change into a nondance expression. Later, Situation D, a process of rediscovery may take place, and the person may return to "traditional" dance.

The urban area may constrict dance performance in the rural area by attracting the latter's participants so that many rural dances must now be held to coincide with the urban work schedule. Drawing upon data from Oraon villages and localities in Ranchi City, India, Vidyarthi (1961) attributes the decline of Adivasi (primitive) dance to Christianity and urbanization. The maintenance and transmission of dances depended on the existence of youth dormitories and the

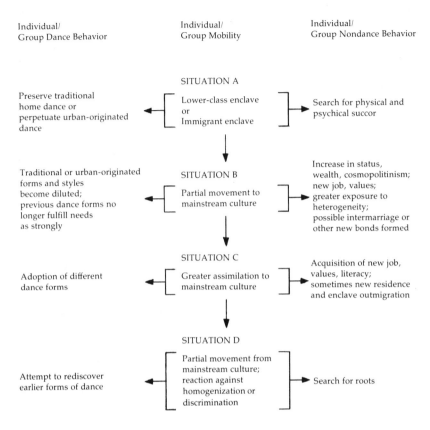

Individual/ Group Dance Behavior	Individual/ Group Mobility	Individual/ Group Nondance Behavior

Figure 12.   Dissolution-disappearance-reemergence of immigrant and lower-class dance forms in the urban area.

Akhra (village dancing ground). The former were abolished in city and village because they were said to be centers of moral corruption. The migrant workers took home new ways of viewing the world and no longer saw the traditional institutions as centers of cultural and educational activities. In the city, the converted Oraons do not dance, or if they do it is a modified, syncretistic blend. Other workers have insufficient time for regular dancing at the Akhra, which still exists and does attract dancers at festival time. Vidyarthi sees a deterioration in the quality of dance "primarily because of the change in economic occupation, educational qualification, and urban way of life" (1961:306).

Keil argues that juju music in Nigeria, urban blues in the United States, and balalaika music in Greece (all of which are used as dance music) degenerated or became diluted when the dominant culture adopted them–commercialization occurred and the idiom was reduced to a common denominator to appeal to the greatest number of people (1973, cf. John Cogley 1973). A similar situation occurred when the Casa de la Cultura Ecuatoriana announced a festival in 1963 to restore interest in the marimba dance and create a national folklore. The setting ceased to be the *casa de la marimba*;[14] it became a saloon, and the dance has become a money-making proposition attracting the mestizo highland tourists. The woman no longer initiates the dance as was the custom, and the distinctive rhythm and style are disappearing. The marimba is being altered to appeal to the nationalist-oriented highlanders (Whitten and Fuentes C. 1966: 179–180). (See Figure 13.)

3d. *Dances of groups of people perceived to be potential threats to the established power structure tend to be restricted.* Colonial records and informant reports indicate that during imperial rule in Africa there were multiple constraints on dancing. For example, in Nigeria after the "Women's War" in 1929, in which unheeded complaints were expressed through the dance medium and then broadcast again leading to violent attempts to make adjustments, authorities feared that dance-play performances in the urban area might foment violence. This led to restrictions, such as requiring permits for public assemblies. For similar reasons, "urban celebrations" in U.S. cities meet with police interference–dancers are asked to move on. Sometimes, the police are incorporated into the dance in an attempt to forestall their intervention (Theeman 1973:342)! In East Africa, some Europeans felt threatened by the *mbeni* dance, its potential for subversiveness through mimicry and mockery, and the extensive social network that developed as part of the process of dance instruction and performance (Ranger 1975). Northern Rhodesia Township Regulations

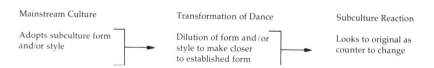

Mainstream Culture	Transformation of Dance	Subculture Reaction
Adopts subculture form and/or style	Dilution of form and/or style to make closer to established form	Looks to original as counter to change

Figure 13.   Mainstream culture adoption of subculture dance form.

proscribed the organization or participation in any dance "calculated to hold up to ridicule or bring into contempt any person, religion or duly constituted authority" (cited in Mitchell 1956:12).

To summarize this section, the third proposition set attempts to explain the moral, economic, or political dynamics which eliminate or modify dance.

Conclusion

The main thrust of this chapter has been to illuminate the significance of dance as reflective, constitutive, and conditioning in the urban area and to convey the challenge of urban, nonverbal communication theoretical issues through the study of a neglected focus of research: dance–urban area interaction. My primary proposition is that, in the urban area, sociocultural factors are the primary determinants of dance concept, process, product, and impact, but these are influenced and modulated by the constraints and opportunities (substrate) of relatively high settlement heterogeneity and density and the concomitant physical infrastructure and minimization of friction space.

On the basis of our current knowledge of dance and the urban area, three sets of propositions which attempt to identify general conditions for specific consequences were discussed. These are summarily presented (see Figure 14):

1. The urban area tends to be a reservoir of ideas and a catalyst

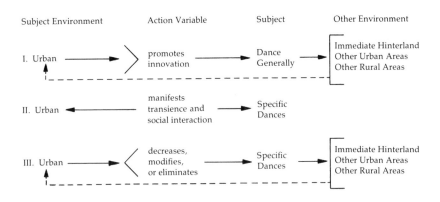

Figure 14.   Urban area—dance relationships.

for dance creativity (used interchangeably with innovation) unless inhibited by sociocultural factors. **1a.** Greater exposure of diverse dance phenomena probably occurs in the urban than rural area. **1b.** Greater opportunity for a creative element to develop tends to exist in the urban area because of the minimization of spatial impediments and potential exposure to diverse dance phenomena, economic base, and location and nature of religious authority. **1c.** The urban area both acts upon rural traditions brought to it and spawns new forms. **1d.** Urban residents tend to be relatively more receptive to a variety of new dance forms than nonurban ones; heterogeneity, tolerance, and cosmopolitanism are determining factors. **1e.** Dance innovations which originate or are observed in urban areas are more likely to be legitimized by style setters and diffused to relatively large numbers of people than are rural innovations which do not get urban exposure. **1f.** The urban area tends to be the locus of legitimization by style setters and of institutionalization of dance forms. (Figure 15 highlights aspects of this proposition set.)

2. Because dances tend to be integral parts of their host sociocultural systems, dances in urban areas manifest urban patterns of social differentiation and interaction. **2a.** Dances in urban areas often provide adaptive vehicles for coping with personal or group need. **2b.** Dances may provide stability by preserving symbols of identity and vehicles for integration. **2c.** They may socialize new urban area participants to urban norms. **2d.** They may criticize the urban condition. **2e.** Dance behavior may correlate with urban sociocultural status aspiration, acceptance, or defiance.

3. The less a dance conforms to the norms of urban decision makers or high status groups, the less likely it is to survive unmodified and/or to be widespread in an urban area. **3a.** Some urban regulations inhibit certain public dance behavior. **3b.** Some economic conditions constrain dance. **3c.** Some dances are eliminated or significantly modified by processes of group sociocultural assimilation to dominant urban area culture or other reference group behavior. **3d.** Dances of groups of people perceived to be potential threats to the established power structure tend to be restricted.

It is essential to reemphasize that the urban area, a kind of culture climax, is the locus of multiple interacting dynamic forces. There is no predetermined or unilinear pattern, but a continuing interplay of complex locally distinct forces and worldwide factors.

These explanatory propositions await in-depth, systematic investigation. We need case studies which explore the interrelations between dance and the urban area in different societal types. The ex-

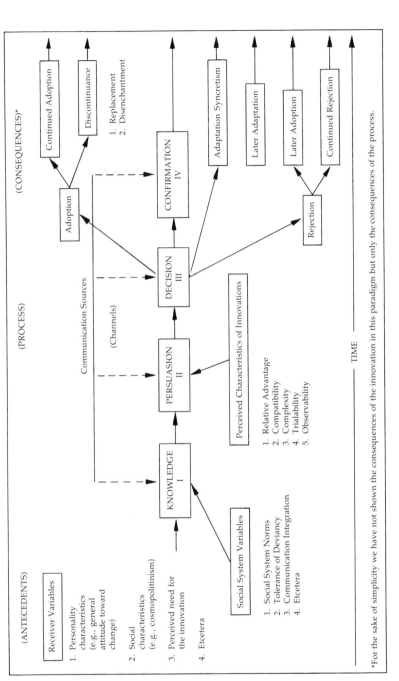

Figure 15. Paradigm of the innovation-decision process (modified from Rogers and Shoemaker 1971:102).

*For the sake of simplicity we have not shown the consequences of the innovation in this paradigm but only the consequences of the process.

ploration of variables apposite to distinct population sectors in cities and cross-cultural studies of comparable population sectors in different cities would be useful. At the current stage of dance studies (cf. Hanna 1979*a*), the distinctions between kinds of urbanism (agrarian, feudal, commercial, and industrial) and city types in terms of historical development are considered irrelevant. These distinctions may prove significant. Further questions include the specific kinds of options that are adopted and rejected or blended in terms of dance context and text (style and structure), and differences in public or private dance behavior.

The introduction to this chapter mentioned that the results of the dynamic interrelations of the urban ecosystem of dance have policy implications. Third World countries and minority groups everywhere are seeking the preservation or revitalization of their own cultures, striving for security or satisfaction in the face of disruptive forces. Many contemporary choreographers are trying to succeed; those who view postindustrial society as "cold, materialistic, and immoral" are seeking artistic, affective counter responses and finding meaning in the experiential (cf. Czikszentmihalyi 1975). Sometimes national, state, and local governments support dance as do private organizations. Since 1957, for example, the Ford Foundation has dispensed a largesse of more than two hundred and fifty million dollars to the arts—patronage equal to that of the popes and kings of yore (Jean White 1973). With movement away from the city center and urban sprawl of megalopolis in the United States, there is a question about where resources should be allocated, how dance schools, study programs, theaters, television, film, and other media should be funded. What are the effects of taxation on theaters, nuisance laws, and assembly permits for performances? What about the use of dance in the school and church? If we come to understand the processes of change, how things happen to occur, were made to occur, can be made to do so, and how they will happen in the future, if we understand the nature of relationships between dynamic living entities—city and dance—we may be better able to meet some of the exigencies and so enhance the quality of human life.

9   Directions for the Future

THIS BOOK PROVIDES a theoretical framework in which to view contemporary and future dance knowledge acquired from disparate times, places, and perspectives. The communication model (Figure 4) encompasses a number of different approaches focusing on the context (sociocultural setting and function) and/or text (movement) of dance. Because the use of one approach will provide only a partial understanding, the model emphasizes the interactions of the dance phenomenon—catalyst, concept, process, performance, result, and impact upon the participants and catalytic environment of dance. My concern is moving toward a theory of dance within which research studies can make contributions toward understanding humans rather than existing as bits of unrelated information. The general source of theory, method, data, and propositions which illustrate the synthetic model in key domains of human existence emanate from the social sciences, humanities, and arts; the specific model accommodates characteristics unique to dance.

This dance communication model draws especially upon anthropology and its subfields and employs two basic principles of anthropology. The first is the comparability of all human cultures, the search for similarities and differences among peoples, and the search for explanations for what is universal to the human species and what is culturally determined and unique to a group. The central question is: What are the underlying psychobiological bases which generate different patterns among individuals through different group and environmental experiences? The comparative approach includes the study of humans today and yesterday, in western and nonwestern societies, in remote tribes, and sophisticated urban settings. The second key anthropological tenet is to understand an individual's culture which is learned through communication; through communication, in turn, the individual may influence the culture. The question is what are the webs of significance a human group spins from its perspectives and from the cross-cultural researcher's perspectives? The intention is to examine the feelings, thoughts, and actions of humans, not as isolated bits and pieces, but in a holistic or systems context. Generative and transformational processes can be examined within this purview. The communication model, adapted to the specific cross-cultural nature of dance as currently known, will provide a framework for considering essential anthropological concerns.

The turbulence of the phase of the anthropological study of dance in which scholars began to reexamine the state of the art (Hanna 1975a, 1979a) catalyzed the development of the model. Extant ones to explain nondance phenomena and to guide future research were not adequate for dance. Similarly, extant theoretical orientations for dance excluded some critical variables. It is the relationship between the text and context that is the most pressing concern from a social science perspective.

This treatise, or reference text for the student somewhat versed in the dynamics and structure of human social life, begins by introducing the subject of dance, identifying necessary and sufficient characteristics: human behavior composed, from the dancer's perspective, of purposeful, intentionally rhythmical, and culturally patterned sequences of nonverbal body movements other than ordinary motor activities, the motion having inherent and aesthetic value. Social scientists study behavior that is observable by the eye. They also investigate what generates the behavior and accounts for its transformations. These interests lead to an exploration of the psychobiological bases of dance, the focus of Chapter 3. Apparently these bases support the proposition that dance is a form of communication distinct from other forms of animal communication.

Subsequent chapters focus on some prominent manifestations of dance in human life. The theoretical model and its related propositions partially explain the possibilities inherent in the cognitive-sensori-affective-motor communication of dance as a vehicle for communicating sociocultural patterns and as an instrument of religious belief and practice, a medium of politics, and a subject and object of human life constrained by the human use of environmental space.

Research Pitfalls

This volume emphasizes some areas that have not been adequately discussed, and it points to gaps in our knowledge, bringing together a disparate literature and summarizing much dance research. The book provides an inventory of hypotheses to test; that is, the propositions offer a challenge to future research. Much work is needed to flesh out the concepts. We have primarily descriptive, historical, humanistic, theoretical, and empirical studies which emphasize text or context. Although the study of dance in written documents goes back to Plato, Aristotle, and Bharata, it is undeveloped in comparison with the study of other expressive forms and performing arts. The book maps out directions for the future of a subject area in the throes of conceptual and methodological development. Commentaries on research problems lace this study so that present weaknesses may be avoided in future work.

There are difficulties arising from the neglect of dance studies and fragmentary accounts in the literature. Unduly biased perspectives pervade the literature. They include ethnocentric, condescending (cf. Chapters 1 and 5 on the colonialists), defensive (indigenes glorifying history or suppressing it in accord with their current values or those they presume an inquirer to hold), personal preference, and historical era biases, although social science has a "no-bias" fantasy. Ongoing translation must occur in communicating about dance, and especially dance in a culture other than one's own.

In addition the problems of secondary analyses include the lack of a common vocabulary to discuss dance, the elimination of some dance from consideration because natives did not use the researcher's term, or because the dance differed from that of the observer's culture. Questions that should have been asked were not; behavior that should have been recorded was not. It is not clear whether descriptions are first-hand observations, second-hand reports of a single informant, or reports of a sample of informants who are representative of their group of society. It is unclear whether a dance description is of a single occurrence or a regular pattern; whether a dance function is manifest (i.e., recognized as such by the dance participants) or latent (i.e., induced or deduced by the analyst).

Given the problems with much secondary dance data (literature and film), purportedly "systematic" comparative armchair studies cannot provide valid conclusions. (See Lomax 1968 and critiques by Kealiinohomoku 1974, Elli Köngäs 1970, Williams 1974, Youngerman 1974.) Furthermore, comparing dance culture areas without considering intracultural variation is puzzling. There is often greater "folk" dance variation between men and women in the same culture than women in one culture area and those in another; women universally share some characteristics. To code what is cultural rather than personal or related to one among several groups requires a representative sample of a group's dances in a society.

Empirical case studies are essential; they are the building blocks of knowledge. Moreover, comparative studies are also necessary; comparison can make familiar what appears strange. The comparative approach focuses the explanation for what occurs in one group or society. It is a useful strategy to force the analyst to try to account for the effect of different variables in similar societies and thus deepen description, analysis, and explanation. Since social science seeks broader theories of humans than a single case study provides, comparative studies assist in determining the generality of a proposition. Over time the accumulation of studies using the dance communication model and the interrelated concepts and propositions presented in this book will tell us more about the nature of human perception, understanding, creation, and performance and how these are influenced by affecting presences and alternate forms of communication. Such comparative studies will yield a more comprehensive picture of what dance is and what dance means. There are, of course, many possible kinds of comparative study: looking at the variation within a culture, examining a single society over time, investigating societies of similar scale and complexity, focusing on societies torn by conflict, and how different parties utilize dance in the political and religious arenas.

Probing for Meaning

The application of the dance model warrants further commentary. Semantic analysis of dance movement is an unplumbed domain (Stone 1975:10). Mehrabian (1972) notes that comprehensive systems of dance notation only describe movements as motion, and there are no guidelines for identifying what they signify. (Arnheim 1972, Langer passim, and Ted Shawn 1974 are among those who have overemphasized the affective dimension of dance.) Thus I developed a semantic grid, Table 2 (Chapter 2), in the process of analyzing my field data and secondary data (Hanna 1979c elaborates the grid).

What we find in research depends heavily on the conceptual tools we have to guide us. If researchers are to analyze meaning for and in behavior, the development of concepts to explicate order in behavior must have high priority. The neglect of the semantic analysis of movement, or emphasis on only one aspect of analysis (textual or contextual), or attention given to a single device (mimetic behavior or conventional sign language) in a single sphere (the movement itself, for example), may be the result of inadequately conceptualizing motional configurations as these operate in different and often multiple devices and spheres of meaning with layers of semantic complexity.

In the grid proposed for semantic studies, the components are devices and spheres of message material which appear inherent in dance behavior viewed in global perspective. In probing meaning the grid can be imposed on the whole dance and used to zoom in on smaller units to bring into focus informant verbalizations, empirical observations, and analyses in line with the pattern of associations of motional configurations. These associations, in turn, are linked with some idea, thing, or emotion. The devices may be used singly, in various combinations, or in differing ratios. Dance meaning may be found in one or more spheres. Revision and expansion may be required as the grid is used to accommodate data which does not fall into the proposed categories. The grid is offered as a tool to probe meaning by placing each unit of dance within each cell of the matrix to confront the possibility (existence/nonexistence) of forms of encoding and the transformation of these forms over time. Adding values and quantification is possible.

Semantic Complexity

In the process of discovering meaning as deeply and broadly as possible, it is important to consider the range of semantic complexity and the sources of symbolism. Without doing this, one cannot adequately use the grid. Considerations of semantic complexity include tacit knowledge, levels of complexity, use of opposites and inversions, ambiguity, synonyms and other manipulations, differences between the message of the dance and its purpose, and the relationship of symbol systems in dance to other symbol systems. Dan Sperber (1974) correctly argues that symbolic forms are unintelligible by themselves. It is necessary to learn the tacit knowledge, the assumptions which are not explicitly stated but within which symbols are embedded. For example, a group may agree a phrase is insulting but be incapable of defining the criteria upon which the judgment rests. A performance is part of a larger whole—the event, culture, and society. It is critical to ascertain what keys or frames a message, that is, the contextual cues for understanding a message and recognizing when one form of encoding transforms into another (cf. Eco 1976:259).

Concretization (mime) is the simplest form of movement symbolism; rising on the scale of complexity are a multitude of transformations of feelings, thoughts, and actions. There may be sets of hierarchical layers of symbols, the layers resembling the skins of an onion, embedded within one another. Roy Ellen (1977) points out that it is necessary to see body part symbols not as single entities but within a system of parts in relation to each other; these symbols may convey information about social relations. For example, in the interpretation of Dylan Thomas' "our eunuch dreams," "one needs to know not only that a eunuch is a man who has been castrated, but also that castration destroys sexual potency, and one must somehow also know that sexual potency is to be taken as a symbol for efficacy in general" (James McCawley 1968:586).

Symbolic complexity may involve opposites and inversions, for example, the symbol for love really meaning hate. What appears as concretization may in fact be intended as metaphor. A symbol may have a patent meaning, while the latent meaning may be contained in a constellation of symbols; the contradiction of meanings perhaps corresponding to structural conflicts (R. Willis 1975). One symbol may have different or condensed meanings; it may be continuously reinterpreted or it may change in intensity over time. The same symbol may have different meanings at different phases in performance. Furthermore, metaphoric equations can operate in two directions at once. Saying the lion is the king of the beasts says something about kings and something about lions. Double metaphors may occur: the representation of an object in turn invokes a cultural context or state of affairs. In symbolism there is a range of specificity.

Ambiguity, different possible interpretations at different levels, exists. Marvin Harris notes that there may be more human repertoires which derive their semantic order from ambiguity and variation than there are repertoires in which orderliness reflects consensus and uniformity (1968:583). Sperber's account of symbolism helps to explain how people deal with ambiguity. He argues that symbolic understanding is not knowledge of something but the knowledge of the meaning of something. (This account is similar to that of the neurologist Brain [1959].) Interpretation, then, is improvisational; it rests upon implicit knowledge and obeys unconscious rules. So, say linguists, do the utterances we emit and understand.

In his comparison of the approach of the structural linguist with the literary analyst, Ragnar Rommetveit makes a point relevant to the study of movement. What the structural linguist labels as "anomaly" may be viewed by the literary analyst as "creative transcendence of conventional use."

> What is conveyed by the artist is in literary analysis *not* assessed by mapping his text on to algorithmically derived constellations of semantic features drawn from a finite universe of "conceptual realities." On the contrary: the artist's [and dancer's] achievement is often evaluated in terms of his capacity to create novel social realities, i.e. to make the reader [or viewer] experience aspects of life which somehow appear to be blurred or even concealed in conventional language [or movement] use. His task may even be defined as a genuinely paradoxical undertaking: he is committed to reveal, by means of words [or dance], what has become invisible as a result of conventional verbalization [and movement]. (1974:21)

The assumption is made that "human discourse takes place under conditions of temporarily shared social realities in a pluralistic world" (ibid.:27).

As is the case for verbal language, dance symbols may have synonyms: a single concept may be manifested by different images. Reincarnation is represented by the Ubakala women's dance for the birth of a child which uses circular, slow, relaxed movement as well as the men's warrior dance which is angular, rapid, and tense. The stylistically similar but occasionally different women's dances for the birth of a child and for a woman's journey to the ancestor world both focus on entry to life segments. Dance symbols may have homonyms, two movements or phases which look alike in most respects and neutralization, the phenomenon whereby a relevant opposition or meaning is cancelled in a particular context. Dance symbols also involve situational qualifiers of space, time, secularity, and sacredness; the juxtapositions or succession of images; and the sequential occurrence of images to produce a synthesis. There may be cross-channel communication, that is, messages sent in the dance differing from those sent in the accompanying song, music, or costume. The message transmitted and the purpose of the dance may be distinct from each other (Rappaport 1971a:66–68). Maring dancers convey messages about military support (those visitors who dance for hosts are expected to fight with them in a future round of warfare) although the avowed purpose is to honor the deceased ancestors. The religious element sanctifies messages.

Symbolic systems in dance may be better understood by analyzing them in relation to other symbolic systems. We know that of the millions of potential stimuli in an individual's environment only certain ones are perceived. Species-specific patterns most likely exist along with culturally specific patterns. A group's general concepts of space, time, energy, mind, and body (which comprise the dance phenomenon) may serve as referents in dance and ascertaining the nature of such perception and meaning helps in understanding how dance is used to communicate emotionally and cognitively. Arthur Koestler's thesis is that the bisociation of two habitually incompatible matrices provides arousal and creates aesthetic impact. In dance the shapes created by the human body with its attendant body image (recollected and unconscious sensations, perceptions, and experiences) may be juxtaposed with the matrices of society or cosmology, that is, the two planes of medium and motif are welded.

Meaning may be deduced through examining how symbolic elements are developed in other aspects of socioculture (cosmology, riddles, proverbs, costume, paraphernalia, music, nondance ritual, myth, polity, economy, social structure, notions of public and private). Barbara Kirshenblatt-Gimblett suggests that it may be necessary to look at movement metaphors in speech and attitudes governing demeanor more generally, for example, "as swift as a lion," "as clumsy as an ox," "social climber" (personal communication). Allusions from these various aspects of socioculture may be part of dance semantics. There may be dominant symbols as Turner suggests. The "holistic" approach of anthropology is essential to interpretation. The point is that *dance* should be studied not as a cultural symbol, but as *a system of meanings*. It is only when dance concept, performance, and nondance facts and fantasies ascertained through wide-ranging ethnographic research are brought together that the logic of the dance system becomes apparent.

Sources of Symbolism

The sources of symbolism also provide clues to understanding the form and content of meaning in movement. Potential categories of reference may include more than environment, subsistence patterns, or the mythic complex (cf. Irving Taylor, 1975:299 on origins of creativity). Symbols may derive from the universal human condition. The Kreitlers (1972:181) argue that there are movements with universally shared meanings: approaching, flight and attack, jumping with joy, and drooping with sorrow. However, Ekman and Friesen (1969) point out that elicitors are not always universal, for example, a funeral may not arouse the same emotion across cultures and their rules may inhibit, simulate, and mask or modulate expression. The roots of symbolism may be internal and innate or sensorially experiential. Merleau-Ponty (1970:267) views the body as a source. Following this tradition Blacking (1977) refers to the latent repertoire of the human body from which cultural transformations are ultimately derived. On the other hand, Douglas (1973) argues that the source of symbolism derives from the social system; the scope of the body as a medium of expression is limited by the controls and the image of the social structure. Gardner's position, with which I agree, combines both biological and social perspectives on the source of symbolism. For him, symbolism is anchored in body images and early bodily experience in culture (1973:109, 1976). Sometimes historical events or the lives of prominent people provide materials for symbolic expression and communication. Among the Ubakala, the source of dance-play symbolism was found in both the body and social fabric.

Data Collection

The value of semantic analyses largely depends on data collection procedures. Therefore, some critical issues in this area warrant comment. Turner (1969) points out that symbols have three major dimensions of significance: exegetic (what informants say about movement), operational (how actors use movement and relate to each other in the process), and positional (how movement symbols relate to other symbol systems). Why not, it may be asked, rely solely upon the actors' analyses? The reason is that participants view behavior from a personal perspective, circumstance, and interest. The analyst can place the behavior in its broader setting without the bias of a participant or indigenous faction. Sperber's notion is that symbol systems are knowledge; interpretation depends on unconscious shared knowledge (1975:35). The anthropologist, he argues, must study symbolic systems consciously by the same procedures used by the native in acquiring them unconsciously: each new item of information is incorporated into information already in the mind and preexisting structures are developed more fully to accommodate new information.

There are a number of ways of *eliciting* informant statements. A combination of procedures may overcome the inadequacies of an individual one. A direct form of inquiry alone may isolate and magnify certain notions and not convey the range, qualifications, and conditions which guide actual behavior. Beginning with informal open-ended questioning and moving to the more specific (including, "Tell me about———, what is it, where, why, how, should, could, would, must, is it the same or different?") is usually best. Ethnoscience procedures for using the ways in which a people talk about activities is relevant for developing culturally appropriate question frames.

Interviewing a broad range of community members, and particularly distinguishing between dancers and observers, may reveal a broad sphere of semantic understanding, competence, and performance, as well as narrower spheres found within categorical groups, ethnic, or factional subcultures (cf. Blacking 1969:19, Fernandez 1965, Pelto and Pelto 1975 on intracultural variation). The ordinary participant, specialist, or observer may differ in perspectives and scope of knowledge. The possibility of meaning varying circumstantially in temporal dimensions and in the channels accompanying movement also needs to be considered.

An interview schedule developed with fixed alternative questions can be administered to a random sample or particular universe (e.g., a population of all dancers) for systematic data gathering to determine the representativeness of responses and how closely observers agree. Krebs (1975) uses film to elicit responses, focusing on the textual aspects of dancing. Of course, what looks like the same dance to an outsider on the basis of text (physical aspect of the dance) may be seen to be a different dance in the context in which it is presented, or in the context of differences in song text, music, costume, or performance group. The Osgood Semantic Differential is a useful measuring technique which combines association and scaling procedures. The subject is presented with a standardized sample of bipolar adjectives for each conceptual meaning to be measured. He or she is then instructed to indicate the direction of his or her association and its intensity on a seven-step scale.

There are certainly problems in eliciting responses. Some meanings may be kept as secrets by selected participants; some differ according to the participant's religion, lineage, or status and may be repressed and/or suppressed for the benefit of broader participation (cf. Fernandez 1965). Most meanings are long forgotten (as one Ubakala spokesman put it, "Time has drowned them") or known to only a few. Meaning may be intrinsic to the dance style and structure and therefore difficult to explain. Some informants may withhold information that they fear may be misused; others may try to boost their culture by portraying it favorably in terms of their perception of the researcher's values. And, as is the case everywhere, most informants find it a formidable task to verbalize about movement (cf. Cottle 1966). It is important to point out that one can identify and react to images and symbols without verbalizing and yet draw correct inferences: there are different ways of knowing and different levels of glossing. As children may use words without knowing the meanings, one may similarly use movements in dance. Motional configurations may be conceptualized as words are.

It is useful to identify informants, publish vernacular texts and translations of informant statements, context, and circumstance of elicitation for purposes of assessing the reliability and validity of analyses. This helps to preclude selecting only concordant features from disparate accounts and to alert the analyst to the fact that the same symbol may have different meanings at different phases in a performance or in different performances. Because of the problems of verbalization, one should not rely completely upon a single source of data. Indigenous informant explanations are critical. But they need to be coupled with analytic observations and analyses of other symbolic systems. This often reveals contradictions and paradoxes. It is necessary to observe how dance is used and how the dancer and audience interact in order to distinguish between the ideal and real, that is, is dance performed and interpreted with the specific meanings people say it should have. Traditional beliefs may contradict ethnographic reality; they may perpetuate the symbolism of sociocultural customs which have disappeared or which persist elsewhere. Thus the researcher infers meaning from the context, antecedents, and consequences.

The distinction between competence (*langue*, or cognitive learning, the acquisition of shared rules of appropriateness, feasibility, and other features of use) and performance (*parole*, dancing with the necessary skills) is relevant to data collection for semantic analysis. The choreographer and dance observer may have the same knowledge (mental conceptualization) as the imitative or improvising dancer, who in addition, must have acquired the skills for dancing (behavioral learning). (In linguistics, according to Howard Maclay [1971:180], the distinction between competence and performance is eroded if semantics is found in deep and surface structure.) It is noteworthy that in imitative dancing, some dancers can translate visual perceptions or other clues from the contextual (pragmatic) realm into dance with little or no intellectualization or corporeal sensations. This is essentially a stimulus-response pattern.

There is no doubt that the problems of valid and reliable symbolic analysis loom large (see Turner 1974:156). Miller (1970) suggests that one kind of verification is one's intuitions as a dancer, choreographer, speaker; there is no objective method for direct appraisal of semantic contents. But by measuring distance between concepts, we can infer something about the coordinates of their universe. Multiple verbal and visual eliciting techniques, with a stratified random sample used in different situations by appropriate investigators (Hanna and Hanna 1966), can help researchers achieve objectivity.

It is to be hoped that I have established that there is a potentially fertile field of semantics to reap if we can but conceive of possible categories wherein to enlarge our stock of relevant distinctions. The results of the application of the grid to a variety of performance types may help in understanding part of what human movement means. This approach does not deny the "affecting presence," immediacy, or self-sufficiency of dance. These dimensions require other concepts and methods of study: using the grid as a taxonomic device—identifying forms of conveying meaning—is not meant to be an end in itself. What is important, is to understand the processes involved in choosing forms and the changes from one form of encoding to another.

Potential Application

The ramifications of such dance research may help us understand the actual and potential importance of dance in everyday life and on special occasions. There are many reports on the value of body movement in life satisfaction, education, and physical and psychological therapy (Martha Davis 1972). Visual "arts" condition our vision of the world. There is evidence of uncommunicative youngsters in regular classes coming to life in participatory arts experiences (Mark Schubart 1972); that concepts can be effectively taught through movement (Claire Schmais 1966); and that the brain damaged and mentally ill will respond to dance experiences (Murphy 1974). Yet, there is little knowledge of the dynamics that make it work. By finding out why some people dance for little or no material reward, we may learn something which will allow us to make everyday life more meaningful.

An increased understanding of dance will promote its efficacious use as one of a number of mental health diagnostic techniques for heterogeneous populations, that is, unserved and underserved cultural groups (Hanna 1978a). The middle class, white, verbally oriented model often results in misunderstanding in diagnosis and treatment when applied to everyone. Therapists using dance need to know how dance and other movement are culturally conceived; what the criteria are for who participates, when, where, how, what is preferred, prescribed, and prohibited; and what movement means to the client. In the healing arts, dance has a number of possibilities. It is useful (1) in comparing different modes of individual and group communication (cross-channel comparison), using the dance a person idiosyncratically and culturally is accustomed to perform or "creative" dance. The comparison can be made in terms of congruent, substitutive, or incongruent messages. Dance can also be useful (2) in comparing pre- and post-treatment assessment; and (3) in revealing information not provided in psychiatric interviews, structured anthropological fieldwork in nondance domains, or spontaneous interaction. It may also be used (4) in identifying problem areas in an individual's exaggerated or excessive use of a limited range of time, space, effort, or flow in movement judged from a baseline range from the individual's specific reference group and culture (cf. Marion North 1972). Cultural efficiency and appropriateness of movement correlate with mental health: psychic conflict produces muscular tension, awkwardness, and ineffectiveness in movement message "reading" and "sending."

In addition to the implications of dance research for life satisfaction, education, and physical and psychological therapy, new insights about the individual and society may emerge. In some cultures dance is used as a channel for behavior not permitted or found embarrassing in other presentational channels. Through the dance medium, individuals may counter habitual motor responses (posture, locomotor movement, gestures) which reflect customary inner thoughts and feelings. The way a person dances (or dresses) often has intimate connection with conscious and unconscious self perception and image conveyed. Dance may reveal compensatory and regressive patterns, displacement, catharsis, sublimation, or play in an expressive and instrumental mode.

Humans live in worlds they create through communication, verbal and nonverbal. Because human creatures have a particular kind of body and nervous system, a large number of potentials are available to them. But each individual is born into a particular culture that selects and develops a small number of these potentials, rejects others, and is unaware of many. Dance is recurrent human thought and action performance by the human body instrument and, as such, is part of the latent repertoire of communicative capabilities peculiar to the human species stretching back thirty thousand years. Paleolithic art provokes some interesting speculations: a trait that is apparently universal in a species and has a neurological substrate is likely to have developed during an age when it had a great and persisting survival value. Subject to the interplay among competitive communicative modalities and sociocultural-historical constraints, dance continues to be a potentially efficacious resource. Existing from time immemorial, dance has times and places of peaking, inhibition, and phoenixlike resurgence.

Generalizations, such as that the significance of dance, kinds of dance, and functions of dance within literate and nonliterate societies differ, need supporting evidence. There are traditional societies which do not give prominent roles to dance; so too, modern societies often underemphasize this expressive-communicative modality. A close look at the United States reveals every kind of dance, function of dance, and a population attributing positive and negative significance to dance. The United States is not a homogeneous "melting pot" and has both literate and illiterate people. Dance may be significant for the same or different reasons in nonliterate and literate societies. For example, dance may be religious behavior both for individuals in highly industrialized societies or for those with minimum technological complexity. Dance in small villages marks social roles; it also does this in large heterogenous modern urban areas. In one of the world's largest, most technological cities, dance permeates the lives of many individuals, from birth to death, as in small villages. This is true, although for most Americans life is segmented into distinct times for work, play, and rest. For members of New York dance cultures, dance is work, play, and rest (e.g., watching others perform or dreaming of dance). Although the verbal overemphasis in the western technological society underevaluates dance, subcultures exist which value it all the more on this account. In part they protest that which is nonsensual.

We know that dance is accessible to empirical observation, technical recording, and analysis. We know that it is subject to test and measurement, logical deductive analysis, and the structural study of the relation of parts to one another, homologies, opposites, inversions, and transformation. Darwin recognized that, in order to understand humans, it is first necessary to understand the means by which humans gather and transmit knowledge in ways similar to and different from their animal forebears. The more we know about dance –its presence, absence, and its resurgence in individual and group life–the more we will know about ourselves: to dance is human.

Appendices

Appendix 1   Dance Movement Data Categories

Movement definition: the visual and/or kinesthetic result of energy release in time and space through muscular response to a stimulus is the essence of dance. Its structure (interrelation of parts) and style (characteristic mode and quality of all the contributing elements) can be analyzed in these terms:

Space (design):
    direction (path the moving body cuts through space)
    level (high–weight on ball of foot; low–body lowered through
       flexing knees; middle–normal stand; elevated; kneeling; sitting;
       lying)
    amplitude (size of movement, relative amount of distance covered
       or space enclosed by the body in action)
    focus (direction of eyes and body)
    grouping (overall spatial pattern of movement in relation to dancer,
       created dance space):
           free form or organized pattern (individual, couple, small
              group, team–linear or circular, symmetrical or asymmetrical)
           physical link (none, parts of body, length of contact)
    shape (physical contour of movement design–includes direction,
       level, amplitude)

Rhythm (time, flow):
    tempo (rate at which movements follow one another)
    duration (relative length of movements, patterns, performance)
    accent (rhythmically significant stress)
    meter (basic recurrent pattern of tempo, duration, and accent)

Dynamics (force, relative amount of energy, effort–tension and relaxation released by the body to accomplish movement):
    space (indulgence–minimum or maximum use; "direct" straight lines or "flexible" curves and deviations)
    flow (control, continuous transfer of energy which qualifies movement–free, unimpeded or bound, hampered)
    locomotion (means of moving from one place to another)
    projectional quality (texture produced by combination of elements –relative quickness or slowness of energy released in space)

Characteristic use of body (instrument of dance):
    posture (movement that activates or is largely supported through the whole body)
    locomotion (movement that involves a change of location of the whole body, e.g., walk, run, leap, hop, jump, skip, slide, gallop)
    gesture (movement of part of the body not supported through the whole body, e.g., rotation, flexion, extension, vibration)

Appendix 2   Ubakala Dance-Play Profiles (Movement Style and Structure)

Dance Group	Use of Space				Level
	Amplitude	Direction	Focus	Grouping	
Group I *Nkwa Ọñu Nwa*	small	counterclockwise 0 front or right side faces directional path	0 center line of direction earthward	0 leaders inside 0 couples in line of direction	low support
Group II *Nkwa Umunna*	small	counterclockwise 0 front or right side faces directional path	sides of line of direction earthward 0 center	0 leaders inside 0	low support middle support
Group III *Nkwa Umu Ọma*	small medium	counterclockwise 0 front or right side faces directional path	line of direction earthward 0 center	0 leaders inside 0	low support
Group IV *Nkwa Edere*	small medium	counterclockwise 0 front, right & back sides face direc- tional path	line of direction earthward diagonally backward	circle couples in line of direction; physical contact	low support middle support knee support
Group V *Nkwa Uko*	small	counterclockwise 0 line, arc, & 0 in 0 center	line of direction earthward diagonally forward	0 couple in 0 center	low support

Appendix 2   Ubakala Dance-Play Profiles (Movement Style and Structure)—*continued*

Use of Space

Dance Group	Amplitude	Direction	Focus	Grouping	Level
Group VI *Nkwa Ese*	small medium large	forward diagonal lines 0s around leader 3 sides of a rectangle with leader cutting through 0	forward line of direction	line 0 arc	low support middle support

Rhythm

Duration

Dance Group	Accent	Pattern	Performance	Meter	Tempo
Group I *Nkwa Ofu Nwa*	first beat fourth sixth	medium	variable	2-beat grouping 4 6	slow even
Group II *Nkwa Umunna*	first				slow even
Group III *Nkwa Umu Oma*				2-beat grouping 3 4	allegro staccato

Table — columns: Dance Group | Flow | Projectional Quality | Gesture | (Meter) | Locomotion | (Tempo). The heading **Dynamics** spans the *Projectional Quality* and *Gesture* columns.

Dance Group	Flow	Projectional Quality	Gesture	Meter	Locomotion	Tempo
		Dynamics	*Dynamics*			
Group IV *Nkwa Edere*	first fourth			2-beat grouping 4		allegro
Group V *Nkwa Uko*						slow even
Group VI *Nkwa Ese*				2-beat grouping 4		allegro
Group I *Nkwa Oñu Nwa*	free and close	sustained swaying yielding sensuous	foot touch handkerchief waving		steps shuffle rotation half-steps	
Group II *Nkwa Umunna*	free and close	sustained undulating sensuous	foot touch handkerchief waving foot brush arms alternatively moving up & down from each other		steps walk	
Group III *Nkwa Umu Oma*	free more expansive marked seriation of patterns	excited brisk vibrating percussive	handkerchief waving foot brush hand brush		fast shuffling walk steps	

Appendix 2 Ubakala Dance-Play Profiles (Movement Style and Structure)—*continued*

Dance Group	Dynamics			
	Flow	Projectional Quality	Gesture	Locomotion
Group IV *Nkwa Edere*	free punctuated boundedness	excited vibrating serendipity	toe slide foot brush shoulder vibration shoulder moving upward	walk steps rotation half-steps
Group V *Nkwa Uko*	free and close	sustained	hip shifts foot touch apron movement with hands	steps
Group VI *Nkwa Ese*	free expanded percussive	excited vigorous vibrating strong reflecting	vibrating pointing of index finger brandishing machete in hand upper torso swing shoulder vibration	bourrée lunge close steps jump hop

Dance Group	Body Patterns						
	Posture	Head	Torso	Arms	Hands	Legs	Feet
Group I *Nkwa Ohu Nwa*	upper torso 45° incline knees flexed	forward as natural extension of spine	pelvic girdle shifts	upper hang naturally lower extend forward	rotate twirling handkerchief	flex & extend rotate	undulate flat or barely arched move close to earth

Group II *Nkwa Umunna*	torso parallel to ground upper torso 20° incline knees flexed	forward as natural extension of spine	upper torso undulation torso contract & release pelvic girdle shift	curved move in opposition to feet	rotate twirling handkerchief	flex & extend rotate	undulate flat or barely arched move close to earth
Group III *Nkwa Umu Oma*	upper torso 15° incline torso parallel to ground knees flexed	forward as natural extension of spine	buttocks bounce	upper hang naturally lower extend forward arms gently follow body line	rotate twirling handkerchief clap	flex & extend, rapid knee action lower leg brushes backward	flat or barely arched move close to earth, away in brushes
Group IV *Nkwa Edere*	upper torso 20° incline upright knees flexed	forward as natural extension of spine	upper torso shimmy	upper hang naturally outward from body lower forward ballroom position & change	rest on partner's body	flex & extend	flat or barely arched move close to earth toe slide toe & heel rotations

Appendix 2   Ubakala Dance-Play Profiles (Movement Style and Structure)—*continued*

Dance Group	Posture	Head	Torso	Arms	Hands	Legs	Feet
			Body Patterns				
Group V *Nkwa Uko*	upper torso 20° incline	forward as natural extension of spine		arm about another's waist upper hang naturally lower extend forward	rest on another's waist bounce apron	flex & extend	undulate flat or barely arched move close to earth
Group VI *Nkwa Ese*	upper torso 20° incline knees flexed	forward as natural extension of spine	inward rotation of shoulder joint upper torso shimmy, downward swing	outstretched forward, sideward, diagonally up & down flexed elbow with lower arm rotation left as shield upper out to sides, lower diag. up to sides	vibrate index finger hold, vibrate machete	flex & extend, rapid knee action, knee lifts	flat bourrée move close to earth, away in hop

Appendix 3   Dance Representation Classificatory Framework

Identification				Function	Date	Group	Location	Size	Sex-Age-Mask-Other of Participant	Sociocultural Context-Activity
Document	Artifact-Technique									
	Lithic	Ceramic	Painting							

Stylistic Characteristics (Features)

Space					Focus		Dynamics			Use of Body		
Direction (group)	Level			Amplitude	Shape	Eyes	Body	Space	Flow	Locomotion Projectional Quality	Face	Posture	Parts & Use
	High	Mid	Low									1 unit	2

Notes

1 Introduction

1. Many anthropologists are beginning to examine dance more critically through their research and teaching. Indicative of the emergent interest in the study of dance from the perspectives of the social sciences is the current doctoral work of more than fifteen anthropology students in the United States and the United Kingdom; a spate of articles and books on dance; the 500 percent growth from 1970 to 1975 of the international, interdisciplinary Committee on Research in Dance (CORD); the 1974 launching of *Dance Research Journal* in which social scientists have been strongly represented; and the increased number of dance papers presented at scholarly association meetings, such as the Annual Conferences on Social Theory and the Arts, American Anthropological Association, Ethnomusicology, and American Folklore Society.

2. *The Anthropology of Dance: A Selected Bibliography* (Hanna 1976, 1978 rev.) was prepared to meet this need. Kealiinohomoku (1976) and Anya Royce (1977) offer valuable insights into the study of dance.

3. Gertrude Kurath is the mentor and psychological supporter of several active anthropologists studying dance from the perspectives of the discipline. In the 1930s she began by producing a few brief articles and news and notes on dance. From 1946 until the early 1970s, she published numerous articles and four books (1964a, 1964b, 1968, 1970; for a list of her work, see Kealiinohomoku and Gillis 1970). Kurath's studies are primarily descriptive, although there is theoretical concern with the diffusion of traits, function, and the interrelation of dance spatial pattern with social structure.

4. See also the surveys by Merriam (1974) and Royce (1974a), who did not point out any significant breakthroughs.

5. For an excellent discussion of the three major dance notation systems and their implications for the anthropological investigation of movement, see Seymour Kleinman (1975). Youngerman (1977)

summarizes Labananalysis, the combination of Laban's notation and effort-shape analysis.

6. I use the ethnographic present for most of the illustrations. However, the reader should bear in mind that the situation may have changed since it was reported.

7. Musicologist Sachs (1937), philosopher Langer (1953, 1957a, 1957b), and psychologists Hans Kreitler and Shulamith Kreitler (1972) have offered general theories of dance. Their conceptualizations are culturally western and thus of limited value for the broader study of dance. Lange's theory (1975) perpetuates some disproved nineteenth-century western notions in Sachs' study. Alan Lomax's (1968) comparative, armchair worldwide study is based on too small a sample to provide valid conclusions. Kurath's corpus of work is valuable as far as it goes. Kealiinohomoku's useful dissertation (1976) presents a generally static theory of dance which is assumed to reflect society; but the theory neglects the potential of dance to contribute to change. Royce's introductory text (1977) improves upon earlier overviews although it slights some critical social science perspectives. Newcomers to the social sciences may choose to begin their odyssey toward understanding dance in human life with this text.

2   Dance?

1. Kaplan points out that definitions are the outcome of the processes of inquiry and communication; specification of meaning is processive, hypothetical, and provisional, and it undergoes modification as inquiry proceeds (1955:527).

2. The result will help the investigator to learn, in the words of Ronald Cohen and Raoull Naroll, "something useful about the theoretical problem he is investigating through the use of the category as a part of his research design" (1973:15).

3. Illustrations of the infinite range of variation upon an ordinary walk, for example, from floridity to leanness, pointed toe, flexed foot, half toe, on toe; small to large, high to low, forward to backward and other directions; slow to fast; light to heavy can be found in most books on teaching modern dance at the college level.

4. The subject of aesthetic discourse calls attention to the issue of dance as art *or* craft; I do not find this to be a particularly fruitful distinction. One of the many problems with the term "art" (Mills 1973 and Roy Sieber 1973 discuss its ethnocentric uses) is that within a group the criteria for and judgment of a work (product) or behavior (performance or product, as a dance which is preserved on film) are not always established by the critics synchronically. Avant garde

phenomena may be rejected at one point in time only to be accepted at another. Judgmental tests are not usually clear-cut. Sieber discusses the "connoisseurship or the right of each age to its ethnocentric aesthetic," and notes "that the history of taste is a story of constantly shifting attitudes which are not cumulative, and which are neither inevitable nor infallible beyond the movement they are in favor" of (1971:128). And Devereux points out that art theories "hobble behind practice, painfully thinking up new and devious ways of justifying unusual, but effective and meaningful modes of communication" (1971:202–203, 194).

5. Morton Wiener et al. (1972) distinguish between communication and observer inference. The observer can infer something about the dancer from his or her movement. The dancer may or may not make this something manifest in an overtly made statement.

6. The technical literature on sign, symbol, and signal is large, mazelike, and contradictory. It is not usually concerned with nonverbal communication, nor dance specifically, within a cross-cultural perspective. I have adapted concepts to accord with the nature of dances I have observed in field settings and that others have reported in the literature. Edmund Leach (1976) provides an introduction to some of the issues involved. My use of terminology comes close to his which, in turn, is a modification of J. Mulder and S. Harvey (1972). My use of sign, metaphor, and metonomy are similar to his index, symbol, and sign, respectively.

7. Sachs (1975) notes that Morris was only concerned with external reality and excluded mental processes from discussion. These are, however, assumed within the theory presented in this chapter.

8. The concretization and iconic signs are symbolic to the extent that they stand for characteristics of objects they denote which do not form part of signs themselves. The use of "icon" is an extension of Robert Redfield's definition, "a representation of a sacred being" (1971:42). See Thomas Sebeok (1976) on the various usages and problems with "iconicity."

9. Let me illustratively examine a war dance. It is symbolic, not actually war, but a way of thinking about it. In a concrete representation of war, the emphasis is on imitative reconstruction (advance and retreat tactics, leadership patterns, tension levels, manner of killing, etc.). A danced war spirit revered as the spirit would be an icon. A stylization might be something like the V gesture for victory. As a metaphor, reference may be to qualities of strength characteristic of war but applied to nonmartial domains of behavior, e.g., economic achievement or graduation from law school. A war dance refering to part of a war action is a metonym. As a signal, a war dance may herald a confrontation or celebration of it.

10. Lomax (1968) suggests dance has heightened redundancy.

Since repetition is certainly an element of affective learning, it may be this quality in dance which contributes to its cardinal educational role in some societies.

11. Ikegami proposed these useful distinctions (I-D, II-D) in his comments on Hanna 1979a.

3   Psyche and Soma

1. The unfolding of innate (species-typical) behavior depends on sufficient and necessary developmental learning and environmental conditions at each stage.

2. Deprivation of exploratory behavior among nonhuman primates, especially in relation to one's mother or juvenile peers, leads to the inability to communicate properly and to fulfill social roles, for example, mating and caring for the young (Jolly 1972:231–235).

3. Spiegel and Machotka give as an example the "method acting" originated by Constantin Stanislavski, Director of the Moscow Art Theater. This method involves the study and re-creation of conditions under which a given form of behavior takes place. Emotionally appropriate behavior is presumed to spontaneously emerge if the actors reconstruct and remember the manifold of internal and external conditions and contingencies related to the character they are playing (1974:24–25).

4. Mechanical and expressive movement were found to differ; the latter was modulated by a state of feeling, or "sentic state," functioning as an algorithm, an inherent manifestation of the central nervous system processes. Clynes elicited emotions among subjects, each seemingly expressing similar structures. Musicians produced similar pulse shapes for each composer when asked to think different pieces using a touch transducer which produces finger pressure recordings.

5. Berlyne (1972:102–117) argues that the study of verbal aesthetic judgments should be supplemented with nonverbal responses to aesthetic material. Verbal judgments such as the Osgood type scales soliciting ratings of pleasingness and interestingness are assumed to reflect important motivational or affective processes within the subject. The psychophysiological measure of momentary arousal (duration of spontaneous exploration and exploratory choice) a stimulus raises includes the galvanic skin response, the duration of electroencephalographic desynchronization, and spectographic analyses of EEG waves.

6. Hanna 1976a provides a fuller exposition of the dance-plays. Fieldwork and some data preparation was carried out with the assistance of a Ford Foundation–Michigan State University Grant (in

conjunction with William John Hanna) and the MSU African Studies Center, 1963–1965.

4 Dance Movement and the Communication of Sociocultural Patterns

1. The filmed dance sample thus represents a consensus of what activity is dance and an esteemed performance. The sample is what linguists call performance, surface manifestations, or *parole*. In addition, the sample reflects generative structure, or knowledge (competence or *langue*).

2. A phrase is the expression of a partial "thought," a group of related movements in a pattern where there are alternations of activity (peaking) and quiescence (pose, rest, energy diminution). A phrase has its own climax and is distinguished by rhythmic pattern and visual configuration of locomotion and/or gesture.

3. Writing about Igbo paintings of crescents, circles, and double-headed arching pythons, Herbert Cole hypothesizes that "they are celestial symbols: the moon, the sun, the rainbow. Such simple motifs fuse the light sky-world of Amadioha [thunder deity and lord of the sky] with the dark earth of Ala, the Great Mother" (1969:87). Although our informants did not identify celestial symbols in the spatial arrangements of dance, it is reasonable to speculate that the importance of the sun, the moon, and rain is reflected in Ubakala dance. On the other hand, the psychologist Arnheim argues that "the primacy of the circle and sphere is of purely perceptual origin" (1969: 277).

4. Arthur Koestler's thesis (1967), that the bisociation of connection of two habitually incompatible matrices or frames of reference create an aesthetic or creative impact, helps explain what makes the *nkwa* work. Dance is physical behavior with psychobiological bases. The human body instrument releases energy through muscular responses to stimuli received by the brain. In organized energy the body or its parts contract and release, flex and extend, rotate, and move from one place to another. In a special domain of motion, and associated with conscious and unconscious experiences and idiosyncratic and culturally derived notions, the body is juxtaposed to sociocultural frames of reference.

5. The sex roles, although distinct, are nevertheless, interdependent. Men receive their birth, nurturance, and, indirectly, their right to partake in political and ritual behavior from women. Women, in turn, receive their birth and politically and ritually ordered environment from men.

6. There is a contrast between male and female movement pat-

tern changes over a lifetime. Male youth and young adult patterns are more alike in energy use than elderly patterns, whereas female young adult and elderly patterns are more similar in energy use than youth ones. In addition to the correlation of movement distinctions with social roles, there appear, on the basis of Charles Adam's analysis of the taped music accompanying the dance-plays, to be musical distinctions as well. Whereas the mothers have an open relaxed tonal range of thirteen semitones, cross-meters of 3:4, and descending melodic contours and sporadic polyphony, the warriors have a wider range of intervals (two octaves), 2:3 tempo, and no clearly discernible melody.

7. The shimmy movement characterizes the warrior–head-hunter dances as well. Potency for unknown endeavors (marriage, politics, or war) appears to be the underlying semantic.

5   Dance in Religion: Practicality and Transcendentalism

1. I chose this area because of my familiarity with it. The concepts and findings discussed in this survey appear to have broader applicability. Delineating subsaharan Africa as an entity is a historical accident—a product of colonialism and traditions of scholarship. The peoples of Africa have also had common experiences, sources of information and energy, which offer another reason for the focus. Dance is, of course, performed in a variety of contexts, some of which have no apparent religious connection. In considering the importance of dance in a society, it is necessary to recognize that there are classes of dance which are differentially ranked. Within a class, a specific dance may be either a major or minor event. And a class of dance may be a concomitant with another class or classes of nondance events, and these may assign rank to the dance.

See Arthur Cole 1942 on the Puritans' negative attitude toward dance in the United States, Margaret Taylor 1967:67–135 on the history of dance in Christianity and its demise with the Renaissance and Reformation, and H. Clive 1961 on the Calvinists. See also Stephen Kern 1975.

2. In this regard, Douglas does not distinguish between magical and sacramental. For her, ritualism signifies heightened appreciation of symbolic action which manifests itself in "belief in the efficacy of instituted signs and sensitivity to condensed symbols" (1973:26). Lest we relegate African behavior to a special category, Douglas' description of the crux of the doctrine of the Eucharist is relevant here: "A real, invisible transformation has taken place at the priest's saying of the sacred words and . . . the eating of the consecrated host has saving efficacy for those who take it and for others. It is based on

a fundamental assumption about the human role in religion. It assumes that humans can take an active part in the work of redemption, both to save themselves and others, through using the sacraments as channels of grace—sacraments are not only signs . . . being instruments" (ibid.:70).

3. The delimiting characteristics of extraordinary behavior for dance seem to fall within Piaget's structural categories of practice play or symbolic play (S. Miller 1973:90). Benefits occurring from such play include the exercise of specific capabilities or skills, learning and exploration, and coping with life.

4. It may be that symbols are less arbitrary than has been believed, as the case of color classification in the languages of the world suggests (Berlin 1970), and Douglas (1973) and Jung (1958) point out in their discussion of the human body and psyche, respectively, as the bases for symbols. Although different groups encode differently, and there are different combinations of elements, there may be a universal total inventory (cf. Lévi-Strauss 1967:90–94). A metaphor can make familiar the strange and generate innovative insights. The Greek roots of the word, meaning "change in motion," emphasize a dynamic "found in the lifelong search for identity, in the interplay between subject and object as the latter gives identity to the former and the former seeks to master it in turn through a new predicate" (James Fernandez 1974:123). Metaphoric predication is a similar kind of translation as synesthesia, translating experience from one sense modality to another.

The distinctions between metaphor and metonym have deep roots in anthropological theory. Tylor distinguishes between metaphor and syntax, and Frazer distinguishes between two types of mental association as the basis for magical beliefs: homeopathic magic depending upon similarity; contagious magic, depending on a law of contact. Thus Leach concludes, "Frazer's homeopathic/contagious distinction is practically identical to the Jakobson–Lévi-Strauss metaphoric/metonymic distinction" (1970:48).

5. A preliminary discussion of "African Dance as Adaptation" appeared in a paper prepared for the Annual Meeting of the Southern Anthropological Society, Columbia, Missouri, February 24–26, 1972.

6. About his observations in Nigeria in the 1920s, Talbot writes, "Dancing takes, to a large extent, the place which prayer occupies in European religions" (1926:802). He argues that dance was a method of worship, attaining union with a god, and increasing the fertility of man and crops through the intervention of a god. And he finds it interesting "to think that it was out of similar dances, from the dithyrambs at the spring festival of Dionysus of which the main object was the magical promotion of the food supply, that the drama of ancient Greece arose" (ibid.:803–804). Of course, in spite of its

periodic proscriptions, dance is a part of the Judeo-Christian heritage. It has been a medium of prayer, an act of praise, an expression of joy, and a show of reverence (Taylor 1967). E. Backman argues that dance in the Christian church was an imitation of the perpetual dance of the angels (sympathetic magic to enable one to enter heaven) and a means of exorcizing evil (1952). H. Clive (1961) draws attention to the passages in the Old Testament in which dance is discussed and presents Calvinist and Lutheran views.

7. Nketia comments on the relationship between possession and music and dancing in Ghana (and apparently widespread in Africa): "It is believed that the state of ecstacy or of possession can be quickly induced and sustained by means of special music closely correlated with specific forms of bodily action. It is believed also that the gods are sensitive to this music. Opportunities are, therefore, sought to call to them while the dancing is going on, in the hope that they will 'possess' the dancers as they are emotionally prepared to receive them" (1957:5). Horton points out that drums are critical to inducing and controlling possession among the Kalabari of Nigeria. If the masquerader is a good dancer, he "should feel the drums 'pushing' him and taking charge . . . at which point he is said to be possessed of the spirit which deigns to mount him" (1969:43). Rodney Needham (1967) and Anthony Jackson (1968) discuss the widespread use of sounds, made by striking or shaking instruments, to create expectancy and alertness for the formal passage from one status or condition to another. Such sounds frame an activity, surpass normal ones, and transcend everyday reality much as the darkening of a theater for a performance in the west. Andrew Neher (1962) and Raymond Prince (1968) point out the psychological and physiological impact of ceremonies involving drums. See Arnold Ludwig 1969 on altered states of consciousness.

8. Hugh Duncan notes that "institutions, like individuals, must parade and display their glamor, if they are to keep their glory alive . . . Superiors, inferiors, and equals use these ceremonies as social stages to display themselves before audiences whose approval sustains their position in the local hierarchy" (1962:262).

9. Dance as a vehicle to release or activate a supernatural potency is related to a commonly held perception in Africa: an ill person does not expect a localized therapeutic effect, but a cure which strengthens the person's whole being (Maquet 1972:105). For the Dogon, reality is expanding energy.

10. In the curing dance of the Bushmen mentioned earlier, for example, "accusations of not having good manners toward guests, of being lazy and indifferent in singing or of abandoning a medicine man while he is still in trance, would be typical. But the next moment the people become a unit, singing, clapping, moving together" (Marshall 1969:380).

11. In terms of distributions, it may well be that the use of mask and possession dances is more common among people of small scale societies or subcultures in large scale societies. In such milieux, an individual plays multiple roles toward the same set of people, and the mask and possession dances are contrivances, modes of distinguishing everyday and extraordinary roles (cf. Horton 1960:70, Douglas 1973).

12. In his introduction to a collection of ten papers on the traditional artist in African societies, d'Azevedo discusses mediation at another level: "The artist emerges as a mediator—explicit or tacitly—between collective and individual striving for expression, a phenomenon reminiscent of the tension in our own society between the alternative roles available to its creative members suggested by Weber's work on religion and Rank's on the artist. This mediation is enacted not only in the context of the relation of artistry to expressive values and myth, but also in social relations involving the exercise of unique creative abilities and the acting out of specific culturally defined roles whose performance and products seem on the one hand to be taken as essentials and on the other hand as expendable if not disturbing elaborations of the normal conditions of society" (1973:13–14).

6   Dance Rites in Political Thought and Action

1. Elias Canetti (1962) speaks of standing as expressing power through height and the independence of support; sitting, through weight and continuance, pressure; lying, as impotence and needing support; reclining as using anything and everything for support; sitting on the ground as denoting absence of needs; squatting as turning in on oneself; kneeling as powerlessness.

2. It should be noted that although dance induces feelings of social solidarity, it also induces the opposite. Whereas in his analysis of Andaman Islander dancing, Radcliffe-Brown found that the individual submits to community action to produce a harmonious unity (1922), in his observations in Central Africa, Evans-Pritchard found dances to be the most frequent occasion of disharmony (1965:74).

Case A. Dance of Anáhuac: For God or Man in Prehistory?

1. There are problems involved in the authors' use of the artifactual material now available to us. We do not know if the existence of artifacts and their quantitative differentiation is representative of actual artifact populations or the accidental product of archaeological discovery in pursuit of answers to very different problems. There

was no random sampling at the relevant time levels to test hypotheses about the purpose of dance and reasons for its change. And many sites are not yet excavated (Michael Coe 1962:91). Another difficulty is that artifact representations are not systematically described or dated. (Appendix 3 is a "Dance Representation Classificatory Framework" which might be a useful way to describe attributes. It is based upon the movement analyses of Rudolf Laban; cf. Ann Hutchinson 1970.) It is useful to classify attributes and consider how these combine in response to the system producing them, that is, to see how these correlate with other phenomena, how specific changes in dance covary with specific historical events in time and space (see Sonia Ragir 1972:178). Style is mostly impressionistically summarized in the literature. Because artifact variations are not plotted over time and correlated with other phenomena, we cannot examine disjunctions, breakings, and reversals of the process of change over time.

Dance is identified by a figure of the human body that deviates from a neutral stance (erect posture, feet together, arms hanging relaxed). This criterion does not distinguish dance behavior from other motor activity such as work, chasing butterflies (cf. Miguel Covarrubias 1957:132), praying, playing ball, fighting, or resting. (E.g., what is the behavioral distinction between the pictures labeled dance and battle, #70 and 78, Sahagún, No. 14, Part IX? The active depiction of a dance, Sahagún, Book 10, XI, p. 39, does not match the static portrayal of a dancer possibly resting in picture #67.) The authors' visual unit of analysis might realistically be any nonverbal communication, a category within which dance falls, rather than dance per se.

The artistic medium creates limitations for depicting dance as do the cultural norms and techniques for representing the human body in motion. George Kubler (1962:62) claims that Aztec manuscript painting is affected by Western conventions of draftsmanship. A stance that deviates from a neutral stance may be chosen merely because it provides a necessary balance for sculptured pieces. Given the problems of an operational definition, it is not too unreasonable to accept the authors' one for purposes of convenience, if these problems are kept in mind.

The second unit of analysis is indicated by the term "dance" and its verbal description from prehistory records, namely the codices, original reports given to Sahagún by members of the Aztec priesthood. Again, we do not know what properties characterized dance and distinguished it from other behavior. Not all people have a word for dance: some include definitional properties not included by others and exclude some which are included.

2. Michael Levin (1973:394) tells us that a "hypothesis, to be

explanatory, must go beyond the data it explains, it must have implications the data themselves do not have." Charles Morgan writes, "what is sought, thus, are hypotheses concerning the social structure of the society which would render the features of the archeological site understandable" (1973:270). The search for explanation points to gaps in knowledge. The discussion which follows attempts to address these points.

3. Mark Leone points out that cultural systems adjust autonomously by selecting from the variability available to them (1972:18). Perhaps dance was an adaptive pattern spreading and differentiating at the expense of less efficient precursors.

4. The later work of Duncan (1962, 1968), Scheflen (1972), Karlins and Abelson (1970), Edelman (1972), Mueller (1973), and George Miller (1973) is particularly relevant to this discussion.

5. In the United States, for example, Mueller suggests that "the preoccupation with consumerism and leisure, fortified on a daily basis by the media, obscures the worker's awareness of its inferior status at work and in society" (1973:116).

6. Sanders and Price write: "As sophisticated and skilled as Olmec art was, however, there is a substantial qualitative and quantitative difference in richness in content between the material remains of Classic and Postclassic periods in Mesoamerica on one hand, and those of even the most elaborate Formative cultures on the other. This increase in quality and quantity must relate to a corresponding increase in the amount and degree of occupational specialization and consequent changes in the character of economic institutions. . . . Monumental architecture is perhaps the best index of the degree of complexity of social systems" (1968:138–140).

7. William Rathje (1972) points out that the quantity, size, and other characteristics of classic Maya funeral pottery are a direct reflection of the scope, divisions, and changes in Classic Maya social stratification. See Shirley Gorenstein 1973 on the variability of traits in culture change.

Case B. Ubakala Dance-Plays: Mediators of Paradox

1. The dance-plays discussed in this chapter are Nkwa Oñu Nwa (Dance-Play for the Birth of a Child), Nkwa Umunna (Relations' Society Dance-Play), Nkwa Umu Ọma (Teenage Dance-Play), Nkwa Edere (Young Girls' Shimmy Dance-Play), Nkwa Uko (Dance-Play for the Death of an Aged Woman), and Nkwa Ese (Dance-Play for the Death of an Aged Man).

2. "Every fresh repetition," wrote Freud, "seems to strengthen this mastery for which [the individual] strives" (1955:14–17, 43). Gustave Bychowski argues that the therapeutic efficacy is not in sheer

repetition but "active reproduction or recreation and . . . transformation through various mechanisms characteristic of artistic production" (1951:393). (See also Hanna 1979c.)

3. Benno Safier points out that rapid motion in dance is especially intoxicating, altering "the state of consciousness, facilitating an orally regressive state of perception and feeling tone without attendant loss of acuity in intellection . . . which gives the feeling of bliss and elation" (1953:242). Dance for recreation, ostensibly the most common kind of dance, is most likely cathartic. A pleasurable expenditure of energy, it is movement differing from everyday behavior.

4. Dance is often restorative in allowing an individual to reassert the impulsive after the strain of adapting and the weariness of conforming (see Wiebe 1969–1970). Safier writes: "Convention dictates which postures, stance, carriage or gait we assume in this or that area of life. Dance is perceived as an escape from this restraint although dance [sic] brings with it its own bondage: in the stylization of movements. At least, dance movements are different from the movements of routine living. Thus dance encourages relaxation both in reality and in illusion" (1953:242).

7   Warrior Dances: Transformations through Time

1. G. Uzoigwe (1975) reports on the dearth of precolonial military studies. When a tradition is stamped out, it is hard to write about it. W. Brelsford (1959) found that there was little descriptive material on war dances in Zambia, attributing this to inspiration lost with the cessation of warfare. Since few anthropologists could observe "illegal" warrior action, many were obliged to rely on the memories of informants, some of whom glorified their history or suppressed it in accord with the values they presumed the inquirer to hold. Furthermore, individuals who considered dance from the contemporary Western perspective of being a segmented, "frivolous" slice of life and not worthy of attention, usually provided the literature on war. "They danced" is the extent of attention to this form of human behavior.

2. This field is retarded because of factors related to the study of the "arts" generally, the study of dance in particular (see Chapter 1), and the factors of the colonial experience and historical time in Africa (discussed in the section on the European impact upon dance and the warrior tradition). The social sciences felt a need to emphasize the "science" in their disciplines and thus neglected the "arts." Discourse, verbal speech, was the primary key to human behavior. In the arts and humanities, systematic focus on nonwestern forms is

also comparatively recent. With respect to the study of dance in particular, scholars reflect the cultures of their own societies and thus have tended to have ethnocentric concepts of dance. Western researchers were most active in Africa and carried with them attitudes of Victorian and Puritanical dislike of the body or shame toward it. Perhaps a voyeuristic appreciation of African dance occurred, but objective reporting may have been psychologically and socially difficult. There was a tendency to perceive dance forms different from one's own as not dance at all. Consequently, if there was no dislike or shame toward the body, there was often a detachment from it and inability to "read" it.

3. Of course, the warrior tradition of Shaka's rule is unique; there were more than one hundred thousand warriors, a million deaths, and domination over a half million population (Walter 1969: 111).

4. In his test of two rival theories, the driver discharge model (in which warlike sports discharged accumulated and aggressive tension), and the culture pattern model (in which aggression is learned and there is a strain toward cultural consistency), Richard Sipes finds the latter model confirmed. War and warlike sports tend to overlap and support each other's presence (1973).

8   The Urban Ecosystem of Dance

1. These probable relationships are based on an overview of the literature on dance, art history, urban studies (especially in anthropology, sociology, and political science), change, field work on dance and urban dynamics (Hanna and Hanna 1981) and visits to cities in Mexico, the United States, U.S.S.R., Europe, and Africa.

2. In contemporary times, the processes of modernization and westernization tend to be concomitants of urban phenomena. No attempt is made to separate them in the discussion. Urban areas are considered to interact with their contiguous rural hinterlands over which they tend to have some dominance. Primary and port cities, especially, also interact with other cities and societies.

3. The space devoted to the first set of propositions is not meant to reflect its relative importance but the number of subpoints.

4. The mass audience does not want change according to Perry Lafferty, vice-president of TV programming: "The TV audience wants to know what to expect, and when you try something different it upsets them [ratings drop]" (reported in Tracey Johnston, "Why 30 Million are Mad about Mary," *New York Times Magazine*, April 7, 1974, p. 30).

5. Ginsburg (1972:271) points out that the trouble with using

the term preindustrial is its implication that cities then became industrial when in fact "there are very few contemporary cities so heavily committed to industrial activity that a great majority of their labor force is engaged in it."

6. Obviously there are always exceptions. For example, the Igbo of Nigeria are noted for their orientation toward innovation, and one finds efforts in rural areas to replicate urban phenomena, for example, building styles, electrification, modern schools, and hospitals. The dynamics of innovations within a dance form (disco dancing, e.g.) differ from receptivity to the innovation of new forms.

7. In his study of American music and dance, between 1920 and 1968, Braun found that of the 102 lyricists and composers of popular songs, twice as many were born in highly urban places than the general population. Furthermore, the "modal personality of the artist was characterized by membership in a minority group, being Jewish, foreign-born, or from the lower class. The arts provide an avenue for upward mobility. Creativity is related to nonconformity and by definition minority status is nonconformist" (1969:149–150).

8. Of course, dance may be eufunctional to rural life as well; the content usually differs. In both places it also may be dysfunctional.

9. Discussing selected urban music, Charles Keil argues (although he has no rural baseline) that the styles that emerge from the dissolution of traditional values and the chaos of the urban milieux are reversed images of the environment—an imposition of clarity and simplicity, and nonflexibility (1973). Alternatively, turmoil can be mirrored and thus symbolically mastered.

10. Traditional dance refers to the dance of an ethnic group which is considered by most members of the group to be their cultural heritage and which has not been created or introduced by most of the current participants (Hanna 1965).

11. Through what is called "creative dance" and "dance therapy" in the United States, educators and therapists argue that individuals can freely express themselves; develop a sense of identity through visual and kinesthetic self-discovery and acceptance of the exposed self; and experience catharsis, accomplishment, self-discipline, and productive interaction with others in a situation, which in some cases, is a family surrogate for the participants. Creative dance provides an opportunity to enact urban life experiences in effigy, to work through past or impending traumatic events, and be exempt from the usual social demands.

12. Upper classes often regard lower class dance forms as vulgar or despicable (cf. Gans 1975:117). On the other hand, a high status group may adopt a lower status dance discovered in the urban area and become less elitist; it usually enriches its own repertoire

in style, structure, and affective excitement (e.g., the incorporation of peasant and "exotic" dance in ballet, the twist at the Junior League Ball). When a group takes over another's style, it is usually modified with syncretistic blends, dilution, or "degeneration" of the original form. (See Figure 13.)

13. The fiesta, which includes dance, is now, however, organized by civic clubs and government branches rather than families and presented publicly rather than in a private patio. Passive observation is the nature of participation for some fiesta-goers; for others it provides emotional catharsis through cult dancing. Increased fiesta attendance involves greater organizational skill and thus diversified and specialized roles. Although in the traditional fiesta there were class differences in the nature of celebration, the upper class emphasizing more sedate, devotional expression, the lower classes focusing on dancing, singing, and drinking, the fiesta now is secularly oriented for diversion, and some commercialization has occurred (Davis 1972).

14. Whether eighteenth-century England or twentieth-century Africa and India, as urbanization, technology, and commercialization increase, the "music hall" seems to take over from the street and role specialization occurs. In New York City, the world center of dance, there has been a revolt against theater constraints, and some dance groups have returned to street performances—sometimes even with the sanction of the city fathers and the arts councils. Thus one could even see dance on Wall Street.

References

Adams, Robert McC.
  1966 *The Evolution of Urban Society: Early Mesopotamia and Pre-Hispanic Mexico.* Chicago: Aldine.
Adelman, Kenneth Lee
  1975 "The Recourse to Authenticity and Négritude in Zaire." *Journal of Modern African Studies* 13(1):134–139.
Albrecht, Milton C.
  1968 "Art as an Institution." *American Sociological Review* 33:383–397.
Alland, Alexander, Jr.
  1973 *Evolution and Human Behavior: An Introduction to Darwinian Anthropology.* 2d ed. Garden City: Doubleday.
  1976 "The Roots of Art." In *Ritual, Play, and Performance,* ed. Richard Schechner and Mady Schuman, pp. 5–17. New York: Seabury Press.
Alloway, Thomas; Lester Krames; and Patricia Pliner, eds.
  1972 *Communication and Affect: A Comparative Approach.* New York: Academic Press.
Allport, Gordon W.
  1961 *Pattern and Growth in Personality.* New York: Holt, Rinehart and Winston.
Alpers, Edward A.
  1972 "Towards a History of the Expansion of Islam in East Africa: The Matrilineal Peoples of the Southern Interior." In *The Historical Study of African Religion,* ed. T. O. Ranger and I. N. Kiambo, pp. 172–201. Berkeley: University of California Press.
Anderson, Alan Ross, and Omar Khayam Moore
  1960 "Autotelic Folk-Models." *Sociological Quarterly* 1:203–216.
Andrew, R. J.
  1972 "The Information Potentially Available in Mammal Displays." In *Non-verbal Communication,* ed. R. A. Hinde, pp. 179–203. Cambridge: At the University Press.

Andrews, Edwards
    1940   *The Gift to Be Simple: Song, Dances and Rituals of the American Shakers*. New York: Dover.
Appelbaum, Richard P.
    1970   *Theories of Social Change*. Chicago: Markham.
Arensberg, Conrad M.
    1972   "Culture as Behavior: Structure and Emergence." *Annual Review of Anthropology* 1:1–26.
    ———, and Arthur H. Niehoff
    1971   *Introducing Social Change*. 2d ed. Chicago: Aldine-Atherton.
Argyle, Michael, and R. Ingham
    1972   "Gaze, Mutual Gaze, and Proximity." *Semiotica* 6:32–49.
Armillas, Pedro
    1958   "Program of the History of American Indians, Part 1: Pre-Columbian America." *Social Science Monograph II*. Washington, D.C.: Pan American Union.
Armstrong, Robert P.
    1971   *The Affecting Presence: An Essay in Humanistic Anthropology*. Urbana: University of Illinois Press.
Arnheim, Rudolf
    1954   *Art and Visual Perception: A Psychology of the Creative Eye*. Berkeley: University of California Press.
    1969   *Visual Thinking*. Berkeley: University of California Press.
    1972   *Concerning the Dance, Toward a Psychology of Art: Collected Essays*, pp. 261–265. Berkeley: University of California Press.
Artaud, Antonin
    1958   *The Theater and Its Double*. New York: Grove Press.
Ashton, Dudley
    1951   "An Ethnologic Approach to Regional Dance." Ph.D. dissertation, University of Iowa.
d'Azevedo, Warren L.
    1973   "Sources of Gola Artistry." In *The Traditional Artist in African Societies*, ed. Warren L. d'Azevedo, pp. 282–340. Bloomington: Indiana University Press.
Backman, E. Louis
    1952   *Religious Dances in the Christian Church and in Popular Medicine*. Trans. E. Classen. London: George Allen & Unwin Ltd.
Bailey, F. G.
    1969   *Stratagems and Spoils: A Social Anthropology of Politics*. New York: Schocken Books.
Banton, Michael
    1957   *West African City*. London: Oxford University Press.
    1966   *Anthropological Approaches to the Study of Religion*. New York: Praeger.

Barnett, H. G.
  1953   *Innovation: The Basis of Cultural Change*. New York: McGraw-Hill.
Barthes, Roland
  1970   *Elements of Semiology*. Trans. Annette Lavers and Colin Smith. Boston: Beacon Press.
Bateson, Gregory, and Margaret Mead
  1942   *Balinese Characters: A Photographic Analysis*. New York: Special Publications of the New York Academy of Sciences.
Baumol, William, and William G. Bowen
  1966   *Performing Arts—the Economic Dilemma: A Study of Problems Common to Theater, Opera, Music and Dance*. Cambridge, Mass.: M.I.T. Press.
Baxter, P. T. W.
  1965   "Repetition in Certain Boran Ceremonies." In *African Systems of Thought*, ed. M. Fortes and G. Dieterlen, pp. 64–78. London: Oxford University Press.
Beck, Brenda
  1975   "The Symbolic Merger of Body, Space and Cosmos in Hindu Tamiland." Paper presented at the Commonwealth Association of Social Anthropologists Conference, Queen's University of Belfast.
Becker, Howard
  1974   "Art as Collective Action." *American Sociological Review* 39 (6):767–776.
Begenau, Don
  1972   "Exploring Social Dance in New York." In *Focus on Dance VI: Ethnic and Recreational Dance*, ed. Jane Harris Ericson, pp. 60–62. Washington, D.C.: American Association of Health, Physical Education, and Recreation.
Benesh, Rudolf, and Joan Benesh.
  1956   *An Introduction to Benesh Dance Notation*. London: A. & C. Black.
Berlin, Brent
  1970   "A Universalist-Evolutionary Approach in Ethnographic Semantics." In *Current Directions in Anthropology*, ed. Ann Fischer, pp. 3–18. Washington, D.C.: American Anthropological Association.
Berlyne, D. E.
  1971   *Aesthetics and Psychobiology*. New York: Appleton-Century Crofts.
  1972   "Affective Aspects of Aesthetic Communication." In *Communication and Affect*, ed. Thomas Alloway, Lester Krames, and Patricia Pliner, pp. 97–118. New York: Academic Press.
Bernal, Ignacio

1969   *The Olmec World*. Trans. Doris Heyden and Fernando Horcasitas. Berkeley: University of California Press.

Biebuyck, Daniel
1973   "Nyanga Circumcision Masks and Costumes." *African Arts* 6(2):20–25, 86, 92.

Birdwhistell, Ray L.
1970   *Kinesics and Context: Essays on Body Motion Communication*. Philadelphia: University of Pennsylvania Press.

p'Bitek, Okot
1966   *Song of Lawino*. Nairobi: East African Publishing House.
1971   *Religion of the Central Luo*. Kampala: East African Literature Bureau.

Blacking, John
1962   "Musical Expeditions of the Venda." *African Music* 3(1):54–78.
1965   "The Role of Music in the Culture of the Venda of the Northern Transvaal." In *Studies in Ethnomusicology* 2, ed. M. Kolinski, pp. 20–53. New York: Oak Publications.
1969   "Songs, Dances, Mimes and Symbolism of Venda Girls' Initiation Schools, Parts I, II, III, IV." *African Studies* 28(1, 2, 3, 4):3–35, 69–118, 149–199, 215–266.
1971   "The Values of Music in Human Experience." In *Yearbook of the International Folk Music Council*, Vol. 1, ed. Alexander L. Ringer, pp. 33–71. Urbana: University of Illinois Press.
1973   *How Musical Is Man?* Seattle: University of Washington Press.
1976   "Dance, Conceptual Thought and Production in the Archaeological Record." In *Problems in Economic and Social Archaeology*, ed. G. Sieveking, I. H. Longworth, and K. E. Wilson. London: Gerald Duckworth Co.
1977   "Towards an Anthropology of the Body." In *The Anthropology of the Body*, ed. John Blacking, pp. 1–28. A.S.A. Monograph 15. London: Academic Press.

Blank, Judith
1973   "The Story of the Chou Dance of the Former Mayurbhanj State, Orissa." Ph.D. dissertation, University of Chicago.

Bloch, Maurice
1974   *Symbols, Song, Dance and Features of Articulation: Is Religion an Extreme Form of Traditional Authority?* Archives Européenes de Sociologie 15:51–81.

Blok, Anton
1975   "A Comment on Physical Strength and Social Power." *Political Anthropology* 1(1):60–66.

Bloom, Lois
1976   "Child Language and the Origins of Language: Origins and Evolution of Language and Speech." Ed. Stevan R. Harnad,

Horst D. Steklis, and Jane Lancaster. *Annals of the New York Academy of Sciences* 280:170–172.

Blumberg, Paul
1963   "Magic in the Modern World." *Sociology and Social Research* 47:147–160.

Boas, Franz
1955   *Primitive Art.* New York: Dover. [Orig. 1927]

Boas, Franziska, ed.
1944   *The Function of Dance in Human Society.* New York: Boas School.

Borgatta, Edgar F., and Jeffrey K. Hadden
1970   "The Classification of Cities." In *Neighborhood, City, and Metropolis,* ed. Robert Gutman and David Popenoe, pp. 253–263. New York: Random House.

Bourguignon, Erika
1968a *Trance Dances.* Dance Perspectives No. 35.
1968b "World Distribution and Patterns of Possession States." In *Trance and Possession States,* ed. Raymond Prince, pp. 3–34. Montreal: R. M. Bucke Memorial Society.
1973a "Psychological Anthropology." In *Handbook of Social and Cultural Anthropology,* ed. John J. Honigmann, pp. 1073–1118. Chicago: Rand McNally.
1973b *Religion, Altered States of Consciousness and Social Change.* Columbus: Ohio State University Press.

Bradbury, R. E.
1957   "The Benin Kingdom and the Edo-Speaking Peoples of South-Western Nigeria." In *Ethnographic Survey of Africa, Western Africa, Part 13,* ed. Daryll Forde, pp. 18–171. London: International African Institute.

Brailsford, Dennis
1969   *Sport and Society: Elizabeth to Anne.* London: Routledge & Kegan Paul.

Brain, Russell
1959   *The Nature of Experience.* London: Oxford University Press.

Brandon, James R.
1967   *Theatre in Southeast Asia.* Cambridge, Mass.: Harvard University Press.

Braun, D. Duane
1969   *Toward a Theory of Popular Culture: The Sociology and History of American Music and Dance, 1920–1968.* Ann Arbor: Ann Arbor Publishers.

Bravmann, Rene A.
1973   *Open Frontiers: The Mobility of Art in Black Africa.* Seattle: University of Washington Press.

Brelsford, W. V.
1959   *African Dances of Northern Rhodesia.* The Occasional Papers,

No. 2. Lusaka: Government Printer for the Rhodes-Livingstone Museum.

Bruner, Edward M.
   1974   "The Expression of Ethnicity in Indonesia." In *Urban Ethnicity*, ed. Abner Cohen, pp. 251–280. New York: Tavistock.

Bruner, Jerome
   1962   "The Conditions of Creativity." In *Contemporary Approaches to Creative Thinking*, ed. H. E. Gruber, G. Terrell, and M. Wertheimer, pp. 12–13. New York: Atherton Press.

Buckley, Walter
   1968   "Society as a Complex Adaptive System." In *Modern Systems Research for the Behavioral Scientist*, ed. Walter Buckley, pp. 490–513. Chicago: Aldine.

Buechler, Hans C.
   1970   "The Ritual Dimension of Rural-Urban Networks: The Fiesta System in the Northern Highlands of Bolivia." In *Peasants in Cities*, ed. William Mangin, pp. 62–71. Boston: Houghton Mifflin.

Burgess, John Stewart
   1928   *The Guilds of Peking*. New York: Columbia University Press.

Bychowski, Gustave
   1951   "From Catharsis to Work of Art: The Making of an Artist." In *Psychoanalysis and Culture: Essays in Honor of Geza Roheim*, ed. George B. Wilbur and Warner Muensterberger, pp. 390–409. New York: International Universities Press.

Byers, Paul
   1972   *From Biological Rhythm to Cultural Pattern: A Study of Minimal Units*. Ph.D. dissertation, Columbia University. Ann Arbor: University Microfilms.

Caldwell, John C.
   1969   *African Rural-Urban Migration: The Movement to Ghana's Towns*. Canberra: Australian National University Press.

Canetti, Elias
   1962   *Crowds and Power*. Trans. Carol Stewart. New York: Viking.

Caplan, Frank, and Theresa Caplan
   1973   *The Power of Play*. Garden City: Doubleday.

Carter, Curtis L.
   1976   "Intelligence and Sensibility in the Dance." *Arts in Society: Growth of Dance in America* 13(2):210–221.

Caso, Alfonso
   1958   *The Aztecs: People of the Sun*. Trans. Lowell Duham. Norman: University of Oklahoma Press.

Castells, Manuel
   1972   *La Question Urbaine*. Paris: Maspero. Cf. *Comparative Urban Research* 3(1):7–13.

Castle, Edgar B.
   1966   *Growing up in East Africa*. London: Oxford University Press.

Chance, Michael R. A., and Ray R. Larsen, eds.
1976   *The Social Structure of Attention*. New York: John Wiley.

Chapple, Eliot
1970   *Culture and Biological Man*. New York: Holt, Rinehart and Winston.

Chigbo, Thomas
1962   "Mine Is the Crusader's Dilemma and I'll Go On Shouting. So Should You." *Nigerian Outlook*, June 1, p. 3.

Chilivumbo, Alifeyo
1969   "Some Traditional Malawi Dances: A Preliminary Account." Mimeographed.

Christensen, James Boyd
1959   "The Adaptive Functions of Fanti Priesthood." In *Continuity and Change in African Cultures*, ed. William R. Bascom and Melville J. Herskovits, pp. 257–278. Chicago: University of Chicago Press.

Clark, Sharon Leigh
1973   "Rock Dance in the United States, 1960–1970: Its Origins, Forms and Patterns." Ph.D. dissertation, New York University.

Clive, H. P.
1961   "The Calvinists and the Question of Dancing in the 16th Century." *Bibliothèque d'Humanisme et Renaissance* 23:296–323.

Clynes, Manfred
1978   *Sentics: The Touch of the Emotions*. New York: Anchor.

Coe, Michael D.
1962   *Mexico*. New York: Praeger.

Cogley, John
1973   "Opinion: Democratization and Culture." *Center Magazine*, May/June, pp. 2–3.

Cohen, Abner
1969   "Political Anthropology: The Analysis of the Symbolism of Power Relations." *Man* 4:215–228.

1974   *Two-Dimensional Man: An Essay on the Anthropology of Power and Symbolism in Complex Society*. Berkeley: University of California Press.

Cohen, Ronald, and Raoul Naroll
1973   "Method in Cultural Anthropology." In *A Handbook of Method in Cultural Anthropology*, ed. Raoul Naroll and Ronald Cohen, pp. 3–24. New York: Columbia University Press.

Cohen, Selma Jeanne, ed.
1974   *Dance as a Theatre Art: Source Readings in Dance History from 1581 to the Present*. New York: Dodd, Mead & Co.

1976   "The State of Sylphs in Academe: Dance Scholarship in America." *Growth of Dance in America: Arts in Society* 13(2): 222–227.

Cole, Arthur
1942   "The Puritan and Fair Terpsichore." *Mississippi Valley Historical Review* 29(1). [Dance Horizons reprint.]
Cole, Herbert M.
1969   "Mbari Is Life." *African Arts* 2(3):8–17, 87.
Collier, John, Jr.
1967   *Visual Anthropology: Photography as a Research Method.* New York: Holt, Rinehart and Winston.
Colson, Elizabeth
1971   *The Social Consequences of Resettlement.* Manchester: Manchester University Press.
Copeland, Roger
1978   "Why Cuba Champions Ballet." *New York Times,* June 11, Sect. 2, pp. 1, 9, 13.
Cottle, Thomas J.
1966   "Social Class and Social Dancing." *Sociological Quarterly* 7 (2):179–196.
Covarrubias, Miguel
1957   *Indian Art of Mexico and Central America.* New York: Alfred A. Knopf.
Cressey, Paul G.
1968   *The Taxi-Dance Hall: A Sociological Study in Commercialized Recreation and City Life.* New York: Greenwood.
Csikszentmihalyi, Mihalyi
1975   *Beyond Boredom and Anxiety: The Experience in Work and Games.* San Francisco: Jossey-Bass.
Custead, Homer John, Jr.
1974   *The Iconography of Śiva Naṭarāja as an Indian Synthesis of Non-Aryan and Aryan Conceptions of Divinity.* Ph.D. dissertation, Florida State University. Ann Arbor: University Microfilms.
Czarnowski, Lucile
1967   "The Sphere of the Folk Forms." In *Focus on Dance TV: Dance as a Discipline,* ed. Nancy W. Smith. Washington D.C.: American Association for Health, Physical Education and Recreation.
Dance News
1949   "Chinese Reds Use Dance Propaganda." 15(2):10–11.
Darwin, Charles
1965   *The Expression of the Emotions in Man and Animals.* Chicago: University of Chicago Press. [Orig. 1872]
Davenport, Richard K.
1976   "Cross-Modal Perception in Apes: Origins and Evolution of Language and Speech." Ed. Stevan R. Harnad, Horst D. Steklis, and Jane Lancaster. *Annals of the New York Academy of Sciences* 280:143–149.
———; C. M. Roger; and I. A. Russell

1973   "Cross-Modal Perception in Apes." *Neuropsychologica* 11:21–28.

Davis, Martha
1972   *Understanding Body Movement: An Annotated Bibliography.* New York: Arno Press.

Davis, Martha Ellen
1972   "The Social Organization of a Musical Event: The Fiesta de Cruz in San Juan, Puerto Rico." *Ethnomusicology* 16(1):38–62.
1973   *Music and Dance in Latin American Urban Contexts: A Selective Bibliography.* Urban Anthropology Bibliographies, Spring.

Dawson, John
1964   "Urbanization and Mental Health in a West African Community." In *Magic, Faith and Healing: Studies in Primitive Psychiatry Today,* ed. Ari Kiev, pp. 305–342. New York: Free Press.

Devereux, George.
1971   "Art and Mythology: A General Theory." In *Art and Aesthetics in Primitive Societies,* ed. Carol F. Jopling, pp. 139–224. New York: E. P. Dutton.

Dewey, John
1922   *Experience and Nature.* New York: W. W. Norton.

De Zoete, Beryl
1953   *The Other Mind: A Study of Dance in South India.* London: Victor Gollancz.

Dittman, Allen T.
1973   *Interpersonal Messages of Emotion.* New York: Springer.

Dlugoszewski, Lucia
N.d.   "Erik Hawkins: Heir to a New Tradition." In *On the Dance of Erik Hawkins,* ed. M. L. Gordon Norton. New York: Foundation for Modern Dance.

Dodson, Don
1974   "The Four Modes of Drum: Popular Fiction and Social Control in South Africa." *African Studies Review* 17(2):317–344.

Doob, Leonard W.
1961   *Communication in Africa.* New Haven: Yale University Press.
1971   *Patterning of Time.* New Haven: Yale University Press.

Doughty, Paul L.
1970   "Behind the Back of the City: Provincial Life in Lima, Peru." In *Peasants in Cities: Readings in the Anthropology of Urbanization,* ed. William Mangin, pp. 30–46. Boston: Houghton Mifflin.

Douglas, Mary
1954   "The Lele of Kasai." In *African Worlds: Studies in the Cosmological Ideas and Social Values of African Peoples,* ed. Daryll Forde, pp. 1–26. London: Oxford University Press.
1963   *The Lele of the Kasai.* London: International African Institute.

1966 *Purity and Danger: An Analysis of Concepts of Pollution and Taboo*. London: Penguin.

1968 "Dogon Culture—Profane and Arcane." *Africa* 38(1):16–25.

1972 "Deciphering a Meal." *Daedalus* 101(1):61–81.

1973 *Natural Symbols*. New York: Vintage.

Drewal, Henry John

1973 "Ẹfẹ/Gẹlẹde: The Educative Role of the Arts in Traditional Yoruba Culture." Ph.D. dissertation, Columbia University.

Duncan, Hugh Dalziel

1962 *Communication and Social Order*. London: Oxford University Press.

1968 *Symbols in Society*. London: Oxford University Press.

Duncan, Otis Dudley

1969 "From Social System to Ecosystem." In *Urbanization and Change: Comparative Perspectives*, ed. Paul Meadows and Ephraim H. Mizruchi, pp. 87–95. Reading: Addison-Wesley.

Durkheim, Emile

1947 *Elementary Forms of Religious Life*. Glencoe: Free Press.

Duvignaud, Jean

1972 *The Sociology of Art*. London: Harper & Row.

Dwyer, D. J.

1972 "Introduction." In *The City as a Centre of Change in Asia*, ed. D. J. Dwyer, pp. vii–xvi. Hong Kong: University Press.

Eco, Umberto

1976 *A Theory of Semiotics*. Bloomington: Indiana University Press.

Edelman, Murray

1972 *Politics as Symbolic Action: Mass Arousal and Quiescence*. Chicago: Markham.

Eibl-Eibesfeldt, I.

1972 "Similarities and Differences between Cultures in Expressive Movements." In *Non-verbal Communication*, ed. Robert A. Hinde, pp. 297–311. Cambridge: At the University Press.

Ekman, Paul

1971 *Universals and Cultural Differences in Facial Expressions of Emotion*, pp. 207–283. Nebraska Symposium on Motivation. Lincoln: University of Nebraska Press.

———, and Wallace V. Friesen

1969 "The Repertoire of Nonverbal Behavior: Categories, Origins Usage, and Coding." *Semiotica* 1:50–98.

Eliade, Mircea

1959 *The Sacred and Profane*. New York: Harcourt, Brace & World (Harvest Book).

Ellen, Roy F.

1977 "Anatomical Classification and the Semiotics of the Body." In *The Anthropology of the Body*, ed. John Blacking, pp. 343–374. London: Academic Press.

Emery, Lynne
1972 *Black Dance in the United States from 1619 to 1970*. Palo Alto: National Press Books.
Erikson, Erik H.
1963 *Childhood and Society*. 2d ed. New York: W. W. Norton.
1966 "Ontogeny of Ritualization in Man." In *A Discussion on Ritualization of Behavior in Man and Animals (June 10–12, 1965)*, ed. Sir Julian Huxley, 251:337–349. Philosophical Transactions of the Royal Society of London.
Errington, Frederick Karl
1974 *Karavar: Masks and Power in a Melanesian Ritual*. Ithaca: Cornell University Press.
Ervin-Tripp, Susan
1976 "Speech Acts and Social Learning." In *Meaning in Anthropology*, ed. Keith H. Basso and Henry A. Selby, pp. 123–153. Albuquerque: University of New Mexico Press for School of American Research.
Evans-Pritchard, E. E.
1928 "The Dance." *Africa* 1:436–462.
1956 *Nuer Religion*. Oxford: Clarendon Press.
1965 *Theories of Primitive Religion*. Oxford: Clarendon Press.
Fernandez, James W.
1965 "Symbolic Concensus in a Fang Reformative Cult." *American Anthropologist* 67:902–929.
1966 "Principles of Opposition and Vitality in Fang Aesthetics." *Journal of Aesthetics and Art Criticism* 25:53–64.
1973 "The Exposition and Imposition of Order: Artistic Expression in Fang Culture." In *The Traditional Artist in African Societies*, ed. Warren L. d'Azevedo, pp. 194–220. Bloomington: Indiana University Press.
1974 "The Mission of Metaphor in Expressive Culture." *Current Anthropology* 15(2):119–145.
Field, M. J.
1940 *Social Organization of the Ga People*. Accra: Government Printing Dept.
1961 *Religion and Medicine of the Ga People*. London: Oxford University Press. [Orig. 1937.]
Firth, Raymond
1972 "Verbal and Bodily Rituals of Greeting and Parting." In *The Interpretation of Ritual*, ed. J. S. La Fontaine, pp. 1–38. London: Tavistock Press.
1973 *Symbols: Public and Private*. Ithaca: Cornell University Press.
Fischer, Claude S.
1975 "Toward a Subcultural Theory of Urbanism." *American Journal of Sociology* 80(6):1319–1341.
Fischer, J. L.

1961   "Art Styles as Cultural Cognitive Maps." *American Anthropologist* 63:79–93.

Fisher, Seymour
1973   *Body Consciousness*. Englewood Cliffs: Prentice-Hall.

Flannery, Kent V.
1972   "Culture History v. Cultural Process: A Debate in American Archaeology. Archaeological Systems Theory and Early Mesoamerica." In *Contemporary Archaeology: A Guide to Theory and Contributions*, ed. Mark P. Leone, pp. 102–107, 222–234. Carbondale: Southern Illinois University Press.

Flett, J. F. and T. M.
1964   *Traditional Dancing in Scotland*. Nashville: Vanderbilt University Press.

Forde, Daryll
1964   *Yakö Studies*. London: Oxford University Press.

Foulks, Edward F.
1972   "The Arctic Hysterias of the North Alaskan Eskimo." *Anthropological Studies No. 10*. Washington, D.C.: American Anthropological Association.

Fouts, Roger S.
1973   "Capacities for Language in Great Apes." Paper prepared for the IX International Congress of Anthropological and Ethnological Sciences, Chicago.

Fraser, Douglas, and Herbert M. Cole, eds.
1972   *African Art and Leadership*. Madison: University of Wisconsin Press.

Frazer, Sir James George
1929   *The Golden Bough: A Study in Magic and Religion, I*. New York: Book League of America.

Freud, Sigmund
1955   *Beyond the Pleasure Principle*. London: Hogarth Press.

Fried, Morton H.
1967   *The Evolution of Political Society: An Essay in Political Anthropology*. New York: Random House.

Friedlander, Ira
1975   *The Whirling Dervishes*. New York: Collier Books.

Fustel de Coulanges, Numa Denis
1956   *The Ancient City: A Study on the Religion, Laws, and Institutions of Greece and Rome*. Garden City: Doubleday Anchor.

Gailey, Harry A.
1970   *The Road to Aba: A Study of British Administrative Policy in Eastern Nigeria*. New York: New York University Press.

Gans, Herbert J.
1975   *Popular Culture and High Culture: An Analysis and Evaluation of Taste*. New York: Basic Books.

Gardner, Howard
  1973 *The Arts and Human Development: A Psychological Study of the Artistic Process.* New York: John Wiley.
  1976 "On the Acquisition of First Symbol Systems." *Studies in the Anthropology of Visual Communication* 3(1):22–37.
Gebauer, Paul
  1971 "Dances of Cameroon." *African Arts* 4(4):8–15.
Geertz, Clifford
  1960 *The Religion of Java.* Glencoe: Free Press.
  1963 *Peddlers and Princes: Social Change and Economic Modernization in Two Indonesian Towns.* Chicago: University of Chicago Press.
  1966 "Religion as a Cultural System." In *Anthropological Approaches to the Study of Religion*, ed. Michael Banton, pp. 1–46. New York: Praeger.
  1973 *The Interpretation of Culture.* New York: Basic Books.
Geis, Gilbert
  1968 "Slum Art, Shoestrings, and Bootstraps." In *The Arts, Youth, and Social Change*, ed. Joan Grant, pp. 42–77. Washington, D.C.: Dept. of Health, Education, and Welfare, Office of Juvenile Delinquency and Youth Development.
Gelfand, Michael
  1962 *Shona Religion: With Special Reference to the Makorekore.* Cape Town: Juta.
Geschwind, Norman
  1973 "The Brain and Language." In *Communication, Language, and Meaning: Psychological Perspectives*, ed. George A. Miller, pp. 61–72. New York: Basic Books.
Giedion, S.
  1960 "Space Conception in Prehistoric Art." In *Explorations in Communication*, ed. Edmund Carpenter and Marshall McLuhan, pp. 71–89. Boston: Beacon.
Ginsburg, Norton
  1972 "Planning the Future of the Industrial City." In *The City as a Centre of Change*, ed. D. J. Dwyer, pp. 269–283. Hong Kong: University Press.
Gluckman, Max
  1954 *Rituals of Rebellion in South-East Africa.* Manchester: Manchester University Press.
  1959 *Custom and Conflict in Africa.* Glencoe: Free Press.
  1960 "The Rise of a Zulu Empire." *Scientific American* 20(4):157–168.
Goffman, Erving
  1959 *The Presentation of Self in Everyday Life.* New York: Doubleday.

Goldfarb, Jeffrey
1976   "Theater behind the Iron Curtain." *Society* 14(1):30–34.
Goodman, Nelson
1975   "The Status of Style." *Critical Inquiry* 1(4):799–812.
Goody, Esther
1972   "'Greeting,' 'Begging,' and the Presentation of Respect." In
The Interpretation of Ritual, ed. J. S. La Fontaine, pp. 39–
72. London: Tavistock Press.
Gorenstein, Shirley
1973   "Tepexi El Viejo: A Postclassic Fortified Site in the Mixteca-
Puebla Region of Mexico." *Transactions of the American Philosophical Society* 63(1).
Gorer, Geoffrey
1962   *Africa Dances*. New York: W. W. Norton. [Orig. 1935.]
Graves, Theodore D., and Nancy B. Graves
1974   "Adaptive Strategies in Urban Migration." *Annual Review of
Anthropology* 3:117–152.
Gray, Robert F.
1965   "Some Parallels in Sonjo and Christian Mythology." In *African Systems of Thought*, ed. M. Fortes and G. Dieterlen, pp.
49–63. London: Oxford University Press.
Greeley, Andrew
1972   *Unsecular Man: The Persistence of Religion*. New York: Schock-
en.
Green, M. M.
1964   *Igbo Village Affairs*. 2d ed. London: Frank Cass and Co.
Greenberg, Joseph H.
1965   "Urbanism, Migration and Language." In *Urbanization and
Migration in West Africa*, ed. Hilda Kuper, pp. 50–59. Berkeley: University of California Press.
Gregory, R. L.
1973   *Eye and Brain: The Psychology of Seeing*. 2d ed. New York:
McGraw-Hill.
Griaule, Marcel
1965   *Conversations with Ogotemmêli*. London: Oxford University
Press.
Grosse, Ernst
1909   "The Dance." In *Source Book for Social Origins*, ed. William
I. Thomas, pp. 577–593. Chicago: University of Chicago
Press.
Gulliver, Pamela, and P. H. Gulliver
1953   *The Central Nilo-Hamites*. London: International African In-
stitute.
Gumperz, John
1974   "Linguistic Anthropology in Society." *American Anthropolo-
gist* 76(4):785–798.

Guthrie, R. Dale
  1976   *Body Hot Spots: The Anatomy of Human Social Organs and Behavior.* New York: Van Nostrand Reinhold.
Hammond, Dorothy
  1970   "Magic: A Problem in Semantics." *American Anthropologist* 72:1349–1356.
Hanna, Judith Lynne
  1965   "Africa's New Traditional Dance." *Ethnomusicology* 9:13–21.
  1970   "Discussion of Rod Rodger's Session: Dance Mobilization as Therapy in the Inner City." In *Workshop in Dance Therapy: Its Research Potentials*, pp. 37–42, 62–63. New York: Committee on Research in Dance.
  1973   "The Highlife: A West African Urban Dance." In *Dance Research Monograph One*, ed. Patricia A. Rowe and Ernestine Stodelle, pp. 138–152. New York: Committee on Research in Dance.
  1974   "African Dance: The Continuity of Change." *Yearbook of the International Folk Music Council* 5:164–174.
  1975a "The Anthropology of Dance: Reflections on the CORD Conference." *Current Anthropology* 16(3):445–446.
  1975b "Dances of Anáhuac—For God or Man? An Alternate Way of Thinking about Prehistory." *Dance Research Journal* 7(2): 39–43.
  1976   *The Anthropology of Dance-Ritual: Nigeria's Ubakala Nkwa di Iche Iche.* Ph.D. dissertation, Columbia University. Ann Arbor: University Microfilms.
  1977a "African Dance and the Warrior Tradition." In *The Warrior Tradition in Modern Africa. Special Issue of Journal of Asian and African Studies*, ed. Ali A. Mazrui, 12(1–2):111–133. Leiden: E. J. Brill.
  1977b "To Dance Is Human: Some Psychobiological Bases of an 'Expressive' Form." In *The Anthropology of the Body*, ed. John Blacking, pp. 211–232. A.S.A. Monograph 15. New York: Academic Press.
  1978a "African Dance: Some Implications for Dance Therapy." *American Journal of Dance Therapy* 2(1):3–15.
  1978b *The Anthropology of Dance: A Selected Bibliography.* R. L. Shep, Seattle; Ge Nabrink, Amsterdam, distributors.
  1979a "Movements toward Understanding Humans through the Anthropological Study of Dance." *Current Anthropology* 20 (2):313–339.
  1979b "Toward a Cross-cultural Conceptualization of Dance and Some Correlate Considerations." Revision of paper presented at 1973 IX ICAES. In *The Performing Arts: Music, Dance, and Theater*, ed. John Blacking and Joann W. Keallinohomoku, pp. 17–45. The Hague: Mouton (World Anthropology).

1979c "Toward Semantic Analysis of Movement Behavior: Concepts and Problems." *Semiotica* 25 (1–2):77–110.

———, and William John Hanna

1966 "The Problem of Ethnicity and Factionalism in African Survey Research." *Public Opinion Quarterly* 30:290–294.

1968a "Heart Beat of Uganda." *African Arts* 1(3):42–45, 85.

1968b "*Nkwa di Iche Iche*: Dance-Plays of Ubakala." *Présence Africaine*, no. 65:13–38.

1981 *Urban Dynamics in Black Africa*. Rev. ed. Hawthorne, N.Y.: Aldine.

Harley, George W.

1950 "Masks as Agents of Social Control in North-east Liberia." *Peabody Museum Papers* 32(2).

Harper, Peggy

1968 "Tiv Women: The Icough Dance." *Studies in Nigerian Dance*, no. 1.

Harris, Marvin

1968 *The Rise of Anthropological Theory*. New York: Thomas Y. Crowell Co.

Hatch, Frank White

1973 *A Behavioral Cybernetic Interpretation of Dance and Dance Culture*. Ph.D., University of Wisconsin. Ann Arbor: University Microfilms.

Hecht, Robin Silver

1973/74 "Reflections on the Career of Yvonne Rainer and the Values of Minimal Dance." *Dance Scope*, Fall/Winter 8(1):5–6.

Hein, Hilde

1969 "Play as an Aesthetic Concept." *Journal of Aesthetics and Art Criticism*.

Heisler, Helmuth

1974 *Urbanisation and the Government of Migration: The Interrelation of Urban and Rural Life in Zambia*. New York: St. Martin's.

Hendin, Judy, and Mihaly Csikszentmihalyi

1975 "Measuring the Flow Experience in Rock Dancing." In *Beyond Boredom and Anxiety*, ed. M. Csikszentmihalyi, pp. 102–122. San Francisco: Jossey-Bass.

Henley, Nancy M.

1973 "Status and Sex: Some Touching Observations." *Bulletin of the Psychonomic Society* 2:91–93.

Herskovits, Melville J.

1938 *Dahomey: An Ancient West African Kingdom*. Vols. I and II. New York: J. J. Augustin.

Hewes, Gordon W.

1973 "Primate Communication and the Gestural Origin of Language." *Current Anthropology* 14(1–2):5–24.

1974 "The Place of Dance in the Evolution of Human Communication." In *New Dimensions in Dance Research: Anthropology and Dance, the American Indian*, ed. Tamara Comstock, pp. 115–130. Proceedings of the Third Conference on Research in Dance, University of Arizona and Yaqui Villages, March 26–April 2, 1972. New York: Committee on Research in Dance.

Hirabayashi, James; William Willard; and Luis Kemnitzer
1972 "Pan-Indianism in the Urban Setting." In *The Anthropology of Urban Environments*, ed. Thomas Weaver and Douglas White, pp. 77–88. Society for Applied Anthropology Monograph Series 11.

Hockett, Charles F., and Robert Ascher
1964 "The Human Revolution." *Current Anthropology* 5:135–168.

Hockings, Paul, ed.
1975 *Principles of Visual Anthropology*. The Hague: Mouton.

Hoerburger, Felix
1965 "Folk Dance Survey." *Journal of the International Folk Music Council* 17(1):7–8.

Hogbin, Ian
1914 *A Guadalcanal Society: The Kaoka Speakers*. New York: Holt.

Holloway, Ralph Jr.
1966 "Cranial Capacity, Neural Reorganization and Hominid Evolution: A Search for More Suitable Parameters." *American Anthropologist* 68(1):103–121.
1976 "Paleoneurological Evidence for Language Origins." In *Origins and Evolution of Language*, ed. Stevan R. Harnad, Horst D. Steklis, and Jane Lancaster, 280:330–348. Annals of the New York Academy of Sciences.

Hopkins, Nicholas
1972 "In the Community." In *Performing Arts Institutions and Young People: Lincoln Center's Study–the Hunting of the Squiggle*, ed. Mark Schubart, pp. 48–55. New York: Praeger.

Horton, Robin
1960 *The Gods as Guests: An Aspect of Kalabari Religious Life*. Lagos: Nigeria Magazine Special Publication.
1962 "The Kalabari World-View: An Outline and Interpretation." *Africa* 32:197–220.
1963 "The Kalabari Ekine Society: A Borderland of Religion and Art." *Africa* 33(2):94–114.
1964 "Ritual Man in Africa." *Africa* 34(2):85–104.
1966 "Igbo: An Ordeal for Aristocrats." *Nigeria Magazine*, no. 90, 168–183.
1967 *African Traditional Thought and Western Science*. I, 37(1):50–71, II, 37(2):155–187.
1969 "Types of Spirit Possession in Kalabari Region." In *Spirit*

Mediumship and Society in Africa, ed. John Beattie and John Middleton, pp. 14–49. New York: Africana Publishing Corporation.

1970 "A Hundred Years of Change in Kalabari Religion." In *Black Africa: Its Peoples and Their Cultures Today*, ed. John Middleton, pp. 192–211. London: Macmillan.

Houlberg, Marilyn Hammersley
1973 "Ibeji Images of the Yoruba." *African Arts* 7(1):20–27.

Howard, James H.
1976 "The Plains Gourd Dance as a Revitalization Movement." *American Ethnologist* 3(2):243–260.

Howell, P. P.
1941 "The Shilluk Settlement." *Sudan Notes and Records* 24:47–66.

Huizinga, Johan
1950 *Homo Ludens: A Study of the Play Element in Culture*. Boston: Beacon Press.

Hull, Richard W.
1972 *Munyakare: African Civilization Before the Batuuree*. New York: John Wiley.

Hunt, Valerie
1968 "The Biological Organization of Man to Move." In *Impulse 1968: Dance, a Projection for the Future*, pp. 51–63.

Hutchinson, Ann
1970 *Labanotation*. Rev. and exp. ed. New York: Theatre Arts Books. [Orig. 1954.].

Huxley, Sir Julian, ed.
1966 "A Discussion on Ritualization of Behavior in Man and Animals (June 10–12, 1965)." *Philosophical Transactions of the Royal Society of London* 251:337–349.

Hymes, Dell
1974 *Foundations in Sociolinguistics: An Ethnographic Approach*. Philadelphia. University of Pennsylvania Press.

Ifeka-Moller, Caroline
1975 "Female Militancy and Colonial Revolt: The Women's War of 1929, Eastern Nigeria." In *Perceiving Women*, ed. Shirley Ardener, pp. 127–158. New York: Halsted Press.

Ikegami, Yoshihiko
1971 "A Stratificational Analysis of the Hand Gesture in Indian Classical Dancing." *Semiotica* 4(4):365–391.

Ilijin, Milica
1965 "Influences Réciproques des Danses Urbaines et Traditionnelles en Yougoslavie." *Journal of the International Folk Music Council* 17(2):85–90.

Ilogu, Edmund
1965 "Christianity and Ibo Traditional Religion." *International Revue of Missions* 54(215):335–342.

Imperato, Pascal James
  1970 "The Dance of the Tyi Wara." *African Arts* 4(1):8–13.
Irons, William
  1974 "Nomadism as a Political Adaptation: The Case of the Yomut Turkmen." *American Ethnologist* 1(4):635–650.
Jackson, Anthony
  1968 "Sound and Ritual." *Man* 3(2):293–299.
Jackson, J. A., ed.
  1969 "Migration." *Sociological Studies* 2. Cambridge: At the University Press.
Jakobson, Roman
  1960 "Closing Statement: Linguistics and Poetics." In *Style in Language*, ed. Thomas A. Sebeok, pp. 350–377. New York: John Wiley.
Johnston, William M.
  1972 *The Austrian Mind: An Intellectual and Social History*. Berkeley: University of California Press.
Jolly, Alison
  1972 *The Evolution of Primate Behavior*. New York: Macmillan.
Jung, C. G.
  1958 *Psyche and Symbol*. New York: Anchor.
Kaeppler, Adrienne Lois
  1967 *The Structure of Tongan Dance*. Ph.D. dissertation, University of Hawaii. Ann Arbor: University Microfilms.
Kagan, Jerome, and Robert E. Klein
  1973 "Cross-Cultural Perspectives on Early Development." *American Psychologist* 28(11):947–961.
Kaplan, Abraham
  1955 "Definition and Specification of Meaning." In *The Language of Social Research*, ed. Paul F. Lazarsfeld and Morris Rosenberg, pp. 527–532. Glencoe: Free Press.
Karlins, Marvin, and Herbert I. Abelson
  1970 *Persuasion: How Opinions and Attitudes Are Changed*. 2d ed. New York: Springer.
Katz, Jerrold J.
  1976 "A Hypothesis about the Uniqueness of Natural Language." In *Origins and Evolution of Language and Speech*, ed. Stevan R. Harnad, Horst D. Steklis, and Jane Lancaster, 280:33–41. Annals of the New York Academy of Sciences.
Kavolis, Vytautas
  1968 *Artistic Expression—a Sociological Analysis*. Ithaca: Cornell University Press.
Kealiinohomoku, Joann Wheeler
  1969–70 "An Anthropologist Looks at Ballet as a Form of Ethnic Dance." *Impulse: Extensions of Dance*, pp. 24–33.
  1972 "Folk Dance." In *Folklore and Folklife: An Introduction*, ed.

Richard M. Dorson, pp. 381–404. Chicago: University of Chicago Press.

1974a   "Dance Culture as a Microcosm of Holistic Culture." In *New Dimensions in Dance Research: Anthropology and Dance, the American Indian*, ed. Tamara Comstock, pp. 99–106. Proceedings of the Third Conference on Research in Dance. New York: Committee on Research in Dance.

1974b   "Review of Choreometrics." *Dance Research Journal* 6(2):20–24.

1976   *Theory and Methods for an Anthropological Study of Dance.* Ph.D. dissertation, Indiana University. Ann Arbor: University Microfilms.

——, and Frank Gillis

1970   "Special Bibliography: Gertrude Prokosch Kurath." *Ethnomusicology* 19(1):114–128.

Kehoe, Alice B.

1973   "Ritual and Religions: An Ethnologically Oriented Formal Analysis." Paper prepared for the IX International Congress of Anthropological and Ethnological Sciences, Chicago.

Keil, Charles

1967   "Tiv Dance: A First Assessment." *African Notes* 4(2):32–35.

1973   "Urban Music." Paper prepared for the Comparative Urban Studies Roundtable at the Graduate Center, City University of New York, November 1.

Keleman, Stanley

1975   *Living Your Dying*. New York: Random House.

Kenyatta, Jomo

1962   *Facing Mt. Kenya*. New York: Vintage Books.

Kepes, Gyorgy, ed.

1972   *Arts of the Environment*. New York: George Braziller.

Kern, Stephen

1975   *Anatomy and Destiny: A Cultural History of the Human Body*. New York: Bobbs-Merrill Co.

Kestenberg, Judith S.; Hershey Marcus; Esther Robbins; Jay Berlowe; and Arhnelt Buelte

1972   "Development of the Young Child as Expressed through Bodily Movement." *Journal of the American Psychoanalytic Association* 19:746–764.

Kilma, Edward S., and Ursula Bellugi

1973   "Teaching Apes to Communicate." In *Communication, Language, and Meaning: Psychological Perspectives*, ed. George A. Miller, pp. 95–106. New York: Basic Books.

Kinney, Sylvia

1970   "Urban West African Music and Dance." *African Urban Notes* 4(4):3–10.

Kirshenblatt-Gimblett, Barbara, ed.
  1976 *Speech Play: Research and Resources for Studying Linguistic Creativity*. Philadelphia: University of Pennsylvania Press.
Kirstein, Lincoln
  1970 *Movement and Metaphor: Four Centuries of Ballet*. New York: Praeger.
Kisselgoff, Anna
  1976 "*Opus '65*, a Dance to the Loss of Innocence." *New York Times*, October 28, p. 59.
  1977 "Ballet: Message from South Africa." *New York Times*, December 9, p. C5.
Kleinman, Seymour
  1975 "Movement Notation Systems: An Introduction." *Quest: The Language of Movement* 23:33–56.
Koestler, Arthur
  1967 *The Act of Creation: A Study of the Conscious and Unconscious in Science and Art*. New York: Dell.
Kramer, Hilton
  1978 "Why America Needs New York as Its Cultural Capital." *New York Times*, April 9, Section 2, pp. 1, 24.
Kraus, Richard
  1969 *History of the Dance in Art and Education*. Englewood Cliffs: Prentice-Hall.
Krebs, Stephanie
  1975*a* "Nonverbal Communication in Khon Dance-Drama: Thai Society Onstage." Ph.D. dissertation, Harvard University.
  1975*b* "The Film Elicitation Technique: Using Film to Elicit Conceptual Categories of Culture." In *Principles of Visual Anthropology*, ed. Paul Hockings, pp. 283–302. The Hague: Mouton.
Kreitler, Hans, and Shulamith Kreitler
  1972 *Psychology of the Arts*. Durham: Duke University Press.
Kubler, George
  1962 *The Art and Architecture of Ancient America*. Baltimore: Penguin.
  1967 *The Iconography of the Art of Teotihuacan*. Washington, D.C.: Dumbarton Oaks.
Kuper, Hilda
  1968 "Celebration of Growth and Kingship: *Incwala* in Swaziland." *African Arts* 1(3):57–59, 90.
  1969 *An African Aristocracy*. London: Oxford University Press. [Orig. 1947.]
Kurath, Gertrude P.
  1960 "Panorama of Dance Ethnology." *Current Anthropology* 1(3): 233–254.
  1964*a* "Iroquois Music and Dance: Ceremonial Arts of Two Seneca

Longhouses." *Bureau of American Ethnology Bulletin 187.* Smithsonian Institution. Washington, D.C.: Government Printing Office.

————, and Samuel Martí

1964b *Dances of Anáhuac: The Choreography and Music of Precortesian Dances.* Chicago: Aldine.

1968 *Dance and Song Rituals of Six Nations Reserve, Ontario.* National Museum of Canada Bulletin 220, Folklore Series 4. Ottawa.

1970 *Music and Dance in Tewa Plaza Ceremonies, New Mexico.* Santa Fe: University of New Mexico Press.

Laban, Rudolf

1974 *The Language of Movement: A Guidebook to Choreutics.* Ed. Lisa Ullman. Boston: Plays.

Ladzekpo, Kobla

1973 "Physician Heal Thyself." *Society for Ethnomusicology Newsletter* 7(4):4.

Lambo, T. Adeoye

1965 "The Place of the Arts in the Emotional Life of the Africa." *AMSAC Newsletter* 7(4):1–6.

Lane, Michael

1970 "Introduction." In *Introduction to Structuralism*, ed. Michael Lane, pp. 11–42. New York: Basic Books.

Lange, Roderyk

1974 "On Differences between the Rural and Urban: Traditional Polish Peasant Dancing." *Yearbook of the International Folk Music Council* 6:44–51.

1975 *The Nature of Dance.* London: Macdonald and Evans.

Langer, Suzanne K.

1953 *Feeling and Form: A Theory of Art Developed from Philosophy in a New Key.* New York: Charles Scribner's Sons.

1957a *Philosophy in a New Key: A Study in the Symbolism of Reason, Rite, and Art.* 3rd ed. Cambridge, Mass.: Harvard University Press.

1957b *Problems of Art.* New York: Charles Scribner's Sons.

Lawler, Lillian B.

1964 *The Dance in Ancient Greece.* Middletown: Wesleyan University Press.

Leach, Edmund

1968 "Ritual." *International Encyclopedia of the Social Sciences*, 13: 520–526. New York: Free Press.

1970 *Claude Lévi-Strauss.* New York: Viking Press.

1971 *Rethinking Anthropology.* New York: Humanities Press.

1972a "Anthropological Aspects of Language: Animal Categories and Verbal Abuse." In *Mythology*, ed. Pierre Maranda, pp. 39–67. London: Penguin.

1972*b* "The Influence of Cultural Context on Non-Verbal Communication in Man." In *Non-Verbal Communication*, ed. R. A. Hinde, pp. 315–343. Cambridge: At the University Press.

1976 *Culture and Communication: The Logic by Which Symbols Are Connected*. New York: Cambridge University Press.

Lee, Richard
1968 "The Sociology of !Kung Bushman Trance Performances." In *Trance and Possession States*, pp. 35–54. Montreal: R. M. Bucke Memorial Society.

Lekis, Lisa
1968 *Folk Dances of Latin America*. New York: Scarecrow.

Lenneberg, Eric M.
1967 *Biological Foundations of Language*. New York: John Wiley and Sons.
1973 "Biological Aspects of Language." In *Communication, Language, and Meaning: Psychological Perspectives*, ed. George A. Miller, pp. 49–60. New York: Basic Books.

Leone, Mark P.
1972 "Preface Issues in Anthropological Archaeology, Introduction." In *Contemporary Archaeology*, ed. Mark P. Leone, pp. ix–xiv, 14–27, 355–358. Carbondale: Southern Illinois University Press.

Lessa, William A., and Evon Z. Vogt, eds.
1972 *Reader in Comparative Religion: An Anthropological Approach*. New York: Harper and Row.

Levin, David Michael
1973 "Balanchine's Formalism." *Dance Perspectives* 55: *Three Essays in Dance Aesthetics*, pp. 29–48.

Levin, Michael E.
1973 "On Explanation in Archaeology: A Rebuttal to Fritz and Plog." *American Antiquity* 38:387–395.

Lévi-Strauss, Claude
1967 *Structural Anthropology*. Garden City: Anchor. [New York: Basic Books, 1963.]
1971 "The Science of the Concrete." In *Art and Aesthetics in Primitive Societies*, ed. Carol F. Jopling, pp. 225–249. New York: E. P. Dutton.

Levy, Jerre
1974 "Psychobiological Implications of Bilateral Asymmetry." In *Hemispheric Function in the Human Brain*, ed. Stuart J. Diamond and J. Graham Beaumont, pp. 121–183. New York: Wiley.

Lewis, I. M.
   1971   *Ecstatic Religion: An Anthropological Study of Spirit Possession and Shamanism*. Baltimore: Penguin.
Lex, Barbara
   1975   "Physiological Aspects of Ritual Trance." *Journal of Altered States of Consciousness* 2(2).
Lienhardt, Godfrey
   1957   "Anuak Village Headmen." *Africa* 27(4):341–355.
Little, Kenneth
   1974   *African Women in Towns: An Aspect of Africa's Social Revolution*. London: Cambridge University Press.
Lloyd, Margaret
   1949   *The Borzoi Book of Modern Dance*. New York: A. A. Knopf.
Lloyd, P. C.
   1966   "Introduction." In *The New Elites of Tropical Africa*, ed. P. C. Lloyd, pp. 1–64. London: Oxford University Press.
Loizos, Caroline
   1969   "Play Behaviour in Higher Primates: A Review." In *Primate Ethology*, ed. Desmond Morris, pp. 226–282. Garden City: Doubleday Anchor.
Lomax, Alan
   1968   *Folk Song Style and Structure*. Washington, D.C.: American Association for the Advancement of Science.
Long, Norman
   1968   *Social Change and the Individual: A Study of the Social and Religious Response to Innovation in a Zambian Rural Community*. Manchester: Manchester University Press.
Luce, Gay Gaer
   1971   *Biological Rhythms in Human and Animal Physiology*. New York: Dover.
Ludwig, Arnold M.
   1969   "Altered States of Consciousness." In *Altered States of Consciousness*, ed. Charles T. Tart, pp. 9–22. New York: John Wiley.
Lyons, John
   1972   "Human Language." In *Non-Verbal Communication*, ed. R. A. Hinde, pp. 49–85. Cambridge: At the University Press.
McCawley, James
   1968   "Review of Current Trends in Linguistics 3," ed. Thomas A. Sebeok. *Language* 44:446–592.
McGuire, William J.
   1973   "Persuasion." In *Communication, Language, and Meaning: Psychological Perspectives*, ed. George A. Miller, pp. 242–255. New York: Basic Books.

MacKay, D. M.
1972   "Formal Analysis of Communicative Processes." In *Non-Verbal Communication*, ed. R. A. Hinde, pp. 3–26. Cambridge: At the University Press.
Mackerras, Colin P.
1972   *The Rise of the Peking Opera 1770–1870*. Oxford: Clarendon Press.
Maclay, Howard
1971   "Overview." In *Semantics*, ed. Danny D. Steinberg and Leon A. Jakobovits, pp. 157–182. Cambridge: At the University Press.
Mahlobo, G. W. K., and E. J. Krige
1934   "Transition from Childhood to Adulthood amongst the Zulus." *Bantu Studies* 8:156–191.
Malcolmson, Robert W.
1973   *Popular Recreations in English Society 1700–1850*. Cambridge: At the University Press.
Malinowski, B.
1936   "Native Education and Culture Contact." *International Review of Missions* 25:480–515.
Mao Tse-Tung
1967   *Selected Works of Mao Tse-Tung*. Vol. III. Peking: Foreign Languages Press.
Manquet, Jacques
1961   *The Premise of Inequality in Ruanda*. London: International African Institute.
1971   *Introduction to Aesthetic Anthropology*. McCaleb Module. Reading: Addison-Wesley.
1972   *Civilizations of Black Africa*. Rev. and trans. Joan Rayfield. New York: Oxford University Press.
Maranda, Elli Köngäs.
1970   "Deep Significance and Surface Significance: Is Cantometrics [Choreometrics] Possible?" *Semiotica* 2(2):173–184.
Marcuse, Herbert
1970   "Art as a Form of Reality." In *On the Future of Art*, pp. 123–134. New York: Viking Press.
Marett, R. R.
1914   *The Threshold of Religion*. 2d ed. London: Methuen.
Marshall, Lorna
1962   "!Kung Bushman Religious Beliefs." *Africa* 32:221–252.
1969   "The Medicine Dance of the !Kung Bushmen." *Africa* 39:347–381.
Martin, Paul S.
1972   "The Revolution in Archaeology." In *Contemporary Archaeol-*

ogy: A Guide to Theory and Contributions, ed. Mark P. Leone, pp. 5–13. Carbondale: Southern Illinois University Press.

Mauss, Marcel
1935   "Les Techniques du Corps." *Journal de Psychologie Normale et Pathologique* 32:271–293.

Mazo, Joseph H.
1974   *Dance Is a Contact Sport*. New York: E. P. Dutton.

Mazrui, Ali A.
1973   "Phallic Symbols in Politics and War: An African Perspective." Paper read at an Interdisciplinary Colloquium on "African Systems of Form," African Studies Center, University of California at Los Angeles.
1975   "The Resurrection of the Warrior Tradition in African Political Culture." *Journal of Modern African Studies* 13(1):67–84.

Mbiti, John S.
1970   *African Religions and Philosophy*. New York: Anchor.

Mead, Margaret
1928   *Coming of Age in Samoa*. New York: W. Morrow.
1940   "The Arts in Bali." *Yale Review* 30(2):335–347.
1946   "Dance as an Expression of Culture Patterns." Paper prepared for the Function of Dance in Human Society, 2d Seminar.

Meadows, Paul
1971   *The Many Faces of Change: Explorations in the Theory of Social Change*. Cambridge, Mass: Schenkman.

Meek, C. K.
1931   *Tribal Studies in Northern Nigeria*. London: Kegan Paul, Trench, Trubner.
1937   *Law and Authority in a Nigerian Tribe*. London: Oxford University Press.

Meerloo, Joost A. M.
1960   *The Dance*. New York: Chilton.

Mehrabian, Albert
1972   *Nonverbal Communication*. New York: Aldine-Atherton.
———, and J. T. Friar
1979   "Encoding of Attitude by a Seated Communicator via Posture and Position Cues." *Journal of Consulting Clinical Psychology* 33:330–336.

Meillassoux, Claude
1965   "The 'Koteba' of Bamako." *Présence Africaine* 24(52):159–193.
1968   *Urbanization of an African Community: Voluntary Associations in Bamako*. Seattle: University of Washington Press.

Menzel, Emil W., and Marcia K. Johnson
1976   "Communication and Cognitive Organization in Humans and Other Animals." In *Origins and Evolution of Language*

and Speech, ed. Stevan R. Harnad, Horst D. Steklis, and Jane Lancaster, 280:131–142. Annals of the New York Academy of Sciences.

Merleau-Ponty, M.
1962   *Phenomenology of Perception*. London: Routledge and Kegan Paul.
1970   "The Spatiality of the Lived Body and Motility." In *The Philosophy of the Body: Rejections of Cartesian Dualism*, ed. Stuart F. Specker, pp. 241–271. Chicago: Quadrangle.

Merriam, Alan P.
1974   "Anthropology and the Dance." In *New Dimensions in Dance Research: Anthropology and Dance. The American Indian*, ed. Tamara Comstock, pp. 9–28. New York: Committee on Research in Dance.

Merton, Robert K.
1957   *Social Theory and Social Structure*. Glencoe: Free Press.

Meyerowitz, Eva L. R.
1962   *At the Court of an African King*. London: Faber and Faber.

Meyersohn, Rolf
1970   "The Charismatic and the Playful in Outdoor Recreation." *The Annals*, no. 389:35–45.

Middleton, John
1960   *Lugbara Religion: Ritual and Authority among an East African People*. London: Oxford University Press.

Miller, George A.
1970   "Empirical Methods in the Study of Semantics." In *Semantics*, ed. Danny D. Steinberg and Leon A. Jakobovits, pp. 569–585. Cambridge: At the University Press.
1973   *Communications, Language, and Meaning: Psychological Perspectives*. New York: Basic Books.

Miller, Stephen
1973   "Ends, Means, and Galumphing: Some Leitmotifs of Play." *American Anthropologist* 75(1):87–98.

Mills, George
1971   "Art: An Introduction to Qualitative Anthropology." In *Art and Aesthetics in Primitive Societies*, ed. Carol F. Jopling, pp. 73–98. New York: E. P. Dutton.
1973   "Art and the Anthropological Lens." In *The Traditional Artist in African Societies*, ed. Warren L. d'Azevedo, pp. 379–416. Bloomington: Indiana University Press.

Mitchell, J. Clyde
1956   *The Kalela Dance*. Paper No. 27. Manchester: Manchester University Press for the Rhodes-Livingstone Institute.

Moedano, Gabriel
1972   *Los hermanos de la Santa Cuenta: Un culto de crisis de origen*

Chichimeca, pp. 599–610. Religión en Mesoamerica: XII Mesa Redonda, Sociedad Mexicana de Antropología.

Mooney, James
1965   *The Ghost-Dance Religion and the Sioux Outbreak of 1890*. Ed. Anthony F. C. Wallace. Chicago: University of Chicago Press. [Orig. 1896.]

Morawski, Stefan
1973   "Politicians versus Artists." *Arts in Society: The Politics of Art* 10(3):8–18.

Morgan, Charles E.
1973   "Archaeology and Explanation." *World Archaeology* 4(3):259–276.

Morris, Charles
1955   *Signs, Language and Behavior*. New York: Braziller.

Morse, Chandler
1961   "The Functional Imperatives." In *The Social Theories of Talcott Parsons*, ed. Max Black, pp. 100–152. Englewood Cliffs: Prentice-Hall.

Moyana, Tafirenyika
1976   "Muchongoyo: A Shangani Dance." *African Arts* 9(2):40–42.

Mubitana, Kafungulwa
1971   "Wiko Masquerades." *African Arts* 4(3):48–62.

Mueller, Claus
1973   *The Politics of Communication: A Study in the Political Sociology of Language, Socialization, and Legitimation*. New York: Oxford University Press.

Mueller, Robert E.
1967   *The Science of Art*. New York: John Day.

Mulder, J. W. F., and S. G. J. Hervey
1972   *Theory of the Linguistic Sign*. Janua Linguarum: Series Minor 136. The Hague: Mouton.

Mumford, Lewis
1938   *The Culture of Cities*. New York: Harcourt, Brace & Co.

Munn, Nancy
1973   "Symbolism in a Ritual Context: Aspects of Symbolic Action." In *Handbook of Social and Cultural Anthropology*, ed. John Honigmann, pp. 579–612. Chicago: Rand McNally.

Munroe, Ruth L.
1955   *Schools of Psychoanalytic Thought: An Exposition, Critique, and Attempt at Integration*. New York: Holt, Rinehart and Winston.

Murphy, Judith, and Ronald Gross
1968   *The Arts and the Poor: New Challenge for Educators*. Washington, D.C.: Department of Health, Education and Welfare.

Nadel, Myron Howard, and Constance Gwen Nadel, eds.

1970   *The Dance Experience: Readings in Dance Appreciation*. New York: Praeger.

Nadel, S. F.

1942   *A Black Byzantium: The Kingdom of Nupe in Nigeria*. London: Oxford University Press.

1947   *The Nuba: An Anthropological Study of the Hill Tribes in Kordofan*. London: Oxford University Press.

Naroll, Raoul

1973   "Galton's Problem." In *A Handbook of Method in Cultural Anthropology*, ed. Raoul Naroll and Ronald Cohen, pp. 927–961. New York: Columbia University Press.

National Research Center of the Arts (NRCA)

1973   *Arts and the People: A Survey of Public Attitudes and Participation in the Arts and Culture in New York State*. Conducted for the American Council for the Arts in Education. New York: ACAE.

Nayacakalou, R. R., and Aidan Southall

1973   "Urbanization and Fijian Cultural Traditions in the Context of Pacific Port Cities." In *Urban Anthropology: Cross-Cultural Studies of Urbanization*, ed. Aidan Southall, pp. 393–406. New York: Oxford University Press.

Needham, Rodney

1967   "Percussion and Transition." *Man* 2(4):606–614.

Neher, Andrew

1962   "A Physiological Explanation of Unusual Behavior in Ceremonies Involving Drums." *Human Biology* 34(2):151–160.

Netting, Robert M.

1971   *Ecological Approach in Cultural Study*. Addison-Wesley Modular Publications No. 6.

New York Times

1976   "Sweating on Palms and Soles." March 7, p. 7.

Nicholas, Ralph W.

1973   "Social and Political Movements." *Annual Review of Anthropology* 2:63–84.

Nigeria Magazine

1957   "Efik Dances." No. 53:159–196.

Nigerian Government

1930a   *Aba Commission of Enquiry: Minutes of Evidence*.

1930b   *Report of the Commission of Inquiry Appointed to Inquire into the Disturbances in the Calabar and Owerri Provinces*, December 1929. Sessional Paper of the Nigerian Legislative Council, No. 28.

Nikolais, Alwin

1971   "Nik—a Documentary," ed. Marcia B. Siegel. *Dance Perspectives* 48, Winter.

Njaka, Mazi Elechukwu Nnadibuagha
1974 *Igbo Political Culture.* Evanston: Northwestern University Press.

Nketia, J. H. Kwabena
1957 "Possession Dances in African Societies." *Journal of the International Folk Music Council* 9:4–9.

Norbeck, Edward
1963 "African Rituals of Conflict." *American Anthropologist* 65(6): 1254–1279.
1973 "Religion and Human Play." Paper prepared for the IX International Congress of Anthropological and Ethnological Sciences, Chicago, September.

North, Marion
1972 *Personality Assessment through Movement.* London: Macdonald & Evans.

Nwabara, Samuel Nkankwo
1965 *Ibo Land: A Study in British Penetration and the Problem of Administration, 1860–1930.* Ph.D. dissertation, Northwestern University. Ann Arbor: University Microfilms.

Nzekwu, Onuora
1963 "The Edda." *Nigeria Magazine,* no. 76:16–28.

Oberg, K.
1940 "The Kingdom of Ankole in Uganda." In *African Political Systems,* ed. M. Fortes and E. E. Evans-Pritchard, pp. 121–164. London: Oxford University Press.

Obianim, Sam J.
1953 "Oshogbo Celebrates Festival of Shango." *Nigeria Magazine,* no. 40:298–310.

Ornstein, Robert E., ed.
1968 *The Nature of Human Consciousness.* San Francisco: W. H. Freeman & Co.

Ortner, Sherry B.
1975 "Gods' Bodies, Gods' Fools: A Symbolic Analysis of a Sherpa Ritual." In *The Interpretation of Symbolism,* ed. R. Willis, pp. 133–170. New York: Halsted.

Ottenberg, Simon, and Phoebe Ottenberg
1960 *Cultures and Societies of Africa.* New York: Random House.

Owomoyela, Okekan
1971 "Folklore and Yoruba Theater." *Research in African Literatures* 2:121–133.

Pagès, G.
1933 "Un Royaume Hamite au Centre de l'Afrique: Au Ruanda sur les Bords du Lac Kivu (Congo Belge)." *Mémoires, Institut Royal Colonial Belge, Section des Sciences Morales et Politiques, Collection, Vol. 1.* Bruxelles: Librairie Folk Fils, Georges van Campenhout, Successeur.

Parrinder, E. G.
  1969 "God in African Mythology." In *Myths and Symbols*, ed. Joseph M. Kitagawa and Charles H. Long, pp. 111–126. Chicago: University of Chicago Press.
Peacock, James L.
  1968 *Rites of Modernization: Symbolic and Social Aspects of Indonesian Proletarian Drama*. Chicago: University of Chicago Press.
Peckham, Morse
  1965 *Man's Rage for Chaos: Biology, Behavior and the Arts*. Philadelphia: Chilton.
Pelto, Pertti J.
  1970 *Anthropological Research: The Structure of Inquiry*. New York: Harper & Row.
———, and Gretel H. Pelto
  1975 "Intra-Cultural Diversity: Some Theoretical Issues." *American Ethnologist* 2(1):1–18.
Perham, Margery
  1937 *Native Administration in Nigeria*. London: Oxford University Press.
Petrosyan, E. Kh.
  1973 "Totemic Dances of Armenia." Paper prepared for the IX International Congress of Anthropological and Ethnological Sciences, Chicago.
Phenix, Philip H.
  1970 "Relationships of Dance to Other Art Forms." In *Dance—an Art in Academe*, ed. Martin Haberman and Toby Meisel, pp. 9–14. New York: Teachers College Press.
Pitcairn, Thomas K., and Margret Schleidt
  1976 "Dance and Decision: An Analysis of a Courtship Dance of the Medlpa, New Guinea." *Behaviour* 58(3–4):298–316.
Pribram, Karl H.
  1976 "Introduction, Neural Parallels and Continuities." In *Origins and Evolution of Language and Speech*, ed. Stevan R. Harnad, Horst D. Steklis, and Jane Lancaster, pp. 728–731. Annals of the New York Academy of Sciences 280.
Prince, Raymond, ed.
  1968 *Trance and Possession States*. Montreal: R. M. Bucke Memorial Society.
Proskouriakoff, Tatiana
  1960 "Historical Implications of a Pattern of Dates at Piedras Negras, Guatemala." *American Antiquities* 25:454–475.
Prost, J. H.
  1973 "Filming Body Behavior." Paper prepared for the IX International Congress of Anthropological and Ethnological Sciences, Chicago.
Pukui, Mary Kawena, and Samuel H. Elbert

1957   *Hawaiian-English Dictionary*. Honolulu: University of Hawaii Press.

Radcliffe-Brown, A. R.
1964   *The Andaman Islanders*. Glencoe: Free Press. [Orig. 1922.]

Ragir, Sonia
1972   "A Review of Techniques for Archaeological Sampling." In *Contemporary Archaeology: A Guide to Theory and Contributions*, ed. Mark P. Leone, pp. 178–192. Carbondale: Southern Illinois University Press.

Ranger, T. O.
1975   *Dance and Society in Eastern Africa, 1890–1970: The Beni Ngoma*. Berkeley: University of California Press.

Rappaport, Roy A.
1971a   "Nature, Culture, and Ecological Anthropology." In *Man, Culture, and Society*, ed. Harry L. Shapiro, pp. 237–267. London: Oxford University Press.

1971b   "Ritual, Sanctity, and Cybernetics." *American Anthropologist* 73(1):29–76.

Rathje, William L.
1972   "Praise the Gods and Pass the Metates: A Hypothesis of the Development of Lowland Rainforest Civilizations in Mesoamerica." In *Contemporary Archeology*, ed. Mark Leone, pp. 365–392. Carbondale: Southern Illinois University Press.

Raum, Otto
1940   *Chaga Childhood*. London: Oxford University Press.

Ravenhill, Philip L.
1978   "The Interpretation of Symbolism in Wan Female Initiation." *Africa* 48:66–78.

Read, Margaret
1938   "The Moral Code of the Ngoni and Their Former Military State." *Africa* 11:1–24.

Reay, Marie
1959   *The Kuma: Freedom and Conformity in the New Guinea Highlands*. Melbourne: Melbourne University Press.

Redfield, Robert
1953   *The Primitive World and Its Transformations*. Ithaca: Cornell University Press.

1971   "Art and Icon." In *Anthropology and Art*, ed. Charlotte M. Otten, pp. 39–65. Garden City: Natural History Press.

———, and Milton B. Singer
1954   "The Cultural Role of Cities." *Economic Development and Cultural Change* 3(1):53–73.

Reina, Ruben E.
1973   *Paraná: Social Boundaries in an Argentine City*. Austin: University of Texas Press.

Reynolds, Peter C.

1976 "Language and Skilled Activity." In *Origins and Evolution of Languages*, ed. Stevan R. Harnad, Horst D. Steklis, and Jane Lancaster, 280:150–166. Annals of the New York Academy of Sciences.

Richards, Audrey I.
1940 "The Political System of the Bemba Tribe—Northeastern Rhodesia." In *African Political Systems*, ed. M. Fortes and E. E. Evans-Pritchard, pp. 83–120. London: International African Institute.
1956 *Chisungu: A Girls' Initiation Ceremony among the Bemba of Northern Rhodesia*. New York: Grove Press.

Richman, Marjorie L., and Gertrude R. Schmiedler
1955 "Changes in a Folk Dance Accompanying Cultural Change." *Journal of Social Psychology* 42:333–336.

Ries, Frank W. D.
1977–1978 "Roman Pantomime: Practice and Politics." *Dance Scope* 12(1):35–47.

Rigby, Peter
1966 "Dual Symbolic Classification among the Gogo of Central Tanzania." *Africa* 36(1):1–17.
1968 "The Symbolic Role of Cattle in Gogo Religion." In *University of East Africa Social Sciences Council Conference, Sociology Papers II*, pp. 440–463. Kampala: Makerere Institute of Social Research.
1972 "Some Gogo Rituals of 'Purification': An Essay on Social and Moral Categories." In *Reader in Comparative Religion: An Anthropological Approach*, ed. William A. Lessa and Evon Z. Vogt, pp. 238–247. New York: Harper and Row.

Rogers, Everett M., with F. Floyd Shoemaker
1971 *Communication of Innovations: A Cross-Cultural Approach*. 2d ed. New York: Free Press.

Rommetveit, Ragnar
1974 *On Message Structure: A Framework for the Study of Language and Communication*. New York: John Wiley & Sons.

Rothstein, David
1972 "Culture-Creation and Social Reconstruction." *American Sociological Review* 37(6):671–678.

Rouch, Jean
1974 "The Camera and Man." *Studies in the Anthropology of Visual Communication* 1(1):37–44.

Royce, Anya Peterson
1974a "Choreology Today: A Review of the Field." In *New Dimensions in Dance Research: Anthropology and Dance. The American Indian*, ed. Tamara Comstock, pp. 285–298. New York: Committee on Research in Dance.
1974b "Dance as an Indicator of Social Class and Identity in

Juchitán, Oaxaca." In *New Dimensions in Dance Research: Anthropology and Dance*, ed. Tamara Comstock, pp. 285–298. New York: Committee on Research in Dance.

1977   *The Anthropology of Dance*. Bloomington: Indiana University Press.

Rudner, Jalmar, and Ione Rudner
1970   *The Hunter and His Art: A Survey of Rock Art in Southern Africa*. Cape Town: C. Struik.

Rust, Frances
1969   *Dance in Society: An Analysis of the Relationship between the Social Dance and Society in England, from the Middle Ages to the Present Day*. London: Routledge & Kegan Paul.

Sachs, Curt
1937   *World History of the Dance*. Trans. Bessie Schonberg. New York: Norton.

Sachs, Nahoma
1975   *Music and Meaning: Musical Symbolism in a Macedonian Village*. Ph.D. dissertation, Indiana University. Ann Arbor: University Microfilms.

Safier, Benno
1953   "A Psychological Orientation to Dance and Pantomime." *Samīksā* 7:236–259.

Sahagún, Fray Bernardino de
1950–1963   *General History of the Things of New Spain. Florentine Codex*. Trans. Charles E. Dibble and Arthur J. O. Anderson. V, pp. 2–5, 7–13. School of American Research and the University of Utah.

Saldaña, Nancy
1966   "La Malinche: Her Representation in Dances in Mexico and the U.S." *Ethnomusicology* 10:298–309.

Salk, L.
1962   "Mother's Heartbeat as an Imprinting Stimulus." *Transactions of the New York Academy of Sciences* 24:753–763.

Sanders, William T., and Barbara J. Price
1968   *Mesoamerica: The Evolution of a Civilization*. New York: Random House.

Schechner, Richard
1969   *Public Domain*. New York: Discus/Avon.
1973   "Drama, Script, Theatre, and Performance." *Drama Review* 17(3):5–36.

Scheflen, Albert E., with Alice Scheflen
1972   *Body Language and the Social Order: Communication as Behavioral Control*. Englewood Cliffs: Prentice-Hall.

Schmais, Claire
1966   "Learning Is Fun When You Dance It." *Dance Magazine* 40 (1):33–35.

Schoffeleers, Matthew, and I. Linden
  1972 "The Resistance of the Nyau Societies to the Roman Cath-
         olic Missions in Colonial Malawi." In *The Historical Study of
         African Religion*, ed. T. O. Ranger and I. N. Kamambo, pp.
         252–273. Berkeley: University of California Press.
Schubart, Mark, ed.
  1972 *Performing Arts Institutions and Young People*. New York:
         Praeger.
Sebeok, Thomas A.
  1976 "Iconicity." *Modern Language Notes* 91:1427–1456.
Service, Elman R.
  1962 *Primitive Social Organization: An Evolutionary Perspective*. New
         York: Random House.
Shapiro, Gary
  1974 "Intention and Interpretation in Art: A Semiotic Analysis."
         Journal of Aesthetics and Art Criticism 33(1):33–42.
Shawn, Ted
  1974 *Every Little Movement: A Book about François Delsarte*. Brook-
         lyn: Dance Horizons.
Shay, Anthony
  1974 "Survival of Extinctions: Traditional Yugoslav Dance Forms
         in a Changing World." *Viltis* 32(5):9–11.
Sieber, Roy
  1971a "The Aesthetics of Traditional African Art." In *Art and Aes-
          thetics in Primitive Societies*, ed. Carol F. Jopling, pp. 127–
          131. New York: E. P. Dutton.
  1971b "Masks as Agents of Social Control." In *Man in Adaptation:
          The Institutional Framework*, ed. Yehudi A. Cohen, pp. 434–
          438. Chicago: Aldine-Atherton.
  1973   "Approaches to Non-Western Art." In *The Traditional Artist
          in African Societies*, ed. Warren L. d'Azevedo, pp. 425–434.
          Bloomington: Indiana University Press.
Siegel, Bernard J.
  1970 "Defensive Structuring and Environmental Stress." *Ameri-
         can Journal of Sociology* 76(1):11–32.
Siegel, Marcia B.
  1974 "New Dance: Individuality, Image and the Demise of the
         Coterie." *Dance Magazine*, April, pp. 38–44.
Simíc, Andrei
  1973 *The Peasant Urbanites: A Study of Rural-Urban Mobility in Ser-
         bia*. New York: Seminar Press.
Simmel, Georg
  1970 "The Metropolis and Mental Life." In *Neighborhood, City,
         and Metropolis*, ed. Robert Gutman and David Popenoe, pp.
         777–787. New York: Random House.
Sipes, Richard G.

1973   "War, Sports and Aggression: An Empirical Test of Two Rival Theories." *American Anthropologist* 75(1):64–86.

Sircar, Manjusri (Chaki)
1972   "Community of Dancers in Calcutta." In *Cultural Profile of Calcutta*, ed. Surajit Sinha, pp. 190–198. Calcutta: Indian Anthropological Society.

Siroto, Leon
1969   "Masks and Social Organization among the Bakwele People of Western Equatorial Africa." Ph.D. dissertation, Columbia University.
1972   "Gon: A Mask Used in Competition for Leadership among the Bakwele." In *African Art and Leadership*, ed. Douglas Fraser and Herbert M. Cole, pp. 57–77. Madison: University of Wisconsin Press.

Sjoberg, Gideon
1960   *The Preindustrial City: Past and Present*. New York: Free Press.

Sklar, Richard L.
1963   *Nigerian Political Parties*. New Jersey: Princeton University Press.

Smith, Alfred, ed.
1966   *Communication and Culture: Readings in the Codes of Human Interaction*. New York: Holt, Rinehart, and Winston.

Sollberger, A.
1965   *Biological Rhythm Research*. New York: Elsevier.

Sorenson, E. Richard
1967   "A Research Film Program in the Study of Changing Man: Research Filmed Material as a Foundation for Continued Study of Non-Recurring Human Events." *Current Anthropology* 8(5):443–469.
———, and Jablonko, Allison
1973   "Research Filming of Naturally Occurring Phenomena: Basic Strategies." Paper prepared for the IX International Congress of Anthropological and Ethnological Sciences, Chicago.

Spencer, Paul
1965   *The Samburu: A Study of Gerontocracy in a Nomadic Tribe*. Berkeley: University of California Press.

Sperber, Dan
1974   *Rethinking Symbolism*. Trans. Alice L. Morton. Cambridge: At the University Press.

Spiegel, John P., and Pavel Machotka
1974   *Messages of the Body*. New York: Free Press.

Spores, Ronald
1974   "Marital Alliance in the Political Integration of Mixtec Kingdoms." *American Anthropologist* 76(2):297–311.

Stearns, Marshall, and Jean Marshall

1968   *Jazz Dance: The Story of American Vernacular Dance*. New York: Macmillan.

Stokoe, William C.
1976   "Sign Language Autonomy." In *Origins and Evolution of Language and Speech*, ed. Stevan R. Harnad, Horst D. Steklis, and Jane Lancaster, 280:505–513. Annals of the New York Academy of Sciences.

Stone, Roslyn E.
1975   "Human Movement Forms as Meaning-Structures: Prolegomenon." *Quest* 23:10–17.

Strauss, Gloria
1977   "Dance and Ideology in China." In *Asian and Pacific Dance*, ed. Adrienne Kaeppler, Carl Wolz, and Judy Van Zile, pp. 19–54. New York: Committee on Research in Dance.

Strongman, K. T.
1973   *The Psychology of Emotion*. New York: Wiley and Sons.

Suess, John G.
1969   "The Performing Arts and the Urban Environment: Some Observations on Relationships." In *The Quality of Urban Life*, ed. Henry J. Schmandt and Warner Bloomberg, Jr., pp. 269–291. Vol. 3, Urban Affairs Annual Reviews. Beverly Hills: Sage Publications.

Sutherland, David Earl
1976   "Ballet as a Career." *Society* 14(1):40–45.

Suttles, Gerald D.
1968   *The Social Order of the Slum: Ethnicity and Territory in the Inner City*. Chicago: University of Chicago Press.
1972   *The Social Construction of Communities*. Chicago: University of Chicago Press.

Sutton-Smith, Brian
1974   "Towards an Anthropology of Play." *Association for the Anthropological Study of Play Newsletter* 1(2):8–15.

Swartz, Marc J.; Victor W. Turner; and Arthur Tuden
1966   "Introduction." In *Political Anthropology*, ed. Swartz, Turner, and Tuden. Chicago: Aldine-Atherton.

Swift, Mary Grace
1968   *The Art of Dance in the USSR*. Notre Dame: University of Notre Dame Press.

Taketomo, Yasuhiko
1969   "An Exploration into Psychodynamics of Time Experience." *Journal for the Study of Consciousness* 2(1):37–54.

Talbot, P. Amaury
1926   *The Peoples of Southern Nigeria*. 4 Vols. London: Oxford University Press.

Tamuno, Tekena N.

1966   "Before British Police in Nigeria." *Nigeria Magazine*, no. 89: 102–116.

Tanner, Nancy, and Adrienne Zihlman
1976   "Discussion Paper: The Evolution of Human Communication: What Can Primates Tell Us?" In *Origins and Evolution of Language and Speech*, ed. Stevan R. Harnad, Horst D. Steklis, and Jane Lancaster, 280:467–480. Annals of the New York Academy of Sciences.

Taylor, Irving A., and J. W. Getzels, eds.
1975   *Perspectives in Creativity*. Chicago: Aldine.

Taylor, Margaret Fisk
1967   *A Time to Dance: Symbolic Movement in Worship*. Philadelphia: United Church Press.

Taylor, Walter
1948   *A Study of Archaeology*. Carbondale: University of Southern Illinois Press.

Ten Raa, Eric
1969   "The Moon as a Symbol of Life and Fertility in Sandawe Thought." *Africa* 39:24–53.

Theeman, Margaret
1973   "Rhythms of Community: The Sociology of Expressive Body Movement." Ph.D. dissertation, Harvard University.

Thompson, Robert Farris
1971   "Sons of Thunder: Twin Images among the Oyo and Other Yoruba Groups." *African Arts* 4(3):8–13, 77–80.

Toffler, Alvin
1970   *Future Shock*. New York: Bantam.

Tracy, Hugh T.
1952   *African Dances of the Witwatersrand Gold Mines*. Johannesburg: African Music Society.

Tracy, Martin
1973   "On the Future of Notation." Paper prepared for the Committee on Research in Dance (CORD) Conference, San Francisco, October 24–27.

Traore, Bakary
1968   "Meaning and Function of the Traditional Negro-African Theatre." In *Colloquium: Function and Significance of African Negro Art in the Life of the People and for the People*, pp. 481–493. March 30–April 8, 1966, 1st World Festival of Negro Arts, Dakar. Paris: Présence Africaine.

Turner, Victor W.
1957   *Schism and Continuity in an African Society: A Study of Ndembu Village Life*. Manchester: Manchester University Press.
1967   *The Forest of Symbols: Aspects of Ndembu Ritual*. Ithaca: Cornell University Press.

1969   *The Ritual Process: Structure and Anti-Structure.* Chicago: Aldine.
1974   *Dramas, Fields, and Metaphor: Symbolic Action in Human Society.* Ithaca: Cornell University Press.
1977   "Commentary on Arts, Values, and Social Action Session." American Anthropological Association Meetings, Houston.

Uchendu, Victor C.
1965   *The Igbo of Southeast Nigeria.* New York: Holt, Rinehart and Winston.

Umeasiegbu, Rems Nna
1969   *The Way We Lived.* London: Heinemann.

Uzoigwe, G. N.
1975   "Pre-Colonial Military Studies in Africa." *Journal of Modern African Studies* 13(3):469–481.

Van Allen, Judith
1972   "Sitting on a Man: Colonialism and the Lost Political Institutions of Igbo Women." *Canadian Journal of African Studies* 6(2):165–181.

Van den Berghe, Pierre, and David P. Barash
1977   "Inclusive Fitness and Human Family Structure." *American Anthropologist* 79(4):809–823.

Van Gennep, Arnold
1960   *Rites of Passage.* Chicago: University of Chicago. [Orig. 1909.]

Vansina, Jan; Raymond Mauny; and L. V. Thomas, eds.
1964   *The Historian in Tropical Africa.* London: Oxford University Press.

Vatsyayan, Kapila
1968   *Classical Indian Dance in Literature and the Arts.* New Delhi: Sangeet Natak Akademi.

Vaughan, James H., Jr.
1973   "Kyagu as Artists in Marghi Society." In *The Traditional Artist in African Societies,* ed. Warren L. d'Azevedo, pp. 162–193. Bloomington: Indiana University Press.

Vidyarthi, L. P.
1961   "Whither Adivasi Dance in Tribal Bihar: Some Preliminary Observations Regarding Impact of Christianity and City on the Oraon Dance Pattern." *Folklore* (India) 2:298–308.

Volland, Anita
1975   *The Arts in Polynesia—a Study of the Functions and Meaning of Art Forms in the Pre-Contact Pacific.* Ph.D. dissertation, University of Pennsylvania. Ann Arbor: University Microfilms.

Wallace, Anthony F. C.
1968   "Psychological Preparations for War." In *War: The Anthropology of Armed Conflict and Aggression,* ed. Morton Fried,

Marvin Harris, and Robert Murphy, pp. 173–182. New York: Natural History Press.

Walter, Eugene Victor
1969 *Terror and Resistance: A Study of Political Violence*. New York: Oxford University Press.

Waterman, Richard A.
1962 "Role of Dance in Human Society." In *Focus on Dance II: An Inter-Disciplinary Search for Meaning in Movement*, ed. Bettie Jane Wooten, pp. 47–55. Washington, D.C.: American Association for Health, Physical Education and Recreation.

Watson, O. Michael
1972 *Symbolic and Expressive Uses of Space: An Introduction to Proxemic Behavior*. McCaleb Module 20. Reading: Addison-Wesley.

Weaver, Muriel Porter
1972 *The Aztecs, Maya and their Predecessors*. New York: Seminar.

Webster's Third International Dictionary
1961 "Dance," pp. 572–573. Cambridge: H. O. Houghton and Co.

Weil, Peter M.
1971 "The Masked Figure and Social Control: The Mandinka Case." *Africa* 41:279–293.

Welch, Claude, Jr.
1975 "Continuity and Discontinuity in African Military Organization." *Journal of Modern African Studies* 13(2):229–248.

Wembah-Rashid, J. A. R.
1971 "Isinyago and Midimu: Masked Dancers of Tanzania and Mozambique." *African Arts* 4(2):38–44.

Wepner, Franklyn
1973 "The Theory and Practice of Orientation Therapy." *Drama Review* 17:81–101.

Werbner, Richard P.
1964 "Atonement Ritual and Guardian-Spirit Possession among Kalanga." *Africa* 34:206–223.

Wescott, Joan
1962 "The Sculpture and Myths of Eshu-Elegba, the Yoruba Trickster: Definition and Interpretation in Yoruba Iconography." *Africa* 32:336–354.
——, and Peter Morton-Williams
1962 "The Symbolism and Ritual Context of the Yoruba Laba Shango." *Journal of the Royal Anthropological Institute* 92(1 & 2):23–37.

Wheatley, Paul
1969 "City as Symbol." Inaugural Lecture Delivered at University College London, November 20, 1967.

1971 *The Pivot of the Four Quarters: A Preliminary Enquiry into the Origins and Character of the Ancient Chinese City*. Chicago: Aldine.

White, Jean M.
1973 "The Modern Maecenas in America." *Washington Post*, March 4, pp. L1, L3.

Whitten, Norman E., Jr., and Aurdio Fuentes C.
1966 "Baile Marimba! Negro Folk Music in Northwest Ecuador." *Journal of the Folklore Institute* 3(2):168–191.

Wiebe, Gerhard
1969–1970 "Two Psychological Factors in Media Audience Behavior." *Public Opinion Quarterly* 33:523–536.

Wiener, Morton; Shannon Devoe; and Stuart Rubinow
1972 "Nonverbal Behavior and Nonverbal Communication." *Psychological Review* 79(3):185–214.

Wild, Stephen Aubrey
1975 "Walbiri Music and Dance in their Social and Cultural Nexus." Ph.D. dissertation, Indiana University.

Williams, Drid
1968 "The Dance of the Bedu Moon." *African Arts* 2(1):18–21.
1972 "Signs, Symptoms, and Symbols." *Journal of the Anthropological Society of Oxford* 3(1):24–32.
1974 "Review of Choreometrics." *Dance Research Journal* 6(2):25–29.
1976 "The Role of Movement in Selected Symbolic Systems." D. Phil. dissertation, Oxford University.
1978 "Deep Structures of the Dance." *Yearbook of Symbolic Anthropology*, ed. E. Schwimmer, pp. 211–230. London: C. Hurst.
——; Rev. J. S.; and J. E. K. Kumah
1970 "Sokodae: Come and Dance." *African Arts* 3(3):36–39.

Willis, R., ed.
1975 *The Interpretation of Symbolism*. New York: Halsted.

Wilson, Edward O.
1975 *Sociobiology: The New Synthesis*. Cambridge, Mass: Harvard University Press.

Wilson, Monica
1954 "Nyakyusa Ritual and Symbolism." *American Anthropologist* 56:228–241.

Wirth, L.
1938 "Urbanism as a Way of Life." *American Journal of Sociology* 44:1–24.

Wittich, Walter Arno, and Francis Schuller
1953 *Audio-visual Materials: Their Nature and Use*. New York: Harper and Brothers.

Wolff, Peter H.

1967   "The Role of Biological Rhythms in Early Psychological Development." *Menninger Clinic Bulletin* 31:197–218.

Wolz, Carl
1971   *Bugaku: Japanese Court Dance*. Providence: Asian Music Publications.

Woodward, Stephanie
1976   "Evidence for a Grammatical Structure in Javanese Dance:
Examination of a Passage from Golek Lambangsari." *Dance
Research Journal* 8(2):10–17.

Youngerman, Suzanne
1974   "Curt Sachs and His Heritage: A Critical Review of World
History of the Dance with a Survey of Recent Studies That
Perpetuate His Ideas." *Dance Research Journal* 6(2):6–19.

1977   "Method and Theory in Dance Research: An Anthropological Approach." *Yearbook of the International Folk Music Council* 7:116–133.

Zander, Alvin
1974   "People Often Work Harder for Group Than for Selves."
Institute for Social Research Newsletter 2(3):2, 7.

Index